W9-BHO-359

Southern Biography Series
William J. Cooper, Jr., Editor

P

P. G. T. BEAUREGARD

Napoleon in Gray

Cabildo, Louisiana State Museum

P. G. T. Beauregard, from an oil painting by Thomas C. Healy

P. G. T. BEAUREGARD

Napoleon in Gray

By T. HARRY WILLIAMS

LOUISIANA STATE UNIVERSITY
PRESS

Baton Rouge

Library of Congress Catalog Card Number 55-7362
Copyright © 1955 by Louisiana State University Press
All rights reserved
Manufactured in the United States of America

ISBN 0-8071-1974-1 (paper)

Louisiana Paperback Edition, 1995
04 03 02 01 00 99   5 4 3 2

FOR
ROBBIE LANE

Preface

Every biographer is certain to be asked one question: why did he pick his particular subject to write a book about? In the case of General Beauregard I might answer: because I wanted to; this paradoxical personality and his dramatic life interested me so much that I was drawn to study him and to try to analyze him. But more impelling than the human lure of his story was the fact that Beauregard was important enough a figure to deserve a biography. He was one of the eight full generals of the Confederacy. He held six independent commands, and for a period he commanded the Army of Tennessee, one of the two principal Confederate field armies. And his postwar career seems to me more fascinating than that of any other Southern general.

Civil War fans, being what they are, are bound to raise the question: was Beauregard a great general? Or, some may ask, was he even a good one? The answer to the first is no, with a caveat for Beauregard that there are few great generals. The answer to the second is yes, with several caveats against him. Beauregard, like other officers in the war, was elevated to army command before he was ready for it. He demonstrated some serious deficiencies and made some bad mistakes. In my opinion he would have developed into a very good field commander—had he been given the chance. But his past errors and his personality quirks had aroused such a distrust of him among the men in the high command that the opportunity was denied. Had things happened a little differently, he might have gone on to become one of the fighting heroes of the Confederacy. As they did happen, he is probably remembered most, as a military man, for his defense of Charleston.

But with Beauregard one can never be sure what he would have become. He was not a consistent personality like Lee. He was a paradox, and his life was a paradox. He was an ardent Southerner, and yet, as a Creole, he was in many ways an alien in the Anglo-Saxon Confederacy. Before a battle he was often visionary and impractical, but once in a fight he was a grim and purposeful soldier.

He affected the manners of a cavalier of the Old South, but after the war he helped to destroy the old agrarian way and to build the New—the industrial—South. One never knows about him. . . .

Perhaps a New York reporter who interviewed him after the war had it right. He said that Beauregard was not a first-class military man but a first-rate second-class man. Maybe the tragedy of the Confederacy was that it did not have enough first-class generals to go around.

For their generous and patient assistance when I was examining their records I wish to thank the staffs of the Southern Historical Collection, University of North Carolina Library; the South Carolina Historical Society; the Division of Manuscripts, Library of Congress; the Department of Archives, Louisiana State University; the National Archives; the Howard-Tilton Memorial Library, Tulane University; the Duke University Library; the Missouri Historical Society; the Emory University Library; the Charleston Library Society; the Confederate Memorial Hall; the Cabildo; the North Carolina State Department of Archives and History; the Confederate Museum; the South Caroliniana Library, University of South Carolina; the Confederate Memorial Institute; and the Florida Historical Society.

Many people helped my research by making suggestions about sources or providing documents. My thanks are due to Dr. J. G. de Roulhac Hamilton, Dr. C. Percy Powell, Mr. J. B. Riggs, Miss Elizabeth Drewry, Dr. V. L. Bedsole, Dr. Robert Woody, Miss Margaret Jemison, Mr. Stanley C. Arthur, Dr. J. W. Patton, Miss Helen McCormack, Miss Elizabeth Jervey, Mrs. Helen Bullock, Dr. J. Harold Easterby, Dr. R. W. Meriwether, the late Miss Stella Drum, Dr. Francis L. Berkeley, Jr., Miss Alberta Johnson, Mr. T. R. Hay, and Dr. Buford Rowland. The aid of others is acknowledged at appropriate points in the notes.

Mr. Otto Eisenschiml read the chapters on Shiloh, and Dr. Frank Vandiver read the entire manuscript. Both contributed valuable suggestions for improvement.

A number of years ago the late Mr. Robert W. Barnwell, Sr., of Florence, South Carolina, who was a close student of the war and a great admirer of Beauregard, talked with me at length about this study and gave me many stimulating ideas. I regret that he did not live to see it completed.

Mrs. Thomas M. Smylie, formerly of the Louisiana State University Press, helped ready my manuscript for publication. The labor of typing it was done by my wife, who also made the index.

Mr. T. S. Kennedy, Pensacola, Florida, readily extended permission to reproduce quotations from the diary of Stephen R. Mallory. The editors of the *Journal of Southern History* allowed me to incorporate sections from two articles of mine which originally appeared in that quarterly.

The maps of Charleston, Manassas, Shiloh, and Petersburg are from the excellent handbooks of the National Park Service, and are used here by the permission of Mr. Herbert Evison, Chief of Information. The Park Service maps are extremely accurate; they provide a graphic picture that for the general reader cannot be excelled. The fine map of the Richmond-Petersburg area was made by Barbara Long for E. B. Long's edition of Grant's *Memoirs*. It is reproduced through the kindness of Mrs. Long and the World Publishing Company.

The Graduate Council of Louisiana State University facilitated my research with two grants-in-aid.

T. HARRY WILLIAMS

Contents

Illustrations

Maps

CHAPTER ONE

The Creole

H<small>E IS THE MOST</small> colorful of all the Confederate generals. He had more glamor and drama in his Gallic-American personality than any three of his Anglo-Saxon colleagues in gray rolled into one. The people of the Confederacy idolized him into a great popular hero, second not even to Lee. He was chivalric and arrogant in the best Southern tradition, but he was more. Something in his resounding name of Beauregard, in his Creole origin in south Louisiana, in his knightly bearing suggested a more exotic environment than the South of Jefferson Davis. A vague air of romance, reminiscent of an older civilization, trailed after him wherever he went. When he spoke and when he acted, people thought of Paris and Napoleon and Austerlitz and French legions bursting from the St. Bernard Pass onto the plains of Italy.

His military career was one of the most unique in the Confederacy and in many ways is more significant to the student of the Civil War than the record of any other Confederate general. It was not confined to one narrow area like Lee's or interrupted by long periods of inactivity like Joseph Johnston's or cut off before the end of the war like Braxton Bragg's. Beauregard was in every important phase of the war from its beginning to its conclusion. He fired the opening gun of the great drama at Fort Sumter. He commanded the Confederate forces in the first great battle of the war at Manassas. In 1862 he was second and then first in command in the West; he planned and fought the first big battle in that theater at Shiloh.

From the West he went to Charleston, and there he conducted the war's longest and most skillful defense of a land point against attack from the sea. In 1864 he returned to Virginia to direct the defense of the southern approaches to Richmond. Later in that year, the government assigned him to command the Division of the West, a huge department with an impressive title and few resources. In the waning months of the war, he was in Georgia and the Carolinas

1

as first and then second in command trying to halt the onward rush of Sherman. He and Joe Johnston surrendered to Sherman in North Carolina the most formidable Confederate army left in the field after Lee yielded to Grant.

He saw most of the war to preserve the Old South. Then, after his cause crashed to defeat and the dream was ended, he was able to adapt himself to the ways of the New South. He was probably more successful than any other prominent Confederate general in making a living and accumulating wealth in the hard years after the war.

And that is why he became a forgotten man in the Southern tradition. When the Southern people made their bitter myths, they constructed them of sacrifice and poverty and frustration. The Southern hero was the reticent and reserved Lee, who lived modestly on a college president's salary, or the grim Jackson, who fell gloriously on the battlefield and escaped having to face the realities of peace. In the Confederate legend there was small room for the prosperous Creole in gay New Orleans who ran railroads and, of all un-Confederate actions, presided over the drawings of a lottery company.

Just below New Orleans the parish of St. Bernard spread its fields of cane and corn, its cypress and live oak forests, and its dark swamps under the warm Louisiana sun. Frenchmen had settled it, and in 1818, only fifteen years after the cession of Louisiana from France to the United States, St. Bernard was proudly and even fiercely French. About twenty miles from the city, in the center of the parish, stood Contreras, the plantation home of the Toutant-Beauregards. Among the gentility of this region of Latin culture, the Toutant-Beauregards ranked high.

Jacques Toutant-Beauregard, the master of Contreras, could trace his French and Welsh lineage back to the thirteenth century. His grandfather, the first of the family to settle in Louisiana, had come out to the colony in the time of Louis XIV. Jacques numbered among his Louisiana ancestors Cartiers and Ducros, names of distinction in the bayou country. His wife was a De Reggio, another first family of St. Bernard. She had a family tree even more impressive than his. The De Reggios claimed descent from an Italian noble family, dukes no less, a scion of which migrated to France and founded a French line that eventually ended up in Louisiana.[1] Jacques could not know that the son who was born to him on May 28, 1818, the third child in what would be a family of seven, would eclipse the eminence of all the Toutant-Beauregards and De Reggios of the past. But he gave the boy a rich, ringing name to befit his ancient heritage. Pierre Gustave Toutant-Beauregard. It would sound well in the future annals of fame. It would also always stamp its bearer as different outside of the bayou country. That sonorous appellation would stand out in the Confederacy like pompano en papillote in a mess of turnip greens.

Young Pierre grew up in an environment that was partly of the plantation South and partly unlike anything Southern. The home in which he lived was a large one-story house, not in the grand tradition of later plantation palaces but a mansion of aristocracy by the standards of its time.[2] The chief crop at Contreras was sugar cane, and there were slaves to plant and harvest it—and to wait on the wants of the white masters. Pierre played with slave boys his own age and as a baby was suckled by a Dominican slave woman. Like other Southern boys, Pierre hunted and rode in the woods and fields of his plantation and paddled his boat in its waterways.[3]

Except that Contreras produced cane instead of the familiar cotton and that he paddled on bayous instead of rivers, the physical features of his formative surroundings were typically Southern. The departure from the plantation pattern was in the cultural influences of his early years. Spiritually his family and south Louisiana were a part of France

[1] On St. Bernard Parish and the delta country, see George W. Cable, *The Creoles of Louisiana* (New York, 1910), 6–8; Harnett T. Kane, *Deep Delta Country* (New York, 1944), *passim*. For the ancestral background of the Toutant-Beauregards, see Grace King, *Creole Families of New Orleans* (New York, 1921), 452–54; T. C. De Leon, *Belles, Beaux and Brains of the Sixties* (New York, 1909), 294–95; Alfred Roman, *Military Operations of General Beauregard* (New York, 1884), I, 2–4; Hamilton Basso, *Beauregard the Great Creole* (New York, 1933), 3–4; J. C. Ducros, "Genealogy of Descendants of Jacques Toutant-Beauregard . . .," MS. in Missouri Historical Society (St. Louis). The Welsh element in the ancestry came from one Tider, a rebel against English authority who had to seek refuge in France. The name was eventually changed to Toutant, and when the last Toutant, a female, married a Beauregard the hyphenated name was adopted.

[2] The house stood until well up into the present century. Abandoned for many years, it became the prey of people who needed wood, and finally collapsed. New Orleans *Times,* November 21, 1866; Kane, *Deep Delta Country,* 66–67.

[3] New Orleans *Times,* September 10, 1882, interview with his wet nurse, Mamie Françoise Similien; Basso, *Beauregard* 5–7.

instead of the South. The Toutant-Beauregards were Creoles, Frenchmen of solid Old World backgrounds who had become feudal aristocrats in the New. They were Latins set down in a semitropical region of rich soil and lush crops that invited the establishment of slave labor. Their elite social position and their habit of commanding slaves made them imperious, proud, sometimes arrogant. They retained many Gallic traits and customs, modified only to suit the Louisiana scene. They loved merrymaking, lusty eating and drinking, luxurious living; they prized manners, breeding, tradition, honor—even to the point of absurdity.

To the American newcomers they seemed to be boastful posers who were also ignorant. They did strut and strike attitudes that were ridiculous to the Americans, and they did ignore, or affect to, the values of American culture. Being provincials, they felt superior to the parvenu Yankees, and at the same time they secretly worried that they were inferior. Feeling that their once-dominant social status was threatened by the incoming American horde, they guarded the old ways of their civilization with an aggressive vanity. They considered themselves cultivated Europeans living in a coarse new world. They might look to New Orleans as the city of their spiritual stimulation, but beyond New Orleans they looked to Paris. If New Orleans was their Paris, Paris was their Mecca.[4]

Pierre's parents intended him to be a Frenchman. French was the language used at Contreras. He probably could not speak English until he was twelve years of age. When he was eight, his father sent him for three years to a private school near New Orleans where all the classes were taught in French.[5] Almost nothing is known of his life in these early years. He seems to have been quiet, studious, and reserved, almost the opposite of what he would be as an adult. Family tradition has preserved certain incidents which are assumed to have significance as revealing his later character. When he was nine, a man teased him before a crowd of relatives and friends, perhaps about failing as a hunter that day. Pierre seized a stick, chased his tormentor into an outhouse, and refused to let him emerge until he apologized. He accepted the apology but refused to shake hands. A little over a

[4] Cable, *Creoles of Louisiana,* 39–40, 139–40; Lyle Saxon, *Fabulous New Orleans* (New York, 1941), 91, 162–63, 169, 189.
[5] Roman, *Beauregard,* I, 4; King, *Creole Families,* 454; Basso, *Beauregard,* 8; J. C. Derby, *Fifty Years among Authors, Books, and Publishers* (New York, 1884), 714.

year later his mother took him to the Church of St. Louis for the children's first communion. As he went up the aisle to the altar, a roll of drums was heard in the street outside. He stopped and looked back, and when the drums sounded again, to the horror of his mother he rushed out of the church. The second episode is supposed to show that even as a child he yearned to be a soldier. It probably meant only that as a country boy he was attracted by a loud and exciting noise. The outhouse story may have real meaning. He would always resent an affront and demand redress, but he seldom forgave.

When Pierre was eleven, his father decided to continue his education by sending him to school in New York City. It was something of a break with Creole custom for a boy to go to school anywhere except New Orleans or France, but the institution he was to attend had a safe Gallic background. Known in the East as the French School, it was operated by two brothers named Peugnet who had been officers under Napoleon Bonaparte. The curriculum emphasized mathematics and commercial subjects. Pierre stayed at the school for four years, coming home only in the Christmas and summer holidays. Here he learned for the first time to speak English, at least fluently, and to write the English language. He worked hard and made good grades in all his subjects. But more interesting to him than the classes were the tales the brothers were always telling of their service with Napoleon. Pierre listened with fascination. He began to read books about Napoleon and his campaigns. In his spare time at New York and during vacations at Contreras, he studied Jena and Austerlitz and all Napoleon's battles. He had found a hero. For the rest of his life he would model himself on the great Corsican. He had also found a profession. Toward the end of his last year with the Peugnets, he came home and announced to the family that he wanted to be a soldier, an officer in the American army. He asked his father to get him an appointment to the United States Military Academy at West Point.[6]

The family objected loudly. Even his father, who went further than most Creoles in associating with Americans, thought this was carrying collaboration too far. Pierre stood his ground. Nothing could change him once he had decided he was right. He would always be this way. He would never give ground on an issue of judgment. In

[6] Roman, *Beauregard*, I, 4–6; Basso, *Beauregard*, 6–8, 15–18; King, *Creole Families*, 454–55.

the end the family yielded to his calm stubbornness. Jacques enlisted political influence to get his son entered at the military academy. Governor A. B. Roman wrote to Representative E. D. White, and White wrote to Secretary of War Lewis Cass to say that Pierre was a fine young gentleman who had been carefully educated and whose family had supported the American cause in the Revolution. The appointment came through almost immediately. Pierre was admitted to the academy as of March, 1834. Without waiting for his father to consent to the appointment in writing, a legal formality, he rushed up to West Point, possibly leaving from the Peugnet school. After arriving at the Point, he wrote Secretary Cass a letter of thanks which did not quite fulfill White's laudatory remarks about his education: "I have written to my father to beg him to inform you weather he wished me to accept it or not; I will submit myself to the answer you will receive from him. . . . I shall endeavour by my conduct during the period I will remain here to merit in some manner the bounty which my country [sic] to bestow upon me."[7]

He enrolled as Pierre Gustave Toutant Beauregard. The hyphen was dropped from his name and would never reappear. Family tradition has it that he deleted the Toutant to secure a better class rating by getting his name up among the B's. This is highly improbable. A cadet's standing at the end of each year was determined primarily by his conduct and grades. A more likely explanation is that he realized the hyphen might subject him to ridicule from other students. The shortening of his name was part of the process by which he was Americanizing himself. In a few years he would lop off the Pierre and sign himself G. T. Beauregard.[8]

The school which the sixteen-year-old Beauregard was entering was the only officer-training institution of importance in the country. Most of the generals that he would fight with and against in the Civil War were the products of its classrooms. West Point was the best school of its kind that an aspiring officer could attend, but as a preparatory seminary for future generals it had glaring deficiencies. In the four years that a cadet spent at the Point he learned, or was

[7] E. D. White to Lewis Cass, February 22, 1834, and P. G. T. Beauregard to Cass, March 23, 1834, in Records of the Adjutant General's Office Relating to West Point (National Archives). Jacques gave his consent in a letter to Cass, April 11, 1834, *ibid.*

[8] Asbury Dickins and John W. Forney (eds.), *American State Papers, Military Affairs,* VII (Washington, 1861), 101; Basso, *Beauregard,* 22–24.

given the opportunity to learn, a lot of mathematics, military engineering, and tactics. The curriculum literally bristled with courses in these subjects. The courses in general education were few in number and superficial in nature. Worst of all, there was little instruction in the higher nature of war—policy, strategy, and military history. Nor were students encouraged to study the theory of war on their own. The technical routine of the academy did not allow time for many visits to the library; and even if it had, the cadets could not have read the best works on war, for these were in French, and the French taught at the school was not sufficient to provide a reading knowledge. This handicap, of course, did not affect Beauregard, who read some of Jomini and learned some lessons he never forgot. In short, West Point turned out good tacticians and narrow specialists; it did not produce men who knew very much about the art of war.[9]

Cadet Beauregard was a grave, reserved, and withdrawn youth, the same kind of person he had been as a boy. Probably nobody at the academy really knew him. When men who had been his classmates tried in later years to recall what he was like, they could remember only that he excelled in sports, rode a horse beautifully, and made high marks.[10] Only one colorful episode was associated with his stay at the Point. He was supposed to have had a tragic love affair with the daughter of Winfield Scott, one of the senior generals of the army. According to the story, highly colored no doubt, he and Virginia Scott became engaged. Her parents insisted that they were too young to marry and that the engagement not be made public. The young couple parted; both wrote, but neither received the other's letters. Beauregard, offended and embittered, soon married another woman.

Several years later he received a summons to come to Virginia on her deathbed. She told him that she had been grieved by his apparent inconstancy but had recently learned that her mother had intercepted his letters. Certain known facts make the tale partially plausible. In

[9] Lloyd Lewis, *Sherman, Fighting Prophet* (New York, 1932), 51–58; T. Harry Williams, *Lincoln and His Generals* (New York, 1952), 4; Dickins and Forney (eds.), *American State Papers, Military Affairs*, V (Washington, 1860), 420–24, 704–708; Hazard Stevens, *Life of General Isaac Ingalls Stevens* (Boston, 1900), I, 29, 31–33, 36–38, 44, 48–49; Edward C. Boynton, *Guide to West Point . . .* (New York, 1867), 9–18, 62–64; *Regulations of the U. S. Military Academy* (Washington, 1904), I–II, *passim*.

[10] De Leon, *Belles, Beaux and Brains*, 295–96; William Howard Russell, *My Diary North and South* (Boston, 1863), 389.

1838, the year Beauregard graduated, Mrs. Scott took her seventeen-year-old daughter to Europe and was gone for five years. In France Virginia was converted to Catholicism. After they returned to the United States, Virginia, without her parents' knowledge, entered a convent, where she died in 1845. Beauregard had married in 1841.[11]

There is no obscurity about his academic record. From the beginning he was an outstanding student. In the annual examinations given in June he stood among the five most distinguished cadets during his first three years, being fourth in 1835 and second in 1836 and 1837. He was also near the top of the conduct roll, with only three demerits in his first year, thirteen the second, and none the third. His teachers predicted a great future for him. He maintained his high position in his senior year. In the final listing of the class of 1838 at graduation, Beauregard ranked second in a group of forty-five.[12] Down the roll at number twenty-three was Irvin McDowell, whom Beauregard would defeat at Manassas in 1861 in the first important battle of the Civil War.

Beauregard also knew in his own class and in preceding classes several men who would serve under him in the Civil War—Jubal Early, William J. Hardee, Jeremy Gilmer, Richard Ewell, and others. Braxton Bragg, who would be one of his most dangerous enemies in the Confederacy, finished in 1837. On the Union side, Beauregard knew Joseph Hooker, Henry W. Halleck, and William T. Sherman. His favorite teacher was artillery instructor Robert Anderson, who would refuse to surrender Fort Sumter to his former pupil in the opening scene of the war. The relations between the two apparently were close, for right after graduating Beauregard served for a time as Anderson's assistant.[13]

A few days after he graduated, Beauregard received his commission as second lieutenant in the corps of engineers, which would entitle

[11] Louise North to Mrs. Charles L. Pettigrew, August 7, 1861, in Pettigrew Family Papers (Southern Historical Collection, University of North Carolina Library) ; Charles Winslow Elliott, *Winfield Scott* (New York, 1937), 415–16.

[12] Dickins and Forney (eds.), *American State Papers, Military Affairs, VI* (Washington, 1861), 50, 1020, VII, 942; Lewis, *Sherman*, 58; George W. Cullum, *Biographical Register of the Officers and Graduates of the U. S. Military Academy* . . . (New York, 1868), I, 548–71. The cadet who ranked first was William Wright, who died in 1845 before realizing the brilliant career expected of him.

[13] Roman, *Beauregard*, I, 6; Beauregard to H. H. Dawson, July 5, 1862, in Beauregard Papers (Division of Manuscripts, Library of Congress), Letter-book, Private Letters, February 28, 1872–December 1, 1875.

him to a salary of about $900 a year, and entered upon the four years of service required of West Point graduates.[14] His first assignment was to Fort Adams, near Newport, Rhode Island. That his superiors in the Engineer Department should send him to Adams was a mark of their confidence in him. Fort Adams, in process of being completed, was the second largest defensive work in the country, being exceeded in size only by Fortress Monroe. Officers liked to be sent there because of the prestige of the location and the pleasant social life in the old resort town of Newport.[15] Beauregard probably liked it too, but he found the climate too hard on his health. Afflicted with a chronic throat ailment since boyhood, he was miserably sick in his first winter at the fort. In the spring of 1839 he had to go to New York to take treatment for a dangerous inflammation of the kidneys that confined him to bed for about two months. His doctors advised him to go south, and Colonel Joseph G. Totten, Chief of the Engineer Department, was willing to let him go. In the fall of 1839 Beauregard, now a first lieutenant, was transferred to Pensacola, Florida, to construct coastal defenses.[16]

He stayed at Pensacola a few months, and then he secured from Colonel Totten a really choice assignment. He was ordered to Barataria Bay on the Louisiana Gulf coast to conduct a topographical and hydrographical survey of the Bay and its islands. He later estimated that he made ten thousand soundings in the course of his work. For the next five years, with one short exception, Beauregard would serve in his native state, first at Barataria and later building or repairing forts near the mouth of the Mississippi. Beauregard, of course, was delighted with his Louisiana assignment. He was in a mild climate, he could visit his family, and he could make frequent trips to New Orleans.[17]

[14] Cullum, *Biographical Register of the Military Academy*, I, 548; Roman, *Beauregard*, I, 6; Dickins and Forney (eds.), *American State Papers, Military Affairs*, VI, 129. Beauregard's first commission, dated July 1, 1838, was in the artillery. On July 7 he received a commission in the engineers. The first part of July was probably the time when he assisted Anderson.

[15] Stevens, *Stevens*, I, 60–61.

[16] Beauregard to J. G. Totten, April 1, June 3, 1839, and Totten to Beauregard, November 20, 1839, in Office of Chief of Engineers files (National Archives).

[17] His work at Barataria was described by Beauregard in a public letter in New Orleans *Republican*, December 20, 1874. His reports in this period are in Engineer Department, Letters Received, Engineer Department files (National Archives) and in the Beauregard Papers (Library of Congress), Letterbook 1.

One day in the city he met an old friend, Charles Villeré, a member of one of the most distinguished Creole families in south Louisiana. Villeré invited the lieutenant to visit his father's plantation, Magnolia, on the Mississippi River about fourteen miles below New Orleans in Plaquemines Parish. Beauregard went, and there he met Charles's beautiful sister, Marie Laure. He fell in love with her at once and courted her ardently and overwhelmingly. They were married in September, 1841. For a while the couple lived at Magnolia, where Marie Laure bore him a son, René. Later Beauregard moved his family to New Orleans, taking a home on St. Louis Street and opening an office to carry on his military duties on Bourbon Street. In a few years another son, Henri, was born.[18]

In August of 1844 Beauregard was ordered to Fort McHenry at Baltimore to act as engineer officer. He would serve at this post until January, 1845. McHenry was an important military center, and a number of officers from the infantry and artillery were stationed there. The social life at the fort was unusually pleasant. Baltimore society viewed the officers as parlor prizes, and they in turn considered the parties and balls and sometimes the belles of the city as the high point of their army careers.[19]

Beauregard worked hard, but he also played.[20] For the first time in his life, as far as the records show, he unbent and let other people see what he was like. He also began to show some of the color that would later be a distinguishing part of his personality. After he got jerked up by the Engineer Department for some sloppiness in his reports, one of his friends teasingly wrote him that he guessed "showy, dashing, popular" officers were no good in the army.[21] It was at about this time that he dropped the P from his name and began signing it

[18] Basso, *Beauregard*, 28–29, 33–34; Roman, *Beauregard*, I, 10; De Leon, *Belles, Beaux and Brains*, 297; Stanley C. Arthur and George C. H. Kernion, *Old Families of Louisiana* (New Orleans, 1931), 62–64.

[19] Samuel G. French, *Two Wars: An Autobiography* (Nashville, 1901), 26.

[20] For Beauregard's reports to Colonel Totten from August–December, 1844, see Beauregard Papers (Library of Congress), Letterbook 1. See also the following letters dealing with construction work at the fort in the Beauregard Papers (Howard-Tilton Memorial Library, Tulane University): Edwin Wilmer to Beauregard, October 5, 26, November 1, 8, 13, 1844; George L. Welcker to Beauregard, October 10, 28, November 1, 18, 21, 1844; H. W. Benham to Beauregard, October 22, 29, 1844; Totten to Beauregard, December 19, 1844.

[21] J. F. Gilmer to Beauregard, November 5, 8, 1844, and Benham to Beauregard, December 16, 1844, in Beauregard Papers (Tulane University).

G. T. Beauregard. When an endorsement on a draft with the new signature showed up in the Treasury Department, an alert bureaucrat wrote him to ask what had become of the P. Almost apologetically Beauregard replied: "It was merely for the sake of brevity, my name being rather a long one I endeavor to shorten it as much as possible. . . ." [22] He was trying to be more human, more American. Whatever repressions his family, his childhood, or his culture had fixed on him were beginning to dissipate.

By February Beauregard was back in Louisiana, working again on the forts around the Mississippi's mouth. [23] One day he sent a civilian employee to Fort Wood with a letter asking the commander of the post for assistance in collecting some supplies of the Engineer Department. Lieutenant John C. Henshaw, temporarily in command, refused to give any help and ordered the messenger to leave. Beauregard was enraged when he heard what had happened. He wrote Henshaw an angry letter in which he called the latter's conduct "arbitrary and unjustifiable." The incident, Beauregard said, reflected on him privately and publicly. Henshaw replied with a letter that Beauregard considered "insulting and abusive" to the point that it would have done "honor to a graduate of Billingsgate." Madder than ever, he thought of cowhiding Henshaw but remembered that he was an officer and hence a gentleman. He then challenged Henshaw to a duel. According to Beauregard, Henshaw tried to avoid a meeting. Beauregard threatened to publish his enemy as a coward if he would not fight. Henshaw claimed that he had not received a challenge and was willing to shoot it out any time.

Finally in April friends of the two officers arranged for them to meet. They were to fight with shotguns, with only one barrel loaded at a time. The first fire was to be at thirty yards; if neither was injured the second was to be at twenty-five; and if a third was necessary, at the same distance. If no injury had been inflicted at this point, either party could request another fire. The two young hotheads were actually ready to start blowing holes in each other when a deputy sheriff appeared and broke up the affair by arresting both of them. [24] Beauregard's conduct throughout the controversy was characteristic

[22] Beauregard to William Selden, March 21, 1845, in Beauregard Papers (Library of Congress).

[23] For Beauregard's letters and reports to Colonel Totten, February, 1845—November, 1846, see *ibid.*, Letterbook 1.

[24] This account is based upon documents in the John C. Henshaw Papers

and revealing. He was always touchy about his honor and always ready to defend it, with shotguns in his youth and blasts of words in later life. He would nearly always consider criticism or opposition some kind of reflection on him, and he would always challenge the offender to make good his words.

In May Colonel Totten confidentially informed Beauregard that Congress might increase the military establishment and that if it did engineer officers could transfer to another branch at a higher rank. Would Beauregard like to change to the artillery or infantry, Totten asked, and what was the lowest rank he would accept? Totten did not say that the dispute between the United States and Mexico over the Texas boundary and other issues might bring the two countries to war, but Beauregard knew that was what his superior was talking about. Eagerly he replied that if the increase was permanent, he would like to join one of the new regiments, that he preferred the artillery, that he wanted the rank of captain at least, and above all that he wanted to be in an outfit that would play an active part in the first campaign.[25]

Dreams of glory were stirring within him, but months of bitter disappointment followed Totten's letter. No promotion, no assignment to a post in the probable seat of war came from Washington. He begged the Engineer Department to send him to General Zachary Taylor's Army of Occupation in Texas as an engineer officer. Back came a curt reply that if the services of any more engineers were needed in Texas his application would be remembered. As he went from one of his dreary little forts to another, he brooded that the war when it came would pass him by. To ease his frustration, he worked out an idea to improve the furnaces used to boil sugar in the south Louisiana mills and asked a friend in Washington how to get a patent.[26]

(Alderman Library, University of Virginia). The Alderman Library supplied me with microfilm of the papers. Beauregard's first letter to Henshaw, March 8, 1845, is in Beauregard Papers (Library of Congress), Letterbook 1. In the Henshaw Papers, see Henshaw to Beauregard, March 11, April 10, 13, 1845; Beauregard to the officers of the Seventh Infantry, March 31, 1845 (explaining the origin of the duel); Beauregard to Henshaw, April 12, 13, 1845.

[25] Totten to Beauregard, May 28, 1845, in Beauregard Papers (Tulane University); Beauregard to Totten, June 12, 1845, in Beauregard Papers (Library of Congress), Letterbook 1.

[26] Welcker to Beauregard, September 12, 1845, in Beauregard Papers (Tulane University); Beauregard to ———, September 18, 1845, in Beauregard Papers (Library of Congress), Letterbook 1.

CHAPTER TWO

The Halls of Montezuma

While Lieutenant Beauregard fretfully dreamed of martial glory the war he had been waiting for started. In May, 1846, the tense relations between the United States and Mexico snapped into open war. Immediately after the news of the declaration of war had been received in New Orleans, Beauregard renewed his application to be sent to General Taylor's headquarters as an engineer officer. Almost frenzied by excitement, he feared that the war would be over before he could get in.[1] He was disappointed in his hope of securing an immediate assignment, and he was wrong in thinking that the United States could defeat Mexico in one short campaign. At the beginning of the Mexican War, the only sizable American army in the field was Taylor's so-called Army of Occupation on the northern bank of the Rio Grande. Taylor and President James K. Polk thought that if the army advanced into Mexico and occupied a part of the country the Mexican government would make peace on American terms. Accordingly Taylor crossed the Rio Grande, defeated the Mexicans in several engagements, and seized a triangle of territory in northeastern Mexico. To the surprise of the naïve planners of the American high command, the Mexicans were not disheartened by their reverses and gave no indication that they were going to quit the war.

Among the points seized by the Americans was the port city of Tampico on the eastern coast, which was used as a base through which to funnel supplies to Taylor's army. To protect Tampico against the unlikely event of a Mexican attack, the Engineer Department had started to construct fortifications around it on the land side. Now Colonel Totten remembered Beauregard's applications for service and his reputation as a fort builder. Late in November the

---

[1] Beauregard to Totten, May 14, 1846, in Beauregard Papers (Library of Congress), Letterbook 1.

impatient lieutenant received instructions to go to Tampico and assume charge of the building of the fortifications. Leaving New Orleans by steamship, he reached Tampico early in December. He would spend the next several months in the picturesque old town which the American officers stationed there loved for its entertainment, its good food, and the beautiful countryside around it.[2]

As was usual with him, Beauregard worked at his job with tremendous energy. His predecessor in charge of the defenses, Captain John G. Barnard, who was to become a lifelong friend, stayed on for a while to help. The works were so constructed as to enable a small garrison to hold the town. When they were completed in late February, Colonel Totten came down to inspect them. In his official report to the Adjutant General's office, he said that the works were admirably devised, and he praised glowingly the skill of Barnard and Beauregard. He also said that he was ordering Beauregard to be ready to join the next big offensive movement of the war, General Winfield Scott's projected campaign to capture Mexico City.[3]

After Taylor's offensive had failed to force Mexico to make a peace, President Polk did what he should have done earlier. He called in Scott, the ranking general in the army and its best soldier, and asked him to devise a plan of victory. Scott responded with a scheme which called for an army under his command to strike at the enemy capital, Mexico City. He proposed that this army be created by taking part of Taylor's forces and uniting them with additional troops from other theaters at Tampico. From Tampico the navy would transport the army to the port of Vera Cruz, farther down on the eastern coast; from Vera Cruz the army could move west on the National Highway to Mexico City. Scott believed that the Mexicans would fight for their capital and that the defeat of their army and the

[2] On Tampico, see John R. Kenley, *Memoirs of a Maryland Volunteer* . . . (Philadelphia, 1873), 235; George C. Furber, *The Twelve Months Volunteer* . . . (Cincinnati, 1849), 390, 416, 434, 435; George Meade, *Life and Letters of George Gordon Meade* (New York, 1913), I, 175, 177, 185; William Starr Myers (ed.), *The Mexican War Diary of George B. McClellan* (Princeton, 1917), 50–51; [George Ballentine], *Autobiography of an English Soldier in the United States Army* (New York, 1853), 134, 137–38; New Orleans *Picayune*, March 19, 1847; New Orleans *Delta*, February 14, 1847.

[3] Beauregard to Totten, November 27, 1846, January 14, 30, February 2, 28, 1847, in Beauregard Papers (Library of Congress), Letterbook 2; Totten to Beauregard, February 20, 1847, *ibid.*; Totten to Captain H. L. Scott, February 19, 1847, in *Senate Executive Documents*, 30 Cong., 1 Sess., Doc. 56, pp. 91–92.

occupation of the city would end the war. In February, 1847, he arrived in Tampico to take command of his gathering forces. Excitement gripped the military and civilian populace as the magnificent-looking general landed while bands played and guns boomed salutes. Everybody had an opinion as to where Scott's expedition was going. At night the soldiers and sailors carried on their speculations in the bars and got gloriously drunk.[4]

Beauregard was one of the few who knew early what Scott's plans were, for he was one of a small group that was intimately associated with the general from the beginning to the end of the campaign. Scott was a fine soldier in every sense of the word. His campaign was brilliantly conceived and, for the most part, brilliantly executed. Although he commanded what is by modern standards a very small army (it never numbered more than fourteen thousand men and sometimes sank as low as nine thousand), he accomplished great results; and his movement ranks high in American military annals. He was a complete general, in that he concerned himself with such matters as logistics, intelligence of the enemy, and psychological warfare. Among the reasons for his success was his astuteness in gathering around him as advisers and helpers men with brains who had received specialized training that he lacked. Among these, the most important was the group of able young engineer officers of which Beauregard was a member, usually known as the Engineer Company. The other members were Major John L. Smith, Captain Robert E. Lee (who dominated the Company), Captain James L. Mason, Lieutenants Isaac I. Stevens, Zealous B. Tower, Gustavus W. Smith (one of Beauregard's closest friends through life), J. G. Foster, and George B. McClellan.[5] Scott employed the engineers in several ways, notably to make reconnaissances before battle and to advise him in forming strategic decisions. In reality the engineer officers were Scott's staff, and they made a good one.

After organizing his army, Scott rendezvoused it at the Isle of Lobos, and then set sail for Vera Cruz. As the fleet approached the city on March 5, the excited soldiers exclaimed at the beauty of the scene before them—the high peak of Orizaba crowned with snow, the hexagonal white walls enclosing Vera Cruz, and the domes and spires of the town glittering in the sun. Some of the officers used up their

[4] Kenley, *Memoirs*, 238–40.
[5] *House Executive Documents*, 30 Cong., 2 Sess., Doc. 1, pp. 279–80.

supply of adjectives in describing the panorama in their diaries; war was still romantic. The more realistic among them noted the artillery pieces (about four hundred of them) bristling from the walls, the strong fortress of Uloa north of the city, and the shifting sand hills all around the town.[6] Scott's first problem was to select a landing place. Fleet commander Commodore David Conner advised a point south of the city. Scott, taking his principal generals and the engineer officers with him, went in a small steamer to inspect the spot, which Scott liked. Before returning to the fleet, Conner ran the steamer close to Uloa to deceive the Mexicans as to Scott's intentions. The Mexicans responded by firing several shots, which were wide of the mark. It was Beauregard's first experience under fire.[7]

On March 9, a beautiful sunny day, Scott put his army ashore. The landing was a model of efficient planning. Expecting opposition, which did not materialize, the first wave of soldiers hit the beach in surfboats, with one hundred men to a boat, while mosquito gunboats shelled the beach from close range to cover the landing. As the operation started, the regimental bands played patriotic airs; spectators lined the walls of Vera Cruz; the officers of the French, Spanish, and English ships watched curiously. When the first landing party planted the American flag in a sand hill, a mighty shout arose from the sailors, and the naval guns fired in salute. By night the entire army of ten thousand was ashore. Lieutenant Beauregard thought it was one of the finest spectacles he had ever seen.[8]

After Scott and the engineers inspected the defenses of Vera Cruz, the commanding general decided not to risk his small army in an assault against the walls. Instead he determined to take the city by

[6] *To Mexico with Scott: Letters of Captain E. Kirby Smith to His Wife* (Cambridge, 1917), 110; Raphael Semmes, *Service Afloat and Ashore During the Mexican War* (Cincinnati, 1851), 105–106, 114.

[7] Justin H. Smith, *The War with Mexico* (New York, 1919), II, 23; Meade, *Meade*, I, 187; *To Mexico with Scott: Letters of Kirby Smith*, 112.

[8] Edward D. Mansfield, *The Mexican War* (New York, 1848), 164–65; [Ballentine], *Autobiography*, 147–48; Semmes, *Service Afloat and Ashore*, 125–28; Myers (ed.), *Mexican War Diary of McClellan*, 53–54; P. S. P. Conner, *The Home Squadron under Commodore Conner in the War with Mexico* (Philadelphia, 1896), 60–82; New Orleans *Picayune*, March 25, 1847; J. Jacob Oswandel, *Notes of the Mexican War . . .* (Philadelphia, 1885), 68; G. T. M. Davis, *Autobiography of the Late Col. Geo. T. M. Davis* (New York, 1891), 125; William H. Parker, *Recollections of a Naval Officer, 1841–1865* (New York, 1883), 84–85. Beauregard's statement is in a sixty-five page manuscript, which he wrote in 1852, now in the Missouri Historical Society (St. Louis), entitled "Reminiscences of an Engineer Officer . . .," 1.

siege. Siege operations as practiced by armies in the nineteenth century were based on the teachings of the great French engineer Vauban. The besiegers would try to completely invest the place they were after, cutting off, if possible, all its lines of supply. Then they would mount batteries to pound the walls. The object was to move the artillery closer and closer to the target. As the batteries advanced, field fortifications and trenches had to be built to protect the guns and to house infantry troops who would guard the pieces against sorties from the garrison.

Obviously in such an operation good engineer officers were of vital importance. Scott's engineers, as they superintended the almost three weeks long siege of Vera Cruz, got their first real taste of war. They also had their first experience of war's dirt and discomfort. Life in the sand hills was not easy. The days were hot, the nights cold. Northers blew down tents, filled trenches with debris, and pelted faces with stinging sand. Lizards, chiggers, fleas, wood ticks, and sand flies afflicted officers and GI's alike. Some of the engineer officers, in a desperate effort to escape the pests at night, greased themselves all over with salt pork before retiring, and slept in canvas bags drawn up to their necks.[9]

Immediately after the army invested Vera Cruz, the engineer officers went to work, reconnoitering as close to the city as was safe and choosing sites for batteries.[10] From then on, they were busy with such jobs as laying out the batteries, building platforms on which the guns would rest, and throwing up epaulements or protective masses of earth in front of the pieces. As the siege progressed, it was evident that the army's siege guns could not damage the walls from a long range, so some of the big pieces from the ships were dismounted and brought ashore.[11] Setting up a battery was hard, tiring work for the engineers who designed them and the enlisted men who did the actual work of building them. During the siege, Beauregard had schedules when he went on duty at 2 A. M. and off at 4 P. M., or

[9] Myers (ed.), *Mexican War Diary of McClellan*, 55; [Ballentine], *Autobiography*, 152, 158; *To Mexico with Scott: Letters of Kirby Smith*, 120, 122; H. J. Moore, *Scott's Campaign in Mexico . . .* (Charleston, 1849), 37–38; Dabney H. Maury, *Recollections of a Virginian in the Mexican, Indian and Civil Wars* (New York, 1894), 34; Furber, *The Twelve Months Volunteer*, 9.

[10] Beauregard, "Reminiscences of an Engineer Officer," 1; Oswandel, *Notes of Mexican War*, 78.

[11] Myers (ed.), *Mexican War Diary of McClellan*, 56–58, 62–63.

started at 2 P. M. and quit at 4 A. M.[12] To get a battery ready required the labor of a hundred men and twenty horses for a day and a night, the men often dragging the guns over sand hills where horses could not go.[13]

One afternoon Colonel Totten directed Beauregard to accompany a detachment that was to lay out a battery about 450 yards from the city. When Beauregard reached the point designated by his superior, he decided, after climbing a tree to survey the terrain, that the place was too advanced and isolated. On his way back to camp to report his objections to Totten, Beauregard saw a ridge which he thought was a better site for the battery. Totten was surprised that Beauregard had not followed orders. The colonel said that he had had the ground well examined. Beauregard said maybe so, but Totten had not examined it from a treetop. Totten agreed to inspect the ground again the next day. This time he admitted that Beauregard was right, and batteries were built on the ridge. Beauregard later claimed that three of the five batteries which finally reduced Vera Cruz were located on sites which he selected.[14] Lieutenant Beauregard was undoubtedly right in his argument with Totten. But he here showed a characteristic that would embroil him in many needless quarrels—a tendency to question the will of a superior and to put the superior in his place with a smart remark.

On another afternoon Lee and Beauregard went on a reconnaissance toward the city and returned to camp after dark. As they emerged from the bush into an open spot, they met a soldier who yelled, "Who goes there?" Before the officers could identify themselves properly he fired, singeing Lee's uniform. The engineers disarmed him and turned him in at camp. The replies of Lee and Beauregard to his challenge were interesting and perhaps revealing. The modest Lee said, "Friends." Beauregard shouted, "Officers!"[15]

[12] During the war, Beauregard kept a small diary, which he called his "Note-Book." It is in the Beauregard Papers (Library of Congress). It will hereinafter be cited as Beauregard MS. Notebook. The above information is taken from various entries for March, 1847.

[13] Moore, *Scott's Campaign*, 9–10; Oswandel, *Notes of Mexican War*, 80, 85; Stevens, *Stevens*, I, 111–14.

[14] Beauregard, "Reminiscences of an Engineer Officer," 2–5; proofsheets of memoirs of William Montgomery Gardner in William Montgomery Gardner Papers (Southern Historical Collection, University of North Carolina Library).

[15] Beauregard, "Reminiscences of an Engineer Officer," 2; W. A. Croffut (ed.), *Fifty Years in Camp and Field: Diary of Major General Ethan Allen Hitchcock, U. S. A.* (New York, 1909), 243.

By March 22 the American batteries were so close to Vera Cruz that they could not only batter the walls but fire into the city itself. The besiegers then began a constant bombardment day and night that lasted for four days. Some of the shells destroyed homes and buildings, and the impressionable Americans, awed by the beauty and the horror of the scene, could hear victims in the town shrieking and moaning.[16] The Mexican commander, shaken by the bombardment and knowing his cause was hopeless, offered to surrender the city. On March 29 the garrison stacked arms in a meadow south of the town as the proud Americans looked on.[17] Proudest of all were the engineer officers, who felt that their skill had enabled Scott to take Vera Cruz with small loss of life. The whole army honored them, they believed. At least Scott and his principal officers honored them, for the official reports to Washington glowed with praise for the engineers. Colonel Totten said they were responsible for the position, form, and arrangement of the trenches and batteries, and commended each officer equally by name.[18]

Lieutenant Beauregard was irked when he read Totten's report. Because he had located most of the batteries which had reduced the city, he thought that he should have had special mention and perhaps should have received a promotion. Afflicted as always by his Napoleonic complex, he wrote, recalling the work of his idol at Toulon: "History tells us that on one occasion, the establishment of a battery stamped a young officer of artillery as a very promising one in the eyes of his superiors!" His wounded spirits were not raised by an attack of fever and diarrhea which hit him after the surrender and confined him to bed for several days.[19]

Scott kept the army in Vera Cruz only long enough to set it up as a base and to collect land transportation. Then he moved the troops west on the National Highway, hoping to get them out of the low country before the hot season struck. The commanding general remained in Vera Cruz to complete his preparations. As the army ad-

[16] Mansfield, *Mexican War*, 170; Moore, *Scott's Campaign*, 15–16; Semmes, *Service Afloat and Ashore*, 137–38; Arthur H. Noll, *General Kirby-Smith* (Sewanee, 1907), 52–53.

[17] Semmes, *Service Afloat and Ashore*, 145–47; New Orleans *Picayune*, April 14, 1847.

[18] Stevens, *Stevens*, I, 116; *Senate Executive Documents*, 30 Cong., 1 Sess., Doc. 1, pp. 220, 241, 244–45, 247–49.

[19] Beauregard, "Reminiscences of an Engineer Officer," 5–6, 10; Beauregard MS. Notebook, March 30–April 7, 1847

vanced, Beauregard accompanied the division of General Robert Patterson, to which he was attached as an engineer officer at Patterson's request. One day Patterson and his staff and Beauregard stopped at one of the numerous homes of Santa Anna, the Mexican commander, and drank the enemy general's health with his own champagne and fought his gamecocks.[20] On April 11–12 the vanguard of the army, led by the divisions of General David Twiggs and Patterson, emerged from the plains into the mountains and found themselves confronting Santa Anna's forces in a strong position around a hill called Cerro Gordo. Santa Anna had chosen his position well. His right rested on a river; north of the river his troops and batteries were posted on high ridges that ran up to the National Highway; north of the highway was Cerro Gordo, on which Santa Anna had mounted batteries. The Mexican general was certain that he could stop any American attack with heavy losses.

In an effort to find out the exact location of the Mexican forces, Twiggs had sent out some officers to reconnoitre around the enemy left. When Beauregard arrived with Patterson's division, he took charge of the reconnaissance. Early on the morning of April 13, with one of Twiggs's officers and an escort, he cautiously followed a mule path that led around Cerro Gordo, and going farther than Twiggs's men the day before, he eventually came to a hill north of Cerro Gordo called Atalaya. He ascended the hill and stayed there surveying the country for over an hour. He was a mile behind the front of the Mexican line. Looking at Cerro Gordo, he decided that it could be carried and the Mexicans flanked out of their position. He so reported to Twiggs when he returned in the afternoon.[21]

On the basis of Beauregard's information, Twiggs decided to attack the Mexicans the next day. A mediocre soldier, his principal notion of war was to attack. He proposed to Patterson and to General James Shields, whose division had just come up, that he strike Cerro Gordo and that Patterson and Shields assail the strong Mexican positions in front. Beauregard was to guide Twiggs's division. Scott's subordinates, in his absence, were planning to commit the army to what could be a decisive battle at the beginning of the campaign, on ground that had not been adequately examined. Patterson, however, had doubts about the plan.

[20] Beauregard MS. Notebook, April 10, 1847.
[21] Beauregard, "Reminiscences of an Engineer Officer," 6–8.

That night he called Beauregard to his quarters and asked the lieutenant for his opinion of Twiggs's scheme. Beauregard said he thought it would succeed but he preferred a different mode of attack. He thought the Americans should concentrate their assault on Cerro Gordo, which was the key to the Mexican position, and make only a deceiving demonstration in front. He feared the result of dividing the army for two simultaneous attacks. Patterson asked him to present his objections to Twiggs, concealing the fact that he had talked to Patterson. Twiggs and Patterson disliked each other heartily. Beauregard then went to Twiggs and asked permission to speak his views about the attack scheduled for the next day. When he had finished, Twiggs said that Beauregard might be right but it was too late to change the orders. "Don't you think we will succeed any how?" asked Twiggs. "Certainly Sir," replied Beauregard, "but I think we ought to throw all the chances in our favor." Twiggs did, however, change his orders that night, when he heard that Scott would arrive the next day. Unwilling to risk the possible disapproval of the commanding general, he called off the attack.[22]

Scott, when he resumed command, was appalled at the thought of attacking the Mexicans in their strong position. Always conscious that he was advancing deep into the enemy country with a small army, Scott always sought to conserve lives by turning a flank of the enemy instead of risking a frontal assault. Now he was determined to find a way around the Mexican left so he could pass a force to the enemy rear. Using the information acquired by Beauregard as a starting point, Scott directed that further reconnaissances be made. On April 15 Lee, Beauregard, and other engineer officers followed Beauregard's trail to Atalaya. While the others ascended Atalaya, Beauregard went on alone toward Cerro Gordo, going almost to its base. Then the fever he had contracted at Vera Cruz hit him again. He returned to camp, marking his path with a hatchet.[23] For the next few days he was so ill that he could barely move about.

This was terribly bad luck for Beauregard. The reconnaissance he had developed so promisingly was taken over by Lee, who found a path by which Scott could bring out a force in the rear of Cerro Gordo. Beauregard missed the credit for completing the reconnaissance, and he also missed the battle of Cerro Gordo on the eighteenth.

[22] *Ibid.*, 8–10; Cadmus M. Wilcox, *History of the Mexican War* (Washington, 1892), 276–79.
[23] Beauregard, "Reminiscences of an Engineer Officer," 10.

So sick he could hardly sit a horse, he had no chance to distinguish himself as Scott turned the Mexican left and swept the enemy from the field.[24]

He was bitter after the battle. He believed that Scott had not dealt fairly with him in the official report. Although the commanding general had been careful to say that the reconnaissance begun by Beauregard was continued by Lee, Beauregard felt slighted. Scott singled out Lee for special praise, while commending all the engineers. Beauregard thought that he should have received credit at least equal to Lee's. Lee had discovered little that Beauregard did not already know, the lieutenant said, and had wasted precious time in useless reconnoitering. Commendation for his work before Cerro Gordo in the reports of Patterson and Twiggs did not assuage his anger. Lee had got the credit in the report that counted. It would not be the last time that he would resent the Virginian.[25]

Hardly pausing after Cerro Gordo, Scott drove his army on and occupied Jalapa on April 20. Beauregard and Lee accompanied the advance division under Twiggs and were among the first officers to reach the town. On the way they had stopped at Santa Anna's hacienda, where they found some maps and drawings of the country. The army paused briefly at Jalapa, while Scott waited for supplies and discharged a number of twelve months volunteers whose terms were up. Most of the engineer officers and an infantry division moved on toward the next stop, Puebla.[26] When the army left Jalapa late in April, the soldiers noted that the fertile farm lands through which they had been marching disappeared as the National Highway wound ever higher into the mountains. The word ran through the ranks that Scott would abandon his base and live off the country. The great adventure of it all thrilled the romantic army, and cries of "On to the halls of the Montezumas" sounded around the campfires. On May 15, the invaders marched into Puebla with bands playing and colors flying. The Americans were now only ninety-three miles from Mexico City. Their only connection with the United States was the tenuous line of communications back to Vera Cruz. If they had not

[24] *Ibid.*, 10–11.

[25] *Ibid.*, 11; *Senate Executive Documents,* 30 Cong., 1 Sess., Doc. 1, pp. 261–63, 277, 295; Winfield Scott, *Memoirs of Lieut.-General Scott . . .* (New York, 1864), II, 444–45, 450.

[26] Beauregard, "Reminiscences of an Engineer Officer," 12; Stevens, *Stevens,* I, 130–31.

known it before, they realized now that they were in a war. As they stood in the grand plaza of Mexico's second city, an army of little more than six thousand in a city of eighty thousand, they could feel the mass hostility of the horde of Mexican spectators pressing upon them.[27]

Scott held the army at Puebla for almost three months. The long pause was for the purpose of organizing the army for the final push on Mexico City. Reinforcements from the states that would bring the army up to fourteen thousand were on the way from Vera Cruz. After they arrived, weeks had to be spent drilling them. Supplies to last the army until it reached Mexico City had to be accumulated. As busy as Scott and his division generals, were the engineer officers. They collected information on the roads leading to the enemy capital and its defenses and made sketches of both for Scott's use. Some of their material they secured from Mexican spies whom Scott had employed at Puebla. Lieutenant Beauregard was in on all the work, but again he became temporarily incapacitated when his horse stepped on his foot and tore a toenail partially off.[28] By the first week of August the reorganizing was completed, and on the seventh the army moved out of Puebla for the last lap of its great march. Five days brought it to the rim of the mountains, and below them the soldiers saw a sight that few ever forgot—the Valley of Mexico with its lakes, towns, and fields spread like a map before them, and barely perceptible in the distance the city they sought.[29]

The army emerged from the mountains at Ayotla, about twenty miles from Mexico City on the National Highway. Straight ahead, the highway ran to the capital on a causeway between lakes and marshes. Commanding the road was a high hill known as El Penon. Two other possible routes were open to the Americans. To the north, or their right, a long, circuitous road skirted the northern shore of Lake Texcoco before reaching Mexico City. To the south, or their

[27] *To Mexico with Scott: Letters of Kirby Smith*, 138–41, 146, 165–66; [Ballentine], *Autobiography*, 219–20, 223–24, 228–30; Moore, *Scott's Campaign*, 96–97.
[28] Semmes, *Service Afloat and Ashore*, 279; R. S. Ripley, *The War with Mexico* (New York, 1849), II, 184–85; Stevens, *Stevens*, I, 144, 148–50; Beauregard MS. Notebook, July 11, 1847.
[29] Semmes, *Service Afloat and Ashore*, 320–21; New Orleans *Picayune*, August 20, 1847; *To Mexico with Scott: Letters of Kirby Smith*, 189–92; Robert Anderson, *An Artillery Officer in the Mexican War . . .* (New York, 1911), 285–87.

left, a shorter road, thought to be in bad condition and possibly impassable, traversed the southern shores of Lakes Chalco and Xochimilco and came out south of the city. Scott naturally wanted to go in on the direct middle route, if possible, so he sent out the engineers to reconnoitre the road ahead and particularly to determine if Santa Anna had fortified El Penon.

On the morning of August 12 Lee and one group went toward the hill while Beauregard and another explored the road toward the right. In the afternoon Lee and Beauregard worked along the northern shore of Chalco and secured information that the road south of the lake was rough but passable. The next day all the engineers were out in the vicinity of El Penon, going as close to the hill as they could. At one point they flushed some Mexican lancers, who ran when the Americans charged. As a result of the reconnaissances, the engineers reported to Scott that Santa Anna, who had not fought since Cerro Gordo, had determined to make a stand in front of the capital and that he had crowned El Penon with artillery. They thought that the position could be taken, but only with heavy losses, because the American army would be largely confined to the causeway as it attacked. Scott, devoted as always to the flanking tactic, then decided to bypass El Penon by taking the southern road, which because of the information supplied by Lee and Beauregard and because of a scout made by another officer he believed to be passable.[30]

As the army swung out south of the lakes, Beauregard accompanied the advance division of General William J. Worth, to which he had been assigned as engineer officer. Consequently he was with the vanguard of the army as it rolled into San Agustin directly south of Mexico City, from which Scott intended to drive north at the capital. Scott, however, had won only a partial success by his flanking movement. He had turned Santa Anna out of El Penon, but the Mexican commander had pulled back and now confronted Scott at San Antonio, a short distance north of San Agustin. The situation was the same as at El Penon. If the Americans advanced, they would have to traverse a narrow causeway covered by artillery fire.

[30] Beauregard, "Reminiscences of an Engineer Officer," 12–16; Wilcox, *History of the Mexican War,* 351–52; Stevens, *Stevens,* I, 164–66; J. F. H. Claiborne, *The Life and Correspondence of John A. Quitman* (New York, 1860), I, 332–34; Scott, *Memoirs,* II, 468–69; Richard M'Sherry, *El Puchero: or, A Mixed Dish from Mexico* . . . (Philadelphia, 1850), 63–64.

As he had done at El Penon, Scott called in his engineers to find a way out of the difficulty. On August 18 he sent one group of them north toward San Antonio. Lee and Beauregard he sent west across a huge lava bed called the Pedregal. Their mission was to find out if the army, or part of it, could cross the molten rocks and reach a road (the San Angel road) on the other side running north. If the Americans could get over the Pedregal, they could flank Santa Anna out of San Antonio. That night Lee and Beauregard reported that they had found a path that could be built into a road. Immediately Scott decided to use the Pedregal route.[31]

The next day the troops of Gideon Pillow and Twiggs were set to constructing a road through the mass of tangled rocks. The engineers were directing the work, conducting batteries to good positions, and exploring toward the Mexican positions on the far side of the Pedregal. The road building was soon halted by the attacks of Mexicans stationed near Contreras on the San Angel road. To stop the attacks, Pillow and Twiggs decided to storm the works around Contreras. The Americans tried to advance but the going was difficult; the enemy was in superior numbers. Meanwhile Scott, from his headquarters, could see Mexican reinforcements coming down the San Angel road. To succor his hard-pressed men, he ordered reinforcements over the Pedregal; Beauregard guided several of these units toward Contreras. One of the newly arrived generals, George Cadwalader, told Beauregard to go back and ask Scott for help.

Disappointed that he might miss the fighting, Beauregard started to recross the Pedregal. As he crossed a ravine, he met General P. F. Smith, the ranking officer on the field, and coaxed Smith to let him stay. Smith, badly in need of a guide to take him to the other troops, readily agreed. After the American forces were united, Smith took Beauregard and Lee and went to reconnoitre the Mexican position. Even though darkness was approaching, Smith decided to attack. Beauregard thought Smith was wrong and tried to get Lee to talk the general out of his decision, but Lee refused. The coming of darkness forced Smith to call off his plan, but he announced that he would attack early the next morning.[32]

[31] Stevens, *Stevens*, I, 169–70; Wilcox, *History of the Mexican War*, 358–59; Scott, *Memoirs*, II, 471.

[32] Beauregard, "Reminiscences of an Engineer Officer," 19–20; Scott, *Memoirs*, II, 474–75; *Senate Executive Documents*, 30 Cong., 1 Sess., Doc. 1, pp. 307, 323, 350–51, Doc. 65, pp. 229–30; Wilcox, *History of the Mexican War*, 363–64.

That night a drenching rain fell on the troops, most of whom were without shelter or fire. Lee, apparently impervious to fatigue, crossed and recrossed the Pedregal, bearing messages between Scott and Smith. Some of the younger officers spent the night in a church, and Lieutenant Beauregard spoke his mind freely to them. He said that Smith was making a mistake and that the army should attack at a later hour in the morning or retrace its route over the Pedregal.[33] There was little sleep for anybody that night, as Smith got his men up and in position at 2:30 in the morning. The engineers, who were to guide the troops to the rear of the enemy camp at Contreras, had to reconnoitre in the darkness. As the army advanced, Beauregard accompanied General Smith at the head of Cadwalader's lead brigade. Through mud and fog the column plodded toward Contreras over a narrow path that delayed the attack until after daybreak. But when it was delivered, it caught the Mexicans completely by surprise. They fled northward as the Americans poured up the San Angel road, their numbers increased by reinforcements that had crossed the Pedregal in the morning. At the same time the forces at San Agustin advanced, and Santa Anna to escape being enveloped abandoned San Antonio and fell back to Churubusco.

To Beauregard fell the honor of bearing to Scott the announcement of the victory at Contreras. Smith sent him to tell the commanding general. Getting a horse, Beauregard rode toward San Agustin. On the way he met Scott, Worth, and their staffs and poured out his news. The delighted old general said, "Young man, if I were not on horseback, I would embrace you." Turning to the staff, Scott said, "Gentlemen, if West Point had only produced the Corps of Engineers, the country ought to be proud of that institution. . . ."[34]

Scott appreciated the magnitude of his victory, and to exploit it to the full he ordered his exuberant troops on to Churubusco immediately. The Americans won their second victory of that hard-fought day when they stormed the enemy lines at Churubusco and drove Santa Anna's disorganized army into the defenses of Mexico City. Beauregard did not participate in the fighting at Churubusco. He was directed to repair the road over the Pedregal, using Mexican prisoners as laborers. He went to the Pedregal, but no prisoners came. Then he heard the sound of firing to the north and started to go to the

[33] Beauregard, "Reminiscences of an Engineer Officer," 20–22.
[34] *Ibid.*, 23–24.

battle. He decided, however, that he should obey orders and stay where he was. Soon he heard that a victory had been won and the road would not be needed. Disappointed that he had missed the fighting, he went to San Agustin and found the other engineers. Here he ate his first meal since breakfast of the previous day, having had only a few pieces of hard bread in the interim.

On the whole, Beauregard felt well satisfied with Contreras and Churubusco. All the reports of his superiors mentioned him and praised his skill and gallantry before and during the battles. As a more tangible reward, he was given the brevet of captain, which meant he had the rank without the pay.[35]

After Churubusco Scott prepared to move on Mexico City itself. The wily Santa Anna then asked for a truce; and Scott, hoping that the peace he knew President Polk desired would follow, agreed. Both sides pledged not to build up their strength during the negotiations. The Mexican violated the agreement; he used the truce as a breathing space to reorganize his defenses. When Scott found this out, he broke off the talks and resumed hostilities. Scott faced a difficult military problem in attempting to capture Mexico City. The capital stood on high ground surrounded by marshes and approached by causeways, three from the south and two from the west. Fortified *garitas*, or gates, guarded each approach. The roads from the south offered the most direct route, but because of the marshes the Americans would be confined to the roads and hence would be subject to a killing artillery fire. The roads from the west were better, and the ground here was higher; but here also was the great fortress of Chapultepec, which would be in the rear of the Americans if they used the western route. If Scott came in from the west, where he would have more room to maneuver, presumably he would first have to take Chapultepec.

Scott's first idea was to use the southern approaches. From September 7–10 he had Lee, Beauregard, and the other engineers out reconnoitering every route. They were to determine if the roads were passable for artillery and the terrain suitable for maneuver and to spy out the defenses of the *garitas*. Once Beauregard and two other

[35] *Senate Executive Documents,* 30 Cong., 1 Sess., Doc. 1, pp. 307, 315, 328, 332, 349–53, and in Appendix, pp. 66–69, 75; Scott, *Memoirs,* II, 480, 501; Beauregard, "Reminiscences of an Engineer Officer," 24–25.

engineers went to within 1,100 yards of the city walls, so close they could see the Mexicans working on their batteries.[36] This kind of reconnoitering was dangerous work, as the engineers well realized.

On one occasion Beauregard was ordered to make a night reconnaissance of the southern gates and, if possible, to enter the city and examine the defenses. Although he protested that such a reconnaisance involved a reckless exposure of life, the order stood. Shortly after midnight Beauregard started out, with a Mexican guide and an escort of four infantry companies. He approached one of the gates with a small group of his men, planning to rush the sentry. He told the guide to answer in Spanish if challenged. When the sentry called for identification, the guide was too frightened to answer. Beauregard, in his best Spanish accent, shouted, "Amigos." Undeceived, the sentry fired. Other pickets rushed up and fired on the Americans.

Beauregard's men became rattled and seemed about to take to their heels. It was a crisis, and Beauregard met it in a way he would employ in other crises later. He struck a pose, without, of course, realizing that he was posing. To his excited soldiers, he addressed the words of Caesar: "Where are you going to, you are mistaken, the enemy is here and not there!" They must have been puzzled by this classical exhortation, but Beauregard's courage rallied them and they drove off the pickets. When artillery fire from the city opened, Beauregard retired his men. The guide escaped by jumping in a canal.[37]

After all the reconnaissances, Scott was still undecided between the southern and western routes. On September 11 he called a conference of his principal officers and the engineers in the church at Piedad to settle the issue. When Scott entered the room, he took a chair and said he would not rise until he had decided the best mode of attack. The commanding general, saying he was thinking out loud, detailed the advantages and disadvantages of each route. Scott said he inclined to the western approach. General Gideon Pillow, President Polk's law partner, spoke in favor of the southern route. Another general said he would like to hear from the engineers. Major Smith, Lee, Tower, and Stevens arose in turn and advocated attack-

[36] Beauregard, "Reminiscences of an Engineer Officer," 27–32; *Senate Executive Documents*, 30 Cong., 1 Sess., Doc. 1, pp. 355, 376, 385, 425–27, Doc. 65, pp. 112–13; Scott, *Memoirs*, II, 508; Wilcox, *History of the Mexican War*, 430–31, 442, 445.

[37] Beauregard, "Reminiscences of an Engineer Officer," 27–29.

ing from the south. Their testimony, especially Lee's, had great weight. Four generals stated they now agreed with Pillow. It was evident that the council would vote for the southern route. At this point several people asked Beauregard, who had come in while Scott was speaking, why he did not give his views. Beauregard replied that he would not unless asked, because he differed from the other engineers. The discussion drew Scott's attention, and he snapped out, "You, young man in that corner, what have you got to say on the subject?" [38]

Beauregard arose to face the council. It was undoubtedly his greatest moment in the war, and he was well prepared for it. He presented a long, reasoned, and often technical argument to support the western route. He had scouted the southern approaches since September 7, he said, and he knew that the enemy defenses on each had increased in strength. An attack from this quarter would be open to the view and the guns of the enemy and over terrain where the army could not maneuver. Remembering his West Point lessons and his reading of Jomini, he lectured the generals, many of whom were politicians in civil life, that it was a sound maxim in war "never to do what your enemy expects or wishes you to do," and obviously the enemy in this case wanted the Americans to attack from the south. The best way to take a city, he continued in a classroom style, was to feint an attack in one quarter and deliver a real one at another point at daybreak. In authoritative military jargon, he told his fascinated listeners that by seizing Chapultepec the Americans would secure a point from which they could move on any part of the circumference of Mexico City even if forced eventually to attack the southern gates. He sat down before an impressed and slightly awed audience.

It had been a good performance, replete with book theory and containing some sound sense. Probably many of the officers did not fully understand him, but they were converted. One general who had endorsed the southern route announced that he was changing his vote. Scott dragged his bulk up from his chair and said, "Gentlemen, we will attack by the western gates. The general officers present here will remain for further orders—the meeting is dissolved." [39] Beauregard must have gone home in a glow that night.

[38] *Ibid.*, 33–37.
[39] Beauregard MS. Notebook, September 11, 1847; Claiborne, *Quitman*, I, 353–55; Croffut (ed.), *Fifty Years in Camp and Field*, 300; Stevens, *Stevens,*

He had carried the council with him against its own will, he had upheld the views of the commanding general, and for once he had outshone Lee.

Once Scott had decided to take Chapultepec, he moved quickly. On September 12 the American batteries opened a concentrated fire on the fortress. Scott kept the bombardment going all day. He expected to breach the walls and then storm the place with infantry the next day. That night Beauregard worked from ten until four-thirty in the morning repairing two batteries which had been damaged by the return fire of the enemy. After resting an hour, he returned to the batteries for the pre-attack firing. In the attack on Chapultepec he was supposed to guide Pillow's division, but actually he did about as he pleased. That morning he told friends he intended to tear down the Mexican flag in the fortress.

As the troops went forward, he joined Colonel Joseph E. Johnston's *voltigeur* regiment. At one point he found a mountain howitzer battery in charge of a sergeant, and stopped and aimed one of the pieces. He rejoined the *voltigeurs* as they went up a hill under heavy fire. Thinking the men needed encouragement, he got a rifle and fired from an exposed position. Before each shot, he would cry to Johnston, "Colonel, what will you bet on this shot?" He crossed the parapet with the first storming parties and rushed through the first open door he saw. His purpose was to get to the top of the walls and find the flag, but he got lost in the maze of the inner works. Bursting up a stairway he saw, to his great disappointment, his friend Captain Barnard hauling the enemy emblem down.[40]

As the victors stood in Chapultepec, with the beaten Mexicans fleeing to the capital, the military situation was highly fluid and slightly confused. Scott sent out orders to his generals to advance toward the city by any available route. Several of them had already started forward, some influenced by a sound instinct to hit the enemy while he was on the run and others hoping to win the glory of being the first to enter Mexico City. Among the latter was John A. Quitman, whose division Beauregard joined as he left Chapultepec to take part in the pursuit. Quitman's engineer officer had been

I, 207; *Senate Executive Documents,* 30 Cong., 1 Sess., Doc. 65, pp. 77–78, 81, 111–12, 123–24, 256–57.

[40] Beauregard, "Reminiscences of an Engineer Officer," 41–45; *Senate Executive Documents,* 30 Cong., 1 Sess., Doc. 1, pp. 190–91, 404–405, 428; New Orleans *Picayune,* September 19, 1847.

wounded, and he was glad to accept the proffered service of Beauregard.

The general asked Beauregard to reconnoitre the road ahead, a broad avenue flanked with ditches and marshy ground and entering Mexico City at the Belen *garita*. As Beauregard went about his work, he crossed a canal by means of a tree lying across it. On the way back, he slipped and fell in the canal. He accompanied Quitman's troops as they moved down the road. A ball from a Mexican musket grazed his shoulder, and another wounded him slightly in the thigh. A little later, as he was standing in the road, a shot struck his side. Momentarily stunned, he revived after a drink of whisky and brandy. To a friend he said, "That is the third bullet that has struck me to-day. I found the other two, and ought to find this one." Unbuttoning his coat, he found that the bullet had gone through a pocket containing his gloves and eyeglasses and had barely pinked the flesh.[41]

By dark Quitman had reached and stormed the Belen *garita*. He then tried to enter the city but was stopped by Mexican fire from an old tobacco factory known as the Citadel. His men exhausted and his artillery ammunition running short, Quitman retired to the *garita* for the night. He was still determined to be the first into the capital, even though he had received word from Scott that Worth was to have that honor. In the darkness Quitman and Beauregard laid out batteries to reduce the Citadel in the morning. While they were looking for a site, Quitman fell headfirst into a canal and Beauregard went down neck deep. At this point the wet and cold captain had been on his feet for two days and nights and in the last thirty-six hours had subsisted on two cups of coffee.[42]

When the Americans arose the next morning, they saw a white flag flying over the Citadel. During the night Santa Anna had evacuated the city. Beauregard, being the only officer present who spoke Spanish, went to the Citadel to ascertain the meaning of the flag. He found there a lone Mexican officer who explained that he had been left to surrender the place. Politely he asked Beauregard for a

[41] Beauregard, "Reminiscences of an Engineer Officer," 46–51; Louisville *Courier-Journal,* April 12, 1893, clipping in Beauregard Papers (Department of Archives, Louisiana State University).

[42] Beauregard, "Reminiscences of an Engineer Officer," 52–58; *Senate Executive Documents,* 30 Cong., 1 Sess., Doc. 1, Appendix, p. 185; Mansfield, *Mexican War,* 300–301.

receipt. In his best theatrical manner, Beauregard replied that American receipts were "written in blood and signed with the bayonet."[43] Sensing his opportunity, Quitman ordered his division to march to the Grand Plaza in the center of the city. Under a splendid sun they wheeled into the square and formed in line as the clock in the great cathedral fronting the Plaza struck seven. The dirty, ragged columns were anything but imposing. Quitman had lost a shoe when he fell in the canal, and Beauregard was covered with mud. But they and not any other division had occupied Mexico City.

The exultant Quitman told Beauregard to ride to Scott with the news. As the young officer rode northward through deserted streets toward the San Cosme *garita*, he was full of romantic thoughts. He remembered Prescott's description of the flight of Cortez and his men from the city over three hundred years before on the very road he was now traveling to announce the victory of another invader. At the outskirts of the city, he met Scott. The old general was irritated by Beauregard's information and snappishly asked if Quitman's division had been in a hurry to forestall Worth.[44]

The fall of Mexico City ended the war. A new Mexican government took over and concluded a peace. Until the negotiations were concluded, the army remained in possession of Mexico City. During these months, Beauregard and the other engineers relaxed and enjoyed some of the social life of the capital. On the day of the occupation Beauregard was taken ill with fever and ague and was in bed for days. He did not entirely recover for several weeks.[45] The officers of the various services, wanting a clubhouse as a center for their entertainment, formed a society, the Aztec Club, that survived for years after the war. Beauregard was a popular member; indeed, he seems to have been generally liked throughout the service.[46] At the club sessions and wherever officers gathered, the recent campaigns were generously rehashed. One day Beauregard was out riding and met Scott and two generals. In one of his heavily playful moods, the

[43] Beauregard, "Reminiscences of an Engineer Officer," 58–59; Claiborne, *Quitman*, I, 365–71; *Senate Executive Documents*, 30 Cong., 1 Sess., Doc. 1, pp. 414–16; Elliott, *Scott*, 547–52.

[44] Beauregard, "Reminiscences of an Engineer Officer," 61–64; Claiborne, *Quitman*, I, 376–78; Fayette Copeland, *Kendall of the Picayune* (Norman, Okla., 1943), 224.

[45] Beauregard, "Reminiscences of an Engineer Officer," 64.

[46] Military Society of the Mexican War, *Aztec Club of 1847* (London, 1928), *passim;* Stevens, *Stevens,* I, 216–17.

old general said to Beauregard, "Young man, I wish to reprimand you, and I wish the whole army was present; but these generals represent it. Why did you advise me to attack by the western gates? You now see the consequences! We have taken this great city and the halls of Montezuma, after a few hours hard fighting and with only a loss of 800 men. Be careful in future, sir, of such bad advice to your seniors."[47]

The commanding general obviously valued Beauregard as an officer, but Beauregard was bitter against Scott after the war. Even though he received the brevet of major for Chapultepec, Beauregard felt that the general had not treated him fairly. In his report of the entire campaign, Scott allotted great but equal credit to Lee, Beauregard, Stevens, Tower, G. W. Smith, and McClellan. Beauregard thought that he should have received special mention, perhaps a paragraph, for supporting Scott's views at the Piedad council.[48] His estimate of Scott as a general was not too high. Rather patronizingly, he liked to refer to Scott as "our glorious old chief." He conceded that Scott was the best general of the war, but he fell short of Beauregard's ideal of a general. There is no evidence that he studied Scott's generalship in the Mexican campaign or learned anything from the general's strategy, as Lee undoubtedly did. Beauregard entered the war with certain rigid ideas about the art of warfare, derived primarily from his study of Napoleon's battles, and a rigid belief that certain rules of war must always be followed. Much of Scott's brilliant strategy was lost on Beauregard because it did not come out of the books. He was shocked at Scott's bold departure from some of the venerated rules of war, which he thought had endangered the American army.[49]

Here was Beauregard's greatest weakness as a soldier. He tended to think of war as something that was in books and that was fought in conformity to a fixed pattern. He could not easily adjust his thinking to an actual situation or improvise new ways of war. Too many times he would go by the rules in the books.

[47] Claiborne, *Quitman*, I, 355n.; Beauregard, "Reminiscences of an Engineer Officer," 38.
[48] Scott, *Memoirs*, II, 533–34; Roman, *Beauregard*, I, 7; Beauregard, "Reminiscences of an Engineer Officer," 38.
[49] Beauregard, "Reminiscences of an Engineer Officer," 65.

CHAPTER THREE

To The Shores of Charleston

O N JUNE 15, 1848, the steamer *Portland* arrived in New Orleans from Mexico with the first soldiers to be returned from the war. Among the passengers were Beauregard and Lee. Beauregard's first official action after getting home was to ask Colonel Totten for leave with pay until November. At this time he was a sick man. The fever and ague he had contracted at Mexico City attacked him at monthly intervals or whenever he exposed himself to bad weather. Not until a year later, after he had taken the water treatment at Biloxi on the Mississippi Gulf coast, did he consider himself cured.[1]

For the next twelve years Beauregard was in charge of what the Engineer Department called "the Mississippi and Lake defences in Louisiana." Ironically·enough, much of his work was done elsewhere; he repaired old forts and built new ones on the Florida coast and in Mobile harbor. In Louisiana his chief task was to repair and make defensible Forts St. Philip and Jackson on the Mississippi about seventy-five miles below New Orleans. These forts were supposed to command the river against a foe attacking from the sea. Much labor was spent on them but not much Congressional money, and they were incomplete when the Civil War started—with fatal results for Beauregard's beloved city.[2]

As he went about his work, Beauregard still carried the bitterness he had brought out of the war. When he heard that the War Department was going to publish a new list of brevets, he wrote to Quitman, now in politics, and asked the general to use his influence to

[1] New Orleans *Picayune,* June 20, 1848; Beauregard to Totten, June 19, 1848, in War Department, Letters Received, Engineer Department files (National Archives); Beauregard to Totten, August 9, 1849, in Office of Chief of Engineer files.

[2] Beauregard's work in this period can be followed in his reports in War Department, Letters Received, Engineer Department files. See also New Orleans *Picayune,* October 26, December 21, 1852, and Beauregard to Captain A. H. Bowman, December 1, 1854, in Beauregard Papers (Tulane University).

get him on the list. It came out, nevertheless, without his name; what was worse, two of the engineer officers with Scott received three brevets. Beauregard had thought Lee would be the only engineer to get three, and he had reconciled himself to the justice of Lee's claim. But to read that a man like Z. B. Tower had secured one more brevet than he was too much. In a fury, he wrote to General P. F. Smith, requesting the general to lay his case before Scott, Totten, and Secretary of War C. M. Conrad. He ticked off his services in Mexico, from Vera Cruz to the Belen *garita*, and asked bitterly: "Well now Genl do you not think that out of these six 'heads' I might at least have received three brevets as well as my friend Tower? especially and above all for the operations against the Garita of Belen! and do you not think that if the matter was properly laid before Mr. Conrad, that he has enough of the 'feu-sacré' about him to 'Give unto Caesar what is Caesar's.' " [3]

Whatever time he could get away from his forts, Beauregard spent at Magnolia, one of the Villeré plantations, where his wife and two sons sometimes lived. Situated below New Orleans on the right bank of the Mississippi, Magnolia was a pleasant place for a tired officer to relax. His oldest son, René, liked to recall in later years how the family sat on the veranda in the evenings watching the moonbeams shine on the leaves of the oak trees and the surface of the river.[4] In March, 1850, Beauregard's domestic happiness was shattered when his wife died giving birth to a daughter. He buried Marie Laure in the family cemetery in St. Bernard. On her tomb was placed an inscription in French which read, in part: "Spirit from Heaven, there you have returned. Sleep in peace, daughter, wife and dear mother." Her grave stood alone through the years and stands alone today; Beauregard would be buried in New Orleans.[5]

In a few years Beauregard married again. His second wife was Caroline Deslonde, also a Creole. She is variously described as being one of four beautiful sisters—and as plain and plump. In marrying

---

[3] Beauregard to John A. Quitman, February 26, 1851, and to P. F. Smith, May 28, 1851, in Beauregard Papers (Tulane University).

[4] René Beauregard, "Magnolia." René prepared a manuscript account of the family's life at Magnolia. Harnett Kane of New Orleans kindly supplied me with a typed copy of the document.

[5] Kane, *Deep Delta Country,* 67–68; De Leon, *Belles, Beaux and Brains,* 203. Mrs. Beauregard's succession is in the Beauregard Papers (Louisiana State University), as is Beauregard's application of September 16, 1852, to be confirmed as "tutor" or guardian of his children.

Caroline, Beauregard acquired a powerful brother-in-law, John Slidell, United States Senator and one of the bosses of Louisiana. The second marriage was childless. It can be surmised that Beauregard was devoted to Caroline but did not love her with the ardor he had devoted to Marie Laure. He worshiped the daughter, Laure Villeré Beauregard, whose mother had died.[6]

It is probable that death did not deeply affect Beauregard. At this period of his life at least, his religious concepts were intellectual rather than spiritual. Three years after Marie Laure had died he wrote a long letter to his friend Barnard in which he discussed his ideas about God and man. Death was not a punishment for sin, he said, but a law of nature: "Death is nothing more than a change of condition that is going on constantly on the surface of the earth a misfortune for the happy but a blessing for the unfortunate. . . ." Anybody of any religion would attain salvation if he lived a good life and believed in a God. He was sure that he was "on the right track" religiously and that he would see Heaven. "I always try to be ready to appear before my Maker, my father—Mother & wife," he ended.[7]

Beauregard tacked his remarks about salvation onto a letter in which he discussed for Barnard the more secular subject of mud lumps in the mouths of the Mississippi. In 1852 the national government appointed a board of army and navy engineers, of which Beauregard and Barnard were members, to survey the problem of keeping the various mouths of the river open to ocean-going navigation. Two dangers at the river passes threatened the development of New Orleans as a port. One was the mysterious mud lumps which would suddenly arise from below the surface to a height as great as fifteen feet, cover large areas, and change the contours of the river overnight. People ascribed the lumps to various causes, some of them fantastic. The explanation generally accepted today is that they were caused by the river sediment resting on the soft clays beneath; the clays escaped from the pressure by emerging at the surface. The second danger resulted from the bars of silt and clay which the river piled up at its mouths as it met the Gulf. Ships drawing over fifteen feet could not pass the bars; sometimes a bar would close one pass

[6] Basso, *Beauregard*, 50, 55; De Leon, *Belles, Beaux and Brains*, 297–99; Russell, *My Diary North and South*, 237.

[7] Beauregard to J. G. Barnard, November 16, 1853, in Beauregard Papers (Tulane University).

completely while the river cut a new opening at another point. If ocean commerce was to move freely on the lower river, a constant-depth channel at one of the passes was vitally needed.

The board of engineers was directed to determine which pass was best suited for large ships and to recommend a procedure for keeping it open. The engineers investigated and advised that towboats be used to dredge a channel at Southwest Pass and to maintain it by constant stirring of the bottom. If dredging did not work, they advocated building jetties at Southwest Pass or a ship canal from the river to the Gulf. The government decided to try the dredging, and Beauregard and another officer were appointed to inspect the activities of the towboats once a month.[8]

Beauregard would carry on these inspections for over a year. He discovered, as might have been predicted, that the towboats could open a channel temporarily but it would refill unless dredged almost constantly.[9] He became convinced that the only fundamental solution was to build jetties or artificial banks on each side of the bars, creating a stronger current that would scour the channel. The mud lumps fascinated him, and he worked out a theory to explain their origin. He believed that they were caused by tubelike openings between the mud layers which permitted the current to eject particles of dirt to areas of the river where the current was less strong. "Them's my ideas," he wrote Barnard. "What do you think of them?"[10] Knowing that jetties would be a long time coming, he invented what he called a "Self-acting Bar-excavator" to be used by ships in crossing the bars. He patented his invention and gave it to the national government.[11] It was probably filed away in the Engineer Department and forgotten. Not until James B. Eads appeared in the 1870's to build

[8] E. L. Corthell, *A History of the Jetties at the Mouth of the Mississippi River* (New York, 1880), 247; instructions from the War Department to Major W. H. Chase, September 15, 1852, in Beauregard Papers (Tulane University); letter by Beauregard in New Orleans *Republican,* December 20, 1874.

[9] Beauregard to Totten, January 12, 1854, and to William Dunbar, January 12, 1854, in Beauregard Papers (Tulane University).

[10] Beauregard to Barnard, November 16, 1853, and to Totten, November 29, 1853, *ibid.*

[11] Beauregard's petition to the Commissioner of Patents, October 26, 1852, Beauregard to J. F. H. Claiborne, February 1, 1855, Totten to Beauregard, December 20, 1853, *ibid.;* Beauregard to Totten, December 14, 1853, in Office of Chief of Engineer files; Beauregard to E. H. Ruffner, April 5, 1877, in Beauregard Papers (Louisiana State University).

his jetties would the problem of the river obstructions be finally solved.

Beauregard's invention of the bar-excavator and his enthusiasm in proclaiming its virtues was one of the reasons some people thought he was a crackpot. He seemed to be always coming up with something new. He also invented a rock and lever for artillery chassis which he claimed would result in more accurate firing at moving objects. The Ordnance Bureau rejected the discovery. He pressed upon the national patent office and the New Orleans newspapers some seeds from Mexico which were guaranteed to cure the bite of a mad dog. Although the seeds were to be dissolved in the best sherry and the mixture taken three times a day, the remedy never became popular, not even in New Orleans.[12]

When Beauregard was not reflecting on mud lumps in 1852, he was thinking about Franklin Pierce, the Democratic presidential candidate, who had also been raised above the surface by the working of currents deep below. Pierce had served briefly as a general in the Mexican War and had been impressed with Beauregard's performance at the Piedad council; the two officers had seen each other frequently during the fighting for Mexico City. After the war they corresponded at long intervals. When Beauregard learned that the Democrats had nominated Pierce, he hastened to write the candidate a fulsome letter of congratulation.[13] It may be conjectured that Beauregard rushed for the Pierce bandwagon because he saw the advantage for his military fortunes of having a friend in the White House. It is equally justifiable to assume that he sincerely admired Pierce. Certainly his zeal for Pierce was not lessened by the fact that General Scott was the Whig candidate.

Beauregard did not stop with a private endorsement of Pierce. When a Whig paper in New Orleans reflected on Pierce's courage in Mexico, he wrote several letters for a Democratic organ defending Pierce. These documents, signed "A Looker on in Venice," were marked by bad diction and a turgid prose of which he became in-

[12] *The Annals of the War* . . . (Philadelphia, 1879), 525–26; Beauregard to the Commissioner of Patents, May 9, 1855, and to Hugh Kennedy, May 26, 1856, in Beauregard Papers (Louisiana State University).

[13] Beauregard to Franklin Pierce, June 9, 1852, in Franklin Pierce Papers (Division of Manuscripts, Library of Congress). See also Beauregard to Pierce, July 8, 1852, and to Claiborne, July 8, 1852, *ibid.;* Beauregard to ———, June 5, 1852, in Beauregard Papers (Tulane University).

creasingly the master. They contained quite as much about Beauregard as they did about Pierce. In one article he repelled a charge that Pierce had not been at the head of his troops in a battle. He explained that a general's proper position was where he could see that his orders were being executed—except when his columns wavered. Then, said Beauregard, obviously projecting himself into the role he was describing, "does it become his duty to put himself at their head and colours in hand, if need be, like Napoleon at Arcola, show his soldiers the way to Victory or to a glorious death!" Prosaic Pierce, from the granite hills of New Hampshire, would never have seen himself as Napoleon. In a concluding purple passage, Beauregard said that the accusations being hurled at Pierce would make foreign nations doubt the soundness of the American political system, not realizing "that the American star far from having reached its calumniating point, has but commenced its brilliant ascent, & that if we are only true to ourselves centuries will yet elapse before it shall have obtained its meridian splendour!" [14]

After Pierce's victory in the election, Beauregard wrote to congratulate his friend. His letter specialized in mixed metaphors. He had been sure that victory would perch upon Pierce's banner but had not expected it to do so with such a brilliant glow; Scott's laurels had been tarnished because in politics he was like Samson shorn of his locks; the friends of Senator Pierre Soulé of Louisiana wanted him appointed to the Cabinet in the hope that the floodtide of democracy would add one more step to the ladder of his fame. In a revealing sentence, Beauregard said that the election proved that a great man's destiny *"must be fulfilled."* [15]

In the midst of his campaign for Pierce, Beauregard heard that his political activities might defeat his assignment to a post that he wanted and had applied for, and that would be the most important position he had yet held—superintending engineer of the New Orleans customhouse. Defiantly he said that he would not take the job if the Whig administration in Washington attached political strings to it.[16] These were fine words, but his real reason for being coy was technical rather than partisan: he wanted a free hand to alter the

[14] Beauregard to the New Orleans *Louisiana Courier*, July 3, 1852, in Beauregard Papers (Tulane University). See also his letter to the same paper, July 7, 1852, *ibid.*

[15] Beauregard to Pierce, November 4, 1852, *ibid.*

[16] Beauregard to Pierre Soulé, August 14, 1852, *ibid.*

construction plan of the building. The national government had started to build the customhouse, intended to house several governmental departments, in 1848. The original plan called for a huge four-story structure covering a larger area than any building in the country, to be constructed of granite in a modified Egyptian style of architecture. By 1860 the government had spent almost $3,000,000 on the building, and it was only partially completed; not until 1881 was it finished to its present height. At all times it was an ugly edifice. Sensitive observers were shocked or repelled by its groined arches, intricate stairways, and damp walls. It had a baleful fascination for Lafcadio Hearn, who said it was "a huge sarcophagus of granite," conveying "an artistic effect of ruin," and hinting of death and the past.[17]

The first builders failed to reckon with the moist, compressible soil of Louisiana. By 1852 the building was settling too fast and unequally; the outer walls were sinking deeper than the interior ones and cracking; one end was said to have sunk twenty feet below the other. The government appointed a board of experts, of whom Beauregard was one, to determine the reason for the building's instability. He and the other members decided that the extensive system of groined brick arches bore too heavily on the soft soil, and advised the use of smaller, iron girder arches.[18] The Secretary of the Treasury, in whose charge the customhouse was, then asked the War Department to lend him Beauregard as superintending engineer; he probably figured that a Louisiana officer of reputation was best equipped to handle the peculiar local engineering problems and to take the brunt of local criticism. At the same time Beauregard had applied for the post, perhaps informally, to Totten, now a general. In the fall of 1852 the government offered Beauregard the appointment, but he refused it. His reason was that the Treasury would not agree to alter the construction plan as recommended by the experts.[19]

A few months later he reversed himself and accepted the assignment. He made it plain to the Engineer and Treasury departments

[17] New Orleans *Picayune*, July 4, 1848; New Orleans *Times*, March 15, 1866, August 22, 1873; Lafcadio Hearn, *Creole Sketches*, ed. by C. W. Hutson (Boston, 1924), 6–10.
[18] Beauregard to four engineer officers, September 10, 1852, in Beauregard Papers (Louisiana State University).
[19] Beauregard to Totten, September 17, October 11, 1852, in Office of Chief of Engineer files; Beauregard to W. L. Hodge, October 29, 1852, in Beauregard Papers (Tulane University).

that his change of mind did not mean that he had changed his opinion of the original plan and that he would not be responsible for any defects in the building resulting from the original mistakes.[20] He must have wanted the position very much, or he would not have yielded his judgment even this much; he would have told the government to throw its job in the Mississippi. Or he may have thought that with Pierce coming into the White House, he would be able to get the plan changed after all. He may only have been holding out for a promotion, because immediately after he accepted the superintendency he was raised to the rank of captain.[21]

Beauregard became superintendent in May, 1853. He would hold the office until 1860. At first he thought that he could handle his new duties and also retain charge of his other engineering work in the state. He soon found that the customhouse demanded most of his time, and he had to ask to be relieved from supervising the improvements at the Mississippi passes. Although he would return at intervals to his forts and his inspections, most of his energy in the next seven years was devoted to the customhouse. He was well paid for his labors. In addition to his pay as captain, he drew eight dollars a day as superintendent.[22] The verdict of other engineers on his superintendency was generally favorable. He installed iron plates on the exterior walls to bind them to the interior ones and to equalize the settling, and piled weights on the higher parts of the building to force them down. Most of his experiments succeeded. Although the building continued to settle, it sank at a more equal rate. Captain Beauregard displayed a testy impatience with people, especially politicians, who criticized his work or tried to interfere with him. They had to leave him alone, he told his superiors in Washington; "I must have elbow room." [23]

[20] Beauregard to Totten, February 26, 1853, in Office of Chief of Engineer files; Beauregard to James Guthrie, May 10, 1853, in Beauregard Papers (Tulane University).

[21] Cullom, *Biographical Register of the Military Academy,* 548–49.

[22] Beauregard to Totten, May 14, 1853, May 21, 1856, in Office of Chief of Engineer files; Beauregard to Totten, January 23, 1854, in Beauregard Papers (Louisiana State University); Stanley C. Arthur, *A History of the U. S. Custom House, New Orleans* (Works Progress Administration, 1940), 40–41.

[23] Beauregard to Guthrie, May 18, 1853, in Beauregard Papers (Tulane University); Beauregard to Bowman, January 10, March 14, September 20, October 10, 1854, in Beauregard Papers (Louisiana State University); Roman, *Beauregard,* I, 8.

Despite his promotion and increased pay, Beauregard was still dissatisfied with his status, still convinced that the army was not treating him justly. He tried to enlist political influence to secure the colonelcy of a new infantry regiment, and talked bitterly about resigning his commission.[24] Late in 1856 he startled the Engineer Department with the news that he was going to Nicaragua to join the filibusterer William Walker, who had seized control of that country. Walker had offered him the rank of second in command of his army, and Beauregard said he thought he would take it. He viewed Walker's undertaking as a noble attempt to establish American institutions in Nicaragua and Anglo-Saxon dominion over a mongrel race of Spaniards and Indians (this was fuzzy thinking for a Creole). "I cannot consent to remain longer in our Service," he said. "I should endeavor to do something for myself. . . . I am a firm believer in *destiny* if my *tide* has arrived." [25]

His threat to resign really alarmed the high brass of the army. Too many capable officers were leaving the service to take more lucrative positions in other fields. The departure of a man of Beauregard's standing and long service would hurt in several ways—a good engineer would be lost and the army's reputation for not holding its best officers would be increased. General P. F. Smith wrote to tell Beauregard that his leaving would be a calamity to the service and the country. Walker was small stuff and would not last long in Nicaragua, Smith accurately predicted, and Beauregard would be making a bad mistake if he tied his career to Walker's. A letter of praise from a respected general like Smith was enough to thrill any captain, but even better was one from Scott himself. The commanding general said that he was deeply concerned that Beauregard was thinking of leaving the army after having won so much distinction in it. Beauregard's brilliant services in Mexico were remembered and appreciated, Scott assured, and he ought not to endanger a bright future by going abroad.[26]

[24] Beauregard to Charles Gayarré, April 11, 1854, in Charles Gayarré Papers (Department of Archives, Louisiana State University); Beauregard to Totten, May 4, 1856, in Office of Chief of Engineer files.

[25] Beauregard to Bowman, December 5, 1856, in Beauregard Papers (Louisiana State University). Appended to Beauregard's manuscript, "Reminiscences of an Engineer Officer," are some extremely flattering letters of recommendation written to Walker in his behalf by Generals Quitman, Twiggs, Patterson, and P. F. Smith.

[26] Roman, *Beauregard*, I, 7–8; Beauregard, "Reminiscences of an Engineer Officer," appended letters.

Such flattery, accompanied by such hints of promotions to come, was the right technique to use on Beauregard. He gave up the Nicaragua project. Back to work at the customhouse he went, still a little dissatisfied and still snapping at people who criticized him. ". . . I would not bend an inch to remain here," he told a friend. "I am always 'ready for a fight' whenever they will say so. I do what is right & for the best, happen what will." Some of his friends wanted him to run for governor, but he hated to become a groveling politician.[27]

He did, however, become a politician, briefly, in 1858, when he ran for mayor of New Orleans. For two years the city government had been controlled by the Know Nothing or American party, which nationally was anti-Catholic and antiforeign but which locally was chiefly pro-crime. A conservative reform element, comprising both Whigs and Democrats, decided to try to beat the Know Nothings in the municipal election of 1858 by nominating the popular Beauregard, who was expected to appeal strongly to the Creoles. In his letter of acceptance, he said that he was a candidate out of a sense of duty to his city. If elected, he promised to create a strong police force to stamp out crime. Discussing national issues, although it was poor politics to do so, considering that he was a coalition choice, he said that he was a state rights Democrat of the progressive school (which meant he was for some change) and a devoted Unionist who would not sacrifice the just rights of the South to those of the nation![28]

The Know Nothings knew enough to realize that Beauregard would be a tough man to beat. To ensure victory, their gangs resorted to terrorism and intimidation, even invading the office of the register of voters and confiscating the voting lists. Beauregard's supporters then organized a vigilance committee consisting of over a thousand armed men. Appropriating some artillery from the state arsenal, they seized the Cabildo and announced they would guarantee an honest election. An appeal which they issued to the public hinted that they would do more. It implied they would take over the city and install Beauregard by force. Undoubtedly it hurt his chances. The Know Nothings demanded arms from the city government so they could fight the vigilantes. For several days New Orleans was an armed

[27] Beauregard to Bowman, August 7, 1857, in Beauregard Papers (Louisiana State University).

[28] A copy of the letter is in a clipping enclosed in a letter from Beauregard to Bowman, June 8, 1858, *ibid.*

camp, with the Know Nothings on the American side of Canal Street and Beauregard's men in the French Quarter.

Despite the threats of violence made by both sides, the election on June 7 was quiet and orderly. The Know Nothing candidate won, primarily because his forces were better organized than the improvised groups backing Beauregard.[29] The captain took his defeat gracefully. In fact, he seemed glad that he had been beaten. To think, he told an army friend, that he had almost sacrificed his commission to help such a disgusting community as New Orleans. For the moment he had turned against his city.[30]

One October day in 1860 Beauregard went down to Fort St. Philip. On his return, as he was stepping ashore from a skiff, he fell in the river. Bystanders saved his life by pulling him out. "I saw the face of God," he said wryly. "He was not looking very pleased with me." [31] In a letter to his friend Barnard describing the incident, he made his only recorded reference to the presidential campaign then reaching its climax. People seemed bent on beating Douglas, Breckinridge, or Bell, he observed, but never troubled themselves about Lincoln, who was the South's most dangerous enemy. His interest in the election and the sectional crisis seemed almost casual. Writing earlier in the year to W. T. Sherman, superintendent of the newly created Louisiana State Seminary of Learning, where Beauregard's two sons were enrolled, he had advised Sherman not to worry about the political situation; with time and patience the present crisis would pass away.[32]

In the letter to Barnard, written when threats of secession were being made all over the Lower South, the principal topic he discussed was who was going to be the new superintendent at West Point. That office had always been held by an engineer officer, but Beauregard had heard that Senator Jefferson Davis (his first hostile contact with that name) was going to try to throw it open to officers

[29] James K. Greer, "Louisiana Politics, 1845–1861," in *Louisiana Historical Quarterly*, XIII (1930), 257–303; John Smith Kendall, "The Municipal Elections of 1858," *ibid.*, V (1922), 357–76; Herbert Asbury, *The French Quarter* (New York, 1938), 295–312.

[30] Beauregard to Bowman, June 8, 1858, in Beauregard Papers (Louisiana State University).

[31] Basso, *Beauregard*, 54.

[32] Beauregard to Barnard, October 2, 1860, in Beauregard Papers (Tulane University); Beauregard to W. T. Sherman, January 12, 1860, in David F. Boyd Papers (Department of Archives, Louisiana State University).

in other branches. Certain senators would fight the proposal, but the engineers must furnish them with arguments. Beauregard had thought of another way to defeat Davis—to bring before the government now the name of a prominent engineer for the appointment. The two best men were Barnard and Montgomery Meigs, but for reasons he did not detail they had no chance.

Then came the climax of the letter. He told Barnard: "After much reflection on the subject, I have consented to sacrifice *$5000* a year & allow my name to be presented for the position, & to do all I can to have you put in charge of the New Custom House here, *on the condition* that you will resign it in my favor whenever I return to this City—for I attach much importance to finishing it." He was asking his brother-in-law, Senator Slidell, to write the Secretary of War that he was ready to obey any order relative to going to West Point![33] Subtlety was not his forte.

Slidell and the other political interests behind the engineers did their work well. In November Beauregard received orders appointing him superintendent as of January, 1861.[34] He started for West Point in December, stopping off in Washington for two days to see General Totten. He found Totten in his office examining sketches of the defenses of Charleston. He told the general that if Louisiana seceded and hostilities between the North and the South started he would have to resign his commission and go with his state. Then he went to New York, where he spent three days with G. W. Smith and other Southern friends who were employed in the city. Presumably they discussed what their course would be if civil war came. Sometime in January he proceeded to West Point and assumed the superintendency on the twenty-third.[35]

It seems incredible, the political situation being what it was, that he even thought of going to the academy or imagined that the government would let him hold the office. In January the Louisiana secession convention was in session, and voted on the twenty-sixth to take the state out of the Union. Either Beauregard was singularly blind to the signs of the times, or, more probably, he wanted the

[33] Beauregard to Barnard, October 2, 1860, in Beauregard Papers (Tulane University).

[34] Roman, *Beauregard,* I, 13; Beauregard to Adjutant General Samuel Cooper, November 20, 1860, in Records of the Adjutant General Relating to West Point.

[35] Roman, *Beauregard,* I, 13–14; Edward C. Boynton, *History of West Point* . . . (New York, 1863), 251.

superintendency on his record as a lever for promotion in the future Confederacy. Soon after he assumed command, a cadet from Louisiana went to his room one night and asked if he should resign. Beauregard replied, "Watch me; and when I jump, you jump. What's the use of jumping too soon?" [36]

Beauregard's superiors were well aware of the mistake they had made in placing an avowed secessionist in charge of the impressionable boys at the nation's only officer-training school. On the day after he became superintendent, Totten wrote him that his orders were revoked and that he was to turn the office over to the previous incumbent. To make sure that Beauregard would understand, this was followed by a directive to the same effect from the Secretary of War. Beauregard readily complied with the instructions. He relinquished the command of the post on the twenty-eighth, ending what is surely the shortest superintendency in the academy's history.[37] He wrote Totten a curious letter of protest about his removal. He could not believe that Totten had acted because of the private talks between them in Washington. Surely his superior understood that he did not intend to resign his commission unless the secession of Louisiana was followed by war: ". . . so long as I remain in the service . . . I shall be most scrupulous in the performance of all my obligations to the Govt. So long as I keep my opinions of the present unfortunate condition of our country to myself, I must respectfully protest against any act of the War Dept. that might cast any improper reflection upon my reputation or position in the Corps of Engineers." As evidence of his integrity, he pointed out that he had persuaded several cadets who wanted to resign to stay until hostilities started.[38]

His letter is an interesting commentary on the influence which state rights legalism had attained over the Southern mind by 1861. Here was an officer in the service of the United States, considering leaving that service to make war against the United States, who could in all sincerity berate the government for removing him from

[36] Morris Schaff, *The Spirit of Old West Point, 1858–1862* (New York, 1907), 195–97; Joseph P. Pearson, *West Point in the Early Sixties* . . . (Troy, N. Y., 1902), 24.

[37] Totten to Richard Delafield, January 24, 1861, Totten to Beauregard, January 24, 1861, Beauregard to Totten, January 26, 28, 1861, in Records of the Adjutant General Relating to West Point; Roman, *Beauregard*, I, 14–15, 421.

[38] Beauregard to Totten, January 25, 1861, in Beauregard Papers (Library of Congress), Miscellaneous Book, January 23, 1861—April 27, 1865.

a position of great military trust where he might endanger the government. An equally strange example is Beauregard's attempt to claim a mileage payment of $165 from the government for his return trip from West Point to New Orleans. The government refused to pay. Even after he had resigned from the army and accepted a general's commission in the Confederacy and commanded a force menacing a Federal garrison in Charleston harbor, he pressed the justice of his claim upon Washington.[39]

After his removal, Beauregard, pursuant to his orders, went to New York, where he caught a steamer to New Orleans. In New York he received a telegram from Governor Thomas O. Moore of Louisiana saying the state had seceded and his services were needed at home. Soon after he arrived in New Orleans, he resigned his commission, effective March 1 or earlier if possible; the government obliged him by making the date February 20.[40] Hardly had he set foot on the local scene when he began to issue a stream of advice to the state military authorities: Forts St. Philip and Jackson were inadequately armed to repel a naval attack; booms should be stretched over the river to hold up an attacking squadron. He saw to it that his recommendations were also presented to the new Confederate government.[41] He had his heart set on being named commander of the state army which the legislature had authorized, but to his disappointment and disgust the appointment went to another. The man who got it was Braxton Bragg, who would be Beauregard's bête noire in the Confederacy.

Bragg, a native of North Carolina, was a West Pointer who had served in the army until 1856, when he resigned to become a planter in Louisiana. He was probably the ugliest and most disliked Southern general. Thin and stooped, he presented a cadaverous appearance; his plain features were distinguished only by huge black eyebrows which met in a tuft above his nose and by a stubby iron-gray beard.

[39] Beauregard to Colonel D. D. Tomkins, March 31, 1861, and to Colonel J. E. Johnston, March 31, 1861, *ibid.,* Letterbook 3.
[40] Beauregard to Cooper, February 9, 1861, and to Totten, February 12, 1861, in Records of the Adjutant General Relating to West Point; Roman, *Beauregard,* I, 15, 423.
[41] Roman, *Beauregard,* I, 17–18, 422; Sarah A. Dorsey, *Recollections of Henry Watkins Allen* . . . (New York, 1866), 66–68; Gustavus W. Smith, *Confederate War Papers* (New York, 1884), 60–61.

Harsh in manner, sour in temper, he made few friends and many enemies.[42]

Bragg must have known that Beauregard would resent his appointment, because immediately after it was made he went to Beauregard's office to explain it and to say that the governor was going to offer Beauregard a colonelcy. Beauregard was out when Bragg called. On his return, being told of Bragg's visit, he sent a note to Bragg declining the governor's commission. He had no personal or military objection to Bragg, he said, but he did object to the injustice being done to himself. He said the same thing to Moore and other friends who urged him to reconsider. His touchy honor was at stake, and he was not going to back down. In at least four letters he used the same phrases—his services were at the command of his state but without military rank and "even unto death." [43] In a dramatic gesture to show he meant the no rank business, he enrolled as a private in the Orleans Guards, a battalion of Creole aristocrats. After he had become a general in the Confederate service and had departed for other fields, his name was still carried on the muster. When it was reached at roll call, the color-sergeant would step forward and say, "Absent on duty." [44]

Beauregard, of course, had no real intention of serving any place as a private. He knew that war was coming, and he was determined to be a general. On February 10 he wrote a letter of congratulation to Jefferson Davis, just chosen as President of the Confederate States, and asked for an appointment in the Confederate Army. To make sure that the new government would be aware of his merits, he got Slidell and other political friends to write letters recommending him for a brigadier generalcy.[45] One day late in February the hoped-for

[42] Sir Arthur J. L. Fremantle, *Three Months in the Southern States* . . . (New York, 1864), 145; Basil W. Duke, *Reminiscences of General Basil W. Duke, C. S. A.* (New York, 1911), 297; Richard Taylor, *Destruction and Reconstruction,* (New York, 1879), 100.

[43] Beauregard to Braxton Bragg, February 9, 1861, in Beauregard Papers (Library of Congress), Miscellaneous Book; Beauregard to Richard Taylor, February 12, 1861 and to Thomas O. Moore, February 19, 1861 and Taylor to Beauregard, February 12, 1861, and Moore to Beauregard, February 17, 1861, in Roman, *Beauregard,* I, 421–23; René Beauregard, "Magnolia"; Beauregard to Albert Fabre, February 18, 1861, in Beauregard Papers (Mirabeau B. Lamar Library, University of Texas). The Lamar Library provided photostats of their Beauregard collection.

[44] Roman, *Beauregard,* I, 16, 316n.

[45] Beauregard to Jefferson Davis, February 10, 1861, in Beauregard Papers (Duke University Library); Beauregard to C. M. Conrad, February 10, and

summons came. Secretary of War Leroy Pope Walker asked Beauregard to come to Montgomery, the Confederate capital, to confer with Davis. Shortly after Beauregard received his call, W. T. Sherman came down to New Orleans from the Seminary of Learning. Calling on Beauregard at the customhouse to give him news of his sons, he found the Creole about to start for Montgomery. Later he saw General and Mrs. Bragg and was treated by both to a jealous denunciation of Beauregard. Bragg railed at a rumor that Beauregard was to be given the command of all Confederate armies.[46]

Beauregard reached Montgomery on February 26. He conferred with Davis until late that night. The President wanted him to go to Charleston and take command of the Confederate and South Carolina forces confronting the Union garrison in Fort Sumter in the harbor of Charleston.

The situation at Charleston was a delicate one. Confederate commissioners were in Washington demanding that the fort be turned over to their government. The Carolina authorities, led by Governor Francis W. Pickens, were itching to take it by force. Pickens asked Davis who should require the surrender, the state or the Confederate government? Davis had to move fast and surely. If the Washington negotiations failed, the surrender of Sumter would probably have to be demanded. The demand must be made by a military representative of the central government acting under its authority. If the demand was refused, the operations against the fort would have to be conducted by a skilled engineer officer. The government could not afford to let some state politician botch up its first military action. Beauregard was the obvious answer to all of Davis' problems. He had a reputation, he was one of the best engineers in the South, and

---

to J. B. Wilkinson, February 18, 1861, in Beauregard Papers (Library of Congress), Miscellaneous Book; Conrad and others to Confederate War Department, February 25, 1861, John Slidell to Davis, February 19, 1861, C. H. Chase to L. P. Walker, March 1, 1861, in Confederate Records of Military Service of Adjutant General's Office (National Archives).

[46] Lewis, *Sherman*, 146–47; William T. Sherman, *Memoirs of William T. Sherman by Himself* (New York, 1891), I, 162. The seminary disbanded in 1861, and René and Henri came home. René secured a commission in the army, but the younger son was placed in school at the Citadel, Charleston. René Beauregard, "Magnolia"; René to Beauregard, May 8, 1861, and Henri to Beauregard, May 8, 1861, in Beauregard Papers (Tulane University); Beauregard to J. P. Thomas, November 16, 1862, in Beauregard Papers (Library of Congress), Letterbook, Private Letters, June 30, 1862—February 9, 1863.

he had a personality that was likely to impress even Charlestonians. On the day after his conference with Davis, he learned that he was going to Charleston as the Confederacy's first brigadier general.[47]

Dispatches and letters went out immediately to Pickens to tell him that Beauregard was coming—and that the general was to have complete control of military operations. Both Davis and Walker used superlatives to describe Beauregard's abilities and his peculiar fitness for the Charleston command. But already he was confusing his Anglo-Saxon colleagues. Walker referred to him as Peter G. T. Beauregard. What Southerner would have a name like Pierre? [48]

As for Peter Beauregard, he was in an ecstasy of glory and rhetoric. The tide of his destiny had come at last. To John G. Barnard, who had upbraided him for joining the Confederacy, he wrote that the South was fighting for the greatest right of a people, to select their own form of government. After the war was over, with the Confederacy victorious of course, he wanted little. He would retire to a farm near New Orleans and live out his years with his family, his books, and a few true friends around him.[49]

[47] Roman, *Beauregard*, I, 19–21; Dunbar Rowland (ed.), *Jefferson Davis, Constitutionalist: His Letters, Papers and Speeches* (Jackson, Miss., 1923), V, 58, hereinafter cited as Rowland (ed.), *Jefferson Davis*.

[48] Roman, *Beauregard*, I, 423–24; Rowland (ed.), *Jefferson Davis*, V, 58–59; *The War of the Rebellion: A Compilation of the Official Records of the Union and Confederate Armies* (Washington, 1880–1901), Ser. I, Vol. I, 259–60, hereinafter cited as *Official Records* (unless otherwise indicated all citations are to Ser. I).

[49] Beauregard to Barnard, March 18, 1861, in Beauregard Papers (Library of Congress), Letterbook 3.

CHAPTER FOUR

The Guns of Sumter

CHARLESTON first saw Beauregard on March 3 when he reached the city and went quietly to Pickens' headquarters at the Charleston Hotel. For the next four years the entire Confederacy would see him through a haze of drama and glory that enveloped no other Southern general.

He is one of the most frequently described generals in Confederate annals. Significantly, nearly every observer noted that he looked French or foreign. He was five feet seven in height and weighed about one hundred and fifty pounds. He had dark hair and eyes and a sallow, olive complexion. His features were marked by a broad brow, high cheekbones, a cropped mustache, and a protruding chin. His eyes fascinated most people; large, melancholy, with drooping lids, they were likened by one man to the eyes of a bloodhound with his fighting instincts asleep but ready to leap into instant action. In manner he was courteous, grave, sometimes reserved and severe, sometimes abrupt with people who displeased him. His expression was fixed, impassive; associates saw him go for months without smiling. He was most likely to erupt into excitement, to show the fire beneath, by suddenly launching into an impassioned defense of the Southern cause. His voice was clear and pleasant, with a barely perceptible French accent. At first acquaintance he impressed people as being modest, industrious, indomitable. Many who saw him thought that he looked like a French marshal or like Napoleon in a gray uniform—which was what he wanted them to think.[1]

[1] A. L. Hull (ed.), "The Correspondence of Thomas Reade Roote Cobb, 1860–1862," in *Publications of the Southern History Association,* XI (1907), 327; Edward A. Pollard, *The Lost Cause* (New York, 1867), 139–40; Edward A. Pollard, *The First Year of the War* (Richmond, 1862), 61n.; John Esten Cooke, *Wearing of the Gray* . . . (New York, 1867), 85–89; John S. Wise, *The End of an Era* (New York, 1900), 330–31; Linton Stephens to R. M. Johnston, August 2, 1861, in Alexander H. Stephens Papers (Emory University Library); Peter W. Hairston to Mrs. Hairston, September 3, 1861, in Peter W. Hairston Papers (Southern Historical Collection, University of North Carolina Library); Fremantle, *Three Months in the Southern States,* 193.

Because he was French and seemed different, he was the victim of all kinds of rumors, most of them baseless. The charge of immorality was, of course, inevitable. Some soldiers believed that he was accompanied on the march by a train of concubines and wagons loaded with cases of champagne. Even in Louisiana it was said, by non-Creoles, that he was unfaithful to his wife, infidelity being allegedly a Creole characteristic.[2] These accusations were given color by the adoration which the women of the Confederacy lavished upon him from the beginning of the war. He might have critics in some quarters, but he was the favorite general of the ladies. They almost smothered him with letters, flags, scarves, small desks, and flowers. One visitor to his office saw two vases of flowers on his table, flanking his maps and plans, and a bouquet of roses and geraniums serving as a paperweight.[3]

His military retinue was a wonderful enough collection in itself to inspire rumor. His staff glittered with former governors and senators serving as voluntary aides. Davis once said that whenever the government had anybody so fine they did not know what to do with him they sent him to Beauregard's staff.[4] A prominent member of the entourage was Frederick Maginnis, a slave whom Beauregard rented as a servant from a woman in South Carolina. Described as "a very white intelligent fellow," Frederick acted important, talked freely about the general's future plans, and posed as a confidant of the great.[5] Another eminent camp follower was a young Spaniard who served as Beauregard's barber and valet. Supposedly he was invested with the function of keeping the forty-three-year-old Beauregard youthful in appearance. In one important respect he failed. At the beginning of the war, Beauregard's hair was jet black. People who saw him a year later were astonished to see that it had turned almost white. His friends attributed the change to worry. Others

[2] Bell Irvin Wiley, *The Life of Johnny Reb* (Indianapolis, 1934), 169; Kate M. Rowland and Mrs. Morris L. Croxall (eds.), *The Journal of Julia Le Grand* (Richmond, 1911), 163, 269.

[3] Russell, *My Diary North and South*, 116–17; Pollard, *Lost Cause*, 139–40.

[4] Mary Boykin Chesnut, *A Diary From Dixie*, ed. by Ben Ames Williams (Boston, 1949), 67.

[5] Colonel L. M. Hatch to Beauregard, June 10, 11, 1861, in Beauregard Papers (Duke University); Beauregard to Mrs. A. F. Baker, June 20, 1865, *ibid.;* Beauregard to Hatch, October 14, 1861, in L. M. Hatch Papers (Southern Historical Collection, University of North Carolina Library); Linton Stephens to R. M. Johnston, August 2, 1861, in Stephens Papers.

said it was because the Federal blockade had stopped the import of dyes.[6]

From Charleston's famous Battery, Beauregard could look out over the harbor and see his military problem spread before him. To his right were James and Morris islands; to his left, Hog and Sullivan's islands. All four were in Confederate possession. On James Island the South Carolina authorities had started to erect batteries at Fort Johnson; they had also begun work on a battery at Cummings Point on Morris. On Sullivan's stood Fort Moultrie, a low brick edifice with walls about as high as those of an ordinary room. Almost directly in front of Charleston on a small island was Castle Pinckney, a tiny, obsolete work of brick. And on a shoal in the center of the harbor, about three miles from the city and almost equidistant between Moultrie and Cummings Point, was Fort Sumter, its unfinished brick and masonry walls rising to a height of sixty feet, garrisoned by fewer than a hundred Federal soldiers commanded by Beauregard's old teacher, Major Robert Anderson.

The Confederates held all points in and around the harbor except Sumter. Beauregard's problem was, if the Federal government refused to give up the fort, to prevent reinforcements from reaching it by sea and ultimately, if his own government so decided, to attack and reduce it. He formally assumed command on March 6. Immediately but tactfully he began to alter and rearrange the armament and batteries established by the Carolinians. They had concentrated their guns at Moultrie and Cummings Point, the two points closest to Sumter. Beauregard, certain that Washington would never yield Sumter, planned to form a circle of fire of which the fort would be the center. From his ring of batteries and forts, he was confident that he could prevent a relieving fleet from reaching Sumter, which was his immediate worry, and eventually, if necessary, batter the fort into submission. He called on Montgomery for more guns of all types and encouraged local inventors who were experimenting with ironclad batteries and floating batteries, one of which was also ironclad. His labors were having a good effect, he informed Secretary of

[6] Louis Moreau Gottschalk, *Notes of a Pianist* (Philadelphia, 1881), 213–14; William Watson, *Life in the Confederate Army* . . . (New York, 1888), 357; Fremantle, *Three Months in the Southern States*, 193; E. John Ellis to E. P. Ellis, March 28, 1862, in Ellis Family Papers (Department of Archives, Louisiana State University).

War Walker. The Carolinians were buckling down to real work: "In the mean time I will go on organizing everything around me." [7]

As he organized, the proud Charlestonians subjected him to a searching scrutiny. They were not accustomed to taking orders from an outsider. Something about him won them; it was his appearance and bearing, said one observer. Charleston went wild about him. It is no exaggeration to say that he was regarded as a demigod. Leading the idolaters was Governor Pickens, who persuaded the Confederate government to enlarge Beauregard's command to include the coastal area around Charleston.[8] The general was not surprised by the worship he had aroused. Indeed, he knew the reason for it. "I am . . . very well pleased with this place," he wrote, "& its people, who are so much like ours in La. that I see but little difference in them." [9] They liked him because he was as haughty as they. A Beauregard did not have to take anything from the aristocrats of Charleston.

By the first week in April the Confederate government had decided that the negotiations going on in Washington for the evacuation of Sumter would be futile. New instructions to Beauregard directed him to act as if he were in the presence of a hostile force with whom at any moment he might be in conflict; all intercourse between the fort and the city, including the exchange of mail and the purchase of supplies by Anderson, was to be stopped. Up to this time the amenities had been properly observed by Beauregard and his old teacher. Anderson received a daily mail and purchased fresh beef and vegetables in the city. One of Beauregard's aides, on a visit to Sumter, heard the officers complaining that they were short of cigars

[7] *Official Records*, I, 25–26, 266–67; Roman, *Beauregard*, I, 29–38; *Annals of the War*, 522–23; Johnson Hagood, *Memoirs of the War of Secession* (Columbia, S. C., 1910), 35–36; Robert U. Johnson and Clarence C. Buel (eds.), *Battles and Leaders of the Civil War* (New York, 1887), I, 66–67, hereinafter cited as *Battles and Leaders*.

[8] F. G. De Fontaine, "The First Day of Real War," in *Southern Bivouac*, II (1886), 73–79; Charleston *Mercury*, March 6, 1861; D. F. Jamison to Beauregard, March 28, April 5, 1861, in Stan V. Henkels' Catalog 1148, *The Beauregard Papers* . . . (Philadelphia, 1916), Pt. II; John Cunningham to William Porcher Miles, March 4, 1861, and William Gilmore Simms to Miles, April 17, 1861, in William Porcher Miles Papers (Southern Historical Collection, University of North Carolina Library); Louise North to Mrs. Pettigrew, in Pettigrew Family Papers; Chesnut, *Diary From Dixie*, 31, 33; Rowland (ed.), *Jefferson Davis*, 60–61; *Official Records*, I, 277.

[9] Beauregard to Walker, April 17, 1861, in Beauregard Papers (Library of Congress), Letterbook 3.

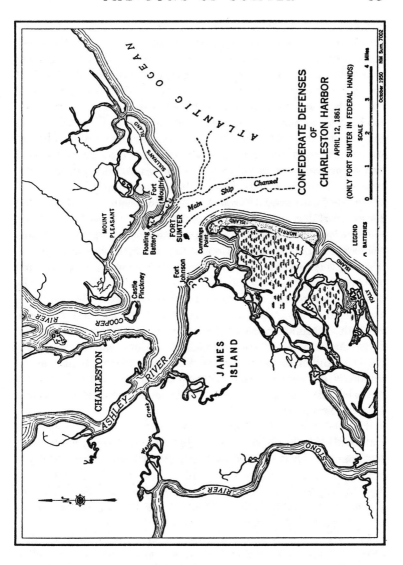

CONFEDERATE DEFENSES
OF
CHARLESTON HARBOR
APRIL 12, 1861
(ONLY FORT SUMTER IN FEDERAL HANDS)

SCALE

0   1   2   3   4 Miles

October 1950   NM Sum. 7002

LEGEND
∩ BATTERIES

ATLANTIC OCEAN

SULLIVANS ISLAND

Fort Moultrie

Floating Battery

MOUNT PLEASANT

FORT SUMTER

Castle Pinckney

Cummings Point

MORRIS ISLAND

Main   Ship   Channel

Fort Johnson

COOPER RIVER

CHARLESTON

ASHLEY RIVER

JAMES ISLAND

Wappoo Creek

STONO RIVER

FOLLY ISLAND

and liquor. On his next trip he took them, with Beauregard's approval, several cases of claret and some boxes of cigars. The game of power politics being played between Washington and Richmond changed this pleasant situation. Beauregard informed Anderson that because of the vacillation shown by the Federal government he was cutting off the mail and the food.[10] At the same time the Washington authorities hardened in their attitude; they determined to hold Sumter. But if it was to be held, the garrison, already short of food, would have to be provisioned. It was decided to send a naval relief expedition, carrying supplies only, to the fort and to notify the Confederate government that the expedition was coming.

On April 8 an emissary from Washington reached Charleston and sought an interview with Pickens. He told the governor that an attempt would be made to provision Sumter and that the United States government hoped no opposition would be made to the expedition. Pickens said that Beauregard commanded at Charleston and decided all military questions. He would have to send for the general. Beauregard came in and heard the news. He said little, knowing that the answer to Washington's challenge would have to be made in Montgomery. He refused to let the agent go to Sumter to see Anderson, and sent him back by train, taking care to delay the train and arrest his telegrams. Then he informed Walker of the import of the message from Washington. An order came back immediately that under no circumstances should he permit provisions to reach Sumter.[11]

The Confederate government was now behind a big diplomatic eight ball. If it let the expedition proceed peaceably to Sumter, the fort could hold out for months, a physical mockery of the new government's claims to sovereignty within its own borders. If it acted to stop the expedition, it would have to use force against the fort or the ships and would place itself in the position of opening war by firing the first shot. The decision was a hard one, but after long discussion Davis and his advisers decided on force. On April 10 an order went to Beauregard to demand the evacuation of Sumter and, if Anderson refused, to reduce the fort. He replied that he would make the demand on the twelfth. Secretary Walker directed him to make it earlier unless there were special reasons for delay. Cryptically

[10] Roman, *Beauregard*, I, 426–27; *Battles and Leaders*, I, 74–82; *Official Records*, I, 248–49.

[11] Roman, *Beauregard*, I, 32–33; *Official Records*, I, 251–52, 289.

Beauregard answered that there were special reasons but did not detail them. His supply of powder was sufficient for only a few hours bombardment, but he did not want to put this information on the wires. He was waiting for a shipment from Augusta which arrived that night.[12] Now he was ready to act.

At about two o'clock on the afternoon of the eleventh, Beauregard sent three aides, Colonel James R. Chesnut, Captain Stephen D. Lee, and Lieutenant A. R. Chisolm, to Sumter with a written demand to Anderson to surrender. They reached the fort at three forty-five and delivered Beauregard's message to the commander. After consulting with his officers for over an hour, Anderson returned to say that he rejected the demand. He put his reply in writing. He walked to the main gate with the Confederates as they departed. A Kentuckian who dreaded the prospect of a fraternal war, he was deeply affected by the interview. He asked if Beauregard would open fire without further warning. After a moment's hesitation, Chesnut said he thought not. Anderson then said, "Gentlemen, if you do not batter the fort to pieces about us, we shall be starved out in a few days." Somewhat astonished by this unexpected information, the aides left for Charleston.[13]

They reported to Beauregard at a little after five. Naturally, the general was interested in Anderson's statement that lack of food might force the Federals to evacuate, and properly he communicated this new factor in the situation to Montgomery. The government snapped at the possibility of securing Sumter without violence. Fresh instructions went out to Beauregard. Walker's quaint and not too clear directive informed him that he was "authorized . . . to avoid the effusion of blood." He was to exercise his delegated power against bloodletting by making another demand on Anderson: if the major would indicate when he would evacuate and if he would agree in the interim not to use his guns against the Confederates if they did not use theirs against him, then Sumter would not be bombarded. If Anderson refused, the fort was to be reduced.[14]

Late at night on the eleventh Beauregard sent his three aides again to Anderson with a letter embodying his new instructions. He

[12] *Official Records,* I, 297; Samuel W. Crawford, *The Genesis of the Civil War* . . . (New York, 1887), 421–22.
[13] *Official Records,* I, 13, 59; Crawford, *Genesis of the Civil War,* 423–24; Roman, *Beauregard,* I, 39.
[14] *Official Records,* I, 301; Roman, *Beauregard,* I, 39–40.

authorized the aides to determine without reporting back whether Anderson met the terms of the ultimatum. The aides reached Sumter after midnight and delivered the letter. Anderson deliberated over it until after three in the morning. He then handed them a written reply. He would evacuate on the fifteenth; he would not fire on the Confederates unless compelled to by some hostile act of theirs or some act showing a hostile intention or unless—and here was the crux of his answer—he received new instructions or additional supplies. Within five minutes the aides decided that Anderson had not met Beauregard's conditions. Chesnut wrote their reply in a casemate: in one hour the Confederate batteries would open on Sumter. Anderson shook hands warmly with them, and said he hoped that if they did not meet again in this world they would in the next. Jumping in their boat, the aides proceeded to Fort Johnson and ordered its commander to start firing. Then they started for Beauregard's headquarters to report. As they headed toward Charleston, they stopped a minute to view the first shot. At four-thirty they heard a report and saw the shell describe a semi-arc and explode over Fort Sumter.[15]

The shot from Johnson was the signal for all of Beauregard's batteries from Morris Island to Sullivan's to begin firing. They banged away at Sumter until nightfall; 2,500 shot and shell were poured at the fort. At first Sumter was silent, but at daylight the flag went up on its walls and its guns opened on Moultrie. The Confederates at Cummings Point wildly cheered this display of Yankee gallantry. To the crowds of spectators on the Battery and the wharves and to the soldiers in both armies it seemed the most wonderful and awful spectacle they had ever witnessed. People believed that a wholesale slaughter must be occurring. And yet on this day and the next it was a singularly safe battle. Beauregard had located his breaching guns out of range from Sumter. With one exception, a rifled gun which had arrived from England the day before the engagement started, his pieces were old smoothbores which from their distant sites could not seriously damage the fort. A competent Southern observer who saw Sumter after the battle said the only effect of the bombardment was to make it look as though it had a bad case of

[15] *Official Records*, I, 14, 60; *Battles and Leaders*, I, 75–76, 82; A. R. Chisolm, "Journal of Events before and during the Bombardment of Fort Sumter—April 1861." A typed copy of Lieutenant Chisolm's MS. journal was generously given to me by Vernon Munroe, New York City.

tachment for his mother. When she died seven years after his birth, however, he took the loss so hard that he never again formed an affectionate association with any woman. To give the boy a change from the Virginia hills, his father got him an appointment to West Point in 1833. "I was not a very exemplary soldier," Early wrote of his Academy years. He tried to leave in 1836 to join the revolution going on in Texas, but his father would not allow it, and Early finished his studies in 1837, graduating eighteenth in his class.

Immediately thereafter Early and many of his classmates went off to Florida to fight the Seminoles. The excitement of military life did not last long. In 1838, Early resigned his commission and returned home to become a lawyer. He dabbled in politics, served without seeing action in the Mexican War, and was an ardent opponent of secession in 1860–61. He served as a member of Virginia's convention which decided the issue, and bravely voted against leaving the Union. But once secession was passed, he saw it as his duty to throw his fortunes with the state "and to defend her soil against invasion." Shortly afterward Governor Letcher commissioned him a colonel in the state forces and sent him to Lynchburg to raise the 24th Virginia.

For the sake of organizational manageability, Beauregard would have done well to break down his command further into divisions of three brigades each. But he did not; the inherent weakness is obvious. With two divisions, the likelihood of orders from Beauregard to either of the division commanders being lost was slim. As it was now, he must get a copy of each order sent to six different brigade commanders. Chances of one or more copies miscarrying were considerable. And in battle, should a brigade not be where Beauregard needed it, the game might be lost.

If his organization could have been better, his energies in erecting his army's defenses could not. As Pickens had said to Bonham, Beauregard was an excellent engineer. He put virtually every man to work, first around Manassas, and then along the approaches to the junction. Bonham he placed at Fairfax Court House, his most advanced position and the focal point at which three main roads from Washington and Alexandria came together. When McDowell advanced, he would have to come through here. Here the first obstructions must be built. Large parties of the South

figure of this arresting scene was Louis T. Wigfall, former United States Senator from Texas, who had turned up in Charleston after his state seceded and had been invited by Beauregard to accept a staff position. Atavistic, blustering, Yankee-hating, Wigfall had been tremendously excited when the flag fell, and with the approval of the commander of Morris Island he set out for Sumter to ask Anderson if he was ready to yield. Curiously, he made his way to the fort without being seen by anybody in the garrison. An astonished Federal gunner about to fire his piece saw Wigfall's fierce face glaring at him through an embrasure. Waving his handkerchief, Wigfall demanded admittance.

After he got in, he asked to see Anderson. Stating that he came from Beauregard, he asked the major to surrender, to stop the fight and the bloodshed (there were no casualties in the entire battle). Anderson inquired what terms Beauregard would offer. Wigfall, who had not seen Beauregard for two days, grandly replied, "Any terms that you may desire—your own terms—the precise nature of which General Beauregard will arrange with you." Anderson said he would accept the conditions offered by Beauregard on the eleventh, namely, that he could transport his garrison to the North and salute his flag on evacuation. Wigfall then left for Charleston to find Beauregard. It was at this point that Anderson puzzled Beauregard by lowering the American flag and hoisting a white one.

Shortly after Wigfall departed, the first set of aides arrived to offer help against the fire. Anderson thanked them for their courtesy but said he could control his own fire. Then he told them that he had surrendered to Wigfall on Beauregard's first terms. The astounded aides said that they were not authorized to treat for an evacuation and neither was Wigfall. Chagrined, Anderson said he would raise the flag again and resume fire. They persuaded him not to until they had explained the matter to Beauregard. Getting him to write out the terms of his agreement with Wigfall, they started for Charleston.

Within a short time the second group of aides landed at the fort bearing Beauregard's surrender demand. Patiently Anderson explained that he had, in effect, already surrendered twice and had accepted the terms of the eleventh. They said they were empowered to offer all of the original terms except the salute to the flag and they were sure Beauregard would agree to this if Anderson would agree to stop fighting. They left for Charleston to report to Beauregard.

By this time the general must have been as confused as Anderson. Not until nightfall did he get the tangled events unsnarled and agree to let Anderson honor his flag.[20] In the excitement of the day, Beauregard had apparently forgotten that he had sent two delegations to Sumter, each one charged with a different function. He betrayed a tendency, which would reappear later, to lose sight of an important detail.

On the fourteenth, a Sunday, the Yankees left Fort Sumter. Anderson paraded the garrison and fired a salute to the flag. On the fiftieth round a gun burst, killing one private and wounding five others, the only casualties of the whole engagement. All the civilities of war were observed. Out of deference to Anderson, Beauregard did not set foot on Sumter until the garrison had departed. As the steamer bearing the Federal troops passed Cummings Point, the Confederates stood respectfully with uncovered heads. Then Beauregard and Pickens headed a gay party of politicians, officers, and ladies to take possession of Sumter. Amidst shouts from the crowds on the Battery and people in boats thronging the harbor and the firing of guns, the flags of the Confederacy and South Carolina were raised above the walls.[21] The Confederacy had Sumter, and had taken it pretty cheaply. From the strictly military viewpoint, Anderson made a mistake in surrendering when he did. The fort was not seriously damaged, nor did Beauregard have the means, then, to damage it. If Anderson had waited, undoubtedly the Federal ships could have run him in supplies at night. Beauregard could have done little to stop them.

The capture of Sumter made Beauregard a Confederate hero overnight. He was the South's first paladin. Extravagant praise of his generalship resounded through the Confederacy. The press lauded him as one of the greatest soldiers in the world. President Davis told Congress that Beauregard had reduced Sumter with the skill to be expected of one with his reputation, and Congress adopted

[20] Mrs. D. Girard Wright, *A Southern Girl in 1861* (New York, 1905), 35–36, 41–44; Russell, *My Diary North and South*, 106–107; Crawford, *Genesis of the Civil War*, 440–42; *Battles and Leaders*, I, 72–73, 77–79; *Official Records*, I, 14–15, 23–24, 29, 30–35, 37–38, 63–65, 427–32; Charleston *Mercury*, April 15, 1861.
[21] *Battles and Leaders*, I, 48; Charleston *Mercury*, April 15, 1861.

a vote of thanks to the general and his army. The South Carolina legislature extended him the privilege of sending two students to be educated in the military schools of the state (he selected his younger son and a nephew). The leaders of the Confederate government wrote him flattering letters of congratulation. Davis, who within a year would be devoting strenuous efforts to destroying him, thanked him for his achievement and for his courtesy to the garrison. Walker crowed that Beauregard had won his spurs. Attorney General Judah P. Benjamin, who would be Davis' first assistant in beating Beauregard down, said he had brought honor to their common state of Louisiana. Already his unusual name was inspiring the amateur poets and song writers to composition; during the war he was the innocent cause of some of the worst verse ever written in America. One piece of doggerel popular after Sumter's fall ran:

> *With cannon and musket, with shell and petard,*
> *We salute the North with our Beau-regard.*[22]

As for the hero, he took the adulation modestly and without surprise. Not one to rest on laurels when work was to be done, he started immediately to rearrange the armament of Charleston to repel a possible Federal attack. Sumter was repaired and strengthened. The batteries bearing on the fort were shifted to cover the entrance to the harbor. He personally reconnoitered the coast from Port Royal to Charleston looking for sites on which to locate additional defensive works.

He talked freely about his plans and the war to William Howard Russell, the English war correspondent. If Russell recorded the general's thoughts correctly, they were marked by rapid shifts of opinion. One day he told Russell the mad Yankees might return to attack Charleston. A week later he talked optimistically about the outcome of the war. Although surprised at the war spirit being shown in the North, he thought it was "the washy sort" and would not last. Besides, he reminded Russell, Southern men had more physical strength than Yankees. The very next night he discoursed on the Northern fanatics and their energetic preparations to attack

[22] Douglas Southall Freeman, *Lee's Lieutenants: A Study in Command* (New York, 1942), I, 3; Rowland (ed.), *Jefferson Davis*, V, 76; James D. Richardson (ed.), *Compilation of the Messages and Papers of the Confederacy* . . . (Nashville, 1905), I, 114; Roman, *Beauregard*, I, 52–53; Russell, *My Diary North and South*, 99.

the South before it was defensible. What he seemed to dread most was a Federal thrust somewhere on the Mississippi River, particularly around New Orleans.[23] "I am surprised that we are not yet prepared on the Mississippi River, when we have had ample time to do so," he wrote Walker in language that could be construed as a criticism of the Secretary. "Could you not find some one to take hold of matters with energy while waiting that I may be sent there. . . ?"[24] Apparently some correspondence, now lost, had been exchanged between Montgomery and Charleston relative to Beauregard going to the Mississippi. Soon after he wrote Walker, he told Russell that he was going to Montgomery to confer with Davis. Work and illness forced him to postpone the trip until the first week in May.[25]

Beauregard, accompanied by Russell, who recognized good copy when he saw it, arrived in Montgomery on the fourth. The next day he met with Davis and Walker. According to an account which he wrote after the war, they asked him to go to Pensacola to help Bragg take Fort Pickens. He told them that Pickens was of no value and that the fate of the Confederacy would be decided on the field and not in ports and harbors. Although his later recollections were not always accurate, he probably spoke as he said. It was like him to lecture his superiors on strategy. Certain it is that at this time he had his first difference with Davis, that he first displayed a tendency, which constantly grew stronger, to instruct the government how to run the war. On the train to Montgomery he had talked with W. L. Trenholm, a Charleston businessman whose family was engaged in foreign trade and had connections with England. Trenholm proposed a scheme by which the government would buy some steamers on which his company would run cotton to England, the cotton to be used to purchase war supplies. Beauregard liked the plan and brought it to the attention of Davis and the Cabinet, who turned it down. After the war Beauregard would say that he supported a project that but for Davis' stupidity would have averted the Confederacy's financial woes. He did not feel so strongly about the issue at the

[23] Roman, *Beauregard*, I, 50–52; Russell, *My Diary North and South*, 116–17, 136–37; Benjamin Allston to R. F. W. Allston, May 1, 1861, in R. F. W. Allston Papers (South Carolina Historical Society, Charleston).
[24] Beauregard to L. P. Walker, April 17, 1861, in Beauregard Papers (Library of Congress), Letterbook 3.
[25] Beauregard to Walker, May 1, 1861, *ibid.*

time; its importance increased with the bitter years. He was piqued that his advice had been ignored, and he made some sharp remarks about the government's procurement policy. But during most of his stay in Montgomery, he was glowing with importance and good humor. Russell saw him in Walker's office measuring off on a map miles of country, as if he were dividing empires.[26] The clash with Davis had been a small one and was ominous only for what is portended.

Beauregard returned to Charleston and resumed work on his plans for coastal defenses north and south of the city. Apparently he and Davis had arrived at an understanding about a future and larger command, for in mid-May he wrote the President that his arrangements for Charleston were about complete and that he would be ready to go anywhere Davis sent him.[27] The government had an assignment waiting for him. On the twenty-sixth he received orders to go to Corinth, Mississippi, and assume command of the defenses of the Mississippi from Vicksburg to the Kentucky and Tennessee borders.[28]

He was ready to leave immediately. But before he departed he gave Charleston a piece of rhetoric to remember him by. In a farewell address to his soldiers, he said that he regretted having to leave Charleston, which he considered his second home. He had hoped to go to Virginia, but his services were required "elsewhere" (no need to let the enemy know his destination) and thither he would go, determined to place as strong a mark as possible on the enemies of the South should they pollute its soil with their dastardly feet. Then, apparently thinking that the Southern people needed a boost in morale and would get it from his address, he exhorted:

> . . . whatever happens at first, we are certain to triumph at last, even if we had for arms only pitchforks and flint-lock muskets, for every bush and haystack will become an ambush and every barn a fortress. The history of nations proves that a gallant and free people, fighting for their independence and firesides, are invincible against even disciplined mercenaries, at a few dollars per month. What,

[26] Roman, *Beauregard*, I, 54–61; Rowland (ed.), *Jefferson Davis*, VIII, 288, 301–303; Russell, *My Diary North and South*, 174–75.
[27] Beauregard to Davis, May 17, 1861, in Beauregard Papers (Confederate Collection, Emory University).
[28] *Official Records*, LIII, Pt. 2, pp. 106, 107.

then must be the result when its enemies are little more than an armed rabble, gathered together hastily on a false pretence, and for an unholy purpose, with an octogenarian [he could never forgive Scott] at its head? None but the demented can doubt the result.[29]

It was a good production and conformed completely to the baroque tastes of the nineteenth century. He would have made a wonderful minister of propaganda.

He was not to go to the West after all. On May 28 he received instructions to proceed to Richmond—now that Virginia had seceded, the capital of the Confederacy. The directive said nothing about the nature of his assignment, only that he was to confer with Davis.[30]

[29] Snow, *Southern Generals,* 228; Charleston *Mercury,* May 30, 1861.
[30] Roman, *Beauregard,* I, 64–66.

CHAPTER FIVE

Napoleonic Planning at Manassas

Beauregard traveled to Richmond by rail. He rode through an almost continuous ovation. At every station, waiting crowds cried for a speech. The hero of Sumter bowed modestly and asked one of his politician aides to speak for him. Admiring women covered him with flowers as he passed. Reaching Richmond on May 30, he found a crowd and a band to welcome him and a carriage and four to take him to a suite at the Spotswood Hotel, where President Davis was quartered. Quietly he told the welcoming committee that he preferred to go to the hotel in another carriage, accompanied only by his staff. The people and the band followed him to the hotel and shouted for him to speak, but Beauregard did not appear. His aloofness made a favorable impression. It was thought that he disliked demonstrations of worship and that he wished to devote all his time in planning destruction for the Yankees.[1]

The next day he conferred with Davis and General Robert E. Lee, who was commander of the Virginia state troops and acting commander of all Confederate forces in Virginia. Until now Beauregard's contacts with Davis had been few and, in a sense, routine. The personal and military relations of the two men had been mostly friendly. From the time of this conference their association would be intimate and important and would affect both them and the cause for which they fought. Their careers would touch at almost every turn. In fact, much of what happened to Beauregard after Sumter can be attributed to Davis. The personality of Davis became a vital part of the Beauregard story. The distinguished-looking President was tall, slender, erect; his face was thin and ascetic. He looked like an in-

[1] John L. Manning to Mrs. Manning, June 2, 1861, in Williams-Chesnut-Manning Papers (Southern Historical Collection, University of North Carolina Library); [Sally A. Putnam], *Richmond During the War* (New York, 1867), 46; Freeman, *Lee's Lieutenants,* I, 2–4; Mrs. Roger A. Pryor, *Reminiscences of Peace and War* (New York, 1905), 135; Richmond *Examiner,* June 1, 1861.

tellectual and had the arrogance of one. His greatest accomplishments had been those of the mind; his mind was the one thing of which he could be proud. He was sensitively proud of the correctness of his opinions and would support a wrong decision to the last. Applause and flattery were his breath of life; opposition and contradiction maddened him. Criticism of himself, his friends, or his policies he regarded as a kind of crime. He could not swallow a dissent or a rebuff in order to use the man who gave it for the common good. He loved to dispute even theoretical points to win a logical victory. Nothing delighted him more than to write a long, lecturing letter to a general who had questioned the wisdom of a Davis decision. It pleased him to show people where they were wrong. He thought they would appreciate his efforts. If he could not convince opponents of their errors, he did not try to conciliate or compromise. He severed relations with them and became their enemy.[2] This was the man who was Beauregard's superior—Beauregard, who specialized in criticism of those above him. They were born to clash.

The conference of May 31 was placid enough. The President had not decided exactly where in Virginia to assign Beauregard. Then Lee explained the strategic situation in northern Virginia, from where he had just returned. He pointed out that the Federals had crossed the Potomac and occupied Alexandria. Their next obvious move was against Manassas, important to the Confederates as a railroad junction. Quickly the President's mind was made up. He would send Beauregard to Manassas, the general of the greatest reputation to the point of greatest danger. Beauregard accepted the assignment calmly. He told Davis that he would leave for Manassas the next morning.

He reached Manassas on the night of June 2 and on the next day assumed command of his troops. His orders read that he was commander of "the Alexandria line" and that he was to act on the defensive. In an address issued to the soldiers, he exhorted them to display the discipline and gallantry exhibited by their Revolutionary

[2] Russell, *My Diary North and South,* 172–73; J. B. Jones, *A Rebel War Clerk's Diary . . .,* ed. by Howard Swiggett (New York, 1935), I, 36–37; Elizabeth Cutting, *Jefferson Davis, Political Soldier* (New York, 1930), 155; De Leon, *Belles, Beaux and Brains,* 49; Clifford Dowdey, *Experiment in Rebellion* (New York, 1946), 6–8; Hamilton J. Eckenrode, *Jefferson Davis, President of the South* (New York, 1923), 115–19; Douglas Southall Freeman, *R. E. Lee: A Biography* (New York, 1934–35), I, 516–18.

forefathers when defending liberty against a foreign tyrant.[3] When news of his presence spread, the South Carolina troops who had served under him at Charleston shouted excitedly, "Old Bory's come!" Soon the army saw much of him. Attended by a small escort and wearing a plain old blue coat of the United States army, he rode all over the camps inspecting his forces and planning defensive sites. As the nervous, grave figure sat his horse at a review or stood on an earthwork giving orders, even the rawest recruit felt that here was a soldier.[4]

Beauregard estimated that he had about six thousand men under his command. Nearly all of them were at Manassas or at the fords of Bull Run, which ran north of Manassas. One regiment occupied an advanced position at Centreville, north of the Run. On the basis of his inspections, he decided that he could not hold the extensive line of Bull Run with his present force. Although new regiments were being recruited in northern Virginia, he feared they would not be ready soon enough.[5] On June 3, the second full day he had been at Manassas, he wrote Davis to ask for reinforcements of at least ten thousand men. After detailing the difficulties involved in defending the numerous fords of Bull Run and the Occoquan River, into which the Run flowed, he said, "I must therefore either be reinforced at once. . . ; or I must be prepared to retire (upon the approach of the enemy) in the direction of Richmond, with the intention of arresting him whenever and wherever the opportunity presents itself; or I must march to meet him at one of said fords, to sell our lives as dearly as practicable." [6] Beauregard was not satisfied with just a dramatic appeal to the government. He also urged the civilians in his department to aid him. Acting on a report that some Federal troops had committed outrages, he issued a proclamation charging that the enemy had invaded Virginia with the warcry of "Beauty and booty." He exhorted the people to rally and expel the "abolitionist hosts" from the land. It was the kind of rhetorical document which he would compose several times in the war and which would always endear him to the populace if not to the government.[7]

[3] Roman, *Beauregard*, I, 66–69.

[4] Cooke, *Wearing of the Gray*, 84–85; An English Combatant, *Battlefields of the South From Bull Run to Fredericksburg* (London, 1863), I, 46–47.

[5] Roman, *Beauregard*, I, 69–70; *Official Records*, II, 831, 841, 846, 879.

[6] Roman, *Beauregard*, I, 70.

[7] *Ibid.*, 73–74; *Official Records*, II, 907.

In the next few weeks reinforcements poured into Manassas. Beauregard's spirits lifted. He spent long hours over his desk studying maps and plans. His headquarters were in a small house on the outskirts of the ugly little town. On the second floor was his apartment, where he worked, ate, and slept. When he was not at headquarters, he was riding the lines, inspecting his forces, directing training of the new units, or mingling with the soldiers. Often he would walk through the camps, stopping to light a cigar at a campfire and talk to the men. Such gestures made him popular. The soldiers felt that he understood their problems and would look after their welfare. According to one GI yarn, a private unknowingly wandered into Beauregard's apartment. Wishing to write a letter, he sat down at a desk and took up pen and paper. Soon he heard a step and saw the general enter. Fearing a rebuke, he stammered an apology. With a smile, Beauregard said, "Sit down and finish your letter, my friend. You are very welcome, and can always come in here when you wish to write." True or not, this tale and others like it bound the army to Beauregard. The morale of the troops was excellent.[8]

The soldiers probably did not know about one evidence of Beauregard's concern for them. After he had been at Manassas a few days, his restless mind turned to the problem of how Confederates could be distinguished from Federals in battle. He came up with a scheme for his men to wear colored scarves, red on one side and yellow on the other, which would extend from shoulder to waist. He pressed his plan on the War Department, with the suggestion that the Richmond ladies could make the scarves. Such a momentous matter could not be decided without being brought to the attention of President Davis, who thought that the identifying symbols were too large and directed that colored rosettes be prepared.[9] The incident was characteristic of Beauregard. His general idea was sound; his specific proposal was extravagant and impractical.

Even though his army was increasing in size, Beauregard was oppressed by fear of attack from a superior Federal force. To strengthen his position, he started a program of feverish fortification building.

[8] English Combatant, *Battlefields of the South*, I, 27-28; Snow, *Southern Generals*, 229–31; [Napier Bartlett], *A Soldier's Story of the War . . .* (New Orleans, 1874), 60; Cooke, *Wearing of the Gray*, 90–92; Mrs. Chesnut, *Diary From Dixie*, 62.

[9] Roman, *Beauregard*, I, 75, 433, 435; A. C. Myers to Miles, June 17, 18, 1861, in Miles Papers.

When some of the soldiers objected that constructing earthworks was
not fit work for gentlemen, he persuaded the planters in the region to
lend him their slaves. He concentrated his fortifications around
Manassas. It was certainly important for the Confederates to hold
the town and its railroad connections. From Alexandria the Orange
and Alexandria Railroad ran twenty-five miles to Manassas and
thence sixty-five miles southwest to Gordonsville, from which Richmond could be reached by rail. The Manassas Gap Railroad ran
west from the town fifty miles to the Shenandoah Valley, where General Joseph E. Johnston commanded a Confederate force of about
eleven thousand. The two lines enabled the Confederates to supply
both armies from the rear; the Manassas road was particularly important as a link to unite Johnston and Beauregard in an emergency.
Nevertheless, Beauregard erred in placing most of his fieldworks
around Manassas. He built almost none on the line of Bull Run itself,
which was the logical line behind which to defend Manassas.[10]

Beauregard also devoted some attention to organizing his services
of supply. His efforts involved him in the first of what would be a
dreary series of controversies with the Richmond bureaucracy. He
wanted to secure his food supplies in the Manassas area, or so he
claimed after the war, but was ordered to get them from Richmond
by Colonel L. B. Northrop, the martinet Commissary General of the
Confederacy. Northrop, after the war, denied that he forbade Beauregard to buy food at Manassas and charged that the general had
supply troubles because he did not know how to organize his railway
transport. The weight of the evidence in the dispute seems to be on
Beauregard's side. Apparently Northrop fixed the prices at Manassas
so low that the farmers preferred to ship their goods to Richmond.

Whatever the merits of the case, Beauregard was profoundly irritated. He complained to Davis that his requests to the War Department were not answered and not even acknowledged. When a requisi-
tion for rope to be used in wells was rejected on the grounds that all
available rope belonged to the navy, he broke out angrily at headquarters, "If they would only send us less law and more rope." An
aide asked, "To hang ourselves with, General?" Bitterly he replied,
"It would be better than strangulation with red tape." [11]

[10] R. M. Johnston, *Bull Run: Its Strategy and Tactics* (Boston, 1913),
21–22, 82; Roman, *Beauregard*, I, 70–71; *Battles and Leaders*, I, 196.

[11] Roman, *Beauregard*, I, 71–75, 432–34; Rowland (ed.), *Jefferson Davis*,
IX, 301; *Battles and Leaders*, I, 261; Charles Marshall, *An Aide-de-Camp of*

By mid-June Beauregard felt that he had his army well enough in hand to plan grand strategy. He prepared a plan of operations which he dispatched to Davis by a staff officer. His views, he informed his superior, "should be acted upon at once." He believed that the Federals were about to attack Johnston. That general should be ordered to fall back from the Valley and unite with Beauregard. Then, by "a bold and rapid movement," the combined forces could retake Arlington Heights and Alexandria, if the enemy was not too strongly posted; all Federal troops in Virginia would have to be recalled to defend Washington. If this junction of forces was not possible, Johnston should be directed to retreat on Richmond; Beauregard would also retire and join him. The combined armies, Beauregard continued, could act on interior lines from Richmond: "we would crush successively and in detail the several columns of the enemy, which I have supposed will move on three or four different lines of operations. With 35,000 men properly handled on our part, I have not the least doubt that we could annihilate 50,000 of the enemy." He ended by exhorting Davis to adopt "a concerted plan" of operations: "otherwise we will be assailed in detail by superior forces, and be either cut off or destroyed entirely." [12]

This curious document reveals much about Beauregard and his generalship. It was his habit to slap together a plan without complete information of the enemy and without regard to the realities of his own resources and then in a glow of enthusiasm to claim that it would accomplish brilliant results. He had no certain evidence that the Federals would attack Johnston first. He ignored the fact that his army and Johnston's lacked the weapons and transport to attack the Washington approaches, just as he overlooked the possibility that the Federals in the abandoned Valley could threaten his rear as he neared Washington. As for the withdrawal on Richmond, his assumption that the Federals would accommodatingly advance in several columns was entirely unwarranted. One of the oddest features of his plan was the manner in which he, a brigadier general, proposed to manipulate the forces of Johnston, a full general by act of Congress. The implication was present that he expected to command the Confederate forces when they were joined.

Lee . . ., ed. by Sir Frederick Maurice (Boston, 1927), 45–46; Basso, *Beauregard,* 119–20.

[12] Beauregard to Davis, June 12, 1861, in Jefferson Davis Papers (Confederate Collection, Emory University Library).

Davis rejected the plan. In a tactful and restrained letter he pointed out to Beauregard some of its faults: the lack of transport and the danger that the Federals would cut Beauregard's communications if Johnston left the Valley. Reinforcements would come to Beauregard, the President assured, and if the armies had to retreat Johnston would join Beauregard. To Beauregard's request for a concerted plan of operations, Davis replied that the present unknown purpose of the enemy required a flexible plan on the part of the Confederacy.[13]

By the latter part of June reinforcements had brought Beauregard's army up to about fifteen thousand. Until now the largest unit in his organization had been the regiment. Thinking that his increasing mass needed a tighter command, he organized, on the twentieth, his nineteen regiments into six brigades. His brigades were uneven in number; three were commanded by generals and three by colonels. The artillery, not too adequate to begin with, was broken up and divided among the brigades. He would probably have achieved better control of his troops if he had organized them into three divisions.[14] As he surveyed his growing forces, Beauregard's mood changed from apprehension to optimism. He told Johnston that he was beginning to believe the Confederates would have to attack if they wanted to get a fight out of the Federals.[15]

A few days later he began a forward movement of three brigades over Bull Run. His purpose, he informed the government, was to protect his advanced position at Centreville and to strike a blow at the enemy if the opportunity offered.[16] Actually he had a more definite plan in mind. Information he had secured from Southern sympathizers in Washington and from other sources indicated a move on Manassas by the Federal army at Washington commanded by General Irvin McDowell.[17] When the Federals advanced, the troops north of the Run would take the first shock of the attack and then retire to the south bank. As the Federals attempted to cross, the

[13] Davis to Beauregard, June 13, 1861, in Roman, *Beauregard*, I, 77–78.

[14] *Official Records*, II, 943–44; Johnston, *Bull Run*, 111–12.

[15] Beauregard to Joseph E. Johnston, June 22, 1861, in Henkels' Catalog 1148, *The Beauregard Papers* . . . (Philadelphia, 1915), Pt. I.

[16] Beauregard to Walker, June 23, 1861, in *Official Records*, II, 947; Roman, *Beauregard*, I, 79.

[17] *Battles and Leaders*, I, 197–98; Beauregard to Myers, July 4, 1861, in Henkels' Catalog, *Beauregard Papers*, Pt. I.

forces at Manassas and other points would advance and attack them in the flank and rear.[18]

He explained this plan in detail early in July to his brigade commanders. The Federals, he said, would march through Centreville and cross Bull Run at Mitchell's Ford on the direct road to Manassas. While the brigade at Mitchell's held the Federals, the others would cross and assail the enemy's most vulnerable flank. Again Beauregard was assuming that the Federals would be obliging enough to do what he wanted. He figured that Mitchell's would be their point of attack because it was his strongest position. The possibility that they might attack at another point he did not consider. Moreover, by improper use of his cavalry he stopped himself from learning the movements of the enemy. Nearly all of the cavalry he placed with General M. L. Bonham's brigade at Mitchell's, in the center of the Bull Run line, where it was in the poorest possible position to detect Federal moves on either flank.[19]

Hardly had he got his brigades over Bull Run when he experienced another change of mood. His intelligence service reported that McDowell was about to advance with forty thousand men. The news plunged him into a fit of apprehension. Characteristically he blamed the government for the peril he thought he was in. At headquarters his staff officers were speaking of Davis as "a stupid fool" and of Secretary Walker as being "beneath criticism & contempt." [20]

Beauregard unburdened his woes in a complaining letter to Louis Wigfall, his former aide at Charleston and now a member of Congress. "How can it be expected that I shall be able to maintain my ground unless reenforced immediately?" he asked. "I am determined to give the enemy battle no matter at what odds against us; but is it right and proper to sacrifice so many valuable lives (and perhaps our cause) without the least prospect of success?" After describing his difficulties in getting help from the War Department, he asked Wigfall to go to Davis and tell the President that he must be properly supported. He ended on a note of unexpected optimism: "Oh, that

[18] Manning to Mrs. Manning, June 20, 1861, in Williams-Chesnut-Manning Papers; Roman, *Beauregard*, I, 79–81.

[19] *Official Records*, II, 448; Jubal A. Early, *Autobiographical Sketch and Narrative of the War Between the States* (Philadelphia, 1912), 4–5; Johnston, *Bull Run*, 129–30; General Thomas Jordan to M. L. Bonham, July 10, 1861, in Beauregard Papers (Library of Congress), Letterbook 4.

[20] Manning to Mrs. Manning, July 7, 1861, in Williams-Chesnut-Manning Papers.

I had the genius of a Napoleon, to be more worthy of our cause and their [the troops'] confidence. If I could only get the enemy to attack me, . . . I would stake my reputation on the handsomest victory that could be hoped for." [21]

Three days later he wrote Davis a letter full of the same forebodings and the same confusion of purpose. He detailed his scheme to lure the enemy to Mitchell's Ford, but now he was afraid the Federals would turn his left. Because of the smallness of his army he would have to act with extreme caution. But if McDowell offered battle, "I shall accept it for my command against whatsoever odds he may array in my front." [22]

When he wrote these letters, Beauregard was thinking in terms of a defensive strategy. Suddenly and without apparent explanation, he shifted to the idea of an offensive movement. On July 13 he sent an aide to Richmond with a proposal for a union of his army with Johnston's. Hardly had the aide left when Beauregard enlarged his plan and sent Colonel James R. Chesnut of his staff to explain it to Davis. The completed design was truly Napoleonic. Johnston, leaving five thousand men in the Valley to contain the Federals, was to join Beauregard with twenty thousand (Johnston had eleven thousand in his command). The combined forces would attack and destroy McDowell. Then Johnston would return to the Valley with his own army and ten thousand of Beauregard's and smash the Federals there. Next Johnston would detach enough men to western Virginia to clear the enemy out of that region. These troops would return and join Johnston, who would then invade Maryland and attack Washington from the rear, while Beauregard, coming up from Manassas, would attack it in front.

In describing the plan to Johnston, Beauregard wrote: "I think this whole campaign could be completed brilliantly in from fifteen to twenty-five days. Oh, that we had but one good head to conduct all our operations!" [23]

Chesnut, speaking from notes, presented the plan on the fourteenth to Davis, Lee, and Adjutant General Samuel Cooper. Both the President and Lee objected to it on two counts. They pointed out

[21] Beauregard to Louis T. Wigfall, July 8, 1861, in Roman, *Beauregard*, I, 81–82.

[22] Beauregard to Davis, July 11, 1861, *ibid.*, 82–83, and in Davis Papers (Emory University).

[23] Roman, *Beauregard*, I, 13–14, 87; *Official Records*, II, 484–85.

that Johnston was too weak to reinforce Beauregard; that the twenty thousand men simply were not there; and that even if the Confederates had enough men to effect a concentration, the Federals would retire into their nearby Washington defenses rather than risk a battle with a superior enemy in the open.[24]

Davis and Lee were right to reject Beauregard's scheme. It was full of holes. The grandiose combinations he proposed to move over northern Virginia might have been executed by experienced generals and armies equipped with efficient staffs and adequate transport services. They were completely impossible for the Confederates in 1861. In assuming a mobility for the Confederate forces that they did not have, Beauregard showed a fatally weak sense of logistics. His plan told much of Beauregard as a soldier. Influenced by Napoleon and Jomini, he always advocated concentration. In the general or fundamental sense he was right. If the numerically inferior Confederates were going to win in Virginia or elsewhere, they would have to concentrate. He saw this, Davis did not. Beauregard's trouble was that he did not know how to fashion a specific plan of concentration that would work. When he tried, the result, as in this case, approached the level of fantasy.

His design of grand strategy rejected by the government, Beauregard turned to studying the movements of McDowell. Of these he was kept informed by as romantic a set of spies as any general ever had in his service. Just before the war started, Colonel Thomas Jordan, his chief of staff, had arranged a spy apparatus in Washington. He asked Mrs. Rose Greenhow, famous capital society dowager and Southern sympathizer, to send him information of important Federal movements. He provided her with a crude cipher. Mrs. Greenhow dispatched her first message early in July: McDowell would advance on the sixteenth. It was carried from Washington by a beautiful girl named Bettie Duvall, who disguised herself as a country girl and rode in a farm wagon to Virginia. Going to the home of friends, she changed her costume to a riding habit, borrowed a horse, and rode to Bonham's headquarters at Fairfax Courthouse. Both Bonham and his young officers were thrilled when she unrolled her long hair, took out Mrs. Greenhow's dispatch, and handed it to the general.

At this time, volunteer girl spies from northern Virginia were

[24] Roman, *Beauregard*, I, 85–87; *Official Records*, II, 505–507, 515.

bursting into Beauregard's lines at every turn, bearing news that the Yankees were coming. They were received with consideration and applause, although their information was generally vague and available in Washington newspapers. To secure more definite news, Jordan sent a man named Donellan to Mrs. Greenhow. He carried a scrap of paper on which Jordan had written in cipher, "Trust bearer." He reached Washington on July 16 and received from her a code message saying McDowell had been ordered to move on Manassas that night. Traveling in a buggy and using relays of horses, Donellan brought the dispatch into the Confederate lines. It was delivered to Beauregard between eight and nine the same night.[25]

Immediately Beauregard ordered his brigades north of Bull Run to retire to their prearranged positions south of the stream. This movement was completed by early morning of the eighteenth. He still nourished hopes of hitting the Federals a counterstroke after he halted them at Mitchell's Ford. A loosely worded order to his brigade commanders, "to all concerned," as he put it, directed them to observe "the special contingencies indicated" as previously instructed. To Davis he sent a telegram summarizing his actions. He would make a stand at Bull Run, he said, but if the enemy force was overwhelming he would have to retire to the Rappahannock River to save his command. He asked the President to notify Johnston of his peril. "Send forward any reinforcements, at the earliest possible instant," he concluded, "and by every possible means." [26]

The government responded to his appeal by speeding on available reinforcements and by ordering Johnston, on the seventeenth, to move to Manassas. Word of Johnston's coming reached Beauregard the next day. He threw the telegram on the table and cried, "Too late, too late. McDowell will be upon me tomorrow with his whole

[25] De Leon, *Belles, Beaux and Brains,* 407–408; Mrs. Burton Harrison, *Recollections Grave and Gay* (New York, 1911), 53–54; Roman, *Beauregard,* I, 89, 117–18; Alfred Roman to Beauregard, December 13, 1861, in Alfred Roman Papers (Duke University Library); Louis A. Sigaud, "Mrs. Greenhow and the Rebel Spy Ring," in *Maryland Historical Magazine,* XLI (1946), 173–74; William Miller Owen, *In Camp and Battle with the Washington Artillery* . . . (Boston, 1885), 25, hereinafter cited as *Washington Artillery;* Hairston to Mrs. Hairston, September 4, 1861, in Hairston Papers; George S. Bryan, *The Spy in America* (Philadelphia, 1943), 177–80; *Official Records,* LI, Pt. 2, p. 688; Mrs. Rose Greenhow, *My Imprisonment and the First Year of Abolition Rule at Washington* (London, 1863), 14–18; *Battles and Leaders,* I, 199–200.

[26] Roman, *Beauregard,* I, 89–90; *Official Records,* LI, Pt. 2, pp. 172–73.

army and we shall have to sell our lives as dearly as possible." [27] Shortly his confidence was restored. That day the Federals felt out the strength of the Confederate position at Blackburn's Ford on the right center of Beauregard's line, and were repulsed. Beauregard rode to the scene of action from his nearby headquarters at the McLean house and observed the enemy retire. This minor action he described extravagantly in his official report, using such phrases as "a flying, baffled foe," whose "heavy masses" broke in "utter rout." [28]

The successful skirmish, coupled with the news of Johnston's advance, caused Beauregard to think again in offensive terms. He sent a courier to Johnston with a proposal for the Valley army to move in two columns. One would come on the Manassas Gap Railroad to join Beauregard. The other would cross the mountains north of the railroad and fall on McDowell's rear while Beauregard attacked in front. Napoleonic to the last, he was suggesting one of the most difficult feats in war—to combine two armies on the battlefield. Johnston rejected the plan on the grounds that his small, green army could not accomplish such a dangerous undertaking.[29] Apparently Beauregard believed until the nineteenth that Johnston would advance as he had recommended. That evening he held a council of his officers and went over his plan. As the conference broke up, he exclaimed, "Now, gentlemen, let to-morrow be their Waterloo." [30]

On the night of the nineteenth or the next day Beauregard learned that the Valley army was coming in one piece on the Manassas Gap Railroad. Johnston and his first troops reached Manassas about noon on the twentieth. The rest of his army, Johnston told Beauregard, should arrive that night. Beauregard outlined for Johnston the situation in his front—McDowell's army was around Centreville—and the

[27] Colonel A. R. Chisolm, in New Orleans *Picayune*, March 1, 1893.

[28] Early, *Autobiographical Sketch*, 6–10; *Battles and Leaders*, I, 201; English Combatant, *Battlefields of the South*, I, 50–52; Roman, *Beauregard*, I, 441–44; *Official Records*, II, 446.

[29] Beauregard, in *Battles and Leaders*, I, 200–201, and in his book, *A Commentary on the Campaign and Battle of Manassas* . . . (New York, 1891), 25–37. Johnston described the incident in *Battles and Leaders*, I, 250, and in his book, *Narrative of Military Operations* . . . (New York, 1874), 38. In both accounts he wrongly said that Beauregard's plan called for all of the Valley army to march to McDowell's rear.

[30] Owen, *Washington Artillery*, 30; Early, *Autobiographical Sketch*, 10–12. Early stated that during the meeting General T. J. Jackson, of Johnston's vanguard, arrived and told Beauregard the entire Valley army was moving as one force but that Beauregard refused to believe him.

disposition of his own line. He also described for Johnston, who was unfamiliar with the region, the terrain of Bull Run. The winding, narrow stream ran between wooded and often precipitous banks and was intersected by numerous fords. Beauregard's front on the Run was eight miles in length. From right to left the fords and the brigade at each, designated by the name of the commander, were Union Mills, Richard Ewell with Jubal Early in reserve; McLean's, D. R. Jones; Blackburn's, James Longstreet; Mitchell's, Bonham; Island, Ball's, and Lewis', P. St. G. Cocke; at the Stone Bridge on the extreme left, N. G. Evans' demibrigade.[31] Taking Mitchell's as the center, Beauregard had four brigades on his right, one in the middle, and one and a half on his left. Before he received one soldier from Johnston, Beauregard had concentrated his forces on the right. This arrangement was curious because the terrain on the right was strong defensively and that on the left was weak. If Beauregard expected to fight a defensive battle, which is what he said in later life he wanted to do, he should have reversed his dispositions. His excuse for massing at the lower fords was that he wished to guard his depots at Manassas from a flank attack.[32] He may have had this reason in mind, but his real purpose was undoubtedly an offensive move against the Federal left.

The two generals then discussed possible strategic movements. Johnston favored an immediate offensive. He assumed that the Federals in the Valley, when they learned he had left, would join McDowell. Therefore, he thought that McDowell should be attacked the next day, before they could arrive. Beauregard agreed completely with the reasoning. He produced a map which showed roads, towns, and streams but no elevations, and pointed out the roads converging on Centreville. He proposed an offensive move against the Federal forces in and around the town. Johnston approved the plan and told Beauregard to execute it. Apparently Johnston understood that the advance was to be made by the entire army.[33]

This statement, and almost any statement about the prebattle planning, is open to qualification. Beauregard and Johnston wrote accounts of what happened during the war and later. Their records

---

[31] Freeman, *Lee's Lieutenants*, I, 48-49; E. P. Alexander, *Military Memoirs of a Confederate* (New York, 1907), 21-22; Johnston, *Bull Run*, 38-42; *Official Records*, LI, Pt. 1, p. 25.

[32] Beauregard, *Commentary on Manassas*, 52-54.

[33] Johnston, *Narrative*, 39-41; Johnston, in *Battles and Leaders*, I, 245; Johnston, in *Official Records*, II, 473-74.

are incomplete and often contradictory of the other. Sometimes one general would change or contravene what he had written earlier. The modern student can only try to connect their versions into an approximately accurate narrative.[34]

Beauregard was delighted with Johnston's decision. In effect, it meant that Johnston, the ranking general, was going to let him direct the battle. During the rest of the day on the twentieth, he arranged Johnston's troops in position as they arrived and also a force under General T. H. Holmes that Davis had ordered to him. By nightfall his dispositions were complete. His line was still heavy on the right. Of the approximately 33,000 men at his command (one brigade of Johnston's army was still absent), he had about 15,500 on his right center. His left was held by fewer than 5,000. The general reserve was four miles from the forces on the far left.[35] Johnston, exhausted by his labors of the last few days, told Beauregard to draft the combat order for the morrow's battle and then retired. Beauregard, who must have been tired himself, worked on the order through the hours of the night.

At four-thirty on the morning of the twenty-first, he presented it to Johnston. The senior officer was surprised to note that the order was framed as if it came from Beauregard and was signed by Beauregard. Johnston was asked to sign only copies intended for distribution among his own troops. Suppressing what feelings of irritation he may have had, Johnston approved the document rather than delay operations.[36]

In considering Beauregard's battle planning, and disregarding the verbal outline which he gave Johnston on the previous day, the combat order may be regarded as his Battle Plan I. In briefest essence, it called for an attack on Centreville to be delivered by four brigades, two moving from the center and two from the left. Six brigades were to cross the fords on the right and support the attack on Centreville or move on other points "according to circumstances." [37]

[34] In describing the planning and the battle, I have given my reconstruction of the documents without arguing their evidence. Anyone who wishes to see the documents debated may examine Freeman, *Lee's Lieutenants*, I. In general, but not completely, my account agrees with Freeman's. As an example of the trouble which the student will encounter, in one account Johnston confused the right and left flanks.

[35] *Official Records*, II, 486; Beauregard, *Commentary on Manassas*, 52–54.

[36] Johnston, *Narrative*, 41; Beauregard, *Commentary on Manassas*, 61–62; *Official Records*, II, 473–74, 486; *Battles and Leaders*, I, 203.

[37] *Official Records*, II, 479–80.

The order was written in vague and confused language and is, from the Confederate viewpoint, one of the most melancholy documents in the war. In the first part of the order he referred to his units as brigades. As he wrote he realized the difficulty of controlling so many brigades on a long front, so he took to calling two brigades a division, even though no divisional organization existed. Having created divisions, he ended up by improvising two corps, although he did not call them by that name. After the fall of Centreville, the army would move forward in two groups, one commanded by Holmes (who was never informed of the arrangement) and the other by an unnamed second in command.

Similar obscurities ran all through the document. Participation was provided for the brigade from the Valley army that had not arrived. No hour was set for the advance to begin. Each section ended, "the order to advance will be given by the commander-in-chief." Did this mean to advance from present positions or new ones to be occupied? Would the order come before or after Bull Run was crossed? And just who was commander in chief? None of these questions could have been answered clearly from the text of the order. This complex, grandiose design would have been difficult to execute even if Beauregard had been an officer with extensive troop experience and if he had at his disposal a trained staff. In the absence of these conditions, the plan was impossible.[38]

It was never to be tried. Shortly after five the sound of firing broke out on the Confederate left. The realities of war were about to confound Napoleonic strategy.

[38] For criticisms of the order, see Freeman, *Lee's Lieutenants*, I, 50–51; Johnston, *Bull Run*, 161–63.

CHAPTER SIX

Beauregard Felix

THE BATTLE OF MANASSAS, the name given to the struggle of July 21 by Southerners, was, as conducted by the Confederate command, a record of bungled orders, sudden shifts in strategy, and final fortunate victory. First of all, it is almost certain that because of poor staff work, Beauregard's combat order was not distributed to most of the brigade commanders who were to lead off the attack. He claimed later that they received copies, and undoubtedly he thought as the battle began that copies had gone out.

But a strange set of people were employed at his headquarters that day. In addition to his not too competent staff, a good many enlisted men and civilian guides who were present were entrusted with the bearing of important orders. Apparently no record was kept of their names, and after the battle, curiously enough, they disappeared and were never heard of again. Beauregard had no idea of the identity of the man who carried one of his most vital orders.[1]

Regardless of whether the order was distributed, it could not be executed. First, it was discovered that a brigade of Johnston's, which was to support the attack on the left, had not arrived. Then, soon after five o'clock reports came in .from Bonham at Mitchell's Ford that the Federals had appeared on his left and that another enemy force was moving on the Warrenton Pike toward the Stone Bridge. The sound of firing along the left was heard at Confederate headquarters at Manassas. All of this indicated to Beauregard an attack on his center and left. If such was the case, his plan for a general offensive could not be immediately put into effect. The combat order temporarily would have to be inoperative.

[1] Freeman, *Lee's Lieutenants,* I, 726–28; *Official Records,* II, 537, 543, 565, LI, Pt. 1, pp. 28, 199; *Battles and Leaders,* I, 246; Beauregard, *Commentary on Manassas,* 51; Early, *Autobiographical Narrative,* 16; James A. Longstreet, *From Manassas to Appomattox* (Philadelphia, 1896), 44–45; Percy Gatling Hamlin (ed.), *The Making of a Soldier: Letters of General R. S. Ewell* (Richmond, 1935), 105–107.

In an instant Beauregard formulated his Battle Plan II. He would launch a diversion on his right to weaken the threatened enemy attack, and if the diversion succeeded he would turn it into a general advance. At five-thirty he sent an order to Ewell at Union Mills Ford on the extreme right. The order directed Ewell to hold himself in readiness to move on Centreville; Holmes would support him in the demonstration. At the end of the directive Beauregard said, "I intend to take the offensive throughout my front as soon as possible." [2]

The confusion and inefficiency prevailing at Beauregard's headquarters were demonstrated by what happened after this dispatch was sent to Ewell. Longstreet, the one brigade commander who had certainly received the combat order of four-thirty and who had crossed the Run, was not informed of the change in plan. He spent most of the day crossing and recrossing and wondering what had happened to the general offensive. Holmes, who was to support Ewell, did not get his instructions until nine. Worst of all, Beauregard or someone on his staff forgot that the order to Ewell had told him to be ready to advance but had not directed him to move. In the turmoil of the moment Beauregard either confused the meaning of his directive to Ewell or thought that he had sent him a second order. Whatever the facts, at about six Beauregard sent an order to Jones at McLean's, received at a little after seven, stating that Ewell had been ordered to take the offensive against Centreville and that Jones was to follow the movement by attacking in his front. The only certainties in all this chaos were that the generals on the left received orders to hold to the last and that Early was directed to place himself where he could support either Longstreet or Jones. [3]

About seven o'clock Beauregard decided to strengthen his left. The equivalent of almost three brigades from the reserve was shifted to the left and left center. All of his actions thus far, it should be emphasized, had been based merely on the report that enemy troops were moving toward the Stone Bridge and on the slow cannonade along the left. No infantry action had been reported to headquarters; no Federal attack had been made at any point on the line. It is remarkable that Beauregard, after placing so much reliance on the movements on his right, did not go personally to that sector to see if his orders were being executed. He and Johnston remained at

[2] Roman, *Beauregard*, I, 447–48; *Official Records*, LI, Pt. 2, p. 186; Beauregard, *Commentary on Manassas*, 65.
[3] *Official Records*, II, 487, 537, 555, 565.

Manassas until sometime after seven. Then they rode to a hill behind Bonham's position at Mitchell's, where they set up field headquarters at eight or eight-thirty.[4]

At this point Beauregard was full of confidence. His left had been reinforced; his troops on the right were making a demonstration. Now was the time to turn the demonstration into an offensive against Centreville. If the Federals were stretching westward toward the Stone Bridge, their left should be particularly vulnerable. He now produced and submitted to Johnston his Battle Plan III, which was to throw five brigades from his right at Centreville. Johnston approved, and Beauregard sent out the orders.[5]

Hardly had Beauregard sat back to consider how his attack would surprise the Federals than surprising news reached him from his signal officer: a Federal column had crossed Bull Run above the Stone Bridge and was moving down on his own left.[6] Immediately Beauregard moved to strengthen the extreme left. Troops already on the left were directed to the Bridge, as was a small infantry unit that had just arrived from Richmond. The sound of firing above the Stone Bridge increased. The signal officer sent word that a large dust cloud had appeared to the northwest. Johnston judged that the cloud meant the Federal army in the Valley was approaching to join McDowell. Although Johnston was worried, Beauregard was not. He still relied on his offensive on the right, when it developed, to bring victory. He dispatched no more troops to the left.

Meanwhile, on the right, the hoped-for offensive was completely stalled. Longstreet, operating under the four-thirty order, was skirmishing north of Bull Run. Jones crossed the Run and looked for Ewell. He did not find him, of course, because Ewell had not received an order to advance. About eight-thirty somebody at headquarters sent instructions to Ewell to cross, but the courier bearing the order never found Ewell. After waiting over two hours, Jones returned to the south bank. Ewell finally got in communication with Jones and learned that he was supposed to have in his possession an order to lead off the offensive. Immediately Ewell sent a courier to Beauregard to explain the snarled situation and to say that he was preparing to advance. The messenger reached Beauregard shortly before ten-thirty. Ewell's news destroyed any hopes of an offensive on the right.

---

[4] *Ibid.*, 474, 491; Beauregard, *Commentary on Manassas*, 79–80.
[5] *Official Records*, II, 491.
[6] Alexander, *Military Memoirs*, 30–31.

It was now too late to develop any move in that sector. Regretfully Beauregard wrote an order for the brigades north of the Run to return.[7] Describing his feelings at the minute, he wrote in a letter: "My heart for a moment failed me! I felt as though all was lost. . . ; but I soon rallied, and I then solemnly pledged my life that I would that day conquer or die! Immediately everything appeared again clear and hopeful. . . ." [8]

It did not look so hopeful to Johnston. As the sound of battle on the left swelled in volume, he became increasingly concerned. He pressed Beauregard to send all available troops to the left. Finally, about eleven-thirty, he cried, "The battle is there. I am going," and rode toward the sound of the firing. Pausing only to order the reserve brigades on the right and center to move to the left, Beauregard joined him.[9] Over four miles of bad roads the generals rode to the scene of action. About twelve-thirty they arrived at an eminence called the Henry house hill or plateau.

Here for the first time they obtained an accurate picture of what had happened on the left during the morning hours. McDowell, demonstrating at the Stone Bridge, had thrown a column of perhaps seventeen thousand men over the Run above the Bridge and had come dangerously close to turning the Confederate left. Only hard fighting by the various unit commanders, acting largely on their own initiative, had stopped the Federals. Even so, the situation was for the Confederates extremely dangerous. The bulk of the Southern forces, excluding the few around the Stone Bridge, had retired under a series of assaults to the brow and eastern edge of the Henry hill, part of which was occupied by the Federals. The Confederate line faced almost west. No officer was in command; some units were standing firm in line; others were shattered, confused, and on the verge of breaking up. Johnston and Beauregard, after taking in the picture, devoted themselves to restoring order and re-forming the lines. Beauregard had the various unit standards advanced forty yards and then ordered the men to form on the colors.[10]

[7] *Official Records,* II, 491, 536-39, 543-44, LI, Pt. 2, pp. 198-99; *Battles and Leaders,* I, 259-61; Hamlin (ed.), *Making of a Soldier,* 106.

[8] Beauregard to Augusta J. Evans, March 24, 1863, in *Official Records,* LI, Pt. 2, pp. 688-89.

[9] *Ibid.,* II, 474-75, 491-92; Johnston, *Narrative,* 47-48; Alexander, *Military Memoirs,* 34. Beauregard also directed the brigades on the right to demonstrate against Federal batteries on the northern bank.

[10] *Official Records,* II, 475, 492; *Battles and Leaders,* I, 210, 248.

With the front stabilized for the moment, Beauregard turned to Johnston and asked him to leave the field. One of them, Beauregard explained, had to be in a position where he could direct movements over the whole field and forward reinforcements. That role belonged to the senior general. The honor of conducting the battle Beauregard claimed for himself. At first the astounded Johnston refused, but in the face of Beauregard's persistence he yielded. He rode back about a mile and a half to a point from which he had a good view of the fighting front.[11]

After Johnston's departure, Beauregard rode along his line and disposed his units to meet the next attack. The Federals were extending their right to try to overlap his left. To meet this danger, he shifted some troops to the left and posted all arriving reinforcements on that sector. As he rode among the men, he made brief speeches to them to stand fast or shouted dramatic statements. Encouraging the commander of the Washington Artillery of New Orleans, he said, "Then hold this position, and the day is ours. Three cheers for Louisiana!" When the standard of a South Carolina unit fell, he cried, "Hand it to me, let me bear the Palmetto Flag." To a Georgia regiment he shouted, "I salute the Eighth Georgia with my hat off! History shall never forget you!" One thrilled observer said later that if Beauregard were ever painted it should be as he appeared that day: eyes flaming, the sallow face blazing with enthusiasm, the drawn sword pointing to the enemy. His horse was killed under him; he calmly took another. During the course of the day he rode four, one of which was a captured Yankee steed.[12]

At two o'clock Beauregard ordered his right to advance against the Federals on the plateau. In a quick attack the Confederates cleared the ground, but the Federals regained it in as quick a counterattack. Nevertheless, Beauregard was not worried about his right; he could hold there. It was the left that concerned him, and the constantly extending enemy right. As arriving reinforcements came up and took their places on the left, he ordered another attack. This time the Confederates swept the enemy from the hill and held the

[11] *Official Records*, II, 475, 491–92; *Battles and Leaders*, I, 210–11.

[12] Owen, *Washington Artillery*, 38; Freeman, *Lee's Lieutenants*, I, 79–80; Cooke, *Wearing of the Gray*, 85–95; Roman, *Beauregard*, I, 105, 109; G. C. Brown to Mrs. David Hubbard, August 22, 1861, in Polk-Brown-Ewell Papers (Southern Historical Collection, University of North Carolina Library); Beauregard to W. M. Gardner, August 24, 1861, in Gardner Papers; *Official Records*, II, 493.

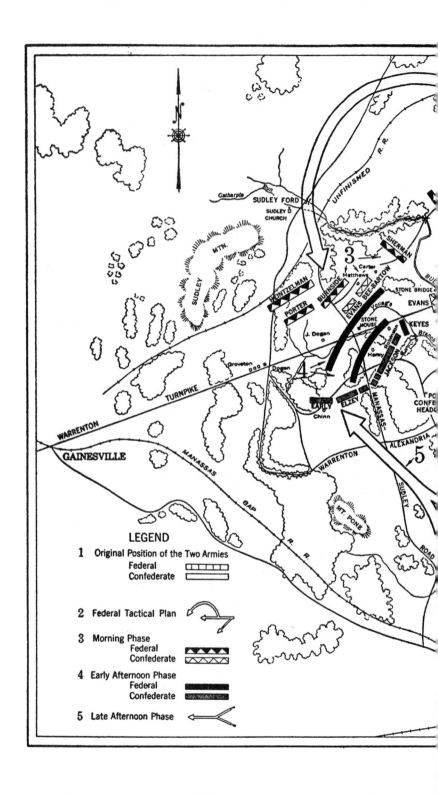

Catharpin Run

SUDLEY FORD

SUDLEY
CHURCH

UNFINISHED

R. R.

SHERMAN

3

Carter

Matthews

BEE-BARTOW

STONE BRIDGE

SUDLEY MTN.

WEINTZELMAN

BURNSIDE

EVANS

Young's

EVANS

BU

SUDLEY

PORTER

STONE
HOUSE

KEYES

J. Dogan

Henry

Robinson

Branch

Groveton

Dogan

4

JACKSON

"PO
CONFE
HEAD

EARLY

ELZEY

Chinn

MANASSAS-

TURNPIKE

WARRENTON

ALEXANDRIA

GAINESVILLE

MANASSAS

5

WARRENTON

SUDLEY

GAP

R. R.

MT. PONE

ROAD

LEGEND

1 Original Position of the Two Armies
    Federal
    Confederate

2 Federal Tactical Plan

3 Morning Phase
    Federal
    Confederate

4 Early Afternoon Phase
    Federal
    Confederate

5 Late Afternoon Phase

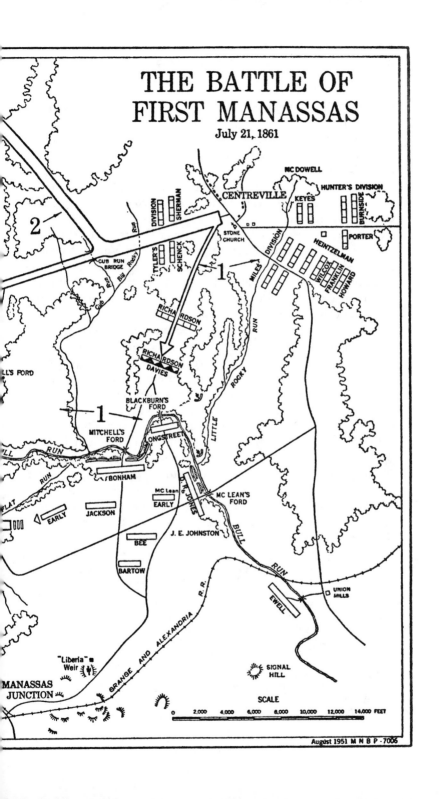

THE BATTLE OF FIRST MANASSAS

July 21, 1861

MC DOWELL

CENTREVILLE

HUNTER'S DIVISION

KEYES

BURNSIDE

DIVISION

SHERMAN

STONE CHURCH

PORTER

TYLER'S

SCHENCK

HEINTZELMAN

MILES' DIVISION

WILCOX

FRANKLIN

HOWARD

CUB RUN BRIDGE

2

RICHARDSON

1

ROCKY RUN

LITTLE ROCKY

RICHARDSON

DAVIES

L'S FORD

BLACKBURN'S FORD

1

MITCHELL'S FORD

LONGSTREET

BONHAM

RUN

RUN

MC Lean

EARLY

MC LEAN'S FORD

FLAT

EARLY

JACKSON

R.R. JONES

BEE

J. E. JOHNSTON

BULL

RUN

BARTOW

"Liberia" Weir

ORANGE AND ALEXANDRIA R.R.

EWELL

UNION MILLS

MANASSAS JUNCTION

SIGNAL HILL

SCALE

0   2,000   4,000   6,000   8,000   10,000   12,000   14,000 FEET

August 1951 M N B P - 7006

ground.[13] The turning point of the battle was now at hand. The missing brigade from Johnston's army had finally arrived at Manassas and was rushed by Johnston to the field, where it formed on the left. Beauregard now had as many men on the plateau as McDowell, perhaps even more. One more brigade would enable him to smash the Federals.

At this moment, about three-thirty, Beauregard looked to the southwest, whence any reinforcements would come. He saw at a distance of about a mile an approaching column. At first he could not tell whether the troops were Confederate or Federal. The fear struck him that this might be the Federal forces from the Valley. Anxiously he peered at the column through his glass. Soon he saw the Federals pull back their line on the extreme right, the first indication to Beauregard that the approaching troops were his own. As they drew closer, he could distinguish the Confederate colors at their head. It was Early's brigade, which had marched from the right of the battle line of the morning to the scene of the final action.[14] Early formed in line on the left of Johnston's brigade. The Federal right was already caving. Exultantly Beauregard ordered an attack along his entire front. The eager Confederates swarmed forward against an enemy on the verge of panic because of a rumor that its flank had been turned. The Federals broke in rout and fled across Bull Run.[15]

Beauregard was a proud figure as he sat his horse and watched the Federals stream up the road to the Stone Bridge. After giving a few directions for pursuit, he rode back to the point where Johnston had set up field headquarters, informed his senior of the outcome of the battle, and returned to him the united command. Johnston directed him to continue the pursuit.[16] At the same time Johnston sent orders to other generals to follow up the Federals.

[13] *Official Records,* II, 494–95; *Battles and Leaders,* I, 212–13.

[14] Beauregard gave a dramatic and an exaggerated account of this incident at an army dinner in October, 1861: New Orleans *Delta,* November 12, 1861; Snow, *Southern Generals,* 232–33. He said that if the column turned out to be Federal he intended to abandon the field, which is improbable, and that he did not recognize the brigade until he saw the Confederate flag at its head. Early said that his brigade was carrying state colors but no Confederate flag. See Beauregard to Early, April 8, 1881, April 14, 1884, and Early to Beauregard, April 29, 1884, in Jubal A. Early Papers (Division of Manuscripts, Library of Congress); Early, *Autobiographical Sketch,* 19–26; Rowland (ed.), *Jefferson Davis,* VIII, 303-304.

[15] *Official Records,* II, 476, 496, 556–57; *Battles and Leaders,* I, 215.

[16] W. W. Blackford, *War Years with Jeb Stuart* (New York, 1946), 35; Roman, *Beauregard,* I, 108–109; *Battles and Leaders,* I, 215.

Little came of the Confederate efforts, however, even though three hours of daylight remained after the Federals had broken at Henry hill. The commanders of some of the pursuing units were unduly cautious and timid in pushing ahead. The available cavalry force was too small to be effective. Johnston and Beauregard spent a lot of time riding around the field instead of personally supervising the chase. Both of them, it may be suspected, were not quite certain of the magnitude of their victory or quite sure what they would encounter north of the Run. Beauregard dispatched orders to one officer on the other side of the stream to "pursue, but cautiously, and he must not attack unless he has a decided advantage." [17] As during the battle, action was taken on the basis of rumors or reports that were not checked. About six-thirty the ominous news spread that a Federal force had passed Union Mills Ford and was moving on Manassas. Hastily Beauregard gathered troops to meet the new threat. The enemy column turned out to be Jone's brigade on its last trip back over Bull Run.[18] By the time the error had been discovered, it was too late to continue operations.

Soon after the Federal rout had started, President Davis arrived on the field. Torn by suspense, he had left Richmond in the morning on a special train. At Manassas he procured a horse and rode to Johnston's field headquarters. Johnston assured him that the battle had been won. Davis, who had been alarmed by the many stragglers he had met on his way, rode around the field to see for himself. Finally satisfied, he made his way back in the darkness to Beauregard's quarters at Manassas, where Johnston soon joined him. After supper he drafted a dispatch announcing the victory to the War Department. While he was working on the document, Beauregard came in from the field. According to a newspaper account, an aide had found him and said Davis was present and wanted to see him. Beauregard replied, "I cannot wait upon the President himself till I have first seen and attended to the wants of my wounded." [19]

After Beauregard's arrival the talk turned to details of the battle. Davis seemed surprised that the pursuit had been stopped. Even though it was after eleven o'clock, he asked if the chase could not be renewed. Johnston and Beauregard, believing it could not, remained

[17] Alexander, *Military Memoirs*, 43–44.
[18] *Ibid.*, 48–49; *Roman, Beauregard*, I, 108–11; *Battles and Leaders*, I, 215–16.
[19] New Orleans *Crescent*, August 7, 1861.

silent. Then Colonel Jordan, Beauregard's chief of staff, said that an officer just back from Centreville reported that the Federals had passed there in a state of rout. To Davis this information was the final proof that a pursuit must be organized. He urged the generals to issue orders. When they did not respond, Jordan, perhaps to relieve the tenseness of the situation, asked Davis if he would dictate the order. The President eagerly agreed. Although he was certainly not familiar with the ground, Davis proceeded to compose a directive providing that Bonham, who had the freshest troops, should move out at once. While he was dictating, someone observed that the officer who had reported on conditions in Centreville had been known in the old army as having an eccentric reputation.

This statement impressed Davis, who was always inclined to judge people by his previous knowledge of them. He remembered the officer, and paused to consider if it was safe to act on his evidence. When it was brought out that the officer had not been to Centreville, as he thought, but to a point near it, Davis was convinced. He conceded that a night advance to Centreville would be impractical and perhaps dangerous. He and the generals decided to move Bonham forward in the morning.

The nature of Bonham's projected advance would be a bitter issue of dispute between Davis and Beauregard to the end of their days. Davis understood that Bonham would be ordered to conduct a full-scale pursuit. Beauregard, who wrote the orders for Bonham, understood that the decision called for a reconnaissance in force and framed his instructions accordingly. It made no difference who was right. Before dawn rain started and fell heavily throughout the next day. The roads turned to mud, and any kind of movement was impossible.[20]

Regardless of whether the Confederates could have exploited their victory by a more vigorous pursuit, they reaped substantial results from the battle. Captured Federal equipment included twenty-eight field guns, thirty-seven caissons, half a million rounds of field ammunition, and other valuable military property.[21] As far as casualties

[20] Roman, *Beauregard,* I, 114–16; *Battles and Leaders,* I, 245; Rowland (ed.), *Jefferson Davis,* VIII, 185–86; Johnston, *Narrative,* 63; Alexander, *Military Memoirs,* 49; Jefferson Davis, *Rise and Fall of the Confederate Government* (New York, 1881), I, 352–56.

[21] *Official Records,* II, 502–503; Susan P. Lee (ed.), *Memoirs of William Nelson Pendleton* ... (Philadelphia, 1893), 153.

were concerned, the figures favored the Confederates. Beauregard had on the field a total of something over 34,000 men. McDowell had probably around 30,000. At the critical point of the battle at the Henry hill, McDowell had at the last some 13,000, Beauregard, 15,000. The Federal casualties were approximately 1,500 killed and wounded and 1,460 prisoners lost to the Confederates, or about 3,000 in all. The total Confederate losses numbered about 2,000, of whom over 1,500 were wounded.[22]

The government and the people were eager to reward Beauregard for the victory. Before breakfast on the twenty-second Johnston suggested to Davis that Beauregard should be promoted. The President replied that he had already thought of this. As the three were eating, Davis gave Beauregard a note that he had written and brought to the table with him. Opening it, Beauregard read: "Appreciating your services in the battle of Manassas and on several other occasions during the existing war, as affording the highest evidence of your skill as a commander, your gallantry as a soldier, and your zeal as a patriot, you are appointed to be 'General' in the army of the Confederate States of America, and with the consent of the Congress, will be duly commissioned accordingly." [23] Beauregard must have thrilled as his eyes ran over the lines. He was now among the top military hierarchy of the Confederacy. Only four men, also full generals, ranked him: Adjutant General Cooper, Albert Sidney Johnston, Lee, and Joseph Johnston.

The public applauded him even more loudly and extravagantly than after the fall of Sumter. Fantastic stories of his exploits at Manassas were spread over the press. Southerners chuckled sardonically at a story in a Northern journal that during the battle he had ridden a headless horse.[24] The tendency was to give more credit to him than to Johnston for the victory. People wrote to tell him that he was *the* great captain of the Confederacy and the best hope for its independence.[25] Musical composers rushed on the market with songs and marches dedicated to his honor; often ornamented with a pic-

[22] Johnston, *Bull Run,* 97–98, 109–10, 255, 260–62, 266–67; *Official Records,* II, 570; Roman, *Beauregard,* I, 111–12; *Battles and Leaders,* I, 194–95.
[23] Johnston, *Narrative,* 59; Roman, *Beauregard,* I, 119.
[24] Freeman, *Lee's Lieutenants,* I, 79-80; Cooke, *Wearing of the Gray,* 89; Mrs. Clement C. Clay, *A Belle of the Fifties* (New York, 1905), 165; Mrs. Chesnut, *Diary From Dixie,* 88.
[25] G. W. Smith to Beauregard, August 12, 1861, and J. S. Preston to Beauregard, August 16, 1861, in Henkels' Catalog, *Beauregard Papers,* Pt. I.

ture of the general on the cover, they bore such flattering titles as "The Beauregard Manassas quick-step" and "Genl Beauregard's grand polka militaire."[26]

As always, the songwriters and the newspaper poets were fascinated by the rhyming possibilities of his name. One particularly atrocious production shrieked:

> *Oh! the North was evil-starred, when*
> *she met thee, Beauregard!*
> *For you fought her very hard with*
> *cannon and petard, Beauregard!*
> *Beau canon, Beauregard! Beau soldat,*
> *Beauregard!*
> *Beau sabreur! beau frappeur! Beauregard,*
> *Beauregard!* [27]

Perhaps the surest mark of his popularity was the appropriation of his name for christening purposes. Babies, racehorses, steamboats, and even female garments were named after him.[28] He continued to be the favorite general of the ladies. They wrote him mash notes in which they begged for a picture or a button from his coat. One idolater ended her request for a picture by asking him to send with it information about "your complexion—color of your hair & eyes." Three young ladies in Federal-occupied Alexandria sent him an entreaty to liberate them, in the shape of a present of three gold shirt buttons; on the back of each button was one word, together spelling "let-us-out." To a like plea from one of the beautiful Cary sisters of Baltimore, Beauregard answered that for her he would plant the Confederate banner on the Washington Monument.[29]

He would receive similar communications for the remainder of the war. Women were always sending him adoring letters, gifts, and

[26] Copies of these compositions may be seen in the libraries of Duke and Emory universities.

[27] De Leon, *Belles, Beaux and Brains,* 263–64; Mrs. Harrison, *Recollections,* 47; Snow, *Southern Generals,* 256–57.

[28] F. D. De Fontaine, *Marginalia; or Gleanings from an Army Notebook* (Columbia, S. C., 1864), 17; Rowland and Croxall (eds.), *Journal of Julia Le Grand,* 269.

[29] Mary S. Waddell to Beauregard, August 21, 1861, in Beauregard Papers (Duke University); Thornton Triplett to Beauregard, August 20, 1861, *ibid.;* Beauregard to Earl Van Dorn, January 10, 1862, in Beauregard Papers (Library of Congress), Letterbook, Official Personal Letters, March 8, 1861— March 31, 1863.

poems which his exploits had inspired them to write. One lady wrote him, late in the war, that she could no longer restrain her emotions for him. She must tell him how she felt even though she overstepped the bounds of maidenly propriety. After this bold beginning, Beauregard must have been let down when he read her concluding sentence: "I could not feel for a father a more tender and earnest affection." [30]

A Richmond editor, surveying all this adulation, bestowed on the hero the title of Beauregard Felix. Among the ancient Romans "felix" meant fortunate, favored of the gods. The name fitted Beauregard because victory so regularly perched on his banners.[31] The classical-minded journalist spoke more aptly than he realized. Beauregard had been lucky to win at Sumter and Manassas. A flip of chance the other way, or a little more determination by his opponents, and the result at either place could have been easily reversed. Particularly at Manassas was it true that success had come without his having done much to bring it about and even despite grave errors on his part that might have brought disaster. Before and during the battle he had demonstrated grave deficiencies as a general. His sense of logistics was weak. The plans of grand strategy he had presented to the government were impossible of execution because they were not based on the realities of available Confederate resources. They were produced in a sort of Napoleonic dreamworld. The same criticism applies to his planning of battlefield strategy. His combat plans at Manassas failed because they were too complex to be carried out by the organization at his disposal. The importance of an efficient staff he would never fully realize.

Beauregard's strategic ideas were derived entirely from Jomini and Napoleon. From his study of these masters he had evolved certain principles of war which he always held to rigidly. Any deviation from them by anybody shocked him. His favorite principle was the one of mass or concentration. "The whole science of war," he wrote, "may be briefly defined as the art of placing in the right position, at the right time, a mass of troops greater than your enemy can there

[30] Mary E. Tucker to Beauregard, sometime in 1864, in Beauregard Papers (Emory University); Rebecca Cameron to Beauregard, March 13, 1865, in Mrs. S. Westray Battle Papers (Southern Historical Collection, University of North Carolina Library).

[31] Cooke, *Wearing of the Gray,* 83.

oppose to you." [32] The various plans of grand strategy which he framed and pressed on the government in 1861 and later were based on this principle. Here was one of the reasons he and Davis quarreled. To him places—cities, even states—were only pawns on the military board. He would willingly give them up to obtain concentrated armies.

Davis dispersed his forces to hold far-flung points. Beauregard thought the President's strategy was suicidal. He wrote in 1862: ". . . our only success lies in throwing all our forces into large armies, with which to meet and successfully overthrow our adversary. The result of one such victory would be worth more to us than the occupation of all our important cities to our enemies." [33] He wanted to win the war quickly, for he realized that in a long struggle the odds favored the stronger North. "I always favored a short & quick War, which should be decided by a few Great Battles," he wrote after it had ended in defeat for his side. [34]

Beauregard's strategic diagnoses were generally sound. If the Confederacy was going to win its independence by force, concentrations of its armies offered the best chance of victory. Yet all of Beauregard's plans of overall strategy and many of his battle designs were rejected by the government. He failed to get them accepted because his specific plans were nearly always unsound: they were not based on realities, and sometimes, as before Manassas, they were almost fantastic.

He failed, too, because of the manner in which he presented his recommendations. He was too quick about everything. His imagination ran away with him. Hardly would he arrive at a place before he had a detailed plan ready. Then he literally threw the scheme at his superiors. Always there was the promise of brilliant success to follow immediately. He rubbed people like Davis and Lee the wrong way. They were offended less, perhaps, by what he said than by the way he said it. He seemed Gallic, excitable, unreliable.

There were marks on the credit side of Beauregard's military ledger. At Sumter and particularly at Manassas he had shown that

[32] Beauregard, *Commentary on Manassas*, 160–61. In 1863 Beauregard had published at Charleston a pamphlet entitled *Principles and Maxims of the Art of War*. It was reprinted in the *Commentary*.

[33] *Official Records*, XV, 744–45.

[34] Beauregard to W. J. Marrin, April 12, 1874, in Henkels' Catalog, *Beauregard Papers*, Pt. II.

he was pugnacious and courageous. He liked to fight, a necessary quality in a battle captain and one which many Northern and Southern generals lacked. At the Henry hill he had handled his men well and had put them in at the right times and places. He could not make war on the map—direct movements of troops he could not see —but he could make it skillfully when his forces were within his range of vision. He could command a small army or a corps in a large one. But judged by what he had shown up to July of 1861, he was unready, if not unfit, to lead a large army.

In the months after Manassas he would demonstrate another weakness. He developed a passion for the use of the pen, for putting all of his opinions on paper. He devoted more attention to warring on Richmond in angry letters than he did to warring on the enemy. It was a quality which many generals of both the North and South shared. They wrote better than they fought. And in the end it would ruin him, as it did the others, with his civil superiors.

CHAPTER SEVEN

Pity for Those in High Authority

WITHIN LESS THAN A WEEK after Manassas, Beauregard was complaining that the fruits of the victory had been lost. Maryland should have been liberated and Washington occupied, he wrote to a member of Congress.[1] The failure of the army to advance he blamed on Richmond. Specifically he blamed Commissary General Northrop. The army could not move because it did not have enough food on hand to last through a campaign of any duration; it could not obtain food because of Northrop's red-tape rules. He also criticized the Commissary General for not supplying the army with sufficient horse and wagon transportation. Although Beauregard bore some responsibility for the situation, the fault was primarily Northrop's. Undeniably the Commissary General was an inefficient and irritating administrator. The army was on short rations.[2]

Frustrated by Northrop's refusal to meet his appeals, Beauregard took more direct action. On August 1 he addressed a letter to two of his former aides, William Porcher Miles and James Chesnut, who were now members of Congress. After describing the sufferings of his men he said:

> They have stood it, though, nobly; but if it happens again, I shall join one of their camps and share their wants with them; for I will never allow them to suppose that I feast while they suffer.
>
> The want of food and transportation has made us lose all the fruits of our victory. We ought at this moment to be in or about Washington. . . . God only knows when we will be able to advance; without these means we can neither advance nor retreat. . . .

[1] Basso, *Beauregard*, 146; Roman, *Beauregard*, I, 118.

[2] Roman, *Beauregard*, I, 120–21; Johnston, *Narrative*, 61, 67; E. P. Alexander to Mrs. Alexander, August 1, 1861, in Edward Porter Alexander Papers (Southern Historical Collection, University of North Carolina Library); *Battles and Leaders*, I, 239.

From all accounts, Washington could have been taken up to the 24th instant, by twenty thousand men! Only think of the brilliant results we have lost by the two causes referred to![3]

Beauregard obviously intended for Miles and Chesnut to transmit his letter to Congress. They read it to the shocked legislators in a secret session. The result was an angry explosion against the Davis administration. Congress called upon the President to report whether he had information showing a want of food in the army. Not quite convincingly, Davis replied that the commissary service was as good as it was reasonable to expect.[4] The contents of the letter inevitably leaked out to the press, leading to criticism of the government for holding Beauregard in leash and to talk of organizing an opposition party. Miles assured the general that no matter how much the administration was displeased with him, Congress and the country were on his side.[5]

The administration was definitely displeased. In the Davis circle people quoted Secretary of the Navy Stephen R. Mallory's remark that the nation's fate was in the hands of self-sufficient, vain military idiots.[6] The President, however, angry as he was, restrained his feelings in writing to Beauregard. In fact, the tone of his letter was patient and friendly, indicating that he was trying to avoid a break with Beauregard. The government was keenly aware of the army's needs, he assured, and would make every effort to supply them. He implied that some of the shortages could have been avoided if Beauregard had submitted "timely requisitions and estimates." Beauregard was unjust to himself in blaming the failure to pursue after Manassas on short supplies. "Enough was done for glory," Davis concluded, and statements of what might have been only stirred up divisions among the people.[7]

In replying to Davis, Beauregard was somewhat evasive and only partly conciliatory. He regretted that his letter had been read in Congress but admitted he had written it to expedite matters. He

[3] Roman, *Beauregard,* I, 121–22.
[4] *Journal of the Congress of the Confederate States of America, 1861–1865* (Washington, 1904–1905), I, 305–306, hereinafter cited as *Journal of the Confederate States Congress.*
[5] Charleston *Mercury,* August 10, 1861; Roman, *Beauregard,* I, 126.
[6] Mrs. Chesnut, *Diary From Dixie,* 102–103.
[7] Davis to Beauregard, August 4, 1861, in Rowland (ed.), *Jefferson Davis,* V, 120–21. In Roman, *Beauregard,* I, 122–23, the letter is misdated August 10.

repeated his charges that the troops were hungry. "I accuse no one, I state facts." Davis he did not blame, because he realized the President could not supervise every bureau. His remarks about taking Washington had been misunderstood. He did not mean it could have been seized immediately after Manassas but at any time thereafter. Then his smoldering feelings broke out: "We have, no doubt, by our success here, achieved 'glory' for our country, but I am fighting for something more real and tangible, i.e., to save our homes and friends from our Northern invaders, and to maintain our independence as a nation. After that task shall have been accomplished, as I feel that I am only fit for private life, I shall retire to my home ... never again to leave it, unless called upon again to repel the same or another invader." [8] The last sentence was evidently intended to assure Davis that Beauregard did not intend to be a rival in the coming Presidential election on November 5, when the Confederate government would change from a provisional to a permanent basis. His friends were urging him to be a candidate; he was the only other person besides Davis whose name was prominently mentioned. After the war Beauregard said he had made a mistake in not consenting to enter the race; anybody would have been a better President than Davis.[9]

After this exchange of letters, the controversy simmered down, for the time being, to a slow boil. Beauregard and his friends were still convinced that Northrop was a dolt and that Davis was wrong to support him. The general continued to believe that the army could not advance, or even retreat if necessary, because of the lack of food and proper transport. To improve his railroad communications, he appointed one Colonel R. A. Snowden as supervisor of railway transportation and sent him to Richmond to advocate a strange scheme to induce private capital to aid in supplying the troops. Needless to say, the colonel was unable to sell the plan. He could not even get to see Davis, who agreed with Northrop that many of the supply troubles of the army were due to Beauregard's neglect of his rail communications. Nor was Beauregard cured of trying to get what he wanted by working through politicians. He asked Vice-

[8] Beauregard to Davis, August 10, 1861, in Roman, *Beauregard*, I, 123–24.
[9] René Beauregard, "Magnolia"; Jones, *Rebel War Clerk's Diary*, I, 88; Beauregard to Augusta J. Evans, April 6, 1867, in Beauregard Papers (Library of Congress), Letterbook, Private Letters, December 16, 1865—April 18, 1867.

President Alexander H. Stephens to use his influence to secure additional artillery for Beauregard's forces. [10] But for the moment he sought to avoid open conflict with the administration. "We have no time now for quarrels and bickerings," he wrote Miles, "but there is no doubt it would be a national good if one or two individuals of our acquaintance could be sent 'on a foreign mission,' somewhere about the Celestial Empire or to Japan." [11]

A casual reading of Beauregard's dispatches might give the impression that life at his headquarters was unduly grim during this period. On the contrary, it was extremely gay. Famous guests came to visit and were served juleps of dark cognac made by his South Carolina aides in large buckets filled with ice and mint. Prince Jerome Bonaparte, touring the United States, came over from the Federal lines, spoke French to Beauregard, and was treated to a review. The beautiful Cary girls, two sisters from Baltimore and a cousin from Alexandria, arrived in camp to thrill the young officers. They slept in a tent on layers of cartridge flannel, their hoop skirts hanging like balloons on a pole overhead, while soldiers stood guard outside. Before they left, they dined with Beauregard on what the general said was his last duck.[12]

Early in August Beauregard persuaded Johnston to undertake a forward movement. After Manassas the Confederates had remained essentially on the Bull Run line, although they occupied places like Centreville just north of it. Beauregard feared that Johnston was content to await another attack at Bull Run.[13] With Johnston's somewhat reluctant approval, Beauregard moved his brigades northward to Fairfax Courthouse and other points. His advance forces went all the way to the heights above Washington on the south side of the Potomac; Beauregard visited them one day and feasted his eyes on the Federal capital. His purpose in advancing was to harass

[10] Roman, *Beauregard*, I, 125–27; Jordan to Miles, August 3, 10, 1861, in Miles Papers; Beauregard to W. G. De Saussure, August 5, 1861, in Beauregard Papers (Charleston Library Society); R. A. Snowden to Beauregard, September 11, 1861, in Beauregard Papers (Duke University); Rowland (ed.), *Jefferson Davis*, V, 124–27; Beauregard to Stephens, August 27, 1861, in Stephens Papers.

[11] Beauregard to Miles, September 4, 1861, in Roman, *Beauregard*, I, 483.

[12] Owen, *Washington Artillery*, 51–52; Snow, *Southern Generals*, 235–36; Robert Stiles, *Four Years under Marse Robert* (New York, 1903), 59; Cooke, *Wearing of the Gray*, 378–80; G. Moxley Sorrell, *Recollections of a Confederate Staff Officer* (New York, 1905), 28–29; Mrs. Harrison, *Recollections*, 59.

[13] Jordan to Miles, August 3, 1861, in Miles Papers.

the Federals on the Potomac and, if possible, lure them into making an attack on ground advantageous to him. "From these advanced positions," he told Johnston, "we could at any time concentrate our forces for offensive or defensive purposes."[14]

Johnston, however, was fearful. Cautious and unaggressive, he thought that Beauregard had placed his advanced units too near the Federal lines. He wanted to abandon the forward positions, but Beauregard insisted they be held for morale purposes if nothing else. With deep misgivings, Johnston assented. But when his eager junior suggested that the whole army move to Fairfax and attempt some kind of offensive, Johnston drew the line. The army was not strong enough, he said, to undertake an offensive so close to the enemy frontier.[15]

Beauregard then proposed another plan. The administration would be asked to reinforce the army from its present size of forty to sixty thousand. With this increased force Johnston and Beauregard would cross the Potomac into Maryland and maneuver in the rear of Washington, forcing the Federals to come out and fight in the open. Beauregard convinced Johnston that it was necessary to strike a decisive blow before the Federals could build up their forces for a spring campaign. Late in September Johnston wrote to Davis asking that the President or the Secretary of War come to Fairfax Courthouse to discuss a possible offensive movement. Davis, thinking that he was the proper person to decide such an important question, made the trip. He arrived on the thirtieth and stayed two days.

On October 1 he conferred with Johnston, Beauregard, and Major General G. W. Smith, who was a close friend of both generals. Smith opened the discussion by asking, "Mr. President, is it not possible to put this army in condition to assume the active offensive?" The generals then broached Beauregard's plan for a move into Maryland. Davis asked how many men would be needed. Smith estimated fifty thousand and Johnston and Beauregard ten thousand more. The President said he could not reinforce the army that much. Generals on other fronts were crying for troops, and their demands had to be met. Even if he could raise the number of men the generals wanted,

[14] Beauregard, *Commentary on Manassas*, 11–12; Roman, *Beauregard*, I, 131–33, 473; Beauregard to A. Herman, September 4, 1861, in Henkels' Catalog, *Beauregard Papers*, Pt. 1.

[15] Roman, *Beauregard*, I, 113–36, 475–77; Beauregard to Davis, September 13, 1861, in Davis Papers (Duke University).

Davis added, it was doubtful if they could be supplied with arms. In lieu of a general offensive, he proposed that a small raiding party be sent over the Potomac to annoy the enemy. Coldly the generals rejected the idea as being impractical and dangerous.[16] The operation he advocated was so inconsequential that it was shocking coming from a director of war. It was characteristic of Davis that he would concern his mind with such a minute matter after refusing to risk something for a great end.

Beauregard was a disgusted man after the conference. Believing that no further action would occur in Virginia before winter closed in, he decided to ask the government to transfer him to New Orleans, which he thought would soon be under Federal attack. In a letter to the new Secretary of War, Judah P. Benjamin, he said that he could not bear to be idle when there was an enemy to fight. Hence, he wished to be assigned to his home state or to some other point of danger.[17] Beauregard's analysis of the situation in Virginia was correct. In mid-October Johnston, more oppressed than ever by what he considered his dangerous proximity to the enemy frontier, withdrew the army to positions farther south. The new line was in the shape of a triangle, with the apex at Centreville and the sides running back to Union Mills Ford and the Stone Bridge. Here the army would shortly go into winter quarters.[18] About the time the withdrawal was made, Beauregard learned that the government would not let him go to New Orleans. The notification came in the shape of a friendly letter from Davis. Beauregard was too valuable in Virginia to be shifted to another theater, the President said. Nor, Davis added, could he anticipate a time when it would be proper to relieve the general from his present position.[19]

Beauregard had another motive for wanting to leave Virginia. He was dissatisfied with the command situation; he resented being placed in what he considered a secondary position. When the armies

[16] Roman, *Beauregard*, I, 136–39, 142–45; Smith, *Confederate War Papers*, 14–20, 33–36; *Official Records*, V, 884–87; Johnston, *Narrative*, 74–77; Davis, *Rise and Fall*, I, 449–51; Rowland (ed.), *Jefferson Davis*, VIII, 506–12.

[17] René Beauregard, "Magnolia"; Roman, *Beauregard*, I, 153–54; *Beauregard to Judah Benjamin, October 5, 1861, typed copy in John F. F. Alexander Papers (Southern Historical Collection, University of North Carolina Library).

[18] Johnston, *Narrative*, 77–78; Roman, *Beauregard*, I, 154–55.

[19] Davis to Beauregard, October 16, 1861, in Rowland (ed.), *Jefferson Davis*, V, 141–43.

of Johnston and Beauregard combined before Manassas, they bore titles. Johnston's was the Army of the Shenandoah; Beauregard's, the Army of the Potomac. After the battle the generals continued the same designations, but the tendency developed to call them both the Army of the Potomac. Beauregard proceeded on the assumption that his forces constituted one of two corps in the army. As a corps commander, he was under Johnston's nominal command, but he was to have complete administrative control over his own unit. In short, he wanted to reproduce much the same situation as had existed on July 21.[20]

To a considerable degree, Johnston let him have his way. At this time the two generals were devoted to each other personally. The small, spruce, compact Johnston, gray of hair, eyes, and beard, admired Beauregard and even tended to let himself be dominated by the younger man. Moreover, Johnston, who was a difficult subordinate, was an easy superior; he was capable of extremely generous impulses to his juniors.[21] For these reasons, the unofficial command relationship which the two had worked out functioned fairly smoothly. In Richmond, however, it was not regarded favorably. Davis thought it violated fundamental principles of military law.[22] The situation was loaded with trouble for Beauregard if he ever took any action which the President considered as infringing on his own prerogatives.

Early in October Beauregard recommended to the War Department the appointment of a certain officer as chief of ordnance of his corps. At the same time he sent an agent to Richmond to recruit a rocket battery company. From the Department he received a reply saying that Davis disapproved of the corps arrangement and preferred one ordnance chief for the whole army. Sensing in this a purpose to make trouble between him and Johnston, he wrote Secretary Benjamin that if he were no longer in command of a corps he wished to be relieved of his false position; otherwise he wanted authority to select his own officers.[23] Before this letter reached Ben-

[20] Beauregard to Davis, September 13, 1861, in Davis Papers (Duke University) and in Roman, Beauregard, I, 477–78.

[21] English Combatant, Battlefields of the South, I, 97–98; Snow, Southern Generals, 277–78; Sorrell, Recollections, 25; Freeman, Lee's Lieutenants, I, 111.

[22] Rowland (ed.), Jefferson Davis, V, 130–31.

[23] Beauregard to Benjamin, October 9, 1861, in Official Records, LI, Pt. 2, p. 339.

jamin Beauregard received a letter from the Secretary dealing with the rocket battery project. The round, smiling, smooth Benjamin, who wrote as though the civil government was his client, informed Beauregard that under Confederate law he had no authority to raise such a company. Beauregard had erred not in motive, said Benjamin, but in judgment.

The general was outraged. He decided that the administration was trying to provoke a quarrel. Very well, they could have it. Ignoring Benjamin, he dashed off an angry letter to Davis. He would leave it to the President to determine who had been guilty of bad judgment, the simple general who had done only what was essential to aid the cause or "the functionary at his desk, who deems it a fit time . . . to debate about the prerogatives of his office and of your Excellency's, and to write lectures on law while the enemy is mustering in our front. . . ." [24] Hardly had Beauregard finished this communication when he received a letter from Benjamin answering his question about his command status. Benjamin clarified the situation simply: "You are second in command of the whole Army of the Potomac, and not first in command of half the army." Irritatingly the Secretary advised Beauregard to read the laws of Congress, where he would learn that there was no legal basis for the existence of a corps. Against the tone of this letter Beauregard also protested to Davis, but mildly. He was beginning to realize that in Benjamin he faced a greater master of words than he. He begged the President to shield him from "these ill-timed, unaccountable annoyances." [25]

Davis was disturbed by the acrimony of the correspondence between Benjamin and Beauregard. In a long, conciliatory letter, he tried to calm his distracted and embittered general. It was only plain military sense, he pointed out, to have one commander for two armies when they were concentrated. As the junior of two generals of the same rank, Beauregard could serve the army best as second in command and first in Johnston's absence. Victory was impossible, Davis ended, unless all could forget thoughts of self in zeal for the common purpose. To this Beauregard replied that if Davis wished a unified command, "we," he and Johnston, would effect it. But he wanted

[24] Beauregard to Davis, October 20, 1861, in Roman, *Beauregard,* I, 158–60.
[25] Benjamin to Beauregard, October 17, 1861, in *Official Records,* V, 904–905; Beauregard to Davis, October 20, 1861, in Roman, *Beauregard,* I, 160–61.

to record his objections that it would not work and might even be disastrous in a field operation.[26]

The government, of course, had no intention of permitting Johnston and Beauregard to create their own kind of reorganization. On October 22 orders from Richmond established the Department of Northern Virginia with Johnston in command. Under Johnston were the Valley District, commanded by Major General T. J. Jackson; the Aquia District, commanded by Major General T. H. Holmes; and the Potomac District, commanded by full General Beauregard. Beauregard felt that he had been degraded to the rank of major general. But as Johnston had not given him the command of the Potomac District, he felt that it would be indelicate to use that title. Out of regard for his senior, he explained later, he continued to style himself as a corps commander.[27]

Because he assumed that he could still do pretty much as he pleased he got in trouble with Benjamin again. When he made certain appointments for his forces, the Secretary informed him that he was proceeding without authority. Only Davis could make these selections. Beauregard was giving the impression that he was usurping power, Benjamin charged. In a letter to Adjutant General Cooper Beauregard denied that he was an usurper. But, he added revealingly, whenever there was a necessity for assuming responsibility "I have never hesitated an instant in my course, leaving it to those in authority and to the country to decide whether I was right or wrong in my conduct."[28]

Davis made a final attempt to persuade Beauregard to stop fighting with Benjamin and to convince him that he was subject to the laws. In a warm letter, the President begged Beauregard to believe that Benjamin was not his enemy. Beauregard had been wrong in disregarding Congressional enactments, and Benjamin had only called attention to his errors. The Secretary had done so, Davis conceded, in the language of a lawyer. As one who had once been a soldier, Davis could understand why Beauregard was offended. But Beauregard should not take Benjamin's lawyer talk too seriously. "Now, my

---

[26] Davis to Beauregard, October 20, 1861, in Rowland (ed.) *Jefferson Davis*, V, 146–49; Beauregard to Davis, October 22, 1861, in Beauregard Papers (Duke University).

[27] *Official Records*, V, 913–14; Roman, *Beauregard*, I, 170–71.

[28] Benjamin to Beauregard, October 23, 1861, in Alfred Roman Papers (Library of Congress); Beauregard to Cooper, October 27, 1861, in Beauregard Papers (Library of Congress), Letterbook 4.

dear sir," the President concluded, "let me entreat you to dismiss this small matter from your mind; in the hostile masses before you, you have a subject more worthy of your contemplation. The country needs all of your mind and your heart. . . . My prayers always attend you; and with confidence, I turn to you in the hour of peril." [29]

At this point Beauregard could have closed the controversy with profit to himself. A more skilled disputant would have written a generous letter of semiapology that would have made Benjamin look petty. Such a letter would probably have won him Davis' support in future dealings with the Secretary. But Beauregard was too fascinated with his pen to stop now. He answered that he accepted Davis' assurances that Benjamin meant no offence. The Secretary, however, would have to be more courteous in his communications. As to Benjamin thinking like a lawyer, Beauregard hoped that he would not be so legal as to strait-jacket the army. This time he had gone too far. He had suggested that the army was above the civil power, above Davis.

The President's patience snapped at last. He replied in a coldly formal letter which omitted the usual ending of "Your friend." He did not feel competent, he said, to instruct Benjamin in matters of style; few were. It was not peculiar for Benjamin to look at an exercise of power in its legal aspect, he continued, "and you surely did not intend to inform me that your army and yourself are outside of the limits of the law." His duty was to see that the laws were executed, he ended grimly, "and I cannot recognize the pretension of any one that their restraint is too narrow for him." [30]

Before the controversy with Benjamin had entered its most bitter stage, Beauregard sent to the War Department his report of the battle of Manassas. He had written a first draft during the summer months but held it until he could collect additional information from the Federal reports. The completed document bore the date of October 14.[31] About nine thousand words in length, it abounded in rhetorical references to things other than the conduct of the battle. In the middle of a description of the fighting at the Henry hill, the

[29] Davis to Beauregard, October 25, 1861, in Rowland (ed.), *Jefferson Davis*, V, 150–51.
[30] Beauregard to Davis, November 5, 1861, in Roman, *Beauregard*, I, 167; Davis to Beauregard, November 10, 1861, in *Official Records*, V, 945.
[31] *Official Records*, II, 505–506. The report is in *Official Records*, II, 484–504. The original manuscript draft is in the Confederate Museum, Richmond.

author burst out: "Oh, my country! I would readily have sacrificed my life and those of all the brave men around me, to save your honor and to maintain your independence from the degrading yoke which these ruthless invaders had come to impose and render perpetual. . . ." [32]

With its customary efficiency, the War Department neglected to forward the report to Davis. The President first learned of its existence when he read a summary of it in a Richmond newspaper. The reporter stated that he had been favored with a "synopsis" of part of the report. Speaking from the synopsis, the reporter said that before Manassas Beauregard had proposed a plan to concentrate his army with Johnston's for the purpose of taking Washington, which scheme the President had rejected. Furthermore, the account continued, Beauregard had experienced great difficulty in convincing Davis of the necessity for bringing about the final junction of the two armies.[33] This report appeared at a time when antiadministration papers were charging that Davis had stopped Beauregard from pursuing the enemy after Manassas and had kept the army inactive for months because of political reasons.[34]

Disturbed and angered, Davis got the report from the War Department and read it. The opening section described the plan of concentration which Beauregard had sent to Richmond by Colonel Chesnut in July. His design had not been accepted, said the general, because of considerations which seemed to counterbalance its advantages. This qualification had not been mentioned in the newspaper synopsis. Nor, the President found, did Beauregard say that the government had been reluctant to order Johnston to him just before the battle. He only implied that he saw the danger before others did. The report was not the criticism of the administration which Davis had been led to believe from the newspaper story.

Nevertheless, the President's wrath mounted. He viewed the introduction to the report as extraneous material which had no place in a battle account. It was an attempt by Beauregard to picture himself as the great strategist of victory. With his usual pedantic reasoning, Davis objected to Beauregard's calling his July proposal a plan, because it had not been presented in writing. On October 30 he addressed a letter of protest to Beauregard. He had been surprised, he

[32] *Official Records,* II, 493.
[33] Richmond *Dispatch,* October 23, 1861.
[34] Charleston *Mercury,* September 28, October 1, 29, 1861.

said, to find that the newspaper synopsis had been sustained by the text of the report. He was surprised also that Beauregard would include such material in a report and that the general claimed he had submitted a plan like the one described. No such scheme had been submitted to him, Davis asserted. Above all, he was surprised because the report looked like "an attempt to exalt yourself at my expense." [35]

When news of the quarrel sifted out to the press, sensational rumors spread in Richmond. It was said that the administration was trying to destroy Beauregard because his name had been mentioned for the Presidency; on another day it was bruited that the general had resigned.[36] As if in answer to these whispers, there appeared in the Richmond *Whig* a public letter from Beauregard. Addressed to the editors, it was obviously intended to reach the country. The heading attracted immediate attention: "Centreville, Va., Within hearing of the Enemy's Guns, Nov. 3, 1861." The text was as remarkable as the heading. After saying that he regretted publication of the synopsis and asking his friends not to worry about the slanders being aimed at him, he proceeded:

> If certain minds cannot understand the difference between *patriotism,* the highest civic virtue, and *office-seeking,* the lowest civic occupation, I pity them from the bottom of my heart. Suffice it to say, that I prefer the respect and esteem of my countrymen, to the admiration and envy of the world. I hope, for the sake of our cause and country, to be able, with the assistance of a kind Providence, to answer my calumniators with new victories over our national enemies; but I have nothing to ask of the country, the Government, or my friends, except to afford me all the aid they can, in the great struggle we are now engaged upon. I am not, and never expect or desire to be, a candidate for any civil office in the gift of the people or of the Executive. The *acme* of my ambition is, after having cast my mite in defence of our sacred cause, and assisted, to the best of my ability, in securing our rights and independence as a nation, to retire into private life—my means then permitting—never

again to leave my home, unless to fight anew the battles
of my country.[37]

This document kept the Richmond rumor pot boiling, but it hurt
Beauregard with the public. The theatrical heading and the exaggerated tone displeased many people, including even some of his
admirers. The general, however, was calmly convinced that he was
following the right course. On the day the letter appeared in print
he answered Davis' communication of October 30. Coolly he enclosed a copy of his letter to the *Whig* with his reply. He charged
that employees of the War and State departments were inspiring
attacks on him in the Richmond press and hinted that Davis had let
these underlings affect his judgment. Denying that he had tried to
exalt himself at the President's expense, he said, "I have always
pitied more than I have envied those in high authority." He refused
to back down on his statement that he had submitted a definite plan
of operations. If Davis wanted proof, he would offer Chesnut's report
of his conference with the President, Lee, and Cooper.[38]

Very definitely Davis wanted the proof. He was industriously
collecting written evidence from Lee, Cooper, and Chesnut that
Beauregard had submitted only a general proposal and not a written,
specific plan.[39] In the midst of his efforts the President had to face
a counteroffensive by Beauregard's friends in Congress. On November 26, in a secret session, they secured the passage of a resolution
asking Davis to furnish reports of all battles not previously communicated to Congress or published in full to the country. Davis
replied that reports of all battles would accompany the report of the
Secretary of War when that document was transmitted to Congress.[40]
Not until January, 1862, while the army was in winter quarters,
would Benjamin complete his report and submit it to the legislators.
Then the controversy between Davis and Beauregard would flare up
again.

After the army pulled back to the Centreville line, Johnston decided that no further operations would be attempted that season by
the Federals. He directed that winter quarters be established. On the
hills around Centreville crude huts sprang up as the army settled

[37] Roman, *Beauregard*, I, 163–64; Richmond *Whig*, November 7, 1861.

[38] Beauregard to Davis, November 7, 1861, in Georgia Portfolio Papers
(Duke University Library).

[39] *Official Records*, II, 509, 511–13, 515.

[40] *Journal of the Confederate States Congress*, I, 478, 486.

down for the cold months. Some units remained in tents until December; even those soldiers in huts, especially if they were from the Deep South, suffered from the unwonted cold. Despite the hardships, the period of winter quarters was for most of the men a time of rest, play, snowball fights, and community sings. Beauregard liked to come to the quarters of the Maryland boys and hear them roll out "Maryland, my Maryland." [41] The general himself did not suffer from the cold. His solicitous female admirers supplied him with gifts of socks, scarves, and comforters. He must have received enough to equip a company.[42]

Before the army entered winter quarters, Beauregard had been pondering a problem that had concerned him earlier—the difficulty of distinguishing Confederate troops from Federals in battle. At Manassas he had observed how hard it was to tell the new Confederate flag from the old flag of the Union. He asked his friends in Congress to get that body to adopt a banner that was different. No change was made; William P. Miles wrote that it was impossible to tear the people away from a desire to retain some reminiscence of the United States flag. Beauregard then decided to design a special flag to be carried only in battle. After conferring with Johnston, Miles, and others, he fixed upon an emblem with a red field crossed by diagonal blue bars on which were white stars. Thus was born the famous Southern battle flag, which later generations of Southerners and Yankees would fondly mistake for the flag of the Confederate States.[43]

With War Department approval of his idea, Beauregard eagerly proceeded to get his first flags made while the army was in winter quarters. They were manufactured in the best tradition of Southern romance. At that time the three Cary girls were on one of their periodic visits to camp. It was decided that they would contribute material from their dresses to make flags for Johnston, Beauregard, and

[41] Randolph H. McKim, *A Soldier's Recollections* (New York, 1911), 53.
[42] Mrs. M. M. G. to Beauregard, September 17, 1861, in Beauregard Papers (Duke University) ; Du Brutz Cutlar to Beauregard, October 1, *ibid.;* Douglas Southall Freeman, *A Calendar of Confederate Papers . . .* (Richmond, 1908), 39, 187.
[43] Roman, *Beauregard,* I, 171–72, 482–86; Miles to Beauregard, August 27, 1861, in Roman Papers (Library of Congress). There are a multitude of letters on the origin of the battle flag in the Beauregard Papers (Confederate Memorial Hall, New Orleans) and in the Confederate Flag Correspondence (Confederate Museum, Richmond).

the dashing Earl Van Dorn. Material for additional flags would be procured from other ladies. Because of the origin of the silk in the first emblems, the backgrounds were more of a feminine pink than a martial red.

On November 28 the flags were formally presented to the troops in solemn ceremonies. An order written by Beauregard was read to each unit. He exhorted the men to remember that the banner was sacred because it had been made by their mothers, wives, and sweethearts: "Under its untarnished folds beat back the invader, and find nationality, everlasting immunity from an atrocious despotism, and honor and renown for yourselves—or death." When the flag was accepted at Van Dorn's quarters, a young officer sprang up, unsheathed his sword, and placed its hilt on the table. His comrades clasped the blade and swore an oath to honor Van Dorn's pledge to Constance Cary to liberate Alexandria and her nearby home.[44]

After the presentation less solemn scenes ensued. At the quarters of the principal generals lavish banquets were spread, and many toasts to independence and womanly beauty were tossed off. Three generals mounted a narrow table at Longstreet's dinner and tried to sing. That stern Puritan, General Edmund Kirby Smith, left one celebration where, as he put it, apple toddy and champagne were "a circulating medium." An aide came to say that the diners, among whom were Beauregard and Johnston, were calling for him to return to make a speech. He refused on the ground that he could not speak soberly to a drunken audience.[45]

No important military operations occurred during the winter. Near Washington George B. McClellan, the Federal commander, was gathering a large army, but he made no aggressive moves. One reason he remained quiet was his own timidity. Another was the exaggerated reports he received and believed of Confederate numbers and armaments. He understood that the Southern lines bristled with artillery pieces. This information was largely the result of clever deception by Beauregard. He had logs trimmed and painted to resemble guns

[44] Roman, *Beauregard*, I, 481; Mrs. Harrison, *Recollections*, 61–63.

[45] Owen, *Washington Artillery*, 60–61; Sorrell, *Recollections*, 34–36, 57–58; Edmund Kirby Smith to Mrs. Kirby Smith, December 3, 1861, in Edmund Kirby Smith Papers (Southern Historical Collection, University of North Carolina Library). Beauregard sent his flag to his wife in New Orleans. When the Federals occupied the city in the spring of 1862, Mrs. Beauregard dispatched it by foreign ship to Havana. It remained there until after the war, when it was returned to Beauregard.

and mounted at points where they could be seen by Yankee observers.[46] During the long months of inaction, the generals had time to reflect on problems of army administration and plan future campaigns. Beauregard occupied himself for a while with a training device to induce his men to fire low and slowly in battle.[47]

Mostly, though, he thought about his grievances against the administration. Although he was determined to have no quarrel with Davis at the present, he remembered the old wrongs and nourished new ones. He complained that his back pay was based on a brigadier general's schedule instead of that of a full general. He continued officially to style himself the commander of a corps, although his shrewd chief of staff, Jordan, begged him to stop the practice. All the time he expected the administration to reopen the fight, to set some trap for him.[48]

In January Davis sent to Congress the report of the Secretary of War. Accompanying it was Beauregard's full report on the battle of Manassas, to which the President attached correcting statements and documents. Most of them were concerned with denying Beauregard's assertion that before the battle he had submitted to the government a comprehensive plan of operations. Immediately Beauregard's friends sprang to his defense. They telegraphed him to ask if he wanted all his report published or if he would consent to omit the opening section, the part dealing with his alleged plan. In lofty and detached manner he replied: "Let Congress do for the best. We must think of the country before we think of ourselves. I believe Burnside's expedition is intended for Wilmington, to cut off railroad to Charleston. Let government look to it." (It was really directed at Roanoke Island). When this telegram was read to Congress, tremendous applause followed. After a secret session of two days, Beauregard's supporters and the administration's agreed to a compromise. It was decided to publish the report without the introduction or the annotations by Davis.[49]

[46] Beauregard to James A. Longstreet, December 5, 1861, in Beauregard Papers (Library of Congress), Letterbook, Official Personal Letters, March 8, 1861–March 31, 1863.
[47] Beauregard to Manning, December 10, 1861, in Williams-Chesnut-Manning Papers.
[48] Jordan to Miles, December 8, 1861, in Miles Papers; Beauregard to A. B. Ryan, November 12, 1861, in Beauregard Papers (University of Texas); Roman, *Beauregard*, I, 189, 488–89; *Official Records*, V, 990.
[49] Roman, *Beauregard*, I, 173–74, 183–85; Davis, *Rise and Fall*, I, 367–71.

This latest brawl in the Davis-Beauregard series occurred when an antiadministration party was forming in Congress and the country. Its leaders were politicians like Vice-President Stephens, Robert Toombs, and certain governors, and powerful editors in Richmond and Charleston. Among its military members were counted Beauregard, Johnston, and G. W. Smith. The group lacked a leader, and some of them figured Beauregard could fill the place. In addition to his reputation, he had important connections. Three of his former aides, Miles, Chesnut, and Roger A. Pryor, were in Congress; Miles was chairman of the committee on military affairs. Another aide, James L. Kemper, was speaker of the Virginia House of Delegates.[50]

The general himself had no political ambitions. He wanted only to be permitted to fight battles as he pleased. He confessed that he could not understand why people were always getting angry at things he wrote. Perhaps, he conceded, he had something to learn about the ways of politicians. He was a little hurt by the treatment he had received from Richmond. His chief of staff noted that he brooded in silence a great deal. "You never saw such a change," Jordan wrote to Miles.[51] Beauregard was also about to undergo a change of scene. The administration decided to remove him from close letter range by sending him to the West.

[50] Thomas R. R. Cobb, "Extracts from Letters to his Wife . . .," in *Southern Historical Society Papers*, XXVIII (1900), 289; Robert McElroy, *Jefferson Davis, the Unreal and the Real* (New York, 1937), I, 333.

[51] Beauregard to Roger Pryor, January 20, 1862, in Beauregard Papers (Library of Congress), Letterbook, Official Personal Letters, March 8, 1861–March 31, 1863; Jordan to Miles, early in 1861, in Miles Papers.

CHAPTER EIGHT

With Albert Sidney Johnston

O NE DAY late in January Roger A. Pryor, one of Beauregard's supporters in Congress and a member of the military affairs committee, came to Centreville. He told Beauregard that the committee and the representatives of the Mississippi Valley states had delegated him to approach the general about transferring to the Western theater. The President, Pryor assured, had agreed to the change. Pryor explained that Beauregard would serve under Albert Sidney Johnston, departmental commander in the West, and would command the left wing of Johnston's forces in Kentucky with headquarters at Columbus on the Mississippi. The situation in the West was critical, Pryor added, and Beauregard's presence would stimulate popular morale.[1]

Although Beauregard claimed after the war that he discouraged Pryor, actually he seems to have been receptive to the offer from the first. The proposed assignment promised more active service and would remove him from the close supervision of Richmond. Any reluctance he expressed was for the purpose of wringing certain concessions from the administration as the price of his departure. He was particularly anxious to avoid giving the impression that he was being forced to leave Virginia against his will. He told Pryor that he would go if these conditions were met: the Western army would be increased to the point where it could start an offensive; he could take with him his staff and a number of experienced officers; and he could return to Virginia when his work in the West was finished. Pryor said that he was not authorized to endorse these demands but he would consult with the War Department. From Richmond he telegraphed vaguely that he was sure Davis would consent to all of Beauregard's wishes.[2]

When Beauregard's political friends heard of the negotiations,

[1] Roman, *Beauregard,* I, 210–11.
[2] *Ibid.,* 211–12.

they urged him not to accept the appointment. They sensed an administration plot to lay him on the shelf. Robert Toombs warned him that while he would not be ordered away, if he left he would never be ordered back.[3] Before he received Toomb's letter, Beauregard decided to take the assignment. Writing to notify Pryor of his acceptance, he said: "I am a soldier of the cause and of my country, ready, at this juncture and during the war, to do duty cheerfully wheresoever placed by the constituted authorities. . . ." His letter was slow in reaching Richmond, and Pryor wired, "May I tell President you will go? say Go." Beauregard replied, "Yes I will go. May God protect our cause."[4] One hour later the letter from Toombs arrived. Unperturbed, the general telegraphed back, "Mississippi Valley in danger. I will be back in time for a move forward." To Joe Johnston he wrote that he had to go to Kentucky temporarily but would return as soon as he had cleared up the confusion there.[5]

In Richmond an acute observer in the War Department wrote in his diary: "Beauregard has been ordered to the West. I knew the doom was upon him!" The opinion of the general's friends was that he had let himself be duped by the administration.[6] The motives of Davis and his advisers in consenting to shift Beauregard to the West are not clear. It is not even certain that the administration initiated the move. Pryor may have originated the scheme out of a desire to push Beauregard's fortunes, but his eagerness to gain the general's assent indicates that he may have been acting as a hatchet man for Davis. Probably he did not present Beauregard's conditions to the government; at least he did not get them approved.

Beauregard's assumption that he could return to Virginia was not justified by Pryor's vague assurances. One thing seems certain: the President was glad to see Beauregard go. His reasons have to be conjectured. Obviously Beauregard was not in any sense being demoted.

[3] *Ibid.*, 489.

[4] Beauregard to Pryor, January 23, 1862, *ibid.*, 490; Pryor to Beauregard, January 24, 1862, and Beauregard to Pryor, January 25, 1862, in Beauregard Papers (University of Texas).

[5] Beauregard to Robert Toombs, January 25, 1862, telegram and letter, in Beauregard Papers (Library of Congress), Letterbook, Official Personal Letters, March 8, 1861–March 31, 1863; Beauregard to Johnston, January 25, 29, 1863, *ibid.* Johnston regretted losing Beauregard: Roman, *Beauregard,* I, 492.

[6] Jones, *Rebel War Clerk's Diary,* I, 107; W. F. Alexander to his father, January 30, 1862, in Jeremy F. Gilmer Papers (Southern Historical Collection, University of North Carolina Library).

He had been second in command to one Johnston, he would have the same relation to another. The Western theater was as important as the Eastern. If Davis considered Beauregard to be a general of doubtful ability, as he probably did, Beauregard could do as much harm in Kentucky as in Virginia. In a letter to a general in the Western army who was a personal friend, Davis stressed that Beauregard was an able engineer and full of resources.[7] Perhaps the President judged that Confederate strategy in the West would have to be defensive and that Beauregard, unfit for field command, would be able to aid Johnston with his skill in fortification. Congressmen from the Mississippi Valley states were demanding that the government give more attention to the West; the assignment of an officer of Beauregard's reputation to that front would ease the pressure. Or maybe Davis was simply fed up with Beauregard's dialectical talents and thought he could escape controversy by shifting the letter writer to a distant post.

Beauregard received his official orders to go to Columbus late in January. After issuing a fervid farewell address to his troops, in which he told them he would return, he departed on February 2. Groups of soldiers followed him through Centreville shouting, "Goodby, General, God bless you, General." As his train moved west, crowds turned out to welcome him at every station. At Nashville he stopped over a day at the request of the state authorities and was presented to the legislature. Later he spoke at a public meeting, sharing the platform with Father A. J. Ryan, the poet-priest of the Confederacy, later to be famous as the author of "The Conquered Banner." On the evening of the fourth Beauregard reached Bowling Green and met for the first time Albert Sidney Johnston.[8]

He saw one of the handsomest and most majestic-looking generals in the Confederate service. Over six feet in height, broad of shoulder and deep of chest, Johnston had a head that was as impressive as his physique. His wavy, dark-brown hair was tinged with gray, as befitted his fifty-nine years. The features of his handsome face, his brow, his nose, his chin, were broad and strong. Commanding in presence,

---

[7] William M. Polk, *Leonidas Polk* (New York, 1915), I, 384.

[8] Roman, *Beauregard*, I, 213, 491–92; *Official Records*, V, 1048, LI, Pt. 2, pp. 455–56; Cooke, *Wearing of the Gray*, 92; Richmond *Dispatch*, quoted in New Orleans *True Delta*, February 15, 1862.

he was grave and dignified in manner. Most people were impressed by him; they deferred to him, accepted his judgments.[9]

In the old army Johnston had had a distinguished career after graduating from West Point. At the beginning of the war he had one of the highest, if not the highest, military reputations in the Confederacy. Davis and others regarded him as a genius. It was predicted that he would be the greatest general of the South. Before he could achieve his promise, he was killed at Shiloh in April, 1862. His death strengthened the opinions held about him. People said that he died just as he was coming into his own, just as he was about to bring victory. During the rest of the war and later, Southerners liked to say, "If only Johnston had lived. . . ." He was like the promising artist who dies young. The critics exclaim that if his life had been spared he would have done something great. The trouble is, no one can ever tell. Nothing that Johnston did in his brief career justifies the belief that he had the elements of greatness. Many things that he did suggest that he was not qualified for high command.

Immediately after Beauregard's arrival at Bowling Green, he and Johnston went into conference. Johnston described his forces and his dispositions. At Bowling Green he had approximately 14,000 men; at points southwest of the town, an additional 11,000. In the center of the Confederate line at Forts Henry and Donelson were 5,500. The force at Columbus on the extreme left numbered 17,000. Thus a line of 150 miles in length was being held by about 48,000 troops. West of the Mississippi in Arkansas, but under Johnston's command, were 20,000 under Van Dorn. Opposing these thin-spread forces was an imposing array of Federal armies. Poised north of Bowling Green was Don Carlos Buell with 70,000 men (of whom probably 57,000 were effectives). In western Kentucky Ulysses S. Grant commanded 20,000. In Missouri Henry W. Halleck, who was also Grant's superior, had a force of about 30,000.[10]

9 William Preston Johnston, *Life of Gen. Albert Sidney Johnston* . . . (New York, 1878), 718, 722, 725–28; Pollard, *First Year of the War*, 342–43; Duke, *Reminiscences*, 71, 100–19; William C. Oates, *The War Between the Union and the Confederacy* . . . (New York, 1905), 307–308; Snow, *Southern Generals*, 430.

10 Roman, *Beauregard*, 213–15; Beauregard, in *Battles and Leaders*, I, 570. These figures differ somewhat from those supplied by Beauregard. He computed the forces in and around Bowling Green at twenty-two thousand. In his official returns at the end of January, Johnston listed them at twenty-eight thousand: *Official Records*, VII, 852–55. Assuming that Johnston knew

The next day Johnston and Beauregard inspected the works defending Bowling Green. They could be easily turned, Beauregard thought. He also got a clearer picture of the whole Confederate line in Kentucky. What he learned shocked his every engineering sensibility. Bowling Green and Columbus, the two flanks, were salients jutting ahead of the center at Forts Henry and Donelson. The Confederates, with numerically inferior forces, were operating on the outside of a circle. The disadvantage of an exterior line was only partially offset by the fact that the Confederates controlled the railroad from Bowling Green to Columbus. Not only were Henry and Donelson in the center thrown back from the flanks, but they were situated, respectively, on two rivers, the Tennessee and the Cumberland, flowing into the Ohio. If the Federals, with the aid of their naval strength, could seize the forts, they would be between the Confederate forces on the flanks and in position to attack one or the other of the isolated fractions.[11]

Beauregard could see no point in trying to hold a weak site like Bowling Green which would have to be evacuated anyway if the Federals advanced. He proposed that it be abandoned and the troops on the right concentrated near the forts. Johnston refused, principally for the reason that such a move would open the line to Nashville to Buell.[12] Johnston's insistence on holding Bowling Green is not as puzzling as his presence there. Here was a general who commanded forces stretching from central Kentucky to Arkansas. Instead of stationing himself at a point where he could supervise all of them efficiently, he stayed at the far right of his line acting as a troop commander of fourteen thousand men, a function which he could well have relegated to one of several capable officers at Bowling Green.

On February 6 Grant attacked and captured Fort Henry. Ironically enough, the Federals moved on Henry when they did partly because of a rumor that Beauregard and large reinforcements were coming from the east. Their hope was to capture at least one of the

the size of his army, he must have given Beauregard a picture something like the one described above. However, there are discrepancies in the various Confederate troop estimates which make accurate analysis difficult.

[11] The forts had been constructed earlier when Kentucky was preserving a fiction of neutrality. Consequently they were located in Tennessee. When the war moved into Kentucky, the Confederates thought it was too late to build new defenses farther north.

[12] Roman, *Beauregard*, I, 215–18; *Battles and Leaders*, I, 576–71.

forts before the expected Confederate help arrived. News of the fort's fall reached Bowling Green the next day. Beauregard, who had had a throat operation just before leaving Virginia, was sick in bed in the Covington House. To his room came General William J. Hardee to discuss the bad turn of events. According to an account which Beauregard composed after the war, he told Hardee that the Confederate forces should be concentrated around Donelson, the next obvious point of attack by Grant. Hardee agreed to present these views to Johnston. Later that day Johnston and Hardee returned to Beauregard's room. Again Beauregard argued for a concentration at Donelson and an attack on Grant. Johnston said that the move was too risky. He favored a withdrawal to Nashville. Beauregard and Hardee then drew up a memorandum embodying Johnston's ideas.[13]

This is Beauregard's after-the-war story of what occurred. The contemporary records indicate it did not happen quite that way. The memorandum, signed by Beauregard and Hardee, was obviously the considered opinion of all three generals after a gloomy conference. It stated that as Henry had fallen and Donelson could not be held, the army at Bowling Green would have to retreat to Nashville for a defense behind the Cumberland River. With Grant astride the Tennessee at Henry, the force at Columbus was separated from the one on the right. For the time, the two wings would have to act separately. Columbus should be evacuated, except for a small garrison, and the main body of troops withdrawn to Humboldt, Tennessee, and, if necessary, even farther south. A desperate effort should be made to hold Island No. 10 and Fort Pillow on the Mississippi. In a message to Richmond Johnston said that Beauregard and Hardee agreed on the necessity for a withdrawal from the present line.[14] Beauregard's endorsement of the memorandum does not mean that he may not have urged the Donelson concentration. He undoubtedly did, at the beginning of the conference, but not with the pertinacity that he remembered.

Regardless of the intensity with which he argued for concentrating at Donelson, it seems certain that he did advocate making the battle for Kentucky at the fort. As was often the case, his strategic instinct was sound. In the initial stage of the Federal move on Donel-

[13] Roman, *Beauregard,* I, 219–21.
[14] The memorandum is in *Official Records,* VII, 861–62; Johnston to Benjamin, February 8, 1862, *ibid.,* 130–31.

son, which started on February 12, Grant advanced with fifteen thousand men. If Johnston had gone to the fort with the bulk of the troops on the right, he could have confronted Grant with a force, counting the garrison, of thirty thousand. He could have struck Grant before Buell arrived. With Grant defeated, Buell undoubtedly would have fallen back to defend the Ohio line. Johnston refused to go to Donelson. He seemed obsessed with the idea that he personally had to conduct the column at Bowling Green to safety. His actions almost defy rational analysis. Having gone on record as believing Donelson to be untenable, he sent at least twelve thousand reinforcements to the fort. These were not enough to stop Grant but were too many to place in a possible trap. Apparently he thought that the garrison could hold off Grant while he got to Nashville and then could extricate itself and join him. In the face of all that he had said to the government about the necessity for a withdrawal, he informed Davis that the purpose of his dispositions was to fight for Nashville at Donelson.[15] The only explanation for these confusions and contradictions is that Johnston was moving temporarily in a fog of mental paralysis induced by the crisis he was facing.

The evacuation of Bowling Green started on the eleventh, and by the sixteenth the army was behind the Cumberland at Nashville. On the thirteenth Beauregard left for Columbus by way of Nashville to assume command of the left wing. Just before leaving, he wrote out for Johnston an outline of the course of action he wished to follow. Departing somewhat from the agreement of February 7, he recommended that Columbus be given up completely, that the defense of the Mississippi be made at Island No. 10 and Fort Pillow, and that the bulk of his forces retire to Jackson, Tennessee, instead of to Humboldt. From Jackson, he explained, he would be in better position to protect the vital railroad lines of west Tennessee. Johnston, busy with the evacuation, said that he would meet Beauregard in Nashville to discuss this new proposal. On the fourteenth Beauregard, still ill, was in Nashville. There he saw Johnston in what would be their last meeting for over a month. Johnston said that with the wings of the army temporarily separated, Beauregard would have to decide things pretty much on his own. Columbus could be yielded, he said, if the government approved.[16]

[15] Johnston, *A. S. Johnston*, 518–19.
[16] Roman, *Beauregard*, I, 221–23.

Before he continued on from Nashville, Beauregard wrote a bitter letter to Pryor. Deploring the weakness of the Confederate forces, he said, "I am taking the helm when the ship is already on the breakers, and with but few sailors to man it. How it is to be extricated from its present perilous condition Providence alone can determine. . . . We must defeat the enemy *somewhere,* to give confidence to our friends. . . . *We must give up some minor points, and concentrate our forces, to save the most important ones, or we will lose all of them in succession.*" [17]

From Nashville Beauregard went to Corinth and on to Jackson. At the latter place he became so ill that he had to stop. While at Corinth he heard from Johnston that Donelson had fallen on the sixteenth. Two days later his superior wired that because of Buell's approach he was withdrawing from Nashville and that for the present Beauregard would have to act as he saw fit—that is, with complete independence.[18] Armed with this authority, the general decided to evacuate Columbus immediately, before the enemy cut its communications. Mindful of Johnston's caution that he secure governmental approval of the move, he put the question up to Richmond. The government readily granted permission.[19] Obviously the purpose to evacuate such an important point, with the enemy within striking distance, should have been guarded with jealous secrecy. The Federals could easily have found out about Beauregard's plan. His colored servant, Frederick Maginnis, blurted out the details at a Negro church meeting in Jackson, where any spy could have heard him.[20]

As he planned the evacuation of Columbus, Beauregard was arranging his forces in a new line. Its right was at Corinth in northeast Mississippi, whence it stretched across the width of Tennessee to Island No. 10 in the Mississippi and New Madrid on the Missouri side. The bulk of his troops were at Corinth, Jackson, Humboldt, and Union City. The line covered Memphis and Corinth, both important railroad centers, and the Louisville and Memphis and the Memphis and Charleston railroads. By using another railroad, the Mobile and

---

[17] Beauregard to Pryor, February 14, 1862, *ibid.,* 224.

[18] *Ibid.,* 224–25, 232–33, 498.

[19] *Ibid.,* 233–36, 499; *Official Records,* VII, 890, 892; Polk, *Leonidas Polk,* II, 74–80.

[20] C. J. Johnson to Mrs. Johnson, February 23, 1862, in C. J. Johnson Papers (Department of Archives, Louisiana State University).

Ohio, he could concentrate rapidly against a Federal force moving on the west side of the Tennessee. Surveying his forces and his communications, his gloom lightened. With a return of optimism came a revival of his offensive spirit. His Napoleonic complex, held in restraint while he was with Johnston, began to operate again now that he was on his own. Visions of a great offensive ran through his mind. Almost instantly he produced a plan.

On February 21 he prepared a confidential circular to the governors of Louisiana, Mississippi, Alabama, and Tennessee. Special couriers carried a copy to each state capital. In the circular he reviewed the recent defeats and their disastrous effects. The Confederacy could not afford to supinely await another attack, he said; the entire Mississippi Valley was in danger of going down. A counterblow must be struck at once. He implored the governors to furnish him with reinforcements to bring his army up to forty thousand. With this force he would march on Paducah, seize the mouths of the Tennessee and the Cumberland, attack Cairo, and threaten, if not capture, St. Louis itself. On the same day he wrote to Van Dorn, describing his plan and asking that general to join him with ten thousand men. "What say you to this brilliant programme which I know is fully practicable, if we can get the forces?" he asked. "At all events, we must do something or die in the attempt, otherwise, all will be shortly lost." [21]

Beauregard's projected offensive violated the terms of his understanding with Johnston. Although Johnston had granted Beauregard complete freedom of movement, he had done so on the assumption that the junior officer would pull back his troops for an eventual union of the two wings. Now Beauregard was proposing, in effect, to take over the command of Johnston's department and plan a new operation. While his actions seem open to criticism, he was doing only what Johnston should have done. Johnston was giving a repeat performance of his course at Bowling Green: he was refusing to act as an army commander. Instead of coming to a central point like Corinth and directing the concentration of his scattered forces, he was guiding his column of seventeen thousand [22] southward through Tennessee. That the urgent problems in his department—the Mississippi defenses, the proper use of Van Dorn's troops—demanded his

[21] Roman, *Beauregard,* I, 240–42, 499.

[22] From Donelson three thousand of the garrison had escaped and joined him.

personal attention seemed not to enter his mind. He was content to fill the role of a major general commanding a corps. In a letter to Benjamin explaining why he had to retreat from Nashville, he said that he was moving his troops toward the west bank of the Tennessee to cross at Decatur so that he could "cooperate or unite" with Beauregard.[23] His language practically admitted that he regarded Beauregard as a co-ordinate commander.

Beauregard's plea for reinforcements brought little results from the governors, but the national government moved to aid him. Braxton Bragg at Pensacola was directed to go to Corinth with ten thousand men, and five thousand were sent up from New Orleans. Beauregard, still plagued by throat trouble and colds and unable to exercise fully the functions of command, was delighted that the experienced Bragg was on the way. He would serve under Bragg when recovered, he told the government, rather than miss his assistance now.[24] Pleased by the apparent support he was getting from Richmond, he warned his brother-in-law, Charles Villeré, now a member of Congress, not to let his name be used in any way against the administration. "*United* we may stand," he wrote, "*divided* we must fall."[25]

On March 5 Beauregard assumed formal command of his forces, whom he styled "The Army of the Mississippi." Heretofore he had dispatched his orders through General Leonidas Polk, who had commanded the troops at Columbus. To the soldiers he issued one of his usual rhetorical addresses exhorting them to fight the cruel invader even to the final sacrifice.[26] A few days later he published what was probably his most widely read composition of the war, his famous appeal to the planters of the Mississippi Valley for bells to provide metal for casting cannon. Opening with an allusion to fighting peoples of the past who had yielded up their church bells for liberty, he continued:

> We want cannon . . . ; and I, your general, intrusted with the command of the army embodied of your sons, your kinsmen, and your neighbors, do now call on you

[23] *Official Records,* VII, 426–27.

[24] *Ibid.,* 912.

[25] Beauregard to Charles J. Villeré, March 1, 1862, in Beauregard Papers (Library of Congress), Letterbook, Official Personal Letters, March 8, 1861—March 31, 1863.

[26] *Official Records,* X, Pt. 2, p. 297.

to send your plantation-bells to the nearest railroad depot, subject to my order, to be melted into cannon for the defense of your plantations.

Who will not cheerfully and promptly send me his bells under such circumstances?

Be of good cheer; but time is precious.[27]

The appeal excited wide attention in the South and the North and in both sections a good deal of ridicule. Bragg thought it smacked of the "Within hearing of the enemy's guns" letter at Centreville. The Confederates already had more guns than instructed men to serve them, Bragg snorted, and there was metal in New Orleans to cast many more. Sensational reports circulated of the number of bells contributed. It was said that nearly five hundred were found in New Orleans when the Federals occupied the city. A coldly factual paper in the Confederate records at the National Archives lists forty-three bells as being offered; of these twenty-nine were declined, probably because the railroads could not transport them.[28]

Beauregard suffered a blow in early March when a Federal force in Missouri captured New Madrid, one of the key points in his system of defense on the Mississippi River. He had thought that New Madrid could hold; when it fell he blamed its commander for putting up a weak resistance. Nevertheless, he hastened to strengthen the armament and the works at Island No. 10 and Fort Pillow, the remaining fortified places on the upper river.[29] Beauregard did not need the fall of New Madrid to tell him that he did not have enough capable officers to organize his troops and defend his line. He had been bombarding Richmond with requests for experienced men. If they were not provided, he threatened, he could not be held responsible for any failures that followed. In a letter to Miles urging the Congressman to stir up the War Department he exploded: "Will not heaven open the eyes and senses of our rulers? Where in the world are we going to, if not to destruction?" Because of his enfeebled condition, he said, he had to have good generals to help him. With ef-

---

[27] Roman, *Beauregard,* I, 518–19.

[28] Bragg to Mrs. Bragg, March 20, 1862, in Braxton Bragg Papers (Duke University Library) ; Snow, *Southern Generals,* 242; "Record of Bells," in War Department Collection of Confederate Records (National Archives).

[29] Roman, *Beauregard,* I, 352–59, 552–63; Jordan to Beauregard's engineer officer, David B. Harris, March 14, 1862, in David B. Harris Papers (Duke University Library).

ficient officers and troops, he could make "a beautiful *ten strike.*" Without them, he could do nothing because "we would lose too much if I failed." Bragg, observing his nervous, distressed superior, thought that but for his aid Beauregard would not be living.[30]

During the weeks of March Johnston was moving his force toward the west bank of the Tennessee and Corinth. After the war Beauregard wrote an account of the Western campaign in which he depicted Johnston as wandering around Tennessee not knowing where to go. Finally Beauregard said to him: my dear but not too bright general, come to Corinth, the logical point of concentration. One of the fiercest of the postwar historical controversies was between Beauregard and the partisans of Johnston as to which general selected Corinth as the place to unite the wings of the Army. The Johnston supporters claimed that their hero had decided on Corinth as early as January, which would make him a rare prophet indeed, and that Beauregard had nothing to do with forming the decision.[31]

Like most of the after-the-war controversies, this one ignored the possibility that both sides may have been right. The contemporary records indicate that Johnston and Beauregard, perhaps independently, settled on Corinth as the rendezvous sometime after the fall of Donelson. They could hardly have missed its advantages. An important railroad center, it was located close to the big bend of the Tennessee. Both generals surmised correctly that Grant would soon move up the river to cut the railroad communications. Corinth was the ideal point to concentrate against him; if they could defeat him, it was also an ideal base from which to jump off for a counteroffensive. The records do show that Beauregard adopted a somewhat superior and chiding tone in his correspondence with Johnston: you ought to hurry to Corinth as soon as possible; you must not let the enemy get between us.[32] In a letter to Johnston written a few days before the separated forces joined, Beauregard outlined a plan of strategy for his superior. He had lost some of his appetite for an offensive. Now he advised a defensive-offensive strategy. He would take a strong position, entice the enemy to attack, and then launch a

[30] Roman, *Beauregard,* I, 509–13; Bragg to Mrs. Bragg, March 20, 1862, in Bragg Papers.

[31] Roman, *Beauregard,* I, 248, 258; Johnston, *A. S. Johnston,* 489–91, 506–507.

[32] Roman, *Beauregard,* I, 248, 510–11.

counterattack which would cut off the Federals from their base on the Tennessee.[33]

Johnston's forces moved into Corinth during the last week in March. The general arrived on the twenty-fourth and met Beauregard. Immediately they plunged into a discussion of the military situation. Beauregard said that Grant's army had moved up the Tennessee and had landed on the west side at Pittsburg Landing, about twenty-five miles from Corinth. It was known that Buell was marching to join him with twenty-five thousand men. To meet the Federal concentration, Beauregard had shifted most of his troops to in and around Corinth. Both generals agreed that a blow should be struck at Grant as soon as possible, before Buell arrived. Then Johnston startled Beauregard by offering him the command of the army in the coming battle. Johnston said he would act as department commander with headquarters in Memphis or Holly Springs. Beauregard refused the assignment. The reason for Johnston's gesture has caused much speculation. His friends ascribed it to his noble character: he generously wanted his junior to receive credit for the victory.[34] Two other and more likely explanations are possible. Under a storm of criticism for the disasters in the West, he may have realized that he had erred in not exercising central command and was now trying belatedly to assume his proper function. Or he may still have wished to avoid large responsibility by placing the greater part of his forces under Beauregard's direct command.

A few days later Beauregard, with Johnston's approval, drew up a plan to reorganize the army. Johnston was designated as commander, Beauregard second in command, and Bragg chief of staff. The new organization contained four corps: the First, under Polk, 9,136 troops; the Second, Bragg, 13,589; the Third, Hardee, 6,789; the reserve corps, John C. Breckinridge, 6,439. In every way Beauregard's arrangements were superior to what had existed before. The command system at the top was filled by the senior generals; the corps organization was compact and should have made for tight control in battle. The only awkward feature was the size of Bragg's corps, which contained more than one third of the army.[35] There

[33] Beauregard to Johnston, March 17, 1862, in Johnston, *A. S. Johnston,* 542.

[34] *Ibid.,* 549–50; *Battles and Leaders,* II, 550, 578; Roman, *Beauregard,* I, 265–66.

[35] *Official Records,* X, Pt. 1, p. 396; Roman, *Beauregard,* I, 267–68.

was little doubt among the men in the various corps as to who the most popular general was. It was the second in command, "the little Napoleon." The soldiers raved about him, one of them later recalled, and accorded him the unmeasured praise given only to genius.[36]

Not much time was allowed Johnston and Beauregard to plan an offensive. Late on the night of April 2 a telegram from the commander at Bethel, about twenty miles north of Corinth, was handed to Beauregard. It stated that the Federals were maneuvering in strength on his front. Immediately Beauregard decided that the Union commanders had divided their forces for an advance on Memphis. He wrote on the bottom of the telegram, "Now is the moment to advance, and strike the enemy at Pittsburg Landing," and told his chief of staff, Jordan, to take it to Johnston. Jordan went to the commander's quarters and gave him the message. Johnston said he would like to discuss it with Bragg; accompanied by Jordan, he crossed the street to Bragg's rooms. Bragg endorsed the proposed move, but Johnston raised objections, the chief one being that the troops needed more training. Jordan, voicing what he knew were Beauregard's views, replied that waiting would only enable the Federals to increase their strength and that an attack now would catch them by surprise. Johnston finally yielded. He authorized Jordan to draft a preparatory order for an advance.

In Bragg's room Jordan wrote a circular order to Polk, Bragg, and Hardee directing them to be ready to move by six the next morning. A similar directive was telegraphed to Breckinridge, commanding the reserve corps east of Corinth. Jordan told an aide to awaken Beauregard at five and tell him that an advance order had been issued. Soon after sunrise Jordan was summoned to Beauregard's quarters. He found the general sitting up in bed writing notes on the backs of telegrams and envelopes. A copy of these Jordan took to his office to use as a basis in framing a directive for the march order to Pittsburg Landing and for the battle order. As he wrote, he also had before him as a model a copy of Napoleon's order for the battle of Waterloo. Before he finished, he went to Beauregard's quarters to sit in on a conference attended by Johnston, Bragg, and Hardee. Jordan said it would take time to write and distribute the

---

[36] William G. Stevenson, *Thirteen Months in the Rebel Army* (London, 1862), 146; F. F. Palms to Henrietta Lauzin, April 4, 1862, in Gras-Lauzin Papers (Department of Archives, Louisiana State University); Henry Morton Stanley, *Autobiography of Henry Morton Stanley* (Boston, 1909), 445.

detailed order. So Beauregard, drawing a rough sketch on the top of a camp table, carefully explained to the corps generals the march routes and the battle order. Without waiting for the written order, which would follow later, they were to have their troops moving by noon. It was then about 10 A.M.[37]

From Corinth to Pittsburg Landing was approximately twenty-five miles and to the first Federal position twenty-two. The Confederates would have to march eighteen miles to reach a point from which they could deploy for battle. Two narrow dirt roads led from Corinth to the Landing. One, the Ridge or Bark Road, ran north and then east. The other started east, turned in a northerly direction to a hamlet called Monterey, and joined the Ridge Road about four miles from Pittsburg. From Monterey the Purdy and Savannah roads led north to intersect the Ridge Road. At the point where the Savannah and Ridge roads crossed, about eight miles from the Landing, was a house known as Mickey's.

Beauregard's written march order directed Hardee to advance on the Ridge-Bark Road, with the head of his column to bivouac that night (the third) at Mickey's. At 3 A.M. on the fourth Hardee was to move on until he approached the enemy position and then deploy in line of battle. Bragg's big corps was to assemble at Monterey and march in two wings on the Purdy and Savannah roads to the Ridge Road. The head of column of the right or Savannah wing was to reach Mickey's before sunset; the head of column of the left or Purdy wing was to reach the intersection at the Ridge Road by night. On the morning of the fourth Bragg was to follow in rear of Hardee on the Ridge Road and form a second battle line. Polk, who had only one division at Corinth (the other was at Bethel), was to leave half an hour after Hardee, bivouac behind the latter that night, and follow his line of march in the morning. At Mickey's Polk was to halt and form as a reserve. His division at Bethel was to move down the Purdy Road and join him.

After the march order had been written, somebody realized that Polk and Bragg might get on the Ridge Road at the same time. Accordingly, Polk was instructed to stop at the Purdy intersection until Bragg's left wing had passed. The reserve corps was to assemble at Monterey after Bragg left and move by the best route to Mickey's

[37] Roman, *Beauregard*, I, 270–72; Jordan, in *Battles and Leaders*, I, 594–96; Beauregard, *ibid.*, 579–81.

or wherever the army was by the morning of the fourth. Beauregard's obvious intention, although not clearly indicated, was to place Polk in Bragg's left rear and the reserve corps in his right rear.[38]

Beauregard's battle order would bring the army into action with the corps arranged one behind the other: Hardee, Bragg, Polk-Breckinridge. Instead of each corps having a specific sector of the Federal line to attack, the first two would advance in parallel lines stretching across a three-mile front. Not only was this formation certain to cause a confusion and mingling of units, but it also meant that Hardee and Bragg would have to give their attention to matters on the entire front.

The order of battle reads strangely when viewed in the light of Beauregard's avowed strategic objective. The Federal army was between two creeks flowing into the Tennessee. While attacking along the whole Federal line, the Confederates planned to turn the enemy left and drive the Federals away from the river and back on the northern creek, where they would have to surrender.[39] This being the objective, the parallel arrangement was faulty. Instead of having a formation in depth on the right, Beauregard's line was equally strong at all points, and his attack was likely to hit each sector of the enemy line with equal strength.

His reasons for the line formation, given after the war, are not quite convincing. He explained that he put Hardee first because that general had the best corps and that he placed Bragg second because many of the latter's troops were recruits and would do better behind Hardee. He also contended that the parallel arrangement was better adapted for the unknown terrain into which the army was advancing.[40] After the war Johnston's partisans charged that Beauregard changed the original order of advance planned by his superior. This accusation they based on a telegram Johnston sent Davis on April 3 announcing that the army was about to advance. Johnston said Polk commanded the left, Bragg the center, and Hardee the right—that is, each corps was assigned a designated sector of the front. Rather than Beauregard altering Johnston's design, it seems probable that Johnston did not know what Beauregard was doing. The hasty planning at headquarters was being done by Beauregard

[38] *Official Records,* X, Pt. 1, pp. 392–95.
[39] *Ibid.,* 397.
[40] *Battles and Leaders,* I, 581–82; Thomas Jordan and J. P. Pryor, *The Campaigns of Lieut.-General N. B. Forrest . . .* (New Orleans, 1868), 149.

and Jordan, with Johnston acting largely as an onlooker. Johnston did not see the written order until the march started, too late to change it even had he wanted to.[41]

It seems plain from the language of the written order of April 3 that Beauregard intended to concentrate the army around Mickey's that night and to attack the next morning. The order was drafted when he thought that the march could be started at an early hour. But the preparations for the movement—the explanations to the corps generals, the framing of instructions—took time. He had to postpone the jump-off until noon. Even then the march did not start. The streets of Corinth were jammed with wagons and troops. As the hours wore on, they remained there. Beauregard blamed Polk for the delay. He said that Polk, not understanding the verbal order, blocked with his troops and his train the line of Hardee's march. Polk said that he could not move until Hardee did and that Hardee did not receive instructions to move until three.

Whatever the facts of the case, which probably were that Beauregard, as at Manassas, forgot to send an order, Hardee did not start until late in the afternoon and Polk until nearly dark. When Polk stopped for the night, he had covered only nine miles.[42] Because of the various delays, Beauregard sometime during the day did the obvious thing. Without preparing new written orders, he recast his time schedule. Now he planned to reach Mickey's by the evening of the fourth and attack on the fifth. In other words, he shoved most of the movements in the written order forward twenty-four hours.[43]

Despite what Beauregard wrote after the war and what historians have written since, the initial delays were not too serious. The movements of Hardee and Polk conformed to the new schedule. Hardee, once started, moved fast. By the morning of the fourth the head of

[41] *Official Records*, X, Pt. 2, p. 387; *Battles and Leaders*, I, 554.

[42] *Battles and Leaders*, I, 596; Roman, *Beauregard*, I, 275–76; Polk, *Leonidas Polk*, II, 90–93.

[43] All accounts of the battle of Shiloh say that from the first Beauregard planned to reach Mickey's by the evening of the fourth and attack on the fifth. This interpretation can be squared with the written order only by assuming that Beauregard meant to get the army to Mickey's, four miles from the Federal position, on the third; advance early on the fourth and spend the day deploying; and attack on the fifth. That Beauregard would waste a day in deployment, when time was so precious to the Confederates, seems absurd. If it be objected that the Confederates did require a whole day to deploy on the fifth, the answer is that the circumstances were unusual and that they never dreamed it would take that long.

his column was at Mickey's, only four miles from where he was to deploy in battle. Before midday Polk reached the Purdy intersection and waited for Bragg's left column to move by. He waited three hours. Finally he received a dispatch from Bragg saying that he was moving his whole corps on the Savannah road and for Polk not to hold up. Polk then went on to Mickey's, his march that day covering seven miles.

Bragg was having all kinds of trouble with his unwieldy corps. Starting late on the afternoon of the third, he did not get the head of his column to Monterey until 11 A.M. on the fourth; his second division arrived late in the afternoon. Although it was only six miles from Monterey to Mickey's, his head of column did not approach the rendezvous until dark. Some of his units were moving in all during the night. Bragg's delays slowed Hardee as well as Polk. He dispatched Hardee in the morning to check his advance until the two corps were closer together. The slowness of his march Bragg ascribed to inefficient guides, the poor condition of the troops, and the improvised organization of the army. Also, he had been held back by his efforts to locate the reserve corps, which had not yet appeared.[44]

On the night of April 4 most of the Confederate army was approximately where it was supposed to be. Tired, bedraggled, and hungry, it was in and around Mickey's and in position to launch an attack on the morrow. Polk's division from Bethel and the reserve corps had not arrived, but they were expected early the next day. As they were to form part of the reserve or third line, the attack could be started in their absence. The worst feature in the situation was the location of Polk's troops. Because of the march mix-up, they were ahead of Bragg. Before Bragg could deploy behind Hardee, he would have to march through Polk.

Soon after midnight a heavy rain started and was still falling at 3 A.M., when Hardee was supposed to move out to form the first battle line. Because of the darkness and the rain, he could not start until dawn. Hardee's corps was not large enough to cover the front between the two creeks. To fill the gap Beauregard had authorized him to place one of Bragg's brigades on his right. By the time Hardee got his own troops and Bragg's unit deployed it was ten o'clock. Then

[44] Johnston, *A. S. Johnston*, 564–65; *Battles and Leaders*, I, 582; Polk, *Leonidas Polk*, II, 93–97; *Official Records*, X, Pt. 1, pp. 463–64, Pt. 2, pp. 390–91.

Bragg began to arrange his own line. The hours were slipping by.[45]

Between six and seven Johnston arrived on the field. He and Beauregard had left Corinth on the fourth; that night they slept at Monterey. Before sunrise they were on their horses and riding toward Mickey's.[46] Impatiently Johnston watched Bragg array his line. The left division was not present. Finally Johnston sent a staff officer to ask Bragg where it was. Bragg said it was somewhere in the rear and he was trying to locate it. Johnston contained himself and waited, for over two hours, according to one account. At twelve-thirty he looked at his watch and exclaimed, "This is perfectly puerile! This is not war!" Riding to the rear, he found the division in the road, its advance blocked by some of Polk's troops. Almost frenzied, Johnston ordered the road cleared. By two it was free, and the last of Bragg's men passed to the front. Bragg now had to deploy the division in line, and Polk had to get his troops up and deployed in Bragg's left rear. Polk, who had been fuming all morning because he could not move till Bragg was out of the way, did not complete his formation until four, at which time his division from Bethel joined him. Soon after the reserve corps arrived. Since morning the Confederates had advanced about two and a half miles. The hour was too late to attack.[47]

As Polk was fixing his line, he was told that Beauregard wanted to see him. He found Beauregard standing in the road talking with Bragg. Speaking with much feeling, Beauregard said, "I am very much disappointed at the delay which has occurred in getting the troops into position." Polk replied that the fault was not his, that he had been held up by the troops ahead of him, meaning Bragg's. Beauregard said that because of the delay the attack would have to be called off. To succeed it had to be a surprise, and with the Confederate army within two miles of the Federal outposts a surprise was impossible at this late hour. The army would have to return to Corinth.

At this point Johnston and several other officers, perhaps attracted by the loud language, came up. Johnston asked what the matter was. Turning to his superior, Beauregard poured out reasons why the attack must be called off. Twenty-four hours had been lost, their

[45] Johnston, *A. S. Johnston*, 560–61; Polk, *Leonidas Polk*, II, 97–98; *Official Records*, X, Pt. 1, p. 567.

[46] *Official Records*, X, Pt. 1, p. 400; *Battles and Leaders*, I, 596–97.

[47] Johnston, *A. S. Johnston*, 560–63; Polk, *Leonidas Polk*, II, 97–99; *Official Records*, X, Pt. 1, pp. 406, 414, 464, 614.

presence was surely known to the Federals. "Now they will be entrenched to the eyes," he cried. He seemed to be unnerved by the miscarriage of his careful plans. Johnston, showing more balance and courage, said that he doubted the Federals knew of their approach and that anyway, having come this far, the army could not turn back. He concluded the informal council by saying, "We shall attack at daylight tomorrow." As he walked off, he said to a staff officer, "I would fight them if they were a million." [48]

Shortly Beauregard's gloomy feelings were cheered. Hardee asked him to ride in front of his men to encourage them. Beauregard expressed reluctance, but when Johnston joined in the request he agreed. He stipulated that there must be no cheering; the noise might betray the presence of the Confederates to listening enemy outposts. Hardee so directed. The order had to be repeated as he cantered down the line, wearing the little red-topped artillery general's cap which he had worn at Manassas. [49]

The soldiers had little to cheer about except the presence of the hero of Manassas. That afternoon the rain stopped, and the sun broke through the mists. The night was clear and cold. For security reasons, the only fires allowed were in holes in the ground. In many units the food rations were short. The weary, wet soldiers, most of whom had been under arms since before dawn, slept on the ground. Beauregard forgot to give orders to set up his tent and had to spend the night in an ambulance wagon. [50]

[48] Polk's report, in *Official Records*, X, Pt. 1, p. 407; Johnston, *A. S. Johnston*, 567–71; *Battles and Leaders*, I, 555, 583–84, 597–98; Roman, *Beauregard*, I, 277–79. Beauregard claimed that Johnston called the council, but the evidence shows clearly it was largely accidental.

[49] *Official Records*, X, Pt. 1, p. 400; Roman, *Beauregard*, I, 530, 533.

[50] Stevenson, *Thirteen Months in the Rebel Army*, 148–49; Roman, *Beauregard*, I, 348.

CHAPTER NINE

Shiloh

THREE CREEKS formed an important part of the terrain of the battle of Shiloh. They bounded the area in which the battle was fought. On the south was Lick Creek, which took its rise about twelve miles from the Tennessee, flowed in a northeast direction, and entered the river south of Pittsburg Landing. On the north was Owl Creek, which flowed parallel with Lick and emptied into Snake Creek, which in turn joined the river north of the Landing. Near the river the distance between the streams was five miles; it was three miles at the point where Grant's army was encamped between Owl and Lick. Owl was the stream on which the Confederates intended to drive the Federals and destroy them.

The land between the creeks was a rolling plateau, rising in places to a height one hundred feet above the river. A few farms dotted the area, but most of it was covered with heavy timber and brush and crossed by ravines. The roads were country dirt ones; most of the primary roads ran in an east-west direction, which made for bad communications for the Confederates. About three miles from the Landing and almost in the center of the area was a little log church called Shiloh, from which the battle would take its name.[1]

On the night of April 5 the two largest armies yet to come together in the war slept within a few miles of each other, the Federal army strangely unaware of the presence of its enemy. As is usually the case with Civil War battles, the estimates of the numbers of the contending forces differ and conflict. It seems certain, however, that Johnston approached the field with close to forty thousand men. In his camps between the creeks Grant had about the same number, possibly a few thousand less. At Crump's Landing four miles downstream (north) from Pittsburg he had another division of about seven thousand. This latter unit did not participate in the fighting on April 6.

[1] Jordan and Pryor, *Forrest*, 117–18; *Battles and Leaders*, I, 465–86, 495–98.

In the battle of that day the two armies seem to have been approximately equal in size.[2]

As the morning of April 6, a Sunday, dawned, a heavy white mist hung low over the woods in front of the Confederate positions. Then the sun broke through and dispelled the fog. Excitedly the romantic Confederates passed the word around that it was another sun of Austerlitz. The clear sky, the bracing air, the freshness of the Southern spring day united to remind the soldiers of the land for which they fought. So did an address by Johnston read to each regiment as it formed in line. Remember the precious stake involved in the coming battle, the commanding general exhorted; remember the mothers, wives, and children hanging on the outcome; remember "the fair, broad, abounding land" and the happy homes that would be desolated by defeat; remember above all the women of the South, whose noble devotion had never been exceeded in any age.[3]

While the troops were forming in line, the generals stood around Johnston's campfire. Apparently another argument over the feasibility of an attack started, with Beauregard again raising objections. It was interrupted by the sound of shots as Hardee's skirmish line encountered the first Federals. Johnston said the battle had started and it was too late to change the dispositions.[4] At five o'clock Hardee's whole line moved forward, followed by Bragg five hundred yards behind. Johnston and Beauregard stood on a slight eminence watching the men advance. The sound of the firing increased as the Confederates drove through the Federal outposts and then lulled temporarily as the attackers moved toward the enemy camps. Shortly before seven Beauregard met Johnston near the latter's headquarters. The commanding general said that the battle had opened in grand style and that he was going to the front. Mounting his horse, he said to his aides, "Tonight we will water our horses in the Tennessee River."[5]

[2] *Official Records*, X, Pt. 1, pp. 112, 398; *Battles and Leaders*, I, 485, 537–39; Johnston, *A. S. Johnston*, 670, 685.

[3] Jordan and Pryor, *Forrest*, 121; Johnston, *A. S. Johnston*, 582; Thomas D. Duncan, *Recollections of Thomas D. Duncan* . . . (Nashville, 1922), 53; letter of Sergeant A. P. B., April 14, 1862, in New Orleans *Evening Delta*, April 21, 1862, clipping in Arthur W. Hyatt Papers (Department of Archives, Louisiana State University); *Official Records*, X, Pt. 2, p. 389.

[4] Johnston, *A. S. Johnston*, 569; Bragg's report, in *Official Records*, X, Pt. 1, p. 464.

[5] *Battles and Leaders*, I, 557, 599; Roman, *Beauregard*, I, 284–85.

One would like to know more of what passed between the two generals in their last meeting, particularly of the command function that Johnston assigned to his junior. After the war Beauregard said that Johnston gave him "the general direction" of the battle.[6] Taken at face value, this statement would mean that Beauregard was to control the principal movements of troops all over the field. Obviously Johnston did not intend him to exercise this power—first, because that would have left nothing for Johnston to do, and second, because Beauregard from his position in the rear could not have directed movements at the front. Johnston's purpose is evident from Beauregard's actions during the day. While the commanding general pressed the attack at the front, Beauregard was to command the troops in the rear sector, particularly the two reserve corps, Polk in rear of Bragg and Breckinridge in rear of Hardee. At the right moment he was to commit them to battle and to send forward any other troops to points where they were needed. This function Beauregard performed until Johnston's death, always moving his headquarters forward as the Confederate front line advanced.

In the Confederate records the battle of Shiloh is a story of headlong attacks, brave fighting, confused and unscheduled advances, and a main objective not attained. As the Confederates drove the surprised Federals before them over the rugged terrain, the lines of the attackers lost their neat line formations. Units from one corps inevitably got mixed with those in another, with a single tangled, irregular line resulting. Finally the corps commanders improvised an arrangement whereby each one directed the attack on a specific area of the front. From left to right the Confederate line was now commanded by Hardee, Polk, Bragg, and Breckinridge. The corps generals devoted most of their efforts to leading charges instead of to organizing their masses and feeding them up to the front. At an early hour many Confederate troops began to straggle off to plunder the Federal camps or to make their way to the rear. These latter Beauregard endeavored to stop with cavalry and organize into battalions to be sent forward again.

Partly because of the actions of the corps generals and partly because of the terrain and stiffening Federal resistance, the initial Confederate advance was slowed. The battle tended to develop into a series of frontal assaults conducted more or less independently. From the Confederate viewpoint the advance was fatally off schedule. The

[6] *Battles and Leaders,* I, 586.

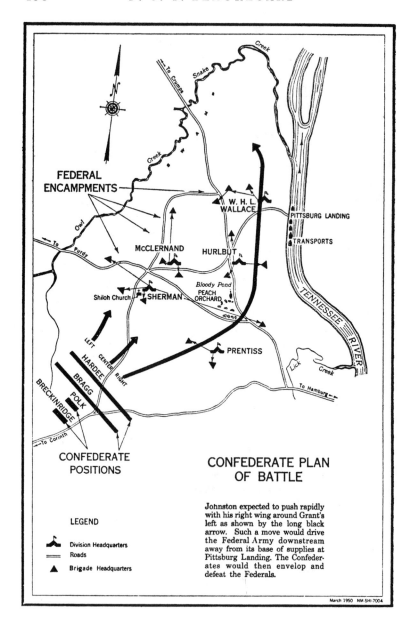

FEDERAL
ENCAMPMENTS

W. H. L.
WALLACE

PITTSBURG LANDING

TRANSPORTS

McCLERNAND   HURLBUT

Bloody Pond

Shiloh Church   SHERMAN   PEACH
                            ORCHARD

TENNESSEE RIVER

PRENTISS

Lick Creek

LEFT CENTER RIGHT

To Hamburg

HARDEE

BRAGG

BRECKINRIDGE

POLK

To Corinth

CONFEDERATE
POSITIONS

CONFEDERATE PLAN
OF BATTLE

Johnston expected to push rapidly
with his right wing around Grant's
left as shown by the long black
arrow. Such a move would drive
the Federal Army downstream
away from its base of supplies at
Pittsburg Landing. The Confederates would then envelop and
defeat the Federals.

LEGEND

Division Headquarters
Roads
Brigade Headquarters

March 1950   NM-SHI-7004

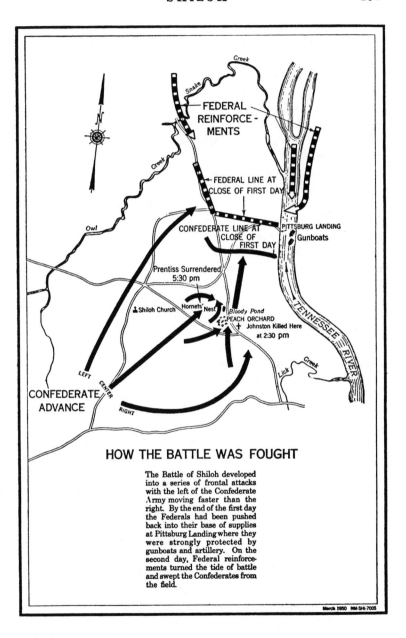

HOW THE BATTLE WAS FOUGHT

The Battle of Shiloh developed
into a series of frontal attacks
with the left of the Confederate
Army moving faster than the
right. By the end of the first day
the Federals had been pushed
back into their base of supplies
at Pittsburg Landing where they
were strongly protected by
gunboats and artillery. On the
second day, Federal reinforcements turned the tide of battle
and swept the Confederates from
the field.

March 1950 NM-SHI-7005

left was moving faster than the right. The Federals were being driven back toward their base on the river instead of northward onto Owl Creek. As the Federals on the Confederate right retired, they came to an old sunken road in a heavily wooded area. In this natural trench General Benjamin Prentiss rallied the remnant of his division; other units later formed on his flanks. Whereas in modern war such a strong position would have been by-passed or contained, the Confederates tried to take it. For hour after hour, while on the left the advance was grinding past Shiloh church, the Confederates flung eleven bloody and vain charges at the place they aptly called the "Hornet's Nest." [7]

Johnston saw what was going wrong with his plan. About noon he moved to the right to personally direct the attack on that vital sector. As he rode among the men, he carried a tin cup in one hand. He had taken it earlier from an officer who had come out of a deserted Federal tent carrying some valuable articles, which he had shown to the general. Johnston rebuked the man for plundering; then, regretting his words, he took the cup, saying, "Let this be my share of the spoils today." Johnston exhorted the men to go forward. Tapping their bayonets with his cup, he said, "These must do the work." At one point where the soldiers were obviously reluctant to charge, Johnston offered to lead them. Shamed, they sprang forward and drove the Federals back.

Johnston sat on his horse watching the retreating Yankees. Governor Isham G. Harris of Tennessee, serving as a volunteer aide, galloped up to the general. He saw Johnston reel in the saddle. "General, are you hurt?" cried Harris. "Yes, and I fear seriously," Johnston replied. A bullet had severed the large artery in his right leg. Maybe a retiring Union soldier had paused and drawn a bead on what he thought was an important officer near the front; maybe a stray ball fired at no one in particular just happened to strike Johnston. Guiding the horses away from the line of fire and holding Johnston with one arm, Harris stopped in a ravine and lifted the unconscious general from the saddle. Other officers gathered around. Any person with the most elementary knowledge of first aid could have stopped the flow of blood and saved Johnston's life. But in the Civil

[7] *Ibid.*, 586–91; Jordan and Pryor, *Forrest,* 121–31; Roman, *Beauregard,* I, 283–307; Johnston, *A. S. Johnston,* 587–609; Duncan, *Recollections,* 58–60; Albert Dillahunty, *Shiloh* (Washington, 1951), 9–15; Otto Eisenschiml, *The Story of Shiloh* (Chicago, 1946), 27–49.

War nobody knew anything about first aid except the medics, and Johnston had sent his surgeon to look after some prisoners.[8] He died at two-thirty. Governor Harris spurred to the rear and delivered the sad news to Beauregard shortly after three.[9]

After the war Johnston's partisans, particularly his son, liked to say that he died at the moment of victory. They claimed that he had achieved triumph elsewhere on the field and was organizing his right for the final push when the fatal bullet hit him. As a matter of fact, victory had not been won anywhere; the Confederate forces were not fighting under a common direction; and Johnston did not have complete control of his forces on the right, let alone on the whole front. By going from unit to unit at the edge of battle, exhorting the men to charge and offering to lead them, Johnston was performing more like a corps or division general than a commander. At the time of his death, he did not have a single staff officer with him, which indicates that he was not exerting much control over the battle.[10] Whatever general direction was being exercised issued from Beauregard.

Up to the time of Johnston's death, Beauregard had been performing the function assigned him by the commanding general— that of ordering movements in the rear of the battle. Soon after the attack started, he set up field headquarters on a high point between the Pittsburg and Purdy roads. From this point he deployed Polk and Breckinridge in columns of brigades and instructed them to follow Bragg and go in wherever they were called to help; if in doubt where to go, they should move toward the sound of heaviest firing. About the middle of the morning, as the Confederate line advanced, he moved up to within half a mile of the abandoned Federal camps. At two o'clock he established his third headquarters of the day near Shiloh church. Always he had his staff riding over the field collecting reports from the front and rounding up stragglers. Any inactive units that he spotted he directed to the front, sending most of them to Hardee on the left. Just before he received the news of Johnston's death, he was about to shift some troops to the center.[11]

[8] Johnston, *A. S. Johnston,* 611–15; Roman, *Beauregard,* I, 537.

[9] J. S. Byers to W. P. Johnston, June 13, 1862, in Mrs. Mason Barret Papers (Howard-Tilton Memorial Library, Tulane University); *Battles and Leaders,* I, 590.

[10] Eisenschiml, *Story of Shiloh,* 39.

[11] *Official Records,* X, Pt. 1, pp. 401–402; *Battles and Leaders,* I, 586–90; Roman, *Beauregard,* I, 285, 289, 294–96.

With Johnston dead, Beauregard assumed command of the army. Immediately he acted to keep the impetus of the offensive rolling. Contrary to what his enemies said during the war and later, he was not ignorant of the situation at the front or indifferent to the outcome of the battle. From the reports of his staff he had a fairly accurate picture of how far the attacks had gone. He knew that the Federal right had retired toward the Landing and that the left was still holding. Ordering that the news of Johnston's death be kept from the men, he directed that the advance continue all along the line. To co-ordinate the attack on the Federal left he ordered Bragg to take charge of the Confederate right and sent General Daniel Ruggles to command the center. The so-called lull of an hour which followed Beauregard's assumption of control was not due to any confusion resulting from the change in command, but to the time involved in shifting additional troops toward the fatal sunken road.[12]

While the Federals from the right were constructing a new and powerful defense line on the bluff above the Landing, the Confederates were concentrating for a final effort against the Hornet's Nest. Ruggles collected over sixty pieces of artillery and pounded the position with a merciless fire. Shaken by the barrage, the Federal troops on the right and left of Prentiss withdrew to the Landing. Prentiss, under orders from Grant to hold to the last, fought on with 2,200 men. Although virtually encircled by attackers, he continued to resist until five-thirty, when he surrendered. If any one man saved the Federal army at Shiloh, Prentiss was the man. Even captured, he and his troops were useful to Grant. A Confederate regiment was detailed to watch over the rich bag of prisoners.

After the surrender of Prentiss, the tired Confederates drifted toward the Federal line around the Landing. The Union forces were massed in a semicircular position with their backs to the river. The line was strongest on the left or south side, where Dill's Branch entered the Tennessee. Here the Federals had assembled fifty artillery pieces to meet the expected attack from the Confederate right. In addition, two Federal gunboats stood by in the river ready to throw their shot when the Confederates advanced. On the Federal right the line faced generally west. For the safety of this sector Grant felt

[12] Roman, *Beauregard*, I, 297–98; *Battles and Leaders*, I, 590; Stanley F. Horn, *The Army of Tennessee* (Indianapolis, 1941), 134–35.

little alarm. Opposite was Hardee, whose pecking assaults indicated he was incapable of mounting a dangerous attack. Besides, Grant's division from Crump's Landing, which had been ordered to the field early in the day and whose commander had confused his route, was finally nearing the scene and would shortly join the troops on the right. Only for his left did Grant fear. Only from their right, where most of their troops were massed, could the Confederates possibly deliver a decisive blow.

They did not have much power to do it here. At this critical moment the Confederates had no reserve to put in to clinch victory. The last unit of Breckinridge's corps had been committed to battle by early afternoon. For the final assault of that bloody day, Bragg could marshal only two relatively fresh brigades from his own corps —not really fresh, for they had been through the carnage of the sunken road. One of them was badly short of ammunition. At Bragg's order they charged, bravely but without much dash, and were repulsed.[13] As they advanced, a part of a regiment from Buell's army appeared in the Federal line. On the previous day one of Buell's divisions had reached the west side of the river. Soon after the battle started Grant ordered it to the field. Its vanguard was just now crossing. Even without the presence of these troops Bragg's attack would have failed. The reports of the brigade commanders told the story: their men were too exhausted to fight.[14]

It was now after six o'clock. From his headquarters at Shiloh church two miles in the rear, Beauregard sent his staff officers to the corps generals with instructions to suspend the attacks and retire to the enemy camps for the night. His reasons for withdrawing, as given in his preliminary report, were that the troops were tired and scattered; darkness was coming on; and the Confederates had substantial possession of the field. In short, Beauregard thought that he had the Federals whipped, that he could do nothing more that day, and that after resting his men he could complete his victory on the morrow.[15]

To the end of his days Beauregard would be criticized and condemned for stopping the attack. It would be said that he let slip the great opportunity for victory in the West: one more assault and

[13] *Battles and Leaders,* I, 590-91; Roman, *Beauregard,* I, 301-304; Jordan and Pryor, *Forrest,* 131-34.
[14] *Official Records,* X, Pt. 1, pp. 551, 555.
[15] *Ibid.,* 386-87.

Grant's army would have been driven into the river and destroyed. Bragg started the criticism, at least officially, when he wrote in his report on April 20 that his troops were starting a final attack with every chance of success when the withdrawal order came. As the years passed, Bragg remembered more and more about the episode, until finally he thought that he had threatened to disobey the order. How Bragg could have imagined, after witnessing what happened to the charge of his two brigades, that he had a chance to seize the Landing defies comprehension. He did not think it two days after the battle. Then he ascribed the Confederate failure to the demoralized and disorganized condition of the troops caused by their want of discipline.[16]

Today Beauregard's decision seems as right as it did to him on the evening of that hard-fought Sunday. He did not know, of course, of the new factor in the battle, the arrival of Buell's troops, that changed the entire situation. Nor, apparently, had he been apprised that the Federal division from Crump's Landing was approaching the field. But he did know that his own men were tired, hungry, and spiritless after thirteen hours of fighting, too exhausted even to cheer when told they had won a victory. He knew that many of the units were scattered, disorganized, and out of control and that the latest attacks had been feebly delivered. These things he had learned from the reports of his aides and other officers; some of them he had seen with his own eyes. As he rode over the rear area of the field he saw groups of men resting on their arms, too weary to move; he saw hordes of stragglers plundering the enemy camps. He saw also the sun going down. He wanted to get his army in hand before darkness. As a matter of fact, with the approach of night, as the reports of the brigade and regimental commanders show, many units were retiring from the line without orders. The withdrawal directive merely recognized an action partially in process of execution. Even with an early start, the disorganization of the Confederate forces was so great that some units did not reach their bivouac until eight o'clock. When all the elements in the situation are weighed, it seems obvious that Beauregard had no recourse but to assemble his army for another attempt the next day.[17]

[16] *Ibid.*, 466–67; Don C. Seitz, *Braxton Bragg* (Columbia, S. C., 1924), 111–13.

[17] Stanley, *Autobiography*, 198; letter of Sergeant A. P. B., April 14, 1862, in New Orleans *Evening Delta*, April 21, 1862, clipping in Hyatt Papers; Roman, *Beauregard*, I, 304–305, 547–50.

That night Beauregard made his headquarters in Sherman's tent near Shiloh church. There came the corps commanders to discuss the events of the day and plan tomorrow's moves. All felt confident that victory had been achieved and that an attack the next day would complete the destruction of the Federal army. Their optimism was confirmed by the receipt of a dispatch from Colonel Ben Hardin Helm, Lincoln's brother-in-law, in northern Alabama that Buell was not marching toward Pittsburg Landing after all but toward Decatur. Captured General Prentiss, who was Jordan's guest and who was having a wonderful time teasing his hosts with predictions of defeat the next day, unwisely said that the report was untrue. They refused to believe him. At Beauregard's direction, Jordan sent a telegram to Richmond announcing the capture of every enemy position and "a complete victory." On the basis of this message, Davis reported to Congress that the Federal army had been practically destroyed.[18]

One Confederate soldier was not so sure the Federals were not being reinforced. Colonel Nathan Bedford Forrest, not yet recognized as a great cavalryman, dressed some of his men in captured Federal coats and sent them into the enemy lines. They reported back that heavy replacements were arriving but that a sudden night attack would push the Federals into the river. Forrest found Hardee and presented his information. The cavalry leader advised an immediate attack or a withdrawal. If the Confederates tried to fight the fresh Federal masses the next day, he said, they would be "whipped like hell." In a rather casual way the corps commander told Forrest to take his intelligence to Beauregard. Forrest was unable to locate the commanding general's headquarters. Once again he sent his scouts to the Federal camps, and again they related that reinforcements were coming in. Once more Forrest sought out Hardee, at two in the morning. This time Hardee told him to return to his regiment and

[18] Roman, *Beauregard,* I, 305; Jordan and Pryor, *Forrest,* 135–36; *Battles and Leaders,* I, 602–603; *Official Records,* X, Pt. 1, pp. 384–85; Richardson (ed.), *Messages and Papers of the Confederacy,* I, 208. Jordan stated, in *Battles and Leaders* (see above), that he received a telegram from Helm in the afternoon and gave it to Beauregard after sunset—that is, after Beauregard had ordered the battle stopped. Beauregard said, in his preliminary report *(Official Records,* above), that he received a message saying Buell had been delayed and would not be able to reach Grant in time to save him. It is possible that two messages about Buell were received and that the one Beauregard mentioned may have come in before the battle ended. In such case, Beauregard may have confused them in his report.

keep a vigilant watch.[19] In such an offhand manner was vital military intelligence often handled in the Civil War.

Forrest's information and his salty analysis of the fate awaiting the Confederates were both correct. That night seventeen thousand of Buell's troops were ferried over the river. With these arrivals, the Crump's Landing division, and the hard core of his own army, Grant had at his disposal on the morning of April 7 at least forty thousand men. Determined to seize the initiative, he launched an attack on the Confederates at daylight. The fighting on the second day was almost an exact reversal of that of the day before. The Confederates were surprised, strategically, because they had expected to be the attackers. During the night and in the early morning hours the Confederate generals had not done too good a job of reorganizing their forces. When the Federals struck, some units were several miles in rear of the first line of encampments. The Confederate line of battle was formed slowly and was not completed until after the Federals had rolled past the Hornet's Nest.

Because of the heavy losses of the previous day and the large number of stragglers who had left the field, Beauregard could put in action only something over twenty thousand troops. From right to left the Confederate line was commanded by Hardee, Breckinridge, Polk, and Bragg. Something of the confusion attending the withdrawal on the preceding night is seen in the fact that Hardee and Bragg had exchanged wings, that Hardee commanded two of Bragg's brigades, and that Bragg directed one of Polk's divisions. Polk arrived on the field late with his other division. As the battle swayed back and forth on a fluid front the Confederate units tended to become more mixed and scattered than on Sunday. Several seem to have been fired on by their own troops. Beauregard noticed one group in a woods who appeared to be clad in white uniforms. At first he thought they were Federals, but he saw they were fighting on the Confederate side. Inquiry developed that they were Louisiana troops. They were equipped with blue coats, and on the day before had been fired into by Confederates. To prevent the repetition of this danger, they had turned their coats inside out.[20]

The impact of the Federal attack forced the Confederates back all along the line. Although the Southern troops resisted stubbornly and

[19] Jordan and Pryor, *Forrest,* 136–37.
[20] Roman, *Beauregard,* I, 316; Basil W. Duke, *Morgan's Cavalry* (New York, 1909), 86.

at points even counterattacked, they could not halt the relentless blue advance.[21] Their failure was not due entirely to inferior numbers or to the lack of a proper reserve. Confederate observers noted that the men seemed to be losing their dash and fire. Even when general officers led them in person to points at the front, they responded feebly. Beauregard himself, on two occasions, seized the colors of slowly advancing regiments and led them forward. When an officer friend reproved him for rashness, he answered, "The order must now be *'follow,'* not *'go'!"* Sometimes a unit, after being placed in line, would stand a short time and then slowly melt away.[22] It was not just that the men were bone-tired after two days of battle; their spirits were close to being broken by the abrupt reversal of fortune, by the sudden snatching away of apparent victory.

Jordan, who had been observing the demeanor of the men, went to Beauregard shortly after two and said, "General, do you not think our troops are very much in the condition of a lump of sugar thoroughly soaked with water, but yet preserving its original shape, though ready to dissolve? Would it not be judicious to get away with what we have?" Beauregard replied, "I intend to withdraw in a few moments." [23]

He too had been studying the soldiers and the situation. Against the fresh, superior Federal forces, the Confederates had no chance of victory. If they remained on the field, they would be pounded to pieces. The only recourse was to get the army away to safety. For an hour Beauregard had been contemplating a withdrawal. Now his mind was made up. Staff officers rode to tell the corps generals to retire, but slowly and in good order. In rear of Shiloh church Beauregard posted a strong rear guard with artillery support. He wanted the Federals to know that although he was leaving, he was doing so with dignity and honor and not in rout and disaster. By four o'clock the Confederates had left the field and were on the road to Corinth.[24]

[21] Roman, *Beauregard*, I, 308–19; *Battles and Leaders*, I, 591–93; Horn, *Army of Tennessee*, 139–42; Dillahunty, *Shiloh*, 16–19; Kenneth P. Williams, *Lincoln Finds a General* (New York, 1952), III, 383–88.

[22] *Official Records*, XI, Pt. 1, p. 402; Seitz, *Bragg*, 113; Roman, *Beauregard*, I, 317; Jordan and Pryor, *Forrest*, 142.

[23] *Battles and Leaders*, I, 603.

[24] Roman, *Beauregard*, I, 318–19; Jordan and Pryor, *Forrest*, 143–46; Johnston, *A. S. Johnston*, 651–53; *Official Records*, X, Pt. 1, p. 388.

No Federals pursued them that day or attacked them that night when they encamped a few miles from the field. Grant's army was in no shape to pursue; it had been too roughly handled. A heavy rain started after dark, making the roads impracticable for artillery the next day. Without supporting artillery, pursuing infantry could easily be checked by a few enemy guns. The next morning Sherman attempted a sort of half-pursuit. The Confederate rearguard turned him back with its cavalry alone.

Even without the presence of harassing Federals, the Confederate withdrawal to Corinth was a grim journey. The weary, discouraged foot soldiers plodded on over the narrow, muddy, almost impassable road; among them jolted the wagons carrying the thousands of groaning wounded. The way of the march was littered with abandoned supplies. Bragg found that few officers were with their men. "The whole road presents the scene of a rout . . . ," he wrote in anger and disgust to Beauregard.[25] The sad job of carrying the wounded to Corinth strained the army's transportation facilities. Shiloh was the first bloody battle of the war. For both sides the casualties were terrific. The Union losses were 1,754 killed, 8,408 wounded, 2,885 captured or missing—a total of 13,047. The Confederate losses totaled 10,697: 1,726 killed, 8,012 wounded, 959 missing.[26]

Of the wounded, probably about five thousand had to be transported in wagons. The scenes that followed their arrival in Corinth were heartrending. Hotels, schools, churches, and homes were converted into hospitals. Many of the wounded were laid out on porches, sidewalks, and the platforms of depots. An appeal for help brought doctors and nurses and students of medicine from all over the surrounding area. They were not enough; medical supplies were short; some of the doctors did not know their business. Eight out of every ten amputations ended in death. Tetanus, erysipelas, and gangrene were rampant. Horrified observers watched a huge pile of amputated limbs in the yard of the Tishomingo Hotel grow ever larger.[27]

Back in Corinth Beauregard radiated satisfaction with the results

[25] Stevenson, *Thirteen Months in the Rebel Army*, 170–71; *Official Records*, X, Pt. 2, p. 400.

[26] D. W. Reed, *The Battle of Shiloh* (Washington, 1909), 23; Thomas L. Livermore, *Numbers and Losses in the Civil War in America, 1861–65* (Boston, 1901), 79–80; *Battles and Leaders*, I, 485, 537–39; Johnston, *A. S. Johnston*, 656.

[27] Wiley, *Johnny Reb*, 263; Horn, *Army of Tennessee*, 148–49; Stevenson, *Thirteen Months in the Rebel Army*, 176–78.

of Shiloh and confidence for the future—if he was adequately rein-forced. In his preliminary report on the battle, he said that the Federal army had been so badly crippled that it was unable to take the field; his own army was more confident than ever of ultimate success.[28] But at the same time he told the government that he feared for the safety of Corinth and asked that the forces defending the South Carolina–Georgia coast be sent to him. Better to lose Charles-ton and Savannah temporarily, he said, than the Mississippi Valley.[29] He was cheered by the impending arrival of Van Dorn from Arkansas. Van Dorn, unable to join Beauregard before Shiloh, was now march-ing to Corinth. Beauregard urged him to hurry. Their combined forces, he wrote, could give the Yankees another whipping. The with-drawal to Corinth had been part of a preconceived plan, he assured Van Dorn; his only regret over Shiloh was that he had not been able to bring off all the supplies he had captured.

Van Dorn took all this gasconade seriously. Believing Beauregard must be flush with materiel, he asked the general to furnish him with some needed arms. Not a whit embarrassed by a request he could not meet, Beauregard answered, "I regret have none; could not remove all I took, but we will take more. Come on." Van Dorn with fourteen thousand troops reached Corinth about April 11, bringing Beauregard's effective total close to fifty thousand.[30]

To the army too Beauregard depicted Shiloh as a victory. In a proclamation announcing Johnston's death, he spoke of the com-manding general as having been killed while leading his columns to triumph. In a congratulatory order to the troops, he said, "Your success had been signal." Only "untoward events" had saved the enemy army from annihilation.[31] The men seemed to believe him. At least they admired him as much as ever. One soldier described for his father a scene when Beauregard rode into their camp a week after the battle. A crowd of soldiers collected around him. In kindly man-ner he asked about their losses and the welfare of their sick. Glimps-ing a wounded man with a bandage about his head, Beauregard rode up to him, extended a hand, and asked, "My brave friend, were you wounded?" Then, realizing he had asked an obvious question, he added, "Never mind, I trust you will soon be well. Before long we

[28] Roman, *Beauregard*, I, 543–44.
[29] *Ibid.*, 568.
[30] *Official Records*, X, Pt. 2, p. 405.
[31] *Ibid.*, X, Pt. 1, p. 397, Pt. 2, pp. 408–409.

will make the Yankees pay up, interest and all. The day of our glory is near." The soldier ended his description by writing: "As he rode away after gracefully bowing to the crowd, a shout such as Napoleon might have heard from the lips of the 'Guard,' went up, 'Hurrah for Beauregard our Chief.' It is strange Pa how we love that little black frenchman, but there is not a man in the army who would not willingly die in following his lead." [32]

The popular verdict on Beauregard was not so unanimously adoring. For the first time his conduct of a battle was widely criticized. Many people thought that on April 6 he should have crushed the Federals with one last attack. His claim that Shiloh was a victory and that the return to Corinth was a planned withdrawal aroused ridicule. A much-quoted newspaper couplet sneered:

> *Here's to Toussaint Beauregard,*
> *Who for the truth has no regard,*
> *In Satan's clutches he will cry,*
> *I've got old Satan, Victori.*

In administration circles in Richmond rumors circulated that during the battle he was lying in a tent—or an ambulance—overcome by melancholia. In one version he was insane and had stayed in his quarters fondling a pheasant. The origin of this tale was that on the first day at Shiloh a soldier had found a pheasant cowering in the brush and had brought it to Beauregard as a present. The general, thinking to give it to a friend in Jackson, directed that it be caged.[33] Like the Confederate hopes of victory, the bird disappeared on the second day.

Shiloh is the most "iffy" battle of the war. Its might-have-beens have fascinated writers. What would have happened if the Confederates had launched their attack on the fifth? What if Johnston had not died? What if Beauregard had made another attack on the sixth? If the Confederates had defeated Grant, would they have smashed Buell and regained the West? Most of the dramatic possibilities of the battle have been exaggerated. If the Confederates had attacked on the fifth, they would have encountered approximately the same size Federal force on that day and the following as

---

[32] E. John Ellis to E. P. Ellis, April 13, 1862, in Ellis Papers.
[33] T. C. De Leon, *Four Years in Rebel Capitals* (Mobile, 1892), 169; Roman, *Beauregard,* I, 344; McElroy, *Davis,* I, 346; Mrs. Chesnut, *Diary From Dixie,* 211; *Battles and Leaders,* I, 346.

they did on the sixth and seventh. One division of Buell's army was on the other side of the Tennessee by midafternoon of the fifth and could have reached the Landing by night. Another could have arrived early the next day.

Only if the Confederates could have made their attack on the fourth, as planned in Beauregard's original order, would they have had a real chance to destroy Grant. On the evening of the sixth Beauregard's cause was lost. Even without Buell's troops, Grant could probably have stopped an attack with the aid of the fresh division from Crump's Landing. But what if a last assault had driven the Federals into the river? The Confederate army would have been so shattered that it could not have followed its success. On the following day, even after a so-called victory, it could muster only some twenty thousand troops. And over the river would have been Buell with twenty-five thousand fresh soldiers. Beauregard could not have advanced for a long time and without reinforcements. Probably he would have had to retire to Corinth to regroup.

In the West Beauregard showed definite improvement as a field commander. The Napoleonic complex, the penchant for grand planning, the tendency to exaggerate the resources available to him—these characteristics were still a part of him but were held in obvious restraint. His battle plan for Shiloh, like the one before Manassas, was whipped up in too short a time. He was yet to learn that a detailed design was not the work of a few hours. The march order from Corinth to the battlefield, while overly optimistic as to the results that could be obtained, was not, as has been sometimes charged, unduly complex. Although his battle arrangement was faulty, it too was innocent of the complexity which had often marred his plans in Virginia. After he took command following Johnston's death, he did all that any general could have done in the circumstances. The withdrawal on the second day was conducted with skill. His one bad mistake was on Sunday night, when he failed to take adequate action to reorganize his army and made no attempt to ascertain the intentions of the enemy. He still tended to overlook an important detail, to assume that the enemy would act as he wanted him to act.

Nevertheless, he gave promise, with continued experience, of developing into a useful field general. The promise was not fulfilled because his career in the field did not continue. Within a few months after Shiloh, Davis removed him from field command and relegated him to the defense of a city under attack from the sea.

CHAPTER TEN

Cock Robin Is Dead

AROUND CORINTH the Confederate defensive line was strong. On a high ridge east of the town the works stretched for three miles from the Memphis and Charleston Railroad on the right to the Mobile and Ohio on the left. From right to left the line was manned by the troops of Hardee, Bragg, and Polk. To the rear and right of Hardee was Van Dorn. Breckinridge's reserve corps was stationed west of Corinth. Even though his position was strong, Beauregard might well have pondered whether either field or permanent fortifications were of much value in the vast Western theater, especially when the enemy controlled the waterways.

Right after the army returned to Corinth, he received the bad news that another supposedly strong point in the Mississippi River defenses had fallen. On April 8 Island No. 10 and its garrison of seven thousand surrendered to the Federals. Its commander, W. W. Mackall, had taken charge late in March, announcing to the officers, "Let me tell you who I am. I am a general made by Beauregard. . . ." After the loss of Island No. 10, Beauregard acted to strengthen the next link in the river chain, Fort Pillow, and directed that works be constructed at Vicksburg.[1] Donelson, Shiloh, Island No. 10—since February the Confederacy had lost over thirty thousand men in the West. The manpower was going fast, and most of it had been lost in attempts to hold fortified places.

Beauregard's line was designed to protect Corinth and its important rail communications against an expected advance of the Federals from Pittsburg Landing. After Shiloh General Halleck, now departmental commander of all Union forces in the West, decided to take the field in person. Leaving his desk in St. Louis, he came to the Landing and took command of the armies of Grant and Buell. From the Mississippi line he brought additional troops freed by the fall of Island No. 10, bringing his total forces to over a hundred

[1] Roman, *Beauregard,* I, 365–67, 384–85; Pollard, *First Year of the War,* 330–32; Beauregard to Harris, April 21, 25, 1862, in Harris Papers.

thousand. Late in April he started for Corinth. New to field command and overly impressed by the surprise which the Federals had suffered at Shiloh, Halleck moved with excessive and unnecessary caution. At the end of each day's march he threw up entrenchments before going into bivouac. It took him approximately the whole month of May to get his army into position before Corinth.

Beauregard knew, of course, of Halleck's advance. He could hardly have failed to note every detail of its crawling onward progress. His first problem was to try to slow or halt Halleck's advance before it neared Corinth. This he tried to do by sending cavalry parties to make raids in Tennessee and Kentucky. He hoped to force Halleck to detach troops to defend his line of communications. His planning was sound enough, but he did not have enough cavalry to bother Halleck.[2] He was also on the alert for a chance to strike a blow at any fraction of Halleck's host that got itself separated from the main army. Early in May he thought he had his chance. One of Halleck's generals, John Pope, advanced at a faster rate than his commander. Aggressive and sometimes rash, Pope pushed his troops forward to Farmington, about four miles east of Corinth, where a swampy area divided him from the nearest Federal forces.

Beauregard formed a plan to trap Pope. While troops from Bragg's corps attacked the enemy in front, Van Dorn was to get on his left flank. In a preattack proclamation to the troops, Beauregard emphasized that for the first time the Confederates were to meet the Federals in strength. "Soldiers, can the result be doubtful?" he asked. "Shall we not drive back into the Tennessee the presumptuous mercenaries collected for our subjugation?"[3]

The results were completely doubtful. The attack in front was delivered on time and successfully, but Van Dorn was unable to get into position. His failure was probably due to Beauregard's lack of exact knowledge of the terrain. Pope retired to safety. Although he had not bagged Pope, Beauregard was fairly satisfied to have driven him back. He realized that an advance by his right might expose his flank on that wing to a counterblow, and he recalled his troops from Farmington to their original line.[4] Later in May Pope advanced again

[2] Roman, *Beauregard*, I, 381, 571–72; Duke, *Morgan's Cavalry*, 92; Cecil F. Holland, *Morgan and His Raiders* (New York, 1943), 95.
[3] *Official Records*, X, Pt. 2, p. 482.
[4] *Ibid.*, VIII, 784–85; Beauregard to Bragg, May 9, 1862, *ibid.*, X, Pt. 2, p. 506; Roman, *Beauregard*, I, 386–87.

to Farmington, and once again Beauregard tried to spring his trap. The outcome was the same disappointment as before. The attack in front was effective, but Van Dorn, although he informed Beauregard that he felt like a wolf and was going to fight like one, could not get his men into action.[5]

As the Federal army approached Corinth, Beauregard considered that he might have to abandon the town. Even without the nearing danger of an enemy attack he did not like it as a base. He once described Corinth as being naturally unhealthful. As a camp site, its greatest deficiency was the lack of an adequate supply of pure water. To secure water, the soldiers dug shallow holes around the camps; these were soon contaminated by refuse. The water smelled so bad that the men held their noses while drinking it. A typhoid-fever epidemic and mass dysentery were the grim results. According to one estimate, as many men died at Corinth in seven weeks during April and May as fell at Shiloh. If Halleck did not drive Beauregard out of Corinth, disease threatened to do so. To increase the general misery, the food furnished by the Commissary Department was insufficient and inferior. Colonel Northrop was up to his old tricks. Beauregard exploded to Richmond in characteristic fashion: "The false views of administration—to say the least—of Colonel Northrop will starve out this army unless I make other arrangements, which I have done." The other arrangements consisted of sending agents to Texas and Arkansas to purchase herds of cattle.[6]

On May 19 Beauregard tried to prepare the government for the eventual evacuation of Corinth. In a letter to General Cooper, he outlined the facts in his situation and the possible moves open to him. Since assuming command at Shiloh, he said, he had received no operational instructions from Richmond. Therefore, he wanted to explain his reasons for holding Corinth at the risk of defeat instead of retiring and drawing the enemy after him. He was maintaining his position because of the town's importance as a railroad center. But, if he had to give it up, his best line of retreat was along the Mobile and Ohio Railroad to Meridian and Montgomery. He would hold Corinth to the last extremity, unless the odds against him were too great

[5] Roman, *Beauregard,* I, 388, 574–77; *Official Records,* X, Pt. 2, pp. 532, 538.

[6] Roman, *Beauregard,* I, 383–84, 572-73; *Official Records,* X, Pt. 1, p. 776; Wiley, *Life of Johnny Reb,* 247; E. John Ellis to E. P. Ellis, April 27, 1862, in Ellis Papers.

or the government wished him to do otherwise. In an indirect fashion, he was asking for a free hand; at the same time he was attempting to protect himself against criticism in Richmond if he had to yield Corinth.

Significantly enough, he communicated with Cooper by letter instead of by telegraph, thus ensuring that he would be free of any immediate binding instructions. His letter did not reach Richmond until about the twenty-sixth. It was answered by Lee, who was serving as Davis' military adviser. Lee expressed disappointment that Beauregard might have to abandon Corinth but approved of the suggested line of retreat.[7] Before Lee's reply could be received, Beauregard was preparing to leave.

On the twenty-fifth he called his corps generals into council. He went over in detail the situation before them. A greatly superior Federal army was closing in on Corinth. From every indication Halleck intended to avoid a direct assault with its attending heavy casualties and take the town by laying siege to it and cutting off its communications. Against such an investment, the Confederates could hold out a long time, but in the end they would have to surrender or retreat under disadvantageous circumstances. The smart thing to do was to retire now. All the generals agreed with this analysis. Hardee was so impressed that he prepared a paper summarizing the results of the deliberations and endorsing the decision. Possibly he did so at Beauregard's request—to give the general another protection against the displeasure of Richmond.

Beauregard told the generals to keep the proposed movement a secret. To deceive the enemy and prevent demoralization among their own troops, they were to spread the rumor that an advance was being planned. Then Beauregard's staff wrote out detailed instructions for each corps commander to follow in the withdrawal. Another conference was held the next day. Carefully Beauregard explained to each general his part in the retirement. He made every one repeat what he was to do and what the others were to do. The time fixed for the evacuation was early on the morning of the twenty-ninth, but delays encountered in moving the supplies forced a postponement of the movement to the following day. At first Beauregard had intended to stop at Baldwin, thirty-five miles to the south. After reaching there,

[7] Beauregard to Cooper, May 19, 1862, in *Official Records,* X, Pt. 2, pp. 529–30; Lee to Beauregard, May 26, 1862, in Roman, *Beauregard,* I, 580–81.

he decided that it would be unsatisfactory as a base and directed that the army continue to Tupelo, fifty-two miles from Corinth. Not until May 28 did he inform Richmond of his purpose. Then he telegraphed Cooper that he was going to Baldwin. "I hope there to be able to beat the enemy in detail," he added.[8]

The evacuation of Corinth was the greatest hoax of the war. Beauregard was a master of hoaxes. When it came to deception, he was like Tom Sawyer; nobody could beat him at throwing in the frills.

Beauregard did not want Halleck to know that the Confederates were leaving; he feared an attack while his army was in march order. To conceal his movement, he employed a set of masterful deceptions. Troops were left behind to keep the campfires burning. Drummers from each brigade stayed to beat reveille at the usual hour. Dummy guns and sentinels were placed where the Federals would be certain to see them. All night an empty train of cars ran back and forth through the town. At frequent intervals it stopped with a loud whistle. Specially detailed troops rushed forth to cheer the arrival of heavy reinforcements. So effective was this device that General Pope reported to Halleck that in the morning he expected to be attacked in force. As the cavalry of the rear guard left Corinth, they removed all road signs and mileposts on the roads leading south. Early the next morning, while the Confederates were marching southward, the Federal army stood cautiously under arms. The smoke from some supplies which Beauregard had burned gave Halleck his first indication that he was watching an abandoned town.[9]

From Corinth the army marched six miles to the Tuscumbia River and halted, ready to fight if pursued. There was no pursuit because Halleck did not discover for a time where Beauregard was going. Slowly the Confederates retired to Baldwin, where again they paused, for several days, to offer battle. From Baldwin Beauregard telegraphed Cooper that the evacuation had been a complete success. On June 9 the army reached Tupelo.[10] Not until it was too late to take up the chase did the Federals find out Beauregard's route of withdrawal. Then some cavalry from Pope's army was sent after the

[8] Roman, *Beauregard,* I, 388–89, 578–86, 395; *Official Records,* X, Pt. 1, pp. 770–71.

[9] Roman, *Beauregard,* I, 390, 582–83, 386–87; E. John Ellis to E. P. Ellis, June 2, 1862, in Ellis Papers.

[10] Beauregard to Cooper, June 3, 1862, in *Official Records,* X, Pt. 1, p. 762; Roman, *Beauregard,* I, 390–91.

Confederates. At one point they captured a few wounded soldiers and a small amount of supplies. Pope's report of this affair occasioned a grotesque misunderstanding. Halleck relayed to Washington news that Pope had seized ten thousand prisoners and fifteen thousand stand of arms. For the remainder of the war Pope would deny that he ever transmitted such a false account, and Halleck would answer that he had received such a report from Pope.

When the story appeared in the Northern and Southern press, Beauregard was naturally concerned. It gave the impression that the retirement had been a rout and that the evacuation represented a defeat. To set the record straight and to apprise the country and the government of the true nature of the withdrawal, he decided to write a public letter to the Mobile *Register*. In this long document, one of his most rhetorical productions, he blistered Pope and Halleck for making false claims. Easily he demonstrated that the number of prisoners and the supplies lost to the enemy were inconsequential. But his real purpose was to prove that the recent movement was not a reverse. "The retreat was conducted with great order and precision, doing much credit to the officers and men under my orders," he said, "and must be looked upon, in every respect, by the country as equivalent to a brilliant victory." [11]

In administration circles, the retreat was viewed as anything but a victory. Even before the evacuation, the friends of Davis had been bitterly critical of Beauregard's course since Shiloh. They sneered that he had done nothing but issue proclamations while the Federals built up their strength for an advance. It was said by some, including Cabinet members, that although the government had increased his army to a hundred thousand men he had not made one move to recover the territory lost in the West. Mary Boykin Chesnut, an intimate of Mrs. Davis, writing in her caustic diary of Beauregard and the aftermath of Shiloh, observed prophetically, "Cock robin is as dead as he ever will be now!" Davis himself was not above flinging a gibe. Writing to his wife right after the withdrawal had begun, he said that if Mississippi troops not lying in camp or retreating with Beauregard were at home they could keep a section of the Mississippi

[11] Pollard, *Lost Cause*, 322–23; Frank Moore (ed.), *The Rebellion Record* . . . (New York, 1864–68), V (1866), 221–22.

River open to the Confederacy.[12] The President may have been thinking of the inevitable collateral results of the retreat to Tupelo. With Corinth lost, Fort Pillow was vulnerable to a flanking movement; on June 1, at Beauregard's instructions, it was abandoned. A little later Memphis surrendered to the Federal navy. The Union gunboats could run all the way down to Vicksburg.

After the withdrawal had been completed, the undercover sniping changed to open attack. The administration was ready to move in on Beauregard. On June 12 Cooper telegraphed Beauregard: "The President has been expecting a communication explaining your last movement. It has not yet arrived." The general replied: "Have had no time to write report. Busy organizing and preparing for battle if pursued. . . . Retreat was a most brilliant and successful one." [13] The next day he decided it would be wise to take enough time to write a report. In this document, he detailed his reasons for evacuating and described how the retreat had been conducted. He had foiled the plans of the Federals, he claimed; they would find Corinth a barren locality and would have to abandon it.[14] His arguments failed to impress Davis. The President told his wife that Beauregard was one of those who could walk only when close to the ground; the general had been placed too high for his mental strength.[15]

Davis' next move was to send a special aide, Colonel W. P. Johnston, Albert Sidney's son, to inspect Beauregard's army and to propound to the general a series of searching questions concerning his recent movements. These questions, which Davis put in writing, were uniformly hostile in nature; they were a merciless inquisition and intended as such. Paraphrased, they ran as follows:

1. What were the purposes of the retreat from Corinth?

2. What were Beauregard's plans for future operations, especially for an offensive?

3. Why had Beauregard not occupied a stronger line around Corinth?

[12] Mrs. Chesnut, *Diary From Dixie,* 220, 225; Benjamin to Slidell, July 19, 1862, in Richardson (ed.), *Messages and Papers of the Confederacy,* I, 263–64; manuscript diary of Stephen R. Mallory, entry of June 21, 1862, typed copy in Southern Historical Collection, University of North Carolina Library, hereinafter cited as Mallory Diary; Davis to Mrs. Davis, June 3, 1862, in Rowland (ed.), *Jefferson Davis,* V, 266.

[13] *Official Records,* XVII, Pt. 2, pp. 594–95.

[14] *Ibid.,* X, Pt. 1, pp. 762–65.

[15] Rowland (ed.), *Jefferson Davis,* V, 277–78.

4. What was the cause of the sickness at Corinth, and were health conditions any better at the new location?

5. Why had Beauregard not cut the Federal line of communications and retaken Nashville?

6. What means were employed to hold the Mississippi after the fall of Island No. 10 and to defend Memphis?

7. What loss of troops and supplies occurred during the withdrawal?[16]

While Colonel Johnston was traveling to the West, Davis was working on a scheme to lay Beauregard on the shelf. From Governor Pickens of South Carolina the President received a complaint that the commander of the coastal defenses, General John C. Pemberton, was unsatisfactory and had no knowledge of the country. Eagerly Davis asked if Pickens could suggest a competent officer who had the required knowledge. Back came the reply Davis must have wanted —Beauregard was the man. Davis informed the governor that Beauregard's health was bad and that the general might welcome a lighter assignment. He urged Pickens to invite Beauregard to come to Charleston.[17] The governor then wrote to Beauregard that he was sorry to hear of his illness, that sea air would be good for him, and that he was needed at Charleston. The President would approve the transfer, Pickens added. Beauregard, who may or may not have seen through the plot, answered: "Would be happy to do so but my presence absolutely required here at present. My health still bad. No doubt sea-air would restore it, but have no time to restore it."[18]

Beauregard's health was indeed bad. His throat ailment continued to give him trouble, and his physical system was generally run down. For months his medical officers had been urging him to take a rest. Now that the army was at Tupelo and no immediate operations were in prospect, they insisted that he go off for a brief period of relaxation. Beauregard agreed to do as they wished. On June 14 they gave him a medical certificate of disability.[19] Although he had just told Pickens that his presence with the army was vital, he decided to go to Bladon Springs, a resort north of Mobile, for a week or ten days. In his absence, Bragg was to command the army. Beauregard decided to leave his command without informing the government of his reasons

[16] *Official Records,* X, Pt. 1, p. 786.
[17] *Ibid.,* LIII, 247; Rowland (ed.), *Jefferson Davis,* V, 274.
[18] Roman, *Beauregard,* I, 591.
[19] *Ibid.,* 403.

and without securing official approval. His action was strange and ill-advised. Here was the commander of the largest field army in the West, whose health was so bad that temporarily he could not perform his duties, proposing to give up his command and to designate another officer as his successor, and all this without a word of explanation to his superiors. Neither step should have been taken until after the fullest conference with Richmond. He was playing directly into the President's hands.

Davis found out about Beauregard's plans by himself violating a rule of military etiquette. On the fourteenth, the day Beauregard received his medical certificate, Davis, by-passing Beauregard, telegraphed Bragg to assume temporary command of the forces around Jackson, Mississippi. Bragg, aware of the arrangements Beauregard was making, referred the telegram to his superior. Beauregard, who must have resented the way in which Davis had addressed his subordinate directly, then wired Cooper that Bragg could not be spared. Bragg would have to command the army while he was absent on sick leave, he explained. This was the first intimation the government had of his purpose. Even now he did not say how long he would be gone or where he was going. "I desire to be back here to retake the offensive as soon as our forces shall have been sufficiently reorganized," he said. "I must have a short rest." [20]

Apparently he realized that his dispatch was incomplete as an explanation, for the next day he wrote Cooper a letter. After repeating his reasons for leaving, he said that he would depart the next day for Bladon Springs, where he would spend a week or ten days. Nowhere in the letter did he even hint that he was asking permission to go; he simply told the government what his schedule was. On the seventeenth he left for Mobile. Bragg wired Richmond that Beauregard had gone and asked for instructions. Davis jumped at the news. Back came a telegram from the President appointing Bragg to the permanent command of the Western department. [21]

Davis took the position then and later that Beauregard had left his command under improper circumstances, that he had, in effect, deserted his post. Before the President removed Beauregard, he discussed the matter with the Cabinet. The members received the im-

[20] Rowland (ed.), *Jefferson Davis*, V, 279; Beauregard to Cooper, June 14, 1862, in *Official Records*, XVII, Pt. 2, p. 599.
[21] Beauregard to Cooper, June 15, 1862, in Roman, *Beauregard*, I, 404–405; Davis to Bragg, June 20, 1862, in Rowland (ed.), *Jefferson Davis*, V, 283.

pression that Beauregard had retreated from Corinth without notice and had abandoned his army without permission; one of them decided that the general's mind had given way under the strain of responsibility. Davis summarized his feelings in a letter to a general who later in 1862 asked him to restore Beauregard to the Western command: "Beauregard was tried as commander of the Army of the West and left it without leave when the troops were demoralized and the country he was sent to protect was threatened with conquest." [22] In a technical sense, the President's accusation was accurate. Beauregard did leave his army without securing official permission. The government, however, could have stopped him before he started. His telegram of the fourteenth to Cooper was received in Richmond the next day, two days before he left, although Davis may not have seen it until the eighteenth.[23] If Beauregard deserted his post, the administration let him do it.

Beauregard first learned of his removal when he reached Mobile. There he received a telegram from Bragg communicating the news. "I envy you," Bragg wrote, "and am almost in despair." Beauregard replied, "I cannot congratulate you, but am happy for the change." He offered Bragg the temporary use of his staff. Immediately after he heard from Bragg, a curt notice from the War Department arrived announcing the change in command. Beauregard's only response was to send his medical certificate to General Cooper with a statement that he would be ready to resume active duty whenever ordered.[24]

In Mobile Colonel Johnston finally caught up with Beauregard. The colonel had been to Tupelo and inspected the army. He saw Beauregard before the general knew he had been dismissed. Although Beauregard did not hide his displeasure at Johnston's instructions, he answered the questions fully and frankly. His replies to the seven queries were as follows:

1. He had retreated from Corinth because of the sickness of the troops and the approach of the Federals, whom he hoped to attack after drawing them on.

2. He would go over to the offensive if the Federals divided their forces or he could feint them into so doing.

[22] Mallory Diary, June 21, 1862; Rowland (ed.), *Jefferson Davis*, V, 284; Davis to Kirby Smith, October 29, 1862, in Kirby Smith Papers.
[23] Rowland (ed.), *Jefferson Davis*, V, 282.
[24] Roman, *Beauregard*, I, 408–409.

3. The line around Corinth was as strong as any that could have been chosen.

4. The bad health of the army was due primarily to bad water; conditions were now improved.

5. If it had been possible to cut the enemy communications, he would have done it; "I shall never be accused of being too slow in taking the offensive or in carrying the war into Africa. . . ."

6. After the fall of Island No. 10, Fort Pillow had been strengthened; when the latter place and Corinth were evacuated, Memphis could not be held.

7. The losses of men and supplies in the retreat were small.

Beauregard, sensing the hostility back of the questions, asked Johnston the purpose of his mission. If Davis questioned the propriety of the withdrawal, said Beauregard, he would ask for a court of inquiry. Johnston replied that he had come only to gather information for the President. The colonel was impressed by Beauregard's answers. In his report to Davis he was almost wholly favorable to Beauregard. He said that the army at Tupelo was in good shape, and he justified completely the evacuation of Corinth. His defense came too late to save Beauregard. The President had made his decision without waiting for the information of his agent.[25]

Beauregard spent the rest of the summer in Mobile and Bladon Springs. In Mobile he was wined and dined by the best families. He found much pleasure in the company of Augusta Evans, author of sentimental novels and the literary light of the town, "whom it would not do for me to see too often," he wrote a friend, "for I might forget 'home and country' in their hour of need and distress." Of her *Beulah,* he said that "many and many pages were read through a flow of tears." [26] He presented her with his pen, with which he had written all of his orders and reports since Sumter. She replied to one of his letters with an epistle of over two thousand words. They corresponded during the rest of the war and for years after its close.[27]

[25] Arthur M. Shaw, *William Preston Johnston* (Baton Rouge, 1943), 73; *Official Records,* X, Pt. 1, pp. 774–86.

[26] Beauregard to H. H. Dawson, July 15, 1862, in Beauregard Papers (Library of Congress), Letterbook, Official Personal Letters, March 8, 1861—March 31, 1863.

[27] Beauregard to Augusta J. Evans, July 24, August 22, 1862, *ibid.,* Letterbook, Private Letters, June 30, 1862—February 9, 1863; William Perry Fidler, *Augusta Evans Wilson, 1835–1909* (University, Ala., 1951), 94–96.

Beauregard devoted most of his time to answering letters from sympathizers and scheming to get restored to active duty. From Tupelo, Jordan sent news that fanned his wrath against Davis. According to the chief of staff, the President's friends were spreading rumors that Beauregard was responsible for the failure to achieve victory at Shiloh and that he had been removed because he had applied for a four months leave. Jordan predicted that when Beauregard reported for duty he would be exiled to a small command like Charleston.[28]

The general replied to Jordan with a letter that revealed how deeply the iron had been driven into his soul. It is surely one of the most extraordinary communications ever penned by a field commander about his civil superior. In the voluminous literature of Davis denunciations it ranks high. Prudently he signed it "G. T. Buenavista":

> I believe you are right in your suppositions relative to the order relieving me of the command of the Department, but I shall make no effort to resume it. If the country be satisfied to have me laid on the shelf by a man who is either demented or a traitor to his high trust—well, let it be so. I require rest & will endeavor meanwhile by study and reflection to fit myself better for the darkest hours of our trial, which I foresee are yet to come. As to my reputation, if it can suffer by any thing that living specimen of gall & hatred, can do—why it is not then worth preserving—and as to glory, you know what Byron and myself think on that subject. I am annoyed to death now, by having everybody looking at me, wherever I go, like a wild beast. . . .
>
> My consolation is, that the difference between "that Individual" and myself is—that, if he were to die to-day, the whole country would rejoice at it, whereas, I believe, if the same thing were to happen to me, they would regret it.

He concluded with a revealing critique of Lee's recent brilliant campaign which had driven the Federals from before Richmond. Lee had done all right, Beauregard conceded, but he would have accomplished more if he had not violated the rules of war by dividing his forces. "I would have attacked differently," said Beauregard.[29]

[28] Jordan to Beauregard, July 7, 1862, in *Official Records,* XVII, Pt. 2, pp. 640–41.
[29] Beauregard to Jordan, July 12, 1862, in Beauregard Papers (Duke University).

Much of Beauregard's correspondence was with anti-Davis editors, who were using his removal as an excuse to attack the administration. He advised one of them, who had sent him some clippings, to moderate his criticisms; it was all right to denounce Davis but too violent a condemnation would lose its effect.[30] He became disturbed, however, when some of his press supporters charged that Bragg had connived at his removal. He admired Bragg and refused to believe that the latter was his enemy. In a private letter to the editors of a Mobile paper, which had denied that there was hostility between him and his successor, he said that Bragg was a true friend and a fine officer; he was glad that the Western command had fallen into such capable hands. Bragg wrote a letter to the same journal claiming that he had done nothing to displace Beauregard. Displaying an utter lack of tact or great cunning, Bragg said that he regretted Beauregard was physically incapable of exercising command. Poor Beauregard, said Bragg, he had seen him become "an old man" in the space of a year.[31]

Bragg's course at this time is hard to follow. Nothing in the records indicates that he intrigued to get Beauregard dismissed. He professed great admiration and friendship for Beauregard. When he devised a plan of operations for his army, he sent it to Beauregard for comment and revision. Yet at the same time he sent Davis accounts of the attacks being made on him by Beauregard's supporters and pictured himself as being smeared because he was known to be a personal friend of Davis.[32] Maybe Bragg realized that he was caught in the middle of a tough fight and was trying to stand in with both sides.

In conducting his press campaign, Beauregard was especially alert to repel charges that he had made any mistakes in the West. He seemed to think that if he was to get his command back his record must stand before the public as spotless. On one occasion he noticed a story in a Savannah paper to the effect that Beauregard had thrown away a great opportunity at Shiloh and had been deceived by General Prentiss about Buell's coming. He sat down and wrote a reply for Jordan to send to the editor. The article stated that its author

[30] Beauregard to H. H. Dawson, July 15, 1862, in Beauregard Papers (Library of Congress), Letterbook, Official Personal Letters, March 8, 1861—March 31, 1863.
[31] Roman, *Beauregard*, I, 592–93.
[32] *Ibid.*, 593–94; Rowland (ed.), *Jefferson Davis*, V, 312.

was a staff officer with Beauregard and knew all that had happened at Shiloh. "Genl Beauregard whose boldness of enterprise & execution is proverbial in his army" had acted prudently in stopping the attack on April 6, wrote Beauregard, and continued with a glowing if not quite accurate account of his conduct at Shiloh.[33] Jordan revised the document and sent it to the Savannah journal. He wrote Beauregard that some members of Bragg's staff were intriguing to damage him and that he was sending a true history of the Western campaign to Edward A. Pollard, editor of the Richmond *Examiner* and a sworn foe of Davis.[34]

As Beauregard's health improved, he nourished hopes of returning to the field and confounding his enemies with a great victory. He told Jordan that he would make his next battle "the most brilliant of the war."[35] Despite everything that had happened, he seemed to think that he would be restored to the Western command. "I hope to do something shortly by taking the offensive with a well-organized army," he confided to a friend.[36] Late in August, his brother-in-law in Congress, Charles Villeré, telegraphed that for "patent reasons" the general's friends wanted him to report for duty immediately. From Bladon Springs Beauregard informed the War Department on the twenty-fifth that he was recovered and ready for an assignment. He wrote Villeré that he would go to Mobile and await his orders. He wanted the Western command, he told Villeré; if he got his army back he had a plan ready by which he expected to regain the Mississippi from Vicksburg to Fort Pillow and to recover Tennessee and most of Kentucky.[37]

The administration had no intention of restoring Beauregard to

[33] This document, undated, is in the Beauregard Papers (Library of Congress), Letterbook, Private Letters, June 30, 1862—February 9, 1863. It was written in July or early in August. Jordan sent it to the Savannah *Republican* on August 8: *Southern Historical Society Papers,* VIII (1880), 415–17.

[34] *Official Records,* XVII, Pt. 2, pp. 679–80.

[35] Beauregard to Jordan, July 12, 1862, in Beauregard Papers (Duke University); Beauregard to Cooper, July 17, 1862, in Beauregard Papers (University of Texas).

[36] Beauregard to J. M. Huger, August 2, 1862, in *Official Records,* XV, 793–94; Beauregard to W. E. Martin, August 3, in Moore (ed.), *Rebellion Record,* VIII (1867), 36.

[37] Villeré to Beauregard, August 21, 1862, and Beauregard to Villeré, August 25, 1862, in Beauregard Papers (Library of Congress), Letterbook, Telegrams and Letters, September, 1862—April, 1864; Beauregard to Villeré, August 27, in War Department Collection of Confederate Records.

his former command or even of assigning him to field duty anywhere. On August 29 orders were drawn appointing him to command the Department of South Carolina and Georgia, with headquarters in Charleston.[38] Because these instructions were mailed to him at Bladon and he had gone to Mobile, they did not reach him for several days. Villeré, however, found out about them immediately. On September 1 he wired Beauregard asking if the general would prefer the trans-Mississippi command to Charleston. This was Beauregard's first intimation that he was not to return to his army. In a sick rage he telegraphed Villeré: "If the country is willing I should be put on the shelf thro' interested motives, I will submit until our future reverses will compel the Govt to put me on duty. I scorn its' motives & present action." The next day, more resigned but still bitter, he made his choice. He informed Villeré: "Am tired of forming armies for others to fight with—hence I prefer Charleston." [39] Even now he could not quite believe that he would be kept from his army for any lengthy period. He urged Villeré to stir up the delegations of the Western states to demand of Davis that he be returned to the West.[40]

Sadly he sent to Bragg and Cooper his plan for an offensive which he had mentioned to Villeré. It was the plan he would have executed, he said, had the President ordered him back to the army he had collected and organized. His design called for two forward thrusts, one through west Tennessee to recapture Fort Pillow and another through east Tennessee to seize Louisville and Cincinnati. Like most of his schemes, it was good in theory but too ambitious for the available resources of manpower.[41] On September 11 he left for Charleston, which he reached on the fifteenth. Governor Pickens and the Charlestonians gave him a warm welcome.[42]

Beauregard's friends in Congress acted on his suggestion to Villeré that the Western states bring pressure on Davis to restore his command. Fifty-nine members signed a petition asking Davis to return him to the West.[43] Two Louisiana Congressmen presented it to the

[38] Official Records, XIV, 601.

[39] Villeré to Beauregard, September 1, 1862, in Roman, Beauregard, II, 1; Beauregard to Villeré, September 1, 2, in War Department Collection of Confederate Records.

[40] Beauregard to Villeré, September 3, 1862, in Beauregard Papers (Library of Congress), Letterbook, Private Letters, June 30, 1862—February 9, 1863.

[41] Roman, Beauregard, I, 413–15; Official Records, XVI, Pt. 2, pp. 544–45.

[42] Roman, Beauregard, II, 2, 435; F. W. Pickens to Davis, September 30, 1862, in F. W. Pickens Papers (Duke University Library).

President on September 13. Davis read the entire document, including the signatures, aloud. Then he sent for the official correspondence relating to Beauregard's removal and read it to the Congressmen. Beauregard had left his army without permission, Davis said angrily; the general should have stayed at his post even if he had to be carried around in a litter. The President ended the interview by saying, "If the whole world were to ask me to restore General Beauregard to the command which I have already given to General Bragg, I would refuse it." [44]

Beauregard really drank the dregs when he learned he would have to stay at Charleston. He believed that his record and his ability entitled him to command one of the two great armies of the Confederacy, which meant that he ranked himself with Lee. His hatred of Davis was as violent as that of the President for him. In a letter to a friend he said: "The barking of Mr. Davis' little man Friday [Benjamin] & of his pack of other curs does not trouble me much. Having no ambitious aspirations, I look upon their futile efforts at decrying me with supreme contempt. . . . When I say I have no ambitious aspirations, I am wrong; I have one, & one only: to deserve at the hands of my countrymen Chevalier Bayard's proud motto 'Sans peur et sans reproche.' " [45]

[43] Roman, *Beauregard*, I, 415–17; the petition, dated September 13, 1862, is in the Davis Papers (Duke University).

[44] Roman, *Beauregard*, I, 417–19; Villeré to Beauregard, September 15, 1862, in Beauregard Papers (Duke University); Edward A. Pollard, *Life of Jefferson Davis* . . . (Philadelphia, 1869), 314–15.

[45] Beauregard to J. R. Randall, October 5, 1862, in Beauregard Papers (Library of Congress), Letterbook, Private Letters, June 30, 1862—February 9, 1863.

Chapter Eleven

Return to Charleston

BEAUREGARD arrived in Charleston on September 15. Before formally assuming command, he inspected the defenses of his department. With his predecessor, General John C. Pemberton, he spent a week examining the works from Charleston to Savannah. Not until the twenty-fourth did he announce his assignment to command. Then he issued a characteristic rhetorical proclamation in which he said he intended to rely on the bravery of his troops to sustain him. Apparently he expected little help from the administration.[1]

Beauregard did not like many of the defense arrangements which Pemberton had made, and he so informed the War Department. Forts Moultrie and Sumter he found to be in good shape but needing some heavier guns. The batteries and works on Sullivan's and Morris islands were incomplete and poorly arranged. The Confederate line on James Island was too long and would have to be shortened. He told the government that he would need more guns, material to build boom obstructions in the harbor, and several gunboats. And of course he thought he should be reinforced. In his command were approximately twenty thousand men, of whom over twelve thousand were in South Carolina and the rest in Georgia. He and Pemberton agreed that the force should be doubled. In essence, Beauregard's plan for the defense of Charleston called for the building and arming of an extensive line that would prevent the Federals from entering Charleston by sea or land.[2]

That the Federals would try to enter was certain. Charleston was high on their list of places wanted. Not only was the city a hated symbol of rebellion to the North; it was one of the biggest loopholes in the Federal blockade of the Atlantic coast. Vessels carrying sup-

---

[1] *Official Records,* XIV, 608–609.

[2] *Ibid.,* 609–12, 615; Roman, *Beauregard,* II, 4–6, 436–39; *Battles and Leaders,* IV, 2–6.

plies in and cotton out plied the harbor almost with the regularity of ferryboats. To operate against Charleston the Federals had a good base. Early in the war they had captured Port Royal, a point off the coast halfway between Charleston and Savannah.

Two modes of attack were open to them. They could throw a combined land and sea attack at one of the islands south of the town and seek to reach Charleston by the back door. Indeed, they had tried this earlier in 1862, putting a force ashore on James Island. The Confederates crushed the invaders before they could push on toward the town. Or, the Federals could send into the harbor their new ironclad ships, deemed by many to be invincible, and try to demolish Sumter and the other inner works with naval fire. If the ships could reduce the forts, Charleston would have to surrender and the port would be closed to blockade runners.[3] This was the plan of attack favored by the Northern Naval Department.

Beauregard thought the Federals would try first to break into the harbor. Soon after he assumed command he called into conference his principal officers and also the naval officers assigned to Charleston. With them he discussed the best defenses to stop the ironclads when they came. Some of the officers thought that a boom of iron or linked logs would constitute a barrier the ships could not break. Beauregard believed a boom might hold up the ships temporarily, but he had little faith that it could keep them out of the harbor. Whatever his defects as a field commander, he was a fine engineer. He saw immediately that the only way to beat back the ironclads was with superior, concentrated firepower. So immediately he began to bombard the government with requests for more and heavier guns, including rifled pieces. In one extremely positive dispatch he said he wanted to increase the armament in the harbor "to the greatest possible extent, as soon as practicable, in all possible ways." Probably to his surprise, the government filled most of his requisitions. He was further surprised but not pleased when his command was extended to include part of the Florida coast. If the government were going to give him more territory to guard, he complained, it ought to give him more men.[4]

Another defensive device which Beauregard thought would be effective was the use of mines or, as they were called in the Civil

[3] *Official Records*, XIV, 614–16, 621–23; Roman, *Beauregard*, II, 10–14, 439–40, 442.

[4] *Official Records*, XIV, 630–31.

War, torpedoes. Across the channel between Moultrie and Sumter the Confederates stretched an intricate rope obstruction. Its primary purpose was to foul the screw propellers of the enemy ships. A few hundred yards in front of it two lines of torpedoes were planted. At low tide the torpedoes floated just below the surface. Each one was loaded with one hundred pounds of powder and was equipped with an automatic fuse invented by Captain Francis D. Lee of Beauregard's staff. When the fuse came into contact with a hard object, such as the side of a ship, the concussion was supposed to ignite the torpedo.[5]

Captain Lee also devised what he and Beauregard called a torpedo-ram. This was a small, swift boat with a pole projecting from its bow under water; at the end of the pole was a torpedo. The idea was for the ram to sneak up on an ironclad, presumably at night, and strike the pole into the vulnerable part of the ship below the water line. On the basis of an experiment that Lee conducted against the hulk of an unfinished gunboat, Beauregard was enthusiastically convinced the rams were practical. He believed they would revolutionize naval warfare. He sent Lee to Richmond to urge the government to build several. With six, he promised, he could hold Charleston against any naval force the Federals could mount. In Richmond Lee's invention got snarled in bureacratic red tape. The Naval Department doubted that it could build vessels for the army. Perhaps there was a feeling that Beauregard had not tested the rams sufficiently—that crazy Frenchman with another crazy idea. Very obviously he had not thought out what would happen to the men in a ram after an explosion at such close range. Their fate would have to await a later and real demonstration.[6]

The attack that Beauregard was preparing for did not come. The Federals were not yet ready. Although Beauregard kept busy with his booms and torpedoes and frequent inspections of the defenses all the way down to Savannah, he had time to think about the larger strategy of the war. Now his fertile mind turned to political expedients that might bring victory. It would be good propaganda, he believed, for the Confederates, in all official papers, to refer to the Federals as abolitionists. He called them that in every dispatch, and

[5] Beauregard, in *Annals of the War,* 514–16.
[6] *Ibid.,* 516; Roman, *Beauregard,* II, 21, 445–46, 454–55; *Official Records,* XIV, 636–37.

urged the government to "proclaim the Black Flag." [7] In the fall Bragg took Beauregard's former army on an offensive into Kentucky. Observing the movement of his successor, the general had another idea.

If Bragg could win and stand on the line of the Ohio River, the Western states of the North might be willing to make peace. Immediately he dashed off identical letters to Congressman Miles and to the governors of South Carolina, Georgia, and Florida: Pickens, Joseph Brown, and John Milton. Without mentioning Bragg's campaign, he proposed that the Southern governors offer to meet with those of the West under a flag of truce at Memphis to decide on a peace treaty to be submitted to both governments. The governors thought the scheme might have possibilities, but they wondered about the propriety of their acting as peacemakers. Wasn't the national government supposed to have something to do with such a matter? Miles frankly told the general that the governors could effect nothing.[8] Beauregard, however, was convinced that he had hit on a practical plan. He assured Brown and the others that he had intended that the conference be held only with the approval of the Confederate government. Now was the time to divide and conquer the enemy, he urged. With Southern resources dwindling, this might be the last occasion on which the Confederacy would be in a position to offer peace. ". . . I place as much faith in *diplomacy* to end a war as in drawn battles . . . ," he wrote.[9]

The more the governors pondered Beauregard's plan the less they liked it. They could not see how it could be practically carried out. Then came news that ended the whole matter. Bragg failed in Kentucky and had to retire to Tennessee. Even Beauregard had to admit that without a Confederate army in Kentucky his scheme had little chance of success. All that he could advocate now was that the governors issue a joint address to the people of the West urging them to cut loose from the Union and get out of the war.[10] This was an

[7] *Official Records*, XVI, Pt. 1, p. 711; *ibid.*, Ser. 2, IV, 916.

[8] Roman, *Beauregard*, II, 30, 450–51.

[9] Beauregard to Brown, October 31, 1862, in Beauregard Papers (Library of Congress), Letterbook, Private Letters, June 30, 1862—February 9, 1863.

[10] *Official Records*, XIV, 667; Beauregard to John Milton, November 11, 1862, in MS. Journal of John Milton (Florida Historical Society, St. Augustine). The officials of the Florida Historical Society kindly furnished me with typed copies of Beauregard items in the Milton Journal.

idea that he would return to several times later. At any favorable turn in the war, he thought, the government should press the West to form a separate confederacy and enter into an alliance with the Confederacy, which should guarantee to the West free navigation of the Mississippi.[11].

With the basic features of Beauregard's peace plan nothing was wrong. Had Bragg gone to the Ohio, it would have been a good propaganda move for the government to wave the olive branch. Beauregard's thinking on the subject showed mental growth. He had come to realize that war is never wholly military but is also partly political and that the Confederacy might not be able to win a military decision. The defect in his proposal was the fantastic notion of having it executed by the governors—the same fault that plagued his military planning. His bold notion of by-passing the central government could not have raised him in favor at Richmond.

Neither did the collapse of Bragg's offensive help him with the administration. The anti-Davis party seized the opportunity to level an attack on the President. Had he not removed Beauregard, their press charged, success instead of failure would have resulted in the West. In Richmond it was whispered that if Bragg had used the plan of operations Beauregard gave him he would have captured Cincinnati. It was also rumored that the government was refusing to give Beauregard certain supplies at Charleston. The general might rise again, people said, but he was just too popular to suit the administration.[12]

By coincidence Beauregard did not get at this time some guns he had been counting on. When he learned that the War Department was sending them elsewhere, he protested to Miles. The government ought to realize, he said, that Charleston was the country's only important center of communication with Europe. He had also on order two seven-inch rifled guns. The Naval Department asked for these for use at Mobile. The question of their disposition was laid before Davis, who decided in favor of the navy. Again Beauregard protested without changing the decision.[13] He was in a bitter mood as the year ended. In a letter to Miles he said that he was not being

[11] Beauregard to Miles, January 5, 1863, in *Official Records*, LIII, 270.

[12] Richmond *Whig*, October 31, November 22, 1862, quoted in Ellsworth Eliot, Jr., *West Point in the Confederacy* (New York, 1941), 162, 183; Jones, *Rebel War Clerk's Diary*, I, 175–76.

[13] Roman, *Beauregard*, II, 39, 42, 255; *Official Records*, XIV, 689.

supported properly, for which he was inclined to blame his old enemy, Northrop. The future of the Confederacy looked dark. The
South lacked good leadership, civil and military. Lee was doing fairly
well, Beauregard admitted, but Stonewall Jackson was really a
greater general.[14]

Beauregard never had to complain that Charleston did not appreciate him. Then as always he was the idol of the city. As people saw
the confident, stocky figure bustling along the Battery or visiting the
forts, they felt a sense of security.[15] Charleston was in a gay mood
that winter. Parties, picnics, and dances were the order of the day
and of the night. The garrisons of Sumter and Moultrie vied in stag-
ing dress parades for the townspeople and their guests. These demonstrations would be followed by a dinner and dance. At every affair
Beauregard, grave and courtly, was the center of attraction, with the
ladies fluttering all about him.[16]

From his female admirers afar he received his usual quota of letters. He corresponded with several women he had met during the
summer at Mobile, which he called "the city of beauties." One of
them wrote him an arch note in which she referred to his sons as
"the busy B's" and to the general as "the king B of the hive." In
reply, Beauregard, speaking for the king, said: "Rest assured that he
will never forget *where* the prettiest & sweetest flowers are to be
found for the honey of his hive." [17] To Miss Augusta Evans he wrote
frequently and always seriously. She told him that she was going to
write a novel about the war and asked him for material about the
battle of Manassas. He sent her a copy of his report, and in a long
letter described his plans and his feelings during the battle.[18]

[14] Beauregard to Miles, December 5, 1862, in Beauregard Papers (Library
of Congress), Letterbook, Private Letters, June 30, 1862—February 9, 1863.

[15] Harriott Middleton to Susan M. Middleton, October 14, 1862, in Mid-
dleton Papers of the Cheves Collection (South Carolina Historical Society,
Charleston); Mrs. Charles M. Cheves to her children, undated, probably
November, *ibid.*

[16] Harriott Middleton to Susan M. Middleton, December 14, 1862, and
Alice Middleton to Harriott Middleton, December 10, 1862, *ibid.; Battles and
Leaders,* IV, 23; Parker, *Recollections,* 307; unsigned article in *Land We
Love,* VI (1869), 212–14.

[17] Beauregard to Mrs. Annie Scott, January 18, 1863, in Beauregard Papers
(Library of Congress), Letterbook, Private Letters, June 30, 1862—February
7, 1863.

[18] Beauregard to Augusta J. Evans, March 24, 1863, in *Official Records,*
LI, Pt. 2, pp. 688–89; Fidler, *Augusta Evans Wilson,* 105–10.

Not all was play with Beauregard that winter. He was planning for the attack that would inevitably come. His son, René, serving on his staff, shared rooms with his father. He would remember later that often he awoke at night to see a light burning in the general's room and Beauregard at work preparing notes to guide his activities the next day. Sometimes he worked in bed. Under his pillow he kept a pencil and a pad of paper so that he could jot down ideas that came to him after he had retired.[19] During these months of measured gaiety and leisurely labor, he received one disturbing piece of news. He learned that his wife in Federal-occupied New Orleans was seriously ill. Ironically, he was informed of this by General Benjamin F. Butler, the Federal commander in New Orleans, whom Beauregard, in common with other Southerners, had denounced as a barbarian for his administration of the captured city. Butler sent the general's brother-in-law and sister, Mr. and Mrs. R. S. Proctor, to Charleston with a letter of sympathy and an offer of a pass and a safeguard if Beauregard wanted to visit his wife and return to Charleston.[20] As far as the records show, Beauregard took no notice of Butler's invitation, nor did he ever reveal that Butler had issued it.

As 1863 opened, Beauregard was advising his friends in Congress what course he and they should follow. To Miles he wrote that should the government wish to send him back to the West to "retrieve" the situation there, his backers were to oppose the move. He wanted to finish his job in Charleston. Besides, the administration had not supported him before in the West and would not again. He did not want to go through the wringer a second time. His brother-in-law Villeré wrote to ask him if now was a propitious time for the opposition to attack the administration. Beauregard replied they must determine this among themselves. He added: "A strong, just, upright & honorable opposition would probably awaken our rulers to a proper sense of their responsibilities & of our true condition." [21] It is probable that Beauregard realized that for the present Charleston was the best place for him to be. If he could throw back the expected Federal attack, his fame would be restored. Then would come the opportunity

[19] René Beauregard, "Magnolia."
[20] Butler to Beauregard, December 5, 1862, in War Department Collection of Confederate Records (National Archives).
[21] Beauregard to Miles, January 7, 1863, and to Villeré, January 13, 1863, in Beauregard Papers (Library of Congress), Letterbook, Private Letters, June 30, 1862—February 7, 1863.

to go on to a bigger command—with the prestige of success behind him.

His greatest need now, he felt, was more troops to defend his extensive department. His effective force numbered about twenty-one thousand. To maintain the morale of his men, he resorted to a strategem he often used—advertising that his army was larger by one-third than it really was and the enemy smaller by a similar proportion. After a battle it was his habit to reverse the figures.[22] Privately he was more frank. He appealed to Governor M. L. Bonham of South Carolina to enforce a *levy en masse* of the male population to meet the Federal attack. When the governor refused, on the grounds that such a conscription would derange the planting interests, Beauregard replied, "With what resources I have I shall make the best battle I can. . . ."[23]

While Beauregard was waiting for the Federals to make their move, he seized every opportunity to annoy them with minor thrusts. Federal gunboats had formed the habit of coming up the Stono River between James and John's islands and shelling the Confederate camps. Often they anchored in the river overnight. The worst offender was the *Isaac Smith*. Beauregard determined to trap her. At points along the river where the ships passed, he had masked batteries erected. On the night of January 30 the unsuspecting *Smith* entered the river and dropped anchor. Suddenly the hidden guns opened on her, and she had to surrender. Repaired and renamed the *Stono,* she became a part of Beauregard's small naval squadron.[24]

On the same night he attempted a more daring exploit. Most of the ironclad ships in the Federal blockading fleet had temporarily gone to Port Royal, leaving a group of inferior vessels, most of them consisting of wooden ships, to watch the harbor. Beauregard had two ironclad gunboats at Charleston. He advised the naval commander to take them out and make a surprise attack on the Federals. Early on the morning of the thirty-first the Confederate ships slipped through the darkness and suddenly appeared in the midst of the blockaders. The fight that followed was disastrous for the Federals. One of their ships was damaged immediately and had to strike its colors. The commander of another badly shot up vessel prepared to

[22] *Official Records,* XIV, 757, XVIII, 839, XX, Pt. 2, p. 490.
[23] Roman, *Beauregard,* II, 461–64.
[24] *Ibid.,* II, 58–60, 462–63; *Battles and Leaders,* IV, 7–8; *Official Records,* XIV, 199–201.

abandon ship but seeing that the Confederates did not realize his condition limped out of the battle. The rest of the fleet, with several other vessels in bad shape, fled the scene.[25]

Beauregard was jubilant when he learned the result. He decided that the victory provided an opportunity for a grand stroke of propaganda. He would declare the blockade of Charleston raised and perhaps persuade some of the European nations to ratify his action. If foreign ships entered the harbor, European recognition of the Confederacy might follow. Then indeed would he be a towering figure in the South. So he issued a proclamation that the blockade had ended, and took the French and Spanish consuls out in the harbor to witness the truth of his words.[26] Nothing came of his adventure in diplomacy because, of course, the blockade had not been broken. When the Confederate gunboats retired, the Federal ships resumed their stations; and when the ironclads returned, the lid was clamped on again. Trying to build up his reputation, Beauregard had overshot the mark. He looked a little ridiculous.

In February Beauregard was certain that the Federals were getting ready to strike. They were increasing their naval strength, he informed Richmond, and the blow would fall on Savannah or Charleston and probably the latter. He asked for the return of some troops he had previously loaned to the commander at Wilmington, North Carolina, the other big Confederate port of entry on the Atlantic coast. The government readily complied with his request. But he was far from satisfied with the strength of his force. He issued one of his purple proclamations to the people of South Carolina and Georgia, calling upon all able-bodied men to join him even if armed only with pikes and scythes. To Richmond he insisted excitedly that he must have additional troops. The War Department replied that he would get what it could give.[27] Beauregard's calls for troops were read, of course, by Davis. The President was irritated. Beauregard was acting in his usual loose and arrogant manner, demanding aid but not explaining why he wanted it. The fellow still had not learned how to treat his superiors and needed to be reminded. Davis dashed off a peevish telegram informing Beauregard that while he would be

[25] Roman, *Beauregard*, II, 56–58; *Battles and Leaders*, IV, 6–7, 28; Parker, *Recollections*, 293–99.

[26] *Official Records*, XIV, 204–206.

[27] *Ibid.*, 758–59, 774–78, 781–82; Rowland (ed.), *Jefferson Davis*, V, 429–30.

reinforced in case of necessity, the government could not act intelligently unless it had exact information of his forces and their positions. Such intelligence Beauregard was to furnish at least every ten days.[28]

By the end of March Beauregard's forces had been increased to a strength of about thirty thousand.[29] The government was giving him little enough, he thought. To Miles he complained that the Confederacy was trying to defend too many coastal towns. The great secret of war was knowing what to give up in order to save more important points. Could not the administration realize that Charleston and Savannah were more important than the North Carolina ports, he asked. With his few and scattered troops he doubted that he could hold the line from Charleston to Savannah, but for Charleston he meant to fight hard. If he met with disaster, the responsibility would not be his but the government's. Aware of an increasing concentration of Federal ships at Port Royal, he knew the enemy was at last ready to strike. "I believe the drama will not much longer be delayed," he wrote, "the curtain will soon rise."[30] Methodically he issued his last-minute instructions. He was as well prepared as he could be.[31]

The curtain was indeed about to rise and with a bang that would alter some Northern concepts about the power of ironclad ships. Proudly the United States Naval Department had assembled at Port Royal an armada that was to batter Fort Sumter into submission. It consisted of nine vessels armed with thirty-three guns of the heaviest caliber used in naval warfare up to that time. Seven of the ships were single-turreted monitors; one was double-turreted. Heading the squadron was the flagship *New Ironsides*, an ironclad frigate. To meet this formidable force the Confederates had in the harbor seventy-seven guns—none of them as heavy as the biggest Federal guns—distributed as follows: at Sumter, forty-four; at Moultrie, twenty-one; on Sullivan's Island, nine; and on Morris, three.[32]

[28] Rowland (ed.), *Jefferson Davis,* V, 433.

[29] Roman, *Beauregard,* II, 105.

[30] Beauregard to Miles, February 10, March 14, 1863, in *Official Records,* XIV, 772–73, 825–26.

[31] *Ibid.,* 846, 851–52; Roman, *Beauregard,* II, 64–65, 465.

[32] Roman, *Beauregard,* II, 68–69. This was the number of guns Beauregard listed as actually engaged. It is not likely that he had many more. In a later account *(Battles and Leaders,* IV, 10–11), Beauregard changed his figures somewhat and claimed he had only sixty-nine guns in action.

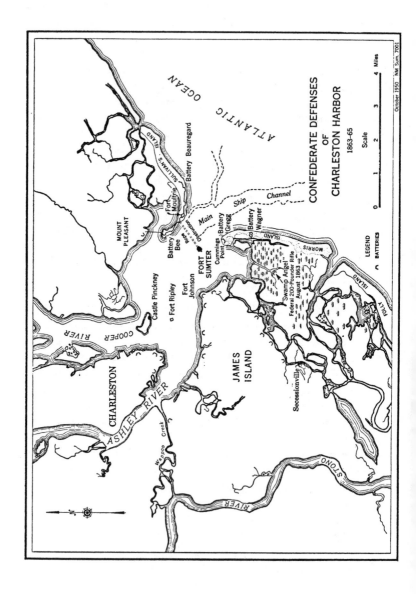

CONFEDERATE DEFENSES
OF
CHARLESTON HARBOR
1863–65

Beauregard as an officer in the army before the war

Engineer officer Beauregard and his first wife, Marie Laure

New Orleans customhouse in 1860, the year Beauregard gave up his job as superintending engineer

Cover of sheet music, "The Beauregard Manassas Quick-Step"

Laure Beauregard Larendon
and Lilian Beauregard Larendon

UNPRECEDENTED ATTRACTION.   OVER TWO MILLION DISTRIBUTED!

L.a.S.L.

Louisiana State Lottery Company

Incorporated by the Legislature for Educational and Charitable purposes, and its franchise made a part of the present State Constitution, in 1879, by an OVERWHELMING POPULAR VOTE.

TO CONTINUE UNTIL JANUARY 1, 1895.

Its GRAND EXTRAORDINARY DRAWINGS take place Semi-annually (June and December) and its GRAND SINGLE NUMBER DRAWINGS take place in each of the other ten months of the year, and are all drawn in public, at the Academy of Music, New Orleans, La.

Famed for Twenty Years, for Integrity of its Drawings and Prompt Payment of Prizes, Attested as follows :

"We do hereby certify that we supervise the arrangements for all the Monthly and Semi-Annual Drawings of the Louisiana State Lottery Company, and in person manage and control the Drawings themselves, and that the same are conducted with honesty, fairness and in good faith toward all parties, and we authorize the Company to use this certificate with fac similes of our signatures attached, in its advertisements."

COMMISSIONERS.

We the undersigned Banks and Bankers will pay all Prizes drawn in the Louisiana State Lotteries, which may be presented at our counters.

R. M. WALMSLEY, Pres. La. Nat'l Bank.   P. LANAUX, Pres. State Nat'l Bank.
A. BALDWIN, Pre. N.O. Nat'l Bank.   CARL KOHN, President Union National Bank.

Semi-Annual Drawing

WILL TAKE PLACE AT THE

ACADEMY OF MUSIC,

NEW ORLEANS, TUESDAY, DECEMBER 16, 1890.

CAPITAL PRIZE, – - $600,000

100,000 Tickets at $40; Halves $20; Quarters $10; Eighths $5; Twentieths $2; Fortieths $1.

—————— LIST OF PRIZES ——————

1 Prize of	$600,000 is	$600,000
1 Prize of	200,000 is	200,000
1 Prize of	100,000 is	100,000
1 Prize of	50,000 is	50,000
2 Prizes of	20,000 are	40,000
5 Prizes of	10,000 are	50,000
10 Prizes of	5,000 are	50,000
25 Prizes of	2,000 are	50,000
100 Prizes of	800 are	80,000
200 Prizes of	600 are	120,000
500 Prizes of	400 are	200,000

—————— APPROXIMATION PRIZES ——————

100 Prizes of	$1,000 are	$100,000
100 Prizes of	800 are	80,000
100 Prizes of	400 are	40,000

—————— TERMINAL PRIZES ——————

999 Prizes of	200 are	$199,800
999 Prizes of	200 are	199,800

3,144 Prizes, amounting to $2,159,600

Club Rates, 55 Fractional Tickets at $1, for $50.

SPECIAL RATES TO AGENTS.   AGENTS WANTED EVERYWHERE.

IMPORTANT. —— HOW TO SEND MONEY.

Remit Currency by Express at our Expense.

NOT LESS THAN FIVE DOLLARS.

Address, **M. A. DAUPHIN**, New Orleans, La.

Give full address and make signature plain.

We pay all charges on Orders of Five Dollars and upwards.

Congress having passed laws prohibiting the use of the mails to ALL Lotteries, we use the Express Companies in answering correspondents and sending Lists of Prizes. Official List of Prizes can be obtained from Local Agents by all holders of tickets.

ATTENTION.—The present charter of the Louisiana State Lottery Company, which is part of the Constitution of the State, and by decision of the Supreme Court of the United States, is an inviolable contract between the State and the Lottery Company, will remain in force under any circumstances **FIVE YEARS LONGER, UNTIL 1895.**

The Louisiana Legislature, which adjourned July 10th, voted by two-thirds majority in each House, to let the people decide at an election, whether the Lottery shall continue from 1895 until 1919. The general impression is that **PEOPLE WILL FAVOR CONTINUANCE.**

Louisiana State Lottery Company handbill, carrying facsimile signature of Beauregard and Jubal Early, as commissioners

Beauregard in 1887

The ironclads crossed the bar of the harbor on April 6 and anchored off Morris Island. Hazy weather obscured the channel, and the pilots objected to taking the ships in. The next day the weather was clear and the water smooth. At one-fifteen in the afternoon the vessels left their anchorage with the ebb tide and headed for the harbor entrance. Slowly and with a certain majesty not lost on the Confederate observers, the iron monsters moved into the main ship channel and steamed in single file toward Sumter. They passed by Morris Island in an ominous silence; the Confederate batteries there fired no shot. But as the ships approached the inner works, the harbor broke into life. The flags of the Confederacy and of South Carolina were raised above Sumter and Moultrie, bands on the parapets played Southern airs, and guns roared in salute.

At three o'clock the lead monitor, the *Weehawken*, came within range of Moultrie and Sumter. Four others were close behind. Moultrie opened fire, Sumter followed, and soon all the guns on Sullivan's and Morris were blazing away. The ships replied, directing most of their shot at Sumter. They moved slowly and hesitantly, their officers searching fearfully for torpedoes and for rope obstructions that might entangle the propellers. The impetus of the Federal advance was also weakened by the *Ironsides,* which had a deeper draught than the monitors. It had trouble maneuvering in the shallower waters off the main channel and in trying to turn about threw the entire line into confusion. Partly because of their cautious approach, the attackers did not reach a range from which they could damage the forts. Most of the ships delivered their volleys from a distance of 1,400 yards. But even if they had been bolder, the monitors would have been unable to run close to the forts. They could not face the terrific weight of the fire from the Confederate works. To try was suicidal. One ship, the *Keokuk,* went to within 900 yards of Sumter and was immediately riddled like a sieve. Several others that attempted to go in were put out of action. At five o'clock the Federal commander, Samuel F. Du Pont, ordered his crippled squadron to retire.[33]

The accuracy of the Confederate firing was amazing and a tribute to Beauregard's training. Even though the monitors were slow and were operating in a narrow channel, they were moving targets and,

[33] *Battles and Leaders,* IV, 11–12, 35–39; Roman, *Beauregard,* II, 67–75, 468–76; *Official Records,* XIV, 245–46, 257–61.

because of their almost submerged hulls, difficult ones. The effectiveness of the Confederate batteries was helped, of course, by the fact that they could hurl a concentrated fire over a small area. During the battle the defenders fired approximately 2,209 shots, of which Moultrie threw 868 and Sumter 810. Beauregard calculated that 520 of the Confederate shots found their target. His estimate is supported by the Federal reports. Every ship in the attacking flotilla was hit. The *Ironsides* was struck 95 times, the *Keokuk* 90, and the *Weehawken* 53; the figures for the other vessels ranged from 35 to 14. Four of the ironclads were seriously disabled, and the *Keokuk,* which got out of the fight, sank the next day off Morris Island. One reason for the large number of hits was that the Confederates had moored buoys in the channel as sighting marks. As the ships came in line with the buoys, the gunners fired with deadly precision.

The monitors, for their part, were unable to deliver much firepower. They threw about 150 shots, of which probably 55 reached a target. Sumter, which was hit 36 times, was barely damaged, and the other works not at all. The puny effort of the monitors was the result of the range from which they had to fire and of limited vision provided by their turrets.[34]

After the battle the fleet went to Port Royal for repairs. Du Pont said that to attempt another attack would be to turn a repulse into a disaster. The Federals learned a bitter lesson from the events of April 7. They knew now that they could not take Charleston by naval action alone. In the words of one of their naval officers, "The harbor was a *cul-de-sac,* a circle of fire not to be passed." Never again would the monitors dare to enter the harbor without the support of land forces. If Sumter was to be destroyed, if the city was to be seized, it would have to be done by a combined operation of the army and navy.[35]

Beauregard was elated by his victory. In his reports to Richmond he emphasized that the action of April 7 proved the monitors were overrated weapons. At the same time he insisted that the country should be proud of the men "who first met and vanquished the iron-mailed, terribly-armed armada, so confidently prepared, and sent forth by the enemy to certain and easy victory." After this last effu-

[34] Roman, *Beauregard,* II, 75; John Johnson, *The Defence of Charleston Harbor* (Charleston, 1890), 58–59; Samuel Jones, *The Siege of Charleston* (New York, 1911), 178–89; *Battles and Leaders,* IV, 12, 37–47.
[35] *Battles and Leaders,* IV, 34, 40, 45.

sion he confided to a friend that he was putting his dispatches in moderate terms to counteract a rumor in Richmond that he exaggerated his successes.[36] With his troops, he made no pretense of restraint. In a congratulatory order he spoke of "the stranded, riddled wreck" of the *Keokuk* and of the ignominious flight of "her baffled coadjutors." The recent triumph, he assured the soldiers, had inspired confidence throughout the country in the ultimate and complete success of the Confederate cause.[37]

It had not done quite that, but it was the first important Confederate exploit of the year. Coming at a time when the situation in the West seemed stalemated and before the spring campaign in Virginia had started, the repulse of the feared ironclads raised Southern morale. It also raised Beauregard's reputation with the public and stirred anew the enemies of the administration to attack Davis for denying a field command to such a brilliant general.[38] His success, Beauregard soon discovered, had not improved his standing with Richmond. When he requested more heavy guns, the government informed him that other departments had prior demands. The high command probably reasoned that Beauregard's victory meant Charleston was already sufficiently armed. To Beauregard the decision was only another case of Davis' animosity. In letters to his Congressional supporters he bitterly criticized the administration for refusing to support him, for failing to recognize his true worth. He pitied a country, he said, which had a President who consulted his prejudices in making appointments. [39]

Determined to increase his battery strength, Beauregard went to the length of getting a Senator friend to present a bill enlarging the artillery force in Charleston. During the debate on this measure another Senator charged that Beauregard was infringing on the prerogatives of the President. The general wrote to his legislative agent that the accusation was false. Probably a little alarmed that his instigation of the bill had been discovered, he denied that he was hostile to Davis. All he asked, he said, was that he not be driven into an unnecessary opposition to the government. "I have my faults and my

[36] Roman, *Beauregard*, II, 75; *Official Records*, XIV, 240–43, 907.

[37] Snow, *Southern Generals*, 259.

[38] Richardson (ed.), *Messages and Papers of the Confederacy*, I, 338; Eliot, *West Point in the Confederacy*, 183.

[39] Roman, *Beauregard*, II, 107; *Official Records*, LIII, 287–89.

deficiencies," he concluded, "but, thank God, selfishness and ambition form no part of my nature."[40]

If the administration thought that Charleston was secure, Beauregard had no such illusions. He believed the Federals would try again, by sea or by land. He renewed his requests to the government for torpedo-rams; with a few of these he was confident he could destroy the blockading monitors. He could not persuade the high command of their utility. In his frustration he said that he felt like Columbus.[41] When the War Department directed him to send reinforcements to Mississippi to aid in the defense of Vicksburg, he dispatched five thousand men but protested to Richmond that he could not give any more without danger to his department. Davis and Secretary of War James Seddon emphasized to him that the Mississippi line was vital to the Confederacy and urged him to furnish additional troops. He replied that any further depletion of his forces would invite an attack. In the face of his insistence, they hesitated to overrule him. The President, however, was profoundly irritated. On one of Beauregard's dispatches, he endorsed that the general's present return of troops did not agree with the last one. Obviously Davis thought that Beauregard was juggling his figures.[42]

In the afterglow of his victory over the ironclads, Beauregard nourished bright hopes of returning to field command. He knew that he had been suggested to replace Pemberton at Vicksburg and that high officers in the Army of Northern Virginia were working to have him brought into that organization as commander of a corps.[43] Lee himself proposed to Davis that Beauregard and most of his troops be brought to Virginia and that Beauregard be given an important post, possibly the command of Lee's own army.[44] Confident that the

[40] Beauregard to J. L. Orr, April 24, 1862, in *Official Records*, XIV, 909–11.

[41] *Ibid.*, 895, 923–24.

[42] *Ibid.*, 924, 932–36; Roman, *Beauregard*, II, 81, 107.

[43] R. S. Ewell to Beauregard, May 8, 1863, in Percy Gatling Hamlin, *"Old Bald Head": General R. S. Ewell* (Strasburg, Va., 1940), 134–35; Longstreet to Lafayette McLaws, June 2, 1863, in McLaws Papers (Southern Historical Collection, University of North Carolina).

[44] Lee to Davis, May 7, 1863, in *Official Records*, XXV, Pt. 2, pp. 782–83. Lee's letter is vaguely phrased and is open to several interpretations. He recommended that Beauregard be brought to Virginia and put in command "here." Douglas Southall Freeman concluded, in *R. E. Lee*, II, 560, that Lee meant for Beauregard to take command of the Army of Northern Virginia. Another possible interpretation is that Lee wanted Beauregard to command in Virginia while Lee undertook an offensive into the North.

tide of his destiny was about to turn for the better, Beauregard decided to help his cause by producing a plan of grand strategy that would win the war for the Confederacy.

Grand planning was almost a vogue with Southern leaders in the gloomy spring months of 1863. And certainly some master design of victory was desperately needed. Even as optimistic a person as Beauregard had to admit that the war was going against the Confederacy.[45] Everywhere Southern armies stood on the defensive. In the West the Federals had overrun large areas of vital territory. The greatest danger spot at the moment was Vicksburg, the key to the defenses of the Mississippi River line, which was under siege by a Federal army led by U. S. Grant. The Confederate high command realized it was imperative to hold Vicksburg. The problem was how to do it. General James Longstreet of Lee's army wanted to detach men from Virginia to Bragg in Tennessee; Bragg could then start an offensive which would relieve the pressure on Vicksburg. Secretary Seddon thought that reinforcements should be sent directly to Mississippi to attack Grant's rear. Lee was uncertain as to what should be done, but eventually he proposed that his army should invade Pennsylvania; a victory on Northern soil would swing the military balance in favor of the South.[46]

Beauregard's plan was similar to Longstreet's, but went far beyond it as a strategic concept. The general submitted his design in a letter to Joseph E. Johnston, now departmental commander of the West. He asked Johnston to lay it before the War Department as his own. He would only indicate the general features of what could be a "brilliant campaign," he told Johnston. He proposed that Lee and other commanders stand on the defensive and from their forces send thirty thousand troops to reinforce Bragg's army in Tennessee. This force, commanded by Johnston, would attack and destroy the Federal army south of Nashville. Then it would move to the Mississippi and cut Grant's communications. Grant would have to loosen his hold on Vicksburg and fight. Of course he would be destroyed. The victorious Confederates could advance into Louisiana and Missouri or eastward to Virginia. While all this was happening, a fleet of Beau-

[45] Beauregard to Pierre Soulé, May 19, 1863, in *Official Records*, Ser. 2, V. 952–53.

[46] *Ibid.*, Ser. 1, XXV, Pt. 2, pp. 790, 842; Longstreet, *From Manassas to Appomattox*, 327–31; John H. Reagan, *Memoirs* . . . (New York, 1906), 121–22.

regard's torpedo-rams would be built in England to recapture New
Orleans. Presto, the war would be over. Beauregard also sent his
plan to Senator Wigfall, urging his former aide to get it adopted by
the War Department but not to reveal that it was Beauregard's. If
he was known as the author, he said, the scheme would be consigned
to the tomb of the Capulets.[47]

In a letter to Villeré, Beauregard enlarged on the possibilities of
his plan and talked frankly about his status in the army. He envisioned the Confederate army crushing all opposition in the West and
then marching into Ohio and persuading the Northwest to leave the
old Union and conclude an alliance with the Confederacy. Of his
own position, Beauregard said it was a peculiar one. If he succeeded,
he increased the hostility of certain persons against him; if he failed,
he incurred their satisfaction and ire. He felt like Sampson shorn of
his locks. To Villeré he said nothing about Johnston commanding
the reinforced army in the West. He remarked that Bragg—or who-
ever took his place—should be able to defeat the Federals. Was he
thinking of himself as Bragg's successor, leading the Confederates
from victory to victory? Probably, because he said that the commander should destroy the enemy by employing European methods
of strategy, which was his way of saying that the commander should
be one who understood, and followed, the rules of war.[48]

There is no record that his plan was ever presented to the government; if it was it was never seriously considered. He had not helped
his cause by dreaming it up. His design was impractical and impossible, largely because it ignored the factors of logistics and resources.
In its wild extravagance, it marked a reversion to his pre-Manassas
habit of producing military fantasies. If Davis saw it, he must have
been more convinced than ever that Beauregard was unfit for field
command.

One man still believed Beauregard's talents could be utilized in
the field. That was Lee, who was then preparing his offensive into
Pennsylvania. To facilitate his own plans, Lee wanted to give Beauregard a role in the coming campaign. Lee's idea was to bring Beauregard and most of his troops to Virginia and make Beauregard commander of a small army in the northern part of the state. While

[47] Beauregard to Johnston, May 15, 1863, and to Wigfall, May 16, 1863,
in *Official Records*, XXIII, Pt. 2, pp. 836–38.
[48] Beauregard to Villeré, May 26, 1863, *ibid.*, XIV, 955.

Lee was invading Pennsylvania, Beauregard would move toward the Potomac as though he were threatening Washington and thus lighten the pressure on Lee. "His presence," wrote Lee to Davis with unconscious irony, "would give magnitude to even a small demonstration. . . ." Lee was late in telling Davis of his purpose to use Beauregard, not apprising the President until the march northward had started. Davis was not enthusiastic about the proposal, but was willing to do as Lee wished. Shortly the President had to inform Lee that Beauregard reported the enemy was in his front and all his troops were necessary to guard his line. In other words, Beauregard did not want to go to Virginia.[49] He did not intend to go any place where he would be in a minor and subordinate position. What he wanted was an independent command, and preferably the direction of his former army in the West.

In June he rebuffed another attempt by the government to give him an unwelcome assignment. The government informed him that the Federal forces on the Carolina-Georgia coast were being transferred to Mobile for an attack on that point. Would Beauregard take part of his troops to Mobile and ascertain the enemy's purpose? If the Federals intended to transfer their strength to the Mississippi line, would Beauregard go to Mississippi and co-operate with Johnston? His answer was that he would not, without an order. He did not believe that the Federal strength in his front had been reduced, and he protested against losing any more men. He gave the administration a hint as to what it should do about him: "As for myself, my earnest desire is to be useful to the utmost extent of my capacities, in any position or command to which it may please the President to assign me; but if left to my own personal preferences, I would desire service in the field, for which I consider myself best fitted by my taste and studies."[50]

When no assignment to field command came, he unloaded his disappointment in a letter to Johnston, who shared his bitterness against Davis. If only the government had adopted his plan to reinforce the Western army, he lamented, how different the situation now would be. "Whereas of what earthly use is that 'raid' of Lee's army . . . in violation of all the principles of war?" he asked. "Is it going to

[49] *Ibid.,* XXVII, Pt. 1, pp. 75–77, Pt. 2, pp. 293–94, Pt. 3, pp. 924–25; Longstreet, *From Manassas to Appomattox,* 335–37.
[50] Beauregard to Samuel Cooper, June 15, 1863, in *Official Records,* XXVIII, Pt. 1, pp. 55–57.

end the struggle, take Washington, or save the Mississippi Valley?" He felt that the Southern cause was close to defeat: "I hope everything will yet turn out well, although I do not exactly see how." [51]

People who saw him in Charleston little dreamed of the resentments and frustrations that smoldered below the surface. One resident described him as looking radiant and reposed. When this man asked if Beauregard would call for volunteers rather than yield Charleston, the general replied, "I certainly shall . . . and rather than give up Charleston I will even make an appeal to the ladies." [52] An English observer found him calm and confident and seemingly satisfied with his position. Beauregard told his foreign guest that he had organized both the Eastern and Western armies of the Confederacy and that war between the North and England was inevitable. At a dinner the visitor heard the general say that Sumter was invulnerable to any attack by the ironclads. In discussing the war, Beauregard said that once he had had many friends in the North but that now he would submit to the Emperor of China before he would return to the old Union. [53]

Beauregard's yearning for field service was soon to be gratified. The Federals were moving on Charleston again, and this time they were coming by land instead of by sea.

[51] Beauregard to Johnston, July 1, 1863, in Beauregard Papers (Duke University).

[52] Thomas Smythe, "Memoranda of an interview with Gen. Beauregard in my own house on the evening of May 20th, 1863" (South Caroliniana Library, University of South Carolina).

[53] Fremantle, *Three Months in the Southern States*, 193–94, 198–99.

CHAPTER TWELVE

The Big Bombardment

THE FAILURE of April 7 rankled with the Federal high command. In Washington plans were considered to destroy Sumter and take the city by a combined army and naval attack. Called in to attend the conferences was General Quincy A. Gillmore, rated as a great artillerist and a master of siege operations. Gillmore was asked if the army could aid the navy to enter the harbor by destroying the offensive power of Sumter. He replied that the army could, by mounting heavy rifled guns on Morris Island, south of the fort. On the strength of his opinion, it was decided to have the army secure possession of the southern end of Morris, reduce the Confederate batteries on the island, and destroy Sumter with rifled artillery. When this was accomplished, the navy would pass into the harbor, supported by fire from Gillmore, and force the city to surrender. Gillmore assumed command of the land forces on June 12, and a little later Admiral John A. Dahlgren replaced Du Pont.[1]

Below Charleston the Federals held a number of islands. One of them was Folly Island, a small, sandy strip, separated from Morris by a narrow inlet. Gillmore's plan was to assemble secretly on Folly a force that would suddenly cross to Morris, surprise the defenders, and occupy most of the island. His preparation period lasted twenty days, during which time he brought in his men, mostly at night, and placed forty-seven guns and mortars to support his assault. His activities were partially concealed from the Confederates at the southern end of Morris by the sand hills and underbrush on Folly. To deceive the Confederates he made a pretense of action at the southern end of Folly, as though he was going to attack James Island.[2]

Beauregard was well aware that a Federal force was on Folly and that it was up to something. The sounds made by the Federals as they assembled their guns could be heard on Morris.[3] He doubted, how-

---

[1] *Battles and Leaders*, IV, 54–55.
[2] *Ibid.*, 56–57; *Annals of the War*, 96–97.
[3] Roman, *Beauregard*, II, 92–94.

ever, that the enemy would try to get at Charleston by the Morris route. He had always considered that they might try to reach the city by moving onto one of the islands. Of the three possible island approaches, he ranked in order of importance to the Federals James, Sullivan's, and Morris. If they took James, they could erect batteries that would command the inner harbor and compel the evacuation of Charleston. From Sullivan's, above the city, they could reduce Sumter, command the harbor entrance, and shell the town. Morris he rated least valuable to the Federals because of its distance from the forts and Charleston. He did not believe that from it they could damage Sumter, fire on the city, or dominate the harbor entrance.[4] Consequently he judged that Gillmore was preparing to strike at James, and it was at James that he concentrated most of his men and guns. The southern end of Morris he left almost defenseless except for a few batteries and a small number of troops. He did not have enough manpower to hold both Morris and James. In the entire area around Charleston he could dispose only 5,860 troops.[5]

Gillmore sprang his attack early on the morning of July 10. Under cover of artillery fire from Folly, an assault force of three thousand crossed the inlet, rushed the weak Confederate works, and by eleven o'clock had occupied three fourths of Morris.[6] Although Beauregard had been caught napping, he affected no alarm at the Federal success. Then and later he denied that he had been surprised. He knew the Federals were preparing to attack, he said; he just did not know at what point. Their possession of Morris was in his opinion no danger to Charleston. The enemy had chosen to break in through a window, he said, and he had no cause to regret their mistaken decision.[7]

The Federals had most of Morris, but the roughest part of their work was still before them. They had to advance to a point where their rifled guns could breach Sumter. The island was about three miles in length; it varied in width from 200 to 300 yards, shrinking even narrower at the upper end. On the western side its white sand surface sloped into a marsh intersected by water courses which separated it from James. The Confederates had concentrated their

[4] *Ibid.*, 110.

[5] Jones, *Siege of Charleston*, 205.

[6] *Battles and Leaders*, IV, 57–58; *Official Records*, XXVIII, Pt. 1, pp. 8–12; *Annals of the War*, 97–98; Hagood, *Memoirs*, 119–21. The attack was preceded on July 8 by a demonstration against James Island.

[7] *Official Records*, XXVIII, Pt. 1, pp. 72–73, Pt. 2, pp. 186–87; *Battles and Leaders*, IV, 13–14.

strongest defenses on the northern end of the island. At its thinnest point stood Battery Wagner, about 2,700 yards from Sumter. In rear of Wagner, on Morris' northern edge, was Battery Gregg, 1,400 yards from the fort. Wagner was one of the strongest field fortifications built in American military history up to that time; even Gillmore's officers paid tribute to the engineering skill that had devised it. Constructed of sand and earth and riveted with turf and palmetto logs, it presented a bastioned front of 275 yards. Flanked on the east by the sea and on the west by marshes, it could be approached only on a strip less than one half the width of its front. This strip could be swept by its own guns and taken in reverse and flank by the batteries of Gregg and James. The barbette guns of Sumter could throw a plunging fire beyond Wagner. Inside the work was a bombproof shelter capable of holding 1,600 men.[8] If Gillmore meant to destroy Sumter, he would first have to take or neutralize Wagner.

He first tried to take it. On the morning after the landing, he ordered an infantry assault. The first wave of Federals reached the parapet, but had to retire when their supports recoiled under a withering fire. Gillmore now decided to establish counterbatteries to breach Wagner before making another attack. For the next week the Federals busied themselves putting into position forty-one guns at distances from the fort varying from 1,300 to 1,900 yards.[9] Beauregard was just as busy changing his defensive arrangements around the harbor. He realized that he did not have enough troops to expel the Federals from Morris and that he probably could not hold the island for long. But he resolved to maintain possession until he could increase his batteries on James and Sullivan's and strengthen Sumter. In his thinking Wagner was an outpost of Sumter and the inner works, to be held long enough to give him time to perfect his other defenses. If he could mount enough guns on James and Sullivan's, he would, when the Federals occupied all of Morris, envelop them in a circle of fire that would hold them away from Charleston.[10] In the press of his activities he did not have time to answer adequately an unfriendly letter from Secretary Seddon asking how the enemy had managed to effect a lodgment on Morris. At his direction new works

[8] *Annals of the War,* 95–96; Jones, *Siege of Charleston,* 229; Quincy A. Gillmore, *Engineer and Artillery Operations against the Defenses of Charleston in 1863* . . . (New York, 1865), 74–75.
[9] *Battles and Leaders,* IV, 58–59; *Official Records,* XXVIII, Pt. 1, p. 73.
[10] Johnson, *Defense of Charleston,* 153–54; *Battles and Leaders,* IV, 16.

went up on James, guns were transferred from Sumter to Moultrie, and the gorge wall at Sumter was protected with wet cotton bales and sand.[11]

One day he stopped his labors long enough to see his old friend and former spy Mrs. Greenhow. She came to Charleston to take ship for Europe on a mission for Davis. He told her the situation was grave and admitted the Yankees had stolen a march on him. She asked, "How is that, General, with your great sagacity?" He replied that if he had had more men the Federals would never have landed on Morris. Gloomily he said that he was being criticized for not stopping them and that he was tired of siege operations. He wanted active service and would like to serve under Lee.[12]

On July 18 Gillmore launched his second attack. At noon all the Federal batteries opened on Wagner, while the monitors came up and shelled it from the sea side. The bombardment was kept up until nightfall. During the entire day the Federals threw over nine hundred projectiles, averaging at times fourteen shots a minute. At the height of the firing the garrison of 1,000 retired to the bombproof and most of Wagner's guns ceased to operate. Gillmore fixed his assault for twilight so that the Confederates on the other islands could not clearly see the attackers. At a little past seven-thirty the Federal batteries slackened their fire, and 6,000 troops, led by a Negro regiment, moved on the fort. As they advanced on the narrow front, the guns of James, Sullivan's, and Sumter got their range. The Federals kept on and approached the ditch in front of the parapet. Suddenly the garrison emerged from its shelter and poured a deadly sheet of musket fire into the blue ranks. It was more than the Federals could stand. They went down in windrows. At one point a part of the assault force struggled to the parapet but was driven out. Gillmore withdrew his troops.

In the brief engagement the Federals lost over 1,500 killed and wounded, while the Confederate casualties were only 174. When the defenders came forth to look at the results of their work, they were horrified by the sight that met them. The dead and wounded lay in piles before the fort, the bodies of both terribly mangled by artillery

[11] *Official Records*, XXVIII, Pt. 1, pp. 74–76, Pt. 2, pp. 198, 205; Roman, *Beauregard*, II, 96, 100, 486–87.

[12] Mrs. Rose Greenhow to Davis, July 16, 1863, in Greenhow Papers (Duke University Library).

fire. Heads, arms, and legs were splattered all over the ditch and the rampart.[13]

Now Gillmore decided to try to breach Sumter from where he was, throwing shells at the fort from a distance of two to two and a half miles. At the same time he would advance parallel lines of entrenchments toward Wagner for the double purpose of getting his artillery in closer range of Sumter and of battering Wagner and Gregg into submission. Eighteen rifled guns were placed to bear on Sumter, and the first parallel line was driven toward Wagner. Each time a new line was finished, the guns, with troops to guard them, moved forward. By mid-August Gillmore had built three parallels and pushed his batteries up over a thousand yards. In the marsh west of Morris the Federals mounted with immense labor a 200-pound Parrott rifle to fire into the city itself from a distance of over five miles. This monster the soldiers called the "Swamp Angel." [14]

While Gillmore was beginning his preparations, Beauregard found time to answer Seddon's letter asking why the enemy had been able to land on Morris. He was too busy, he told the secretary, to write a full reply; later he would present a detailed report. The Federals had got on Morris because he had lacked labor to build defensive works and men and guns to hold all the islands. He was prolonging the contest on Morris in order to prevent the Federals from using it as a base against Sumter. To carry out his purpose he needed more long-range guns and proper ammunition. On Beauregard's dispatch Davis endorsed: "I hope some clear comprehension of the causes which enabled the enemy to approach Morris Island . . . will be given in the promised report." [15] Beauregard was not alone in trying to evade blame for the developing danger to Charleston. In the city a prominent resident noted that "all parties" were devoting what time they could spare from speculating in imports to censuring somebody else for Gillmore's success.[16]

It would be almost a month before Gillmore would complete his preparations. During that period the Federals shelled Wagner and

[13] *Battles and Leaders,* IV, 59, 74–75; *Annals of the War,* 98–99; *Official Records,* XXVIII, Pt. 1, pp. 76–77; Hagood, *Memoirs,* 143; D. B. Harris to Mrs. Harris, July 18, 1863, in Harris Papers.

[14] *Battles and Leaders,* IV, 60–61, 72–73; *Annals of the War,* 99–101.

[15] Beauregard to Seddon, July 20, 1863, in *Official Records,* XXVIII, Pt. 1, pp. 57–59.

[16] John Preston to James Chesnut, July 20, 1863, in Williams-Chesnut-Manning Papers.

Sumter every day and sometimes at night. For their after-dark firing they used a large calcium light that illuminated the whole island. Sometimes the bombardment was light and sometimes heavy, although the heaviest was light compared to what was to come later.[17] Beauregard begged the government for all the big guns it could spare. Anticipating the eventual loss of Morris and the neutralizing of Sumter, he wanted them for his works on James and Sullivan's. If he could complete what he always called his circle of fire, he believed he could keep the Federals out of the harbor. The government had but few guns to send and those few, to Beauregard's anguish, were delayed in transportation.[18]

Beauregard realized that when Gillmore got his batteries closer Sumter would be pounded mercilessly and would lose much of its value as a defensive point. Therefore, he had working parties at the fort day and night removing its best guns to Moultrie and other places on Sullivan's Island. "These matters cannot be attended to with too much expedition," he directed. By August 16 only forty guns remained at Sumter, the minimum he judged necessary for its defense.[19] To perfect his arrangements, Beauregard needed time. Wagner, coming under an ever more deadly bombardment, had to hold out. The commander of the garrison, now reduced to less than a thousand, told him that the men were becoming dispirited and hopeless. Beauregard replied that the fort must be held and fought to the last extremity consonant with legitimate warfare. He assured the garrison it would be withdrawn at the proper moment.[20]

By August 17 Gillmore was ready to open on Sumter. That day the Federals threw 948 shells at the fort, of which 448 struck inside of the walls and 232 outside. At the same time they fired on Wagner and pushed their parallel lines ahead. This was the beginning of a sustained bombardment that would last until September 2. In the week after the seventeenth the Federal batteries hurled nearly 5,000 shots at Sumter. In that seven days, 2,643 shells exploded inside the fort and 1,699 against the exterior.

17 *Official Records,* XXVIII, Pt. 1, pp. 77–83.
18 Rowland (ed.), *Jefferson Davis,* V, 572; Roman, *Beauregard,* II, 120–23, 494–95; *Official Records,* XXVIII, Pt. 2, p. 219.
19 *Official Records,* XXVIII, Pt. 1, pp. 79–81, 83–84; Roman, *Beauregard,* II, 499.
20 Roman, *Beauregard,* II, 120–21, 124, 494. For background on the siege of Wagner, see Paul Hamilton Hayne, "The Defence of Fort Wagner," in *Southern Bivouac,* I (1886), 599–608.

Gillmore was using guns the like of which had never before been employed in siege warfare. Hitherto the heaviest caliber piece used in land batteries had been a 100-pounder. Gillmore introduced 200- and 300-pounders, that is, guns firing projectiles weighing 200 and 300 pounds. In the siege of Sumter the power of modern long-range artillery was first developed.[21]

Sumter had not been built to stand up against a pounding like this. Nearly all of its guns were put out of service, its walls were cracked and weakened, and a hole eight by ten feet was blown in the upper casemates of the west face. When the brick masonry walls were struck by shells, they tended to crumble and slope down toward the water. To replace the lost material, the Confederates brought in sand by night and dug up dirt from the parade ground. In one respect the accumulating debris made the outer walls stronger; shells could make little impression on the mass of earth and masonry. In another way the sloped nature of the debris presented a new danger: an assault party could easily climb the exterior ramparts. To guard against the latter possibility, wire entanglements were placed near the base of the walls and sharpened wood pikes mounted on the crest.[22]

By August 21 the "Swamp Angel" was ready to go into action. Gillmore sent a letter to Beauregard demanding the evacuation of Sumter and Morris Island; if Beauregard refused, Gillmore threatened to fire on Charleston. The letter was delivered to Beauregard's headquarters while he was absent inspecting some fortifications. By some oversight it was unsigned, and Beauregard's officers sent it back. Gillmore then committed an act of questionable honesty. He ordered the big gun to open on the city and returned the communication with his signature. Beauregard was justly indignant. In a blistering letter he rejected the ultimatum and told Gillmore what he thought of him: "It would appear, Sir, that despairing of reducing these works, you now resort to the novel measure of turning your guns against the old men, the women and children, and the hospitals of a sleeping city—an act of inexcusable barbarity." Gillmore,

---

[21] *Official Records*, XXVIII, Pt. 1, pp. 84–85, 596–606, 608–22, Pt. 2, p. 288; Roman, *Beauregard*, II, 126–27; *Battles and Leaders*, IV, 61; *Annals of the War*, 101–102, 109–10.

[22] Roman, *Beauregard*, II, 126–27; *Battles and Leaders*, IV, 26.

he predicted, would win "a bad eminence in history—even in the history of this war." [23]

The "Swamp Angel" threw a number of shells into the city. They caused more fear and inconvenience than actual damage. Banks moved their resources out of range and hospitals were evacuated. A good many people decided they would be safer in the upper part of town. Others resolved to sit it out where they were, with tubs of water scattered throughout their houses. The chief complaint of those who stayed was that the screaming of the shells interrupted their sleeping. On the thirty-sixth round the gun burst. Gillmore's enormous labors in mounting it had gone for nothing. [24]

From August 24 to September 2 the Federals continued to bombard Sumter. Beauregard wondered how long the fort could take it. He sent his engineer officers to confer with the commandant, Colonel Alfred Rhett, and his officers. The officers of Sumter were disagreed as to how long it could be held, with Rhett more pessimistic than the others. The engineers reported that Sumter could be defended for many days and recommended that Beauregard and not the commandant decide when it should be evacuated. Beauregard approved their opinion. He directed that Sumter must be fought to "the last extremity," which he defined as the moment when it became impossible to maintain possession without unnecessary loss of life. [25]

The Federal shells seemed to be bringing the moment nearer. After heavy firing by Gillmore's batteries in the last days of August, the ironclads took up the attack. On the night of September 1-2 the *New Ironsides* and five monitors pounded the fort at close range for five hours. The naval action ended the first sustained bombardment of Sumter. Since August 17 the Federal guns had fired close to seven thousand shells. The damage to the fort was tremendous. The western wall was badly cracked, most of the southern wall was down, and the

[23] Roman, Beauregard, II, 140–42; *Official Records*, XXVIII, Pt. 2, pp. 57–59; *Battles and Leaders*, IV, 66. The statement that Beauregard's officers returned Gillmore's letter without the general's having seen it is conjectured. Beauregard's letter to Gillmore is vague but implies this is what happened.

[24] *Battles and Leaders*, IV, 72–74; Louis G. Young to Mrs. A. R. Young, August 22, 1863, and to Henry Gourdin, August 22, 1863, in Gourdin-Young Papers (Emory University); Mrs. H. A. De Saussure to Mrs. Joseph Glover, August, 1863, in Henry William De Saussure and Wilmot Gibbes Papers (Duke University).

[25] Roman, *Beauregard*, II, 512–14; *Official Records*, XXVIII, Pt. 1, pp. 85–86, 614.

eastern wall was almost demolished. Nearly every casemate had been breached. Not a single barbette gun was in working order; when the ironclads attacked, Sumter had fired not a shot in reply.[26] Jubilantly Gillmore considered that his work was done. Sumter was neutralized; now he could turn his attention to Wagner.

While Sumter was being battered to pieces, Gillmore had pushed his parallels and his guns closer to Wagner. By August 26 the Federal sappers had driven to within two hundred yards of the fort; by September 2 they had reduced the distance to less than a hundred yards.[27] Beauregard, alarmed by the rapid advance of the enemy, called his officers into conference on the fourth to ask them how long Morris Island could be held. For ten days at the most, they told him gloomily —until the Federals had completed their approaches. After listening to their reports, Beauregard decided to hold the island as long as possible but to remove the heavy guns from Wagner and Gregg.[28] Gillmore had no intention of permitting the Confederates to make a leisurely evacuation. He resolved upon a supreme effort to reduce Wagner—to hit it with what might be termed a double artillery attack. His plan was to silence the guns in the fort with a bombardment by mortars: guns with a high trajectory fire that could drop shells into the fort. With the artillery in Wagner unable to operate, the Federal sappers could work unmolested. At the same time he would breach the bombproof shelter with heavy rifles, forcing the garrison to surrender or keeping it penned up while infantry rushed the rampart.

At daylight on the fifth Gillmore began his attack. Seventeen mortars shelled the fort, fourteen Parrott rifles fired at the bombproof, ten light siege rifles swept the approaches to the rear, and the *New Ironsides* hurled its shot from the sea side. The bombardment was unceasing and lasted for forty-two hours, the Federals firing during the night with the aid of calcium lights. In this period the Federals threw over three thousand shots at Wagner. The effect was all that Gillmore had wished for. Under the hail of fire the Confederates could not operate their guns. The sappers worked in complete se-

[26] *Official Records,* XXVIII, Pt. 1, pp. 86–87; Roman, *Beauregard,* II, 147–48, 513; Beauregard to Harris, September 3, 1863, in Harris Papers.

[27] *Annals of the War,* 102–103; *Official Records,* XXVIII, Pt. 1, pp. 85–87; *Battles and Leaders,* IV, 62–63.

[28] *Confederate Archives: A Calendar of the Ryder Collection of Confederate Archives at Tufts College* (Boston, 1940), 54–56; *Official Records,* XXVIII, Pt. 1, pp. 87–88, 100–102.

curity, even wandering up to the ditch in front of the fort and inspecting it. Inside the fort most of the garrison had to stay in the bombproof. There they were safe enough, but they suffered terribly from heat and thirst. Their suffering was intensified, since they were tired men to begin with. Because of the pressure of the shelling on previous days Beauregard had been able to relieve the garrison only about every five days.[29]

The outcome was as clear as the calcium lights that lit up the scene at night. Wagner was doomed. If the Confederates attempted to man the parapet and work their guns, they would be slaughtered. If they stayed under shelter, the Federals would penetrate to the parapet and rush it before the garrison could emerge from the bombproof. On September 6 the commander at Wagner, Colonel L. M. Keitt, dispatched message after message to Beauregard saying that the fort could not be held. Unless Wagner was evacuated, said Keitt, the garrison would be sacrificed. Beauregard sent his best engineer, Colonel D. B. Harris, to inspect the works. Reluctantly Harris recommended that Wagner must be abandoned.[30] Beauregard then prepared detailed orders for the evacuation of Wagner and of the island. First the garrison of Wagner was to withdraw to Gregg; then the troops of both forts would go in rowboats to steamers that would take them to James Island. Special details were left behind in Wagner and Gregg to blow up the magazines, the two explosions to be simultaneous.

On the night of September 6–7 the Confederates departed from Morris Island. The Federals did not discover the movement until the last boats were leaving the shore. Only one part of Beauregard's plan did not go according to schedule. The demolition parties failed to blow up the magazines, and failed for a characteristic Confederate reason—the fuses would not work.[31]

After a siege of fifty-eight days the Federals had possession of Morris Island. Beauregard had held them off long enough to enable him to remove his heavy guns from Sumter to other works and to strengthen the inner defenses of the harbor. He had conducted his

[29] *Official Records,* XXVIII, Pt. 1, pp. 88–89; Battles and Leaders, IV, 23, 63–64; *Annals of the War,* 104–106; Hagood, *Memoirs,* 189–90; J. F. Gilmer to Mrs. Gilmer, September 6, 1863, in Gilmer Papers.

[30] *Official Records,* XXVIII, Pt. 1, pp. 89–90; D. B. Harris to Mrs. Harris, September 9, 1863, in Harris Papers.

[31] *Official Records,* XXVIII, Pt. 1, pp. 90–91; Charles C. Jones to his mother, September, 1863, in Georgia Portfolio Papers.

operations with great skill. The only possible criticism of his defense of Wagner was that it had been too passive: he might have slowed even more the Federal approach to the fort had he employed sorties and other delaying tactics.[32] It was questionable if the Federals had gained much by taking Morris and silencing Sumter. Their big problem was still before them. They could not capture Charleston or close the port unless the fleet could get into the inner harbor. The disabling of Sumter did not open the harbor. To enter it the iron-clads would have to pass the channel obstructions and brave the fire of Beauregard's batteries on Sullivan's and James islands. The next round was to belong to Admiral Dahlgren and the navy.

Dahlgren was eager to play his part. On September 7 he demanded the surrender of Sumter. The fort's commander, Major Stephen Elliott, who had replaced Rhett, referred the ultimatum to Beauregard. The general's answer was: "Tell Admiral Dahlgren to come and take it."[33] The admiral tried to come. He considered a plan to take all the ironclads into the harbor for one bold attack. This he abandoned when he sent some of the monitors in to feel out the mines rumored to be in the channel and they caught such a fire from Moultrie that they had to retire. Dahlgren then decided to make a small-boat assault on Sumter. A picked force of marines and sailors would be landed at the base of the wall at night; they would surprise the garrison, said by Dahlgren to be no more than a corporal's guard, and the Federals would have the fort. Dahlgren asked Gillmore to help by organizing a similar assault by the land forces. Gillmore agreed but said the two columns should be under a common command—under an army officer. Dahlgren rejected this arrangement. He and Gillmore then proceeded to set up separate attacks to be made at the same time. Interservice rivalry prevented a concert that might have produced success.

Dahlgren scheduled his assault for the night of the seventh. Under a clear, starlit sky, four hundred sailors and marines crowded into small boats. A tug pulled them to within eight hundred yards of the fort and cast them loose. The sailors took up oars and rowed toward the dim mass of Sumter. On the parapet sentinels saw the barges approaching and gave the alarm. As the boats came in close, the Confederates hailed them. The Federals gave no answer. Suddenly a

[32] Hagood, *Memoirs*, 181–84.
[33] Roman, *Beauregard*, II, 155; Gillmore, *Engineer and Artillery Operations against Charleston*, 335.

signal rocket shot up from Sumter. Beauregard had expected an attempt like this; his plans to meet it had been carefully worked out. The guns of James and Sullivan's opened on the waters near the fort. A Confederate gunboat steamed up and fired into the attackers. The garrison of three hundred lined the walls and hit the first line of boats with rifle fire, hand grenades, brickbats, and pieces of masonry. Only a few of the Federals got ashore, and these had to surrender immediately. Five boats were captured, and the rest fled. Gillmore's expedition was delayed by low tide and never got into the fight.[34]

The small-boat assault ended for a period the first great offensive against Sumter and Charleston. Sumter was battered, but it was still a formidable barrier to the Federals. Even under fire the Confederates had managed to rebuild the ramparts. With dirt, sand, and logs, they strengthened the damaged walls, bringing in much of the material at night in boats. The end result was to transform the character of Sumter. It had been a brick masonry fort; now it was a powerful earthwork, more impervious to shells than before.[35]

Beauregard's greatest worry now was not Sumter but Moultrie and the other works on Sullivan's Island. Sumter had become, in effect, an infantry outpost. Moultrie was the gate to the harbor. From Cummings Point at the end of Morris the distance to Sumter was three-fourths of a mile; from Sumter to Sullivan's it was a mile. If Gillmore mounted guns at the point, as he obviously would, he might be able to destroy the batteries on Sullivan's. The fleet could then enter the harbor, and it would be all over. There was little Beauregard could do to prevent the Federals from placing batteries to bear on Moultrie. His biggest guns did not have sufficient range to reach Cummings Point effectively. In summary, his difficulty was that the enemy could get within range of Moultrie but could stay out of its range. Beauregard's chief engineer was depressed as he contemplated the prospect. All that he could see ahead was an unequal fight in which the Federals fired in perfect safety and the Confederates repaired damages. "As long as the contest is one of work and shooting at long range," he wrote gloomily, "no people can beat the infernal Yankees." [36]

[34] *Battles and Leaders,* IV, 49–51; Roman, *Beauregard,* II, 156–57; *Official Records,* XXVIII, Pt. 1, pp. 724–27; J. F. Gilmer to Mrs. Gilmer, September 8, 1863, in Gilmer Papers. Beauregard expected an attack, because the Confederates had learned the code used by the Federals with their signal flags and could decipher some of the messages.

[35] Roman, *Beauregard,* II, 158–66.

[36] J. F. Gilmer to Mrs. Gilmer, September 9, 11, 1863, in Gilmer Papers.

CHAPTER THIRTEEN

Return to Virginia

I T WAS QUIET after the big bombardment. For almost two months the Federals made no major move against Sumter or the other works. Admiral Dahlgren was convinced that the navy by itself could not force an entrance into the harbor; he feared the firepower of Beauregard's new batteries and the mines rumored to be in the channel. Many of his monitors had been damaged in the recent operations, and these had to be repaired. General Gillmore was occupying himself with erecting new batteries at Cummings Point. He acted as though his part of the operation was largely accomplished. He had neutralized Sumter, which was all he had contracted to do originally, and he did not have sufficient force to seize it.

Beauregard was busier than the Federals. At Sumter he put the garrison at work repairing the damages of the bombardment. Sand and dirt were brought in to strengthen the outer walls, a central bomb-proof was constructed, and some heavy guns were returned to the fort. As he usually did in a period of quiet on his own front, Beauregard turned his mind to making plans for generals in other theaters. Now he began to think about Bragg in the West. Bragg had defeated the Federals in September at Chickamauga and had shut them up in Chattanooga, but he was not making much progress toward getting them out and recovering the Tennessee line. Beauregard worked out a plan, which he sent to Bragg, asking that general to present it to the government as his own. Beauregard proposed that in Virginia the Confederates stand on the defensive. From Lee's army and other sources Bragg would be reinforced with thirty-five thousand troops; Bragg could then cross the Tennessee, flank the Federals out of Chattanooga, and smash them in a showdown battle. After that Bragg could aid Lee in Virginia. "I fear any other plan will, sooner or later, end in our final destruction in detail. . . ," Beauregard gloomily told Bragg. "Our resources are fast getting exhausted; our people, I fear, are getting disheartened; for they see no bright spot in the horizon to revive their drooping hopes. . . ." [1]

Bragg was having his troubles at the moment. After Chickamauga he and his generals engaged in a bitter brawl as to why the results of the battle were not more decisive. Bragg blamed the generals, they blamed him. One officer was shipped to Mississippi and another suspended, two corps generals wrote to the War Department that Bragg was unfit for command, and finally the majority of the generals sent a petition to Davis asking for Bragg's removal. Faced by what was almost a revolt by the officers of the principal army in the West, Davis decided to handle the matter personally—by going to Bragg's headquarters. He arrived at about the same time that Beauregard's letter reached Bragg. The President's idea of how to soothe the situation was peculiar. He called the generals before him and in Bragg's presence asked them what they thought of their commanding general. Several of them told him: Bragg should be removed. After this painful interview Davis talked with individual officers but came to no decision about changing commanders.

A few days later he again summoned the generals to council. This time he asked if the army could take the offensive and if any general had a movement in mind. Bragg presented, in general terms, Beauregard's plan, without, of course, naming the author.[2] Beauregard displayed an unusual interest in getting his scheme adopted. He sent his brother Armand to Bragg's camp to act as an observer and to push his plan with Bragg. Before the council Armand talked to Bragg but avoided meeting Davis. Both Armand and Bragg reported to Beauregard that the President had received the plan favorably and would support it. But—and here was the fatal catch—he could not weaken Lee's army.[3] Davis promised to try to find reinforcements elsewhere. He never found them, nor did he relieve Bragg. So ended in talk the Confederacy's last chance to recover the Tennessee line and redress in part the disasters of Gettysburg and Vicksburg.

On his return trip to Richmond Davis stopped off at various points to deliver speeches. He reached Charleston on November 2. Beauregard and other military and civic dignitaries met him at the rail-

[1] Beauregard to Bragg, October 7, 1863, in Roman, *Beauregard*, II, 162–64.

[2] Sorrell, *Recollections*, 200–201; Longstreet, *From Manassas to Appomattox*, 464–68; *Official Records*, XXX, Pt. 2, pp. 65–66, 138, Pt. 4, pp. 705, 734–36.

[3] *Official Records*, XXX, Pt. 4, pp. 734–36, 745–46.

way station and conducted him to the City Hall. Here Davis addressed a large crowd. He paid tribute to the defenders of Sumter, giving special praise to the fort's commandant, Major Stephen Elliott, and predicted that Charleston, strengthened by additional aid from the government, would be able to hold out. Let us trust to our commanding general, he said, let us forget personal feuds.[4] After his speech Davis retired to the home of former Governor William Aiken, where he was to stay while in the city. Aiken, before the President's arrival, had arranged for the military and civil leaders to meet Davis at a dinner. Beauregard, in a stiff little note, informed Aiken that he could not attend: "I thank you for your kind invitation . . . it would afford me much pleasure to dine with you—but candor requires me to inform you that my relations with the President being strictly official, I cannot participate in any act of politeness which might make him suppose otherwise." [5]

The general was enraged by Davis' address. Major Elliott had been the only individual mentioned by name. This Beauregard interpreted as a deliberate affront to him. Undoubtedly Davis did not intend it that way. After all, he had referred to the commanding general. But what really angered Beauregard was probably the President's allusion to personal feuds. Beauregard unburdened his feelings in a letter to Augusta J. Evans. Davis had "done more than if he had thrust a fratricidal dagger into my heart! he has *killed* my *enthusiasm* in our holy cause! . . . May God forgive him—I fear I shall not have charity enough to pardon him." [6]

In the lull after the big bombardment Beauregard had an opportunity to test out his idea of destroying the blockading ships with torpedo boats. Some Charleston citizens put up money to build a cigar-shaped vessel named the *David*. About twenty feet long and five in diameter, the boat was operated by a small engine and carried in front a spar torpedo with seventy-five pounds of powder. The plan of Beauregard and the builders was to send the *David* out at night to ram the *New Ironsides*. On a hazy evening in October the attempt was made. A crew of four steered the *David* to where the *Ironsides* was anchored. The Confederates ran in close to the unsuspecting

[4] Charleston *Daily Courier,* quoted in Rowland (ed.), *Jefferson Davis,* VI, 73–78; Roman, *Beauregard,* II, 167–68.

[5] Beauregard to William Aiken, October 31, 1863, in War Department Collection of Confederate Records (National Archives).

[6] Beauregard to Augusta J. Evans, November 25, 1863, *ibid.*

Federals and struck the *Ironsides* with the torpedo six feet under the waterline. The water thrown up by the explosion extinguished the fires in the *David's* engine compartment, and the boat drifted to sea under heavy shelling from the *Ironsides* and other ships. The crew jumped overboard. Two of them were captured; the other two got back in the boat and started the fires going. They eluded the blockaders and managed to return to Charleston. The results of the test were inconclusive. The *Ironsides* was jolted and had to be taken to Port Royal for repairs, but she was not seriously hurt. Obviously the torpedo boats, as Beauregard envisioned them, did not carry enough explosive power to sink an ironclad.[7]

Late in October Gillmore heard that Beauregard was remounting guns in Sumter. The Federal general decided to resume the bombardment, hoping to keep the fort neutralized while the navy prepared for another attack. On the twenty-sixth the new batteries at Cummings Point opened fire. Twenty-nine heavy mortars and rifled guns pounded the fort from a range of less than a mile. At first the volume of fire was as great as in the big bombardment; later the Federals were satisfied to maintain a slower shelling. This second sustained bombardment lasted for forty-one days and nights, through November and into December. At intervals the Federals threw some shells into the city. Some buildings were hit, and Beauregard decided to move his headquarters to the upper part of town.

Against Sumter the guns fired mainly at the southeast face or sea front, which heretofore had escaped heavy shelling. Now it was breached along half its length; its upper casemates were demolished. Every day the Federal observers could see the fort shrink in height as the debris from the battered ramparts slid down to the lower casemates. The effect of the shelling was much the same as in the previous August. Although the Confederates could not work their guns in reply, the Federal guns did little real damage to Sumter. The accumulating debris tended to smother the shells and make the fort stronger than ever. In the bombproof the garrison was comparatively safe; only twenty-two deaths were recorded during the bombardment. The greatest danger to the fort was that the Federals might try a small-boat assault and rush over the low walls. Gillmore contemplated such a move but remembering the navy's disastrous attempt decided against it. He thought the navy should now move in

---

[7] *Annals of the War*, 520–21; *Official Records*, XXVIII, Pt. 1, pp. 731–35.

and take Sumter. Admiral Dahlgren insisted that he could not attack without more monitors. Beauregard's defenses were too strong, he said, and his whole squadron might be destroyed. The additional monitors never came, and during Beauregard's tenure of command the Federals made no further major moves against Charleston. In the second bombardment Beauregard could thank his stars that the Federals, in their obsession with Sumter, forgot about Moultrie.[8]

One of Beauregard's engineer officers, laboring at Sumter day and night, found in the ruined walls and the desperate resistance of the defenders something strangely beautiful and romantic. Trying to describe his feelings to his family, he wrote of the rugged outline of the ramparts against the night sky, the lanterns in unseen hands that guided men piling sandbags on the walls, the sentinels hunched over small fires in the casemates. "That ruin is beautiful . . . ," he exclaimed, "but it is more than this, it is emblematic also . . . is it not in some respects an image of the human soul, once ruined by the fall, yet with gleams of beauty and energetic striving after strength, surrounded by dangers and watching, against its foes. . . ."[9]

In the winter of 1863-64, with active operations suspended, Beauregard had little to do but think about himself. He spent much of his time brooding about his role in the war, his hatred of Davis, and the future of his cause. He expressed his feelings in letters to his political friends. Placed together in chronological order, these letters form a revealing record. They show a man who is ambitious but unsure of what he wants, who is heartsick at the injustice he thinks his civil superiors have done him, who believes that his country is doomed.

To Pierre Soulé: I fear they intend to send me to the West at the eleventh hour and without adequate resources. I hear that if Lee defeats the Federals he will go west and I will be sent to Virginia. I do not want to command an army whose job is to watch a defeated foe. My health is too bad for me to take the field, but if I have to I desire

[8] *Battles and Leaders,* IV, 24–25, 66–67; Roman, *Beauregard,* II, 171–76; *Official Records,* XXVIII, Pt. 2, p. 489; J. F. Gilmer to Mrs. Gilmer, November 22, 1863, in Gilmer Papers; Frank Barnes, *Fort Sumter* (Washington, 1952), 33–35. The latter work contains an excellent summary of the entire siege.
[9] Captain John Johnson to his sisters, December 19, 1863. A copy of this letter was furnished me by Colonel R. P. Johnson, a descendant of Captain Johnson.

P. G. T. BEAUREGARD

the command of my former army.[10] We must concentrate our forces at a decisive point. I send you a plan, the sixth one I have proposed to the government. Let the western army be reinforced from Virginia and other sources to a size of one hundred thousand; let its commander be permitted to proceed without hampering restrictions from Richmond. "It is concentration and immediate mobility that are indispensable to preserve us." [11]

To W. P. Miles: When I think of "the persistent inability and obstinacy of our rulers," I become despondent and fear that we may be "finally crushed." [12]

To Charles Villeré: Next spring and summer will see our defeat. My usefulness in the war is ended. If a war starts in Europe, I will offer my services to some nation there. Why hasn't the Confederacy produced a great captain like Napoleon? Is it not because "we have a power near the *throne* too egotistical and jealous to allow such a genius to develop itself whilst saving the country?" [13]

To Miles: Thanks for sending me a copy of the resolution of Congress praising my defense of Charleston. How different is the action of the legislators from the jealousy of the President. "The curse of God must have been on our people when we chose him out of so many noble sons of the South, who would have carried us safely through this Revolution!" [14]

In his dark bitterness Beauregard resolved to leave the army. He prepared a letter to Adjutant General Cooper asking that he be relieved of duty until such time as he could be assured of the support of the government. He listed eight points to prove he lacked the confidence of his superiors: criticism of his actions at Morris Island by the Secretary of War, the failure of the War Department to promote his officers, the refusal of the government to assign him to field serv-

[10] Beauregard to Soulé, November 28, December 5, 1863, in War Department Collection of Confederate Records. On December 31 Lee proposed to Davis that Beauregard be given the western command; *Official Records,* XXXI, Pt. 3, p. 779.

[11] Beauregard to Soulé, December 8, 1863, in Roman, *Beauregard,* II, 177–79, and to Soulé, December 11, in *Official Records,* XXXI, Pt. 3, pp. 812–13.

[12] Beauregard to Miles, December 18, 1863, in *Official Records,* XXXI, Pt. 3, pp. 843–44.

[13] Beauregard to Villeré, December 22, 1863, in War Department Collection of Confederate Records (National Archives).

[14] Beauregard to Miles, February 4, 1864, *ibid.* The resolution of Congress is in Richardson (ed.), *Messages and Papers of the Confederacy,* I, 425.

ice, and others. After he wrote the letter he reflected on it and decided not to send it. But he filed the document carefully in his papers.[15]

The most interesting military event of the winter, from Beauregard's viewpoint, was the attempted use by the Confederates of a submarine. This craft was built under the supervision of a resident of Mobile, Horace L. Hundley, who offered it to Beauregard. The submarine was twenty feet long, three and a half feet deep, and five feet wide, and carried a crew of seven to eight men. It was propelled by a screw worked from the inside by the crew. On either side of the boat were fins. When these were depressed while the sub was in motion it sank; when they were elevated it rose to the surface. Supposedly it could submerge for hours. Behind it the vessel dragged a torpedo. The idea was for the submarine to approach a Federal ship at night, submerge and pass under it, and arise on the other side. This would bring the torpedo into contact with the side of the ship from which the sub had approached; a trigger on the torpedo would go off at the shock of the impact, firing the torpedo.

On a practice submersion in the harbor the submarine demonstrated a technical defect. It sank but did not rise. When the vessel was later raised, the members of the crew were found dead, in attitudes of horrible distortion. The naval officers wanted to try another test, and another crew volunteered. Beauregard, horrified at what had happened, forbade any more submersions. He suggested to a lieutenant who had helped construct the craft that it be used as a torpedo boat like the *David* and be sent out to sink the *Housatonic,* one of the blockading ships. This officer agreed to the transformation, and the sub was equipped with a spar torpedo. One night in February it stole upon the *Housatonic* and rammed her; the resulting explosion sank the Federal ship. The attacker went down with its victim, either destroyed by the force of the detonation or drawn into the *Housatonic's* vortex. Years later searchers found the two vessels lying side by side on the bottom of the harbor.[16]

Early in March Beauregard went to Florida. His troops there had just repelled an attempt by the Federals at Jacksonville to advance into the interior. He wanted to examine the situation and to determine if a further blow could be dealt the enemy. One day he was handed a telegram from Mobile. It told him that his wife in New

[15] Beauregard to Cooper, February 7, 1864, in Beauregard Papers (Library of Congress).

[16] *Annals of the War,* 519–20; Roman, *Beauregard,* II, 181–84.

Orleans had died on March 2. Immediately he returned to Charleston, knowing that there he would shortly receive letters from her family giving him details of her death. All during the war he had managed to correspond with his wife in Federal-occupied New Orleans and to get replies from her. Their messages were transmitted through an intermediary, one A. Lefort, who was a member of the crew of a French naval vessel that frequently put in at New Orleans. Apparently Lefort would pick up a letter from the general at Mobile, a Confederate port, and deliver it to New Orleans; a letter from Mrs. Beauregard he would take to Mobile on a return trip. It was on Lefort that Beauregard was relying now for word from home.[17]

Soon the news came. A letter from his wife's sister, Julia Deslonde, told him of his Caroline's last hours. In a long letter of reply to Julia, he said that he had half expected the sad event. He knew that for two years she had been seriously ill, and he had received no letter from her since December. He seemed fascinated with what she must have thought as she was dying: "My poor Caroline must have often asked herself on her bed of pain if she would ever see me again, and, more than once in her agony, her wandering thoughts must have directed themselves toward these battle lines in order to bid me an eternal goodbye. I well know that her beautiful soul, her generous and patriotic heart preferred the salvation of the country to the joy of seeing me. She must have said 'The country comes before me' [he had written the words now and they became real]—sublime words which I desire that you have carved on her tomb." [18]

Many people wrote Beauregard letters of condolence. From these sources and others he learned that a Northern-subsidized newspaper in New Orleans had charged that Mrs. Beauregard's illness had been aggravated by the desertion of her traitor husband. This tasteless accusation fanned popular wrath; at least six thousand people attended her funeral in a kind of grim protest. He may not have known that General N. P. Banks, the Federal commander in New Orleans,

[17] A. Lefort to Beauregard, May 6, June 7, 24, 1863, in Edwin M. Stanton Papers (Division of Manuscripts, Library of Congress). These are translations of letters in Beauregard's papers that were captured at the end of the war.

[18] Beauregard to Julia Deslonde, April 2, 1864, in War Department Collection of Confederate Records (National Archives). Mrs. Beauregard was buried in the cemetery of St. John the Baptist Catholic church at Edgard, Louisiana. For aid in locating her burial place I am indebted to Mr. Lubin F. Laurent and Mrs. May Champagne of Edgard. Her tomb is unmarked, but according to Mr. Laurent it had at one time a marble slab bearing the inscription which Beauregard devised.

provided a steamer to carry her body upriver for burial in her native parish of St. John the Baptist.[19] In replying to those who had written, Beauregard spoke harshly of the "Vandal" Yankees among whom his wife had died. He almost seemed to regard her death as a political or military event. In one letter he said that he would like to rescue at the head of an army "her hallowed grave." In another he said, "Our Independence shall have cost me dearly; but our country is welcome to the sacrifice." [20]

Beauregard was always proud of the way he thought his wife had died, but after the war he denied her a place in the myth of the heroic Southern women who had labored for the success of the Confederacy. He seemed to forget that she had been a semi-invalid in an occupied city. In 1866 John Esten Cooke, the Virginia novelist, considered writing a book of sketches of prominent Confederate women. He proposed to include Mrs. Beauregard, and asked Augusta J. Evans to approach the general for permission. Miss Evans did so, but Beauregard said his wife did not deserve such notice. "I thank you, Miss Augusta, for your kind and considerate offer. . . , which I would accept with pleasure, if the one I loved so dearly had done more than to pray and suffer in silence for the success of our sacred cause," he wrote. "Her last words were indeed worthy of a Roman matron, but what are words to the acts of those noble hearted women —yourself included—who devoted their time and labor to assisting and taking care of the sick and wounded—besides encouraging the fainthearted. . . . These are the heroic women whose names and conduct should be transmitted to future generations. . . . I beg then, and entreat in the name of the South, that you should have your biography published. . . ." [21]

[19] Basso, *Beauregard,* 235; Roman, *Beauregard,* I, 10; unidentifiable newspaper clipping, March 14, 1864, in Beauregard Papers (Missouri Historical Society).

[20] Snow, *Southern Generals,* 267–68; Beauregard to W. E. Martin, April 5, 1864, in War Department Collection of Confederate Records (National Archives). In the latter collection are also Beauregard to Mrs. C. G. Shepard, April 7, 1864, to Numa Augustin, April 10, 1864, to S. W. Ferguson, April 11, 1864, to B. M. Palmer, April 18, 1864. Descriptions of Mrs. Beauregard's illness and of her funeral are in Polyxene Reynes to Emile Reynes, January 21, 1864, Uranie Reynes to Emile Reynes, March 3, 8, 1864, in Reynes Family Papers (Department of Archives, Louisiana State University). For copies of these letters I am indebted to Miss Joan Doyle.

[21] Beauregard to Augusta J. Evans, October 26, 1866, in Beauregard Papers (Library of Congress), Letterbook, Private Letters, December 16, 1865— April 18, 1867.

As the spring of 1864 opened, Beauregard's military star was rising. A Richmond editor pointed out that he was the only Confederate general to come out of 1863 with larger laurels, and entreated Davis to restore him to command in the West. Vice-President Stephens, in a speech before the Georgia legislature denouncing the government's conduct of the war, paid special tribute to the able defender of Charleston. Even the chiefs of the inner Davis circle thought it might be politic to court him. One of them suggested that maybe "the Beauregard clique" in Congress might be detached from the opposition to Davis.[22]

In a minor and passive way Beauregard became involved in the Confederacy's strategic planning for 1864. The man who brought him into the picture was General James Longstreet, commander of the First Corps in Lee's army. Late in 1863 Longstreet had taken most of his troops west to join Bragg. After the failure of the Confederates to recapture Chattanooga, Longstreet, who had quarreled with Bragg, had been permitted to go off on an independent expedition into East Tennessee. He failed to accompish anything and was chased by the Federals up to near the Virginia border. At this point he began to evolve plans of grand strategy for the government. He proposed that Beauregard with most of his troops move to join Longstreet's forces. Together they would invade Kentucky, threaten the railroad line supplying the Federals, and then force the enemy to retire from Chattanooga. At the same time the Confederate army in northern Georgia under Joe Johnston, who had succeeded Bragg, would advance into Kentucky. The united forces would then be in position to undertake a smashing offensive. In Longstreet's plan Beauregard was to lead the first column entering Kentucky.

Longstreet presented his scheme in person to Davis; it was carefully considered by the President and presented in written form to the generals who would participate in it. Everybody but Longstreet questioned the soundness of the design. The logistical difficulties in such a complicated movement were obviously too great, as even Beauregard admitted. The President finally rejected the plan, but neither he, Bragg, now his military adviser with the title of general in chief, nor Johnston could think of anything to put in its place.

[22] Richmond *Whig,* March 10, 1864, quoted in Eliot, *West Point in the Confederacy,* 160–61; Henry Cleveland, *Alexander H. Stephens* . . . (Philadelphia, 1866), 763; G. B. Hodge to W. P. Johnston, April 5, 1864, in Barret Papers.

Longstreet was convinced that one reason Davis opposed the plan was that he would not entrust an important field command to Beauregard. This thought may have entered Davis' mind, but larger reasons determined his decision.[23]

As for Beauregard, he had no hopes of securing field service or of leaving what he now referred to as the Department of Refuge. Convinced that the enemy would attempt no active operations against Charleston and suffering from fatigue and his chronic throat ailment, in April he applied to the War Department for leave. He wanted to go to his favorite resort, Bladon Springs near Mobile, for a rest. Approval of his request did not come, but a document of a different nature did. A telegram from Bragg asked if he would come to Virginia to serve in the field. On the fourteenth he answered, "Am ready to obey any order for the good of the service." He then received a directive to proceed to Weldon, North Carolina, near the Virginia border, where instructions would be sent him.[25]

Beauregard left Charleston on the twentieth and reached Weldon two days later. From there he wired Bragg that he was on the scene but had found no instructions. "In the mean time," he said, "will give general direction to everything." Bragg replied that Beauregard was to command the Department of North Carolina and Cape Fear, which included Virginia south of the James River, and sent a staff officer to Weldon to explain the military situation to Beauregard. When Beauregard formally assumed command the next day, he renamed the department, apparently on his own initiative, the Department of North Carolina and Southern Virginia.[26]

After talking with the staff officer, Beauregard understood his assignment and his military problem. The Confederate high command was preparing for the big Federal offensive expected to start in May. In northern Virginia stood the Army of the Potomac, technically commanded by George Meade but actually directed by General in Chief Grant, who traveled with it. It was obviously poised for an advance against Lee's army and Richmond. Just as obviously the Federals were mounting an important diversion to aid their main

[23] *Official Records*, XXXII, Pt. 2, pp. 790–92, Pt. 3, pp. 627–28, 637–42, 656, 736; Longstreet, *From Manassas to Appomattox*, 543–47; Johnston, *Narrative*, 291–97; Sorrell, *Recollections*, 229.
[25] Roman, *Beauregard*, II, 193; *Official Records*, XXXIII, 1283.
[26] *Official Records*, XXXV, Pt. 2, pp. 444–45; Roman, *Beauregard*, II, 195, 539.

offensive. They held various points on the Virginia–North Carolina coast. From any one of these they could launch an attack that might sever the railroad lines supplying Richmond and Lee's army. The high command figured that the Federal advance would be along the line of the James, but they did not know exactly where the blow would fall. The Federals might strike at Petersburg, the most important railroad center south of Richmond, or at the railroad between the two, or at the line between Petersburg and Weldon; they might even menace Richmond itself.

To guard against any of these eventualities, Lee himself had suggested that Beauregard, with as many of his troops as could be spared, be brought to North Carolina or the James. Beauregard's mission, then, was to protect and hold the southern approaches to Richmond. It was an important mission. Without possession of these approaches, Lee's army could not be supplied and could not maneuver or hold Richmond. If that condition ever resulted, the war would be practically over.[27]

Beauregard's department was large, the boundaries of it vaguely defined, and the command responsibility in it confused. Commanding on the Cape Fear line, with headquarters at Wilmington, North Carolina, was W. H. C. Whiting. Gathering to attack New Berne on the Carolina coast was a force under Robert Hoke, who was operating under orders from Bragg although he was in the department of George Pickett, whose headquarters were at Petersburg. Beauregard assumed that the northern boundary of his department was the James and Appomattox rivers. These streams joined at City Point, but north of City Point on the James was Drewry's Bluff, heavily fortified to guard the river approach to the capital. Was the Bluff under Beauregard's jurisdiction? North of the James was the Department of Richmond, an independent command under Robert Ransom; only if Ransom crossed the James to co-operate with Beauregard would he come under the latter's control. The final complication was that Lee, in an emergency, could exercise authority to the southern boundary of Whiting's department.

As Beauregard learned more about his department, he decided that his troops were too small in number and too scattered in location. Convinced that the enemy would soon strike at Petersburg, he told Bragg he wanted to concentrate his forces and to bring in rein-

[27] *Official Records,* XXXIII, 1282–83.

forcements. He asked that the operation against New Berne be called off and Hoke placed under his direct command. The reinforcements he proposed to get from his former command in South Carolina. Not so sensitive for the safety of Charleston now that he was away from it, he advised that two brigades, those of Johnson Hagood and Henry A. Wise, be brought north to serve with him or Lee. The high command responded that New Berne could be captured before any danger to Petersburg developed; Beauregard agreed this might be possible, and counseled Hoke how to proceed. The government also directed Hagood and Wise to join Lee. This did not displease Beauregard. He reasoned that he might get some of the men in the two brigades; besides, Lee would now be less likely to draw on Beauregard for added strength.[28]

Since his arrival at Weldon, Beauregard had acted like a model subordinate. He had been prompt in making reports and restrained in making requests. He seemed to realize that in coming into the Richmond area he was coming into closer contact with Davis and would have to watch himself. Writing to Bragg he observed, sensibly, that events might make it necessary for him to operate north of the James. In such case he would be glad to serve under Lee: "I would take pleasure in aiding him to crush our enemies and achieve the independence of our country." In due course his letter came to Davis for perusal and endorsement. When the President read Beauregard's well-meant offer, he boiled. Did the Frenchman still think he didn't have to obey the rules unless he wanted to? Angrily Davis wrote on the letter: "I did not doubt the readiness of General Beauregard to serve under any General who ranks him. The right of General Lee to command would be derived from his superior rank."[29] Even in this hour of the Confederacy's peril, the President could not cease to be a martinet or forget his hatred of Beauregard.

Before the Confederates could complete their preparations on the southern approaches, the Federal offensive developed. On May 5, in an operation designed to coincide with Grant's movement in northern Virginia, an army of twenty-two thousand men under the command of Benjamin F. Butler ascended the James on transports. The next day Butler seized City Point on the south side of the James, only eight miles from Petersburg; this was an ideal point from which

[28] *Ibid.,* LI, Pt. 2, pp. 876, 880, 882, 886; Roman, *Beauregard,* II, 195–97, 541.
[29] *Official Records,* XXXIII, 1326–28.

to operate against Petersburg and the railroads. Instead of staying there, he landed most of his troops at Bermuda Hundred, between the James and the Appomattox rivers. This position was strong defensively but faulty as an offensive base. From it Butler could hit the Richmond–Petersburg railroad, but to reach Petersburg or the line south of it he would have to cross two streams, Swift Creek and the Appomattox.

The Federal movement caught the Confederates unprepared and placed Petersburg, and hence Richmond, in terrible danger. Beauregard was still at Weldon. Hagood and his brigade were below Petersburg on a train en route to Richmond; Wise was preparing to follow. Hoke was ready to deliver his attack on New Berne, but he was about to be called off. Davis, fearful of the threat poised by Grant's offensive, on the fourth had ordered Beauregard to send Hoke with all speed to Lee. In Petersburg Pickett was getting ready to leave for an assignment north of Richmond when the blow fell. He had, in effect, one regiment to defend the town and the railroad to Richmond. Naturally concerned, he informed Beauregard and the War Department of his situation. From the Department he received no acknowledgment, no reply whatever. At the moment the high command was too occupied with the danger developing in Lee's front to worry about what was happening twenty-three miles away at the back door.[30]

Beauregard answered Pickett promptly. He directed Pickett to take command of any troops arriving in Petersburg on their way to Richmond and to detain Hagood's brigade and use it. Beauregard added that he was sick and could not travel; for the present Pickett was to remain in command. Then Beauregard informed Bragg that Petersburg was in danger and that he had instructed Pickett to halt Hagood. Bragg, obsessed with northern Virginia, replied that the brigade must come to Richmond; he wired Pickett not to stop the troops. Like a good subordinate Beauregard repeated Bragg's decision to Pickett. Also like a good subordinate who believed his superiors were acting on the basis of inaccurate information, he tried to get the decision changed. Again he warned Bragg that a crisis was at hand and again he insisted that Hagood's was the only force that could meet it. Impressed by the reports of Beauregard and Pickett, Bragg finally woke up to the situation south of the James. On the morning of the sixth he authorized Pickett to halt Hagood.[31]

[30] *Ibid.*, XXXVI, Pt. 2, p. 957; Rowland (ed.), *Jefferson Davis,* VI, 246–47.

In the next few days the feared crisis did not quite develop. For this the Confederates could thank the reinforcements that reached Pickett, and Butler's incapacity for field command. Union cavalry destroyed two railroad bridges south of Petersburg, and Butler's troops tore up a small section of track on the line to Richmond. These blows severed the line of communications between Weldon and Richmond, forcing the Confederates to detour men and supplies, but Butler could have done much more. He could have seized Petersburg, the key to all the railroads in the region, and forced the evacuation of Richmond. Instead he moved slowly, timidly, giving the Confederates time to concentrate.

While events were breaking fast around Petersburg, Beauregard remained at Weldon supervising the northward movement of Wise and Hoke. He seemed to be in no hurry to go to Petersburg. To Whiting he wrote, "I do not yet know whether I will take an active part in the great Drama about to be enacted around Richmond." He added mysteriously, "I fear, however, to be 'a little too late.' " [32] From Davis he received a telegram saying it was hoped Beauregard could proceed to Petersburg and "direct operations before and behind" him. For the President, this was sheer flattery. At the bottom of the document Beauregard wrote dryly, "Much obliged, but not often so hopeful regarding me." [33] He notified Davis that he was still sick but hoped to leave the next day.[34] Not until the eighth did he take his departure. Was he trying to avoid command responsibility? Or was he reluctant to come closer to Richmond and Davis?

No sign of indecision or lack of confidence marked him when he reached Petersburg early on the morning of May 10. Hoke's force and other reinforcements arrived the same day. Beauregard was his old self—assured, optimistic, organizing everything, producing plans on the instant. He wired Bragg: "Have just arrived. Will take the offensive as soon as practicable." A little later he notified the President's adviser: "Hope to be in position for offensive to-morrow night." [35]

[31] *Official Records,* XXXVI, Pt. 2, pp. 956–57, LI, Pt. 2, pp. 891, 895; Roman, *Beauregard,* II, 548–49.

[32] Beauregard to W. H. C. Whiting, May 5, 1864, in Beauregard Papers (Library of Congress), Letterbook, April 22, 1864—November 15, 1864.

[33] Rowland (ed.), *Jefferson Davis,* VI, 248; Henkels' Catalog, *Beauregard Papers,* Pt. II, 59.

[34] *Official Records,* LI, Pt. 2, p. 894.

[35] *Ibid.,* 915.

CHAPTER FOURTEEN

On The Petersburg Line

B EAUREGARD's assurance to Bragg that he would undertake an immediate offensive was based on information he had received that the Federals were withdrawing from Bermuda Hundred. He planned to form a junction with Ransom, who had crossed to Drewry's Bluff with part of the Richmond garrison, and attack Butler before he could leave. To verify his reports of the Federal movements, he prepared to send reconnaissance parties toward Bermuda.[1]

Beauregard's information was wrong. Butler, instead of withdrawing, was preparing to advance toward Drewry's Bluff. Another danger to the capital appeared in the presence of a large enemy cavalry force moving toward the city from the north. On the night of May 10-11 Beauregard received a telegram from Secretary Seddon warning that Richmond was in "hot danger." Although the secretary did not see fit to tell Beauregard what the specific threats to the city were, he did give the general a sound analysis of the strategic situation and a sound order what to do. He directed Beauregard to leave Petersburg at the earliest moment and join his troops with Ransom's at Drewry's Bluff. Thus placed, the united Confederate forces would be in position to counter any move the Federals might make against Richmond or Petersburg.[2]

A juncture with Ransom was a part of Beauregard's plan. With no objection, he ordered Hoke's division to march to Drewry's Bluff. He was not willing, however, to admit that his chance for an offensive had disappeared, and he had no intention of letting Seddon exercise a rigid control over his movements. After Hoke started Beauregard received information that Butler was evacuating Bermuda Hundred. Immediately he directed Hoke to move toward Bermuda and press the Federals. At the same time he informed Bragg that he had changed Hoke's orders and asked for approval. No reply from

[1] Roman, *Beauregard*, II, 199, 555.
[2] *Official Records*, XXXVI, Pt. 2, p. 986.

Bragg came, but one from Seddon did. In emphatic language the secretary told Beauregard to obey the original directive. After another exchange of telegrams Beauregard countermanded his order to Hoke.[3]

Seddon was pained by the episode, and told Beauregard so. The general was pained too. He said that he was serving in the field at great danger to his health and that if his actions were not approved he wanted to be relieved. He informed Bragg that he would "insist" on receiving orders from only one source—from Bragg, as Davis' military representative.[4] All of his sensitivity about official persecution was coming to the fore as he neared Richmond.

Beauregard did not follow Hoke's troops and the other forces that were going to Drewry's Bluff. He had asked Whiting to come up from Wilmington to take command at Petersburg. Before leaving he wanted to confer with Whiting and to collect two brigades arriving from Weldon. His delayed departure irritated the War Department. On May 12 the Federal cavalry force penetrated the outer defenses of the capital; on the same day Butler approached Drewry's Bluff and probed at the fortifications. The high command felt that the commanding general should be at the point of danger. The general, however, was taking his time. Not until the thirteenth did he leave Petersburg. At three in the morning on the next day, in a driving rain, he rode up to the Drewry House with his escort and reinforcements and assumed command. On the way he had defeated a small Federal force and passed the enemy flank. The dramatics could hardly have been better.[5]

No fear for the capital, no sense of urgency weighed on Beauregard. The enemy cavalry force had retired down the James, and he did not seem to think it would return. For the threat of Butler he had no anxiety. With at least twenty thousand troops under his command, he believed, as he had at Petersburg, that he could dispose of Butler whenever he was ready. In short, his own front was secure, and he did not have to give it much attention. As he had done so many times before in similar situations, Beauregard turned his thoughts to somebody else's front. At what was undoubtedly his last opportunity to prove himself a useful officer by tending to his

[3] *Ibid.*, 920, 991, LI, Pt. 2, p. 919.
[4] *Ibid.*, XXXVI, Pt. 2, p. 992, LI, Pt. 2, p. 920.
[5] Roman, *Beauregard,* II, 200; *Battles and Leaders,* IV, 196–97; Hagood, *Memoirs,* 231–32.

business, he could not resist dabbling in grand strategy. He produced one of his plans.

Immediately after his arrival he called into conference Colonel Harris, his chief engineer, and Colonel W. H. Stevens, engineer of the Richmond defenses. They discussed the events at Drewry's Bluff and also the situation on Lee's front. After an hour's conversation Beauregard announced that he had a plan to save the Confederate cause in Virginia and that he wanted Stevens to communicate it to the President. His design was based upon his favorite principle of concentration. Lee was to fall back toward the Richmond defenses and send Beauregard ten thousand men; five thousand additional troops from the capital garrison were to join Beauregard. With these reinforcements Beauregard would attack Butler's right flank while Whiting moved up from Petersburg to hit his right rear. The assault would separate Butler from his base at Bermuda and force him back on the James, where he could be destroyed. Beauregard expected this result to be accomplished by the fifteenth. Then he would cross the James and attack Grant on his left flank while Lee struck from the front. Grant would be destroyed, and the road to Washington would be open.[6]

This plan, which Beauregard had outlined verbally and not put in writing, Stevens took to Richmond. Not being able to see Davis, who was ill, he went to Bragg. He described the scheme and asked Bragg to issue orders approving its execution. Bragg replied that he would have to consult Davis, who would not be accessible until a later hour. In the meantime, said Bragg, he would ride out and talk with Beauregard. At about six, three hours after Beauregard himself had arrived at the Bluff, Bragg was at the Drewry mansion. He and Beauregard proceeded to discuss the grand design. Beauregard argued for it, Bragg voiced objections. The President's adviser said that the time required to make the concentrations would tip off the Federals, who would entrench in front of the Bluff and later seize Petersburg. A retreat by the army north of the capital would endanger its safety

[6] Beauregard to Henry A. Wise, October 3, 1873, in *Southern Historical Society Papers,* XXV (1897), 206. After the conference Beauregard wrote out a copy of the plan for Bragg. Although it was dated May 14, it was not delivered to Bragg until five days later; Roman, *Beauregard,* II, 200–202, 213–14. The plan is also described in *Battles and Leaders,* IV, 197–99. In these various accounts by Beauregard there are minor discrepancies but no serious differences.

and expose strategic areas to capture. Besides, ended Bragg, Beauregard already had enough force to smash Butler.[7]

In a last attempt to convince Bragg, Beauregard cried: "Bragg, circumstances have thrown the fate of the Confederacy in your hands and mine. Let us play our parts boldly and fearlessly! Issue those orders and I'll carry them out to the best of my ability. I'll guarantee success!"[8] Bragg was not persuaded. Promising only to submit the plan to Davis, he departed.

Later in the morning the President came to Beauregard's headquarters to discuss the scheme. His objections to it were the same as Bragg's. Vainly Beauregard protested that his proposal was the only course that would enable the Confederates to change from a passive defense to the offense. Davis refused to give his approval. He said that Beauregard should attack Butler immediately and try to destroy him; if that result could be attained part of Beauregard's troops could be detached to the point of real danger, Lee's front. To aid Beauregard the President promised to restore Ransom's troops which had been returned north of the river to meet the cavalry thrust. Beauregard agreed that he would bring up Whiting and make the attempt. To ensure that Beauregard would have unquestioned authority in the coming operation, the War Department issued an order extending his command to include Drewry's Bluff and all of Virginia south of the James.[9]

Beauregard's plan probably would not have worked. It is doubtful if the Confederates could have accomplished two such concentrations in the time he envisioned. As always, he ignored the vital factor of logistics. And as always, he inspired distrust by producing a design immediately after he arrived on the scene and by promising grandiose results to follow its adoption. Davis and Bragg rejected the scheme instantly and with some scorn. Their attitude seemed to be, this is what you would expect from Beauregard. But if Beauregard's plan

[7] After the war Beauregard claimed that Bragg endorsed the plan and promised to get Davis to approve it. However, when Bragg received Beauregard's document cited in the preceding note, he immediately drew up for Davis a memorandum detailing his objections to the plan. It is asssumed that he voiced to Beauregard on the fourteenth the same arguments he penned for Davis on the nineteenth. Beauregard's memory of Bragg's attitude was obviously incorrect.

[8] *Southern Historical Society Papers*, 207, punctuation and capitals supplied.

[9] *Ibid.; Battles and Leaders*, IV, 199; Davis, *Rise and Fall*, II, 511–13; Rowland (ed.), *Jefferson Davis*, VI, 253; *Official Records*, XXXVI, Pt. 2, p. 1002.

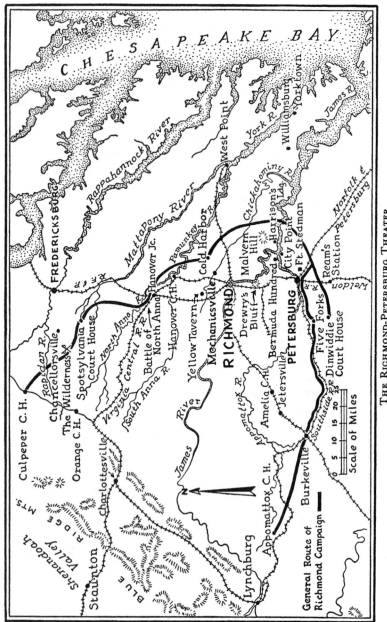

THE RICHMOND-PETERSBURG THEATER

was not likely to succeed, the Davis-Bragg policy promised little better. Beauregard's proposal *might* have brought immediate victory —or immediate defeat. The Davis-Bragg strategy of shifting forces above and below Richmond to halt successive attacks could stave off defeat but could end in nothing but failure.

On May 15, while the high command worried whether the next blow would fall on Richmond or on Lee's army, Beauregard began to plan his battle against Butler. Even now he manifested no sense of anxiety or haste. As he saw the situation, there was ample time for him to complete his preparations. He decided that he would allow Whiting approximately two days to join him at the Bluff. Then, with his forces concentrated, he would attack on the seventeenth.

He informed Bragg of his purpose in a telegram that reached Richmond early in the morning. His dispatch threw the jittery high command into a near panic. Seddon endorsed on the document that the delay would be fatal, and rushed it to Davis. The President agreed, and called for Bragg. Bragg, as always, concurred with his superior's views. He wired Whiting to move at once to Drewry's Bluff. Then he sent a telegram to Beauregard explaining the order to Whiting and impressing the necessity for an immediate movement. Beauregard should make his attack the next day, said Bragg.[10]

Before Bragg's telegram arrived at the Bluff, Beauregard had decided to change his plan. Instead of bringing Whiting to Drewry's he would bring him to Port Walthall Junction, south of the Federal position. Then, as Beauregard attacked Butler in front, Whiting would strike at the enemy rear. The revised movement would bring Whiting to the scene on a shorter line of march and would enable Beauregard to launch his attack on the sixteenth. Beauregard was proposing one of the most complex and difficult feats in war—to move two separate forces to a field of battle and unite their attack. He had suggested much the same role for Whiting in his grand design of the fourteenth. Davis had not liked the idea then; Beauregard must have known he would not like it now.

Beauregard had just finished writing his instructions for Whiting when he received Bragg's telegram. He was not going to be stopped now by interference from Richmond. At the end of his letter to Whiting he wrote: "I have just received a telegram from General Bragg, informing me that he has sent you orders to join me at this

---

[10] *Official Records,* XXXVI, Pt. 2, p. 1004, LI, Pt. 2, p. 934.

place. You need not do so, but follow to the letter the above instructions."[11] Then he sent dispatches to Davis and Bragg explaining that his changed plan had necessitated a change in Whiting's orders. Davis disliked the new arrangements but accepted them as the best hope of getting speedy action from Beauregard.[12]

In the afternoon Beauregard called his division commanders, Ransom, Hoke, and Alfred Colquitt, to headquarters to go over the battle plan. At daybreak Ransom on the Confederate left was to attack the enemy right and cut the Federals off from Bermuda Hundred. At the same time Hoke would pin down the Federal left with demonstrations; when Ransom broke the Federal right, Hoke was to smash ahead. Colquitt was to act as a reserve, ready to aid either wing. At Port Walthall Junction Whiting was to await the sound of the battle. Then he was to move forward and hit the enemy in rear or flank. As Beauregard foresaw the battle, Butler would be "environed by three walls of fire" and completely destroyed. Beauregard was certain that his plan would work. As he rode along his lines that evening he was in a gay mood. He asked the men if they were not tired of defensive fighting. When they answered affirmatively, he said that he was going to change it for them.[13]

On the morning of the sixteenth a heavy fog hung over Drewry's Bluff. Shortly before five Ransom started his division through the mist toward the Federal lines; in about an hour he carried the first breastworks and captured several hundred prisoners. Apparently the battle was off to a good start and would proceed as Beauregard had planned. Actually Ransom had accomplished little, and his movement had developed some serious weaknesses. His casualties had been numerous, his ammunition supply was running low, and several units had gone astray in the fog. He could see almost nothing of the enemy position. To Beauregard he sent word that he was halting to re-form his line and that he needed help. Beauregard sent him a brigade from the reserve.[14]

Soon after Ransom moved, Hoke started his advance. He cleared his front but soon encountered stiff resistance. On the left Ransom

[11] *Ibid.*, XXXVI, Pt. 2, p. 200; *Battles and Leaders,* IV, 200.
[12] *Official Records,* LI, Pt. 2, pp. 934, 1077; Rowland (ed.), *Jefferson Davis,* VI, 256.
[13] *Official Records,* XXXVI, Pt. 2, pp. 200–201; Roman, *Beauregard,* II, 203–205; Hagood, *Memoirs,* 235.
[14] *Official Records,* XXXVI, Pt. 2, pp. 212–13.

heard that Hoke was in trouble, and sent some of his troops to aid his comrade. Led by inexperienced brigade commanders, they merely drifted to the right and never joined Hoke. To strengthen Hoke Beauregard shifted more units from the reserve to the front. They were not enough. Hoke was stalled and even had to pull back some of his troops to prevent them from being flanked. On the other wing Ransom too reported that he could not advance, at least until he straightened his lines.[15]

From his field headquarters Beauregard had anxiously followed the battle's course. When the news of Ransom's initial success was received, Beauregard exclaimed, "Wait until I get my left well in." At intervals he sent telegraphic reports to Bragg, and until the middle of the morning he was confident of victory.[16] About eight Beauregard heard the sound of firing from the south, which he interpreted to mean that Whiting was advancing and would soon hit the enemy in rear. With Whiting coming up, it was no longer so important for Ransom to continue his costly advance. Indeed, Ransom had reported that the safety of his command would be endangered by another attack. Consequently, at ten, Beauregard directed his commander on the left not to resume the offensive.[17]

The resistance of the Federals had forced Beauregard to modify his plan. Originally he had envisioned Whiting's advance as a relatively minor part of his encircling movement. Now Whiting's force had become the only instrument that could bring victory. At nine Beauregard sent by courier an urgent directive to Whiting: "Press on and press over everything in your front, and the day will be complete." A half hour later he repeated the message.[18] Then he settled down to the grim job of waiting. With him was Davis, who had come out from Richmond to observe the battle. Hours passed. At a little before two firing broke out again from the south. Davis smiled and said, "Ah, at last!"[19] Both men listened anxiously. The sound died away, and all was quiet.

Beauregard decided, correctly, that the firing had come from Whiting's cavalry instead of from his main body. He was not quite

[15] *Ibid.*, 202–203, 237.

[16] Owen, *Washington Artillery,* 316; Roman, *Beauregard,* II, 560; *Official Records,* XXXVI, Pt. 2, pp. 196–97.

[17] *Official Records,* XXXVI, Pt. 2, p. 202.

[18] *Ibid.*

[19] Owen, *Washington Artillery,* 318.

ready, however, to give up the battle. On the right he moved Hoke forward and pressed the enemy back slightly. He wired Bragg that he hoped to organize another general attack. At intervals he sent prodding and finally pathetic pleas to Whiting to advance. The last one, dispatched at eight-thirty at night, when operations had ceased, exhorted: "Remember Dessaix at Marengo and Blucher at Waterloo." [20]

As darkness approached Beauregard sadly recognized that his plan to destroy Butler had failed. The most that he could accomplish now was to drive the Federals back to their base at Bermuda Hundred the next day. Peremptory orders to Whiting directed him to join the main army in the morning. For the fighting of the sixteenth Beauregard had to be satisfied with a partially held field, five captured guns, and 1,400 prisoners. His own casualties numbered 2,506.[21]

Early the next morning Beauregard prepared to attack. Soon he discovered that the Federals had left his front and were retiring toward Bermuda Hundred. Although he moved rapidly in pursuit, he could not catch them. By the end of the day Butler was safely behind the fortified lines of his base. Here in the confluence of the James and the Appomattox the Federals were secure against any attack that Beauregard could deliver. But if Beauregard could not get at them, he could easily prevent them from getting out. Opposite the Federal works he constructed a string of fortifications about three miles in length, the so-called Howlett line. This line shut Butler up between the two rivers as though, in Grant's phrase, he was corked in a bottle. Beauregard described the Federal commander's predicament in similar terms: "He now rests there, hemmed by our lines, which have since, been advanced . . . and now completely cover the southern communications of the capital, thus securing one of the principal objects of the attack." [22]

As the pursuit of the seventeenth started, Whiting's troops had joined Beauregard. Their general did not come with them; he had given up his command to another officer. At last Beauregard learned why Whiting had not attacked during the battle. It was a fantastic and tragic story. In briefest terms, Whiting had started to advance, and then, in an apparent mental paralysis, had stopped and refused

[20] *Official Records,* XXXVI, Pt. 2, p. 198; Roman, *Beauregard,* II, 560–61.
[21] *Official Records,* XXXVI, Pt. 2, pp. 198–206.
[22] Hagood, *Memoirs,* 249–51; Roman, *Beauregard,* II, 208.

to go on. People in the army and out believed that he was drunk or under the influence of narcotics. His own explanation was that he was sick and exhausted from his labors at Petersburg and disordered in body and mind.[23]

Beauregard had always admired Whiting, and now he treated him with great kindness. In a letter he told his subordinate that he had made a bad failure, but publicly Beauregard defended Whiting from the charge of drunkenness. When he wrote his report of the battle, he said only that Whiting's delay was one reason the victory was not complete. In fact, in his report, Beauregard criticized Ransom at least as severely as he did Whiting. He charged that Ransom had exaggerated the obstacles in his front and had sent in misleading reports.[24] Personal motives may have prompted Beauregard to make excuses for Whiting and to assail Ransom. In the final analysis, the responsibility for Whiting's movement rested on Beauregard. It was he who had insisted that Whiting move to the field instead of to Drewry's Bluff; it was he who had changed Whiting's orders. Criticism of Whiting could easily turn into criticism of Beauregard.

In Richmond there was some criticism. Colonel Northrop, an old enemy, denounced the general as a charlatan whose blunders were ruining the Confederacy. The men in the high command said little, but they were evidently far from satisfied with the results of the battle. Seddon commented a little later that Beauregard's explanation of why the victory was incomplete was open to serious question. Davis, describing the engagement for Lee, observed dryly: "Our success . . . was equal to anticipated." [25]

Actually Beauregard's victory had substantially changed the strategic situation in Virginia, as Davis well knew. Because Beauregard's line was short, he could hold Butler corked with a relatively small force. This meant that part of Beauregard's army could be withdrawn to aid Lee. Lee realized immediately the value of Beauregard's success; he asked Davis to send him some of the troops on the Howlett line. The President replied that he had ordered 3,337 men to Lee and would dispatch 1,600 more. These depletions left

[23] Hagood, *Memoirs*, 236; Reagan, *Memoirs*, 191; *Official Records*, XXXVI, Pt. 2, pp. 256–60, 312, 1026.

[24] *Official Records*, XXXVI, Pt. 2, pp. 203–205, 1026.

[25] Jones, *Rebel War Clerk's Diary*, 215; *Official Records*, XXXVI, Pt. 2, p. 204; Rowland (ed.), *Jefferson Davis*, VI, 256–57.

Beauregard with a force of approximately 15,000 troops of all arms.[26]

Whatever his critics might think of Drewry's Bluff, Beauregard was as confident as ever of his abilities as a general and a strategist. Two days after the battle he had another plan of grand strategy ready for Bragg's consideration. This design was a reversal of his scheme of the fourteenth. Now Lee was to fall back toward Richmond, and Beauregard with fifteen thousand troops would move up to join him. Together they would crush Grant; then Beauregard would return and destroy Butler. "Without such concentration," he said, "nothing decisive can be effected, and the picture presented is one of ultimate starvation." [27]

This proposal received little more consideration from the high command than the previous one. Davis wrote in official comment that Lee's ability was too well known to permit an officer from another theater to suggest what moves he should make. Furthermore, said the President, if Beauregard could spare fifteen thousand troops for the proposed attack, he could reinforce Lee with ten thousand now, which would enable Lee to defeat Grant.[28] Davis informed Beauregard that Lee must be strengthened and that Beauregard's army was the best source from which to draw help. If Beauregard wished to accompany and command his troops, added the President, the administration would be most willing. Beauregard had been playing the game of military semantics too long to fall in this trap. He replied: "With regard to re-enforcing General Lee, I shall be most happy to do so whenever you shall judge proper to order it." [29]

After Drewry's Bluff the high command ceased to regard Beauregard's army as an independent force with a mission of its own. The Confederate planners considered it a pawn to be used in the larger strategic situation in Virginia or a reservoir from which to reinforce Lee. While Beauregard and Butler had fought between Richmond and Petersburg, Grant had struck the Confederate army in northern Virginia. After the savage battles of the Wilderness and Spotsylvania, he slid off to his left, hoping to get between Lee and Richmond and

---

[26] Douglas S. Freeman (ed.), *Lee's Dispatches* . . . (New York, 1915), 187; *Official Records,* LI, Pt. 2, p. 945; Roman, *Beauregard,* II, 222–23; *Battles and Leaders,* IV, 205; Rowland (ed.), *Jefferson Davis,* VI, 256–57.

[27] *Official Records,* XXXVI, Pt. 2, pp. 1021–22.

[28] *Ibid.,* LI, Pt. 2, p. 945; Rowland (ed.), *Jefferson Davis,* VI, 257–58.

[29] Rowland (ed.), *Jefferson Davis,* VI, 258–59; *Official Records,* XXXVI, Pt. 3, pp. 818–19.

force Lee to battle. By the last week in May he had reached a point fifteen miles northeast of Richmond. To counter this move Lee shifted to his own right, bringing his army closer to the capital.

Lee's movement also brought him closer to Beauregard. The proximity of the forces north and south of the James suggested to Lee the possibility of a concentration. Confederate intelligence indicated that some of Butler's troops had been removed by water to join Grant. If the report was true, Beauregard would be able to contain Butler with a smaller force. When Richmond asked Beauregard to check the accuracy of the information, he replied that the Federals seemed to be increasing their strength. A few days later he conceded that Butler might be reinforcing Grant.[30] Lee was convinced that Beauregard could safely leave the Bermuda Hundred line with most of his troops and move north of the James. In three letters to Davis Lee said that he would retire nearer to Richmond if Beauregard would indicate a convenient point where their forces could meet.[31]

Beauregard showed no desire to join Lee. He told the government that he was containing an enemy force twice as large as his own. His argument partially convinced the President. Davis suggested to Lee that perhaps Beauregard's troops were as well employed as they could be.[32] Lee was not quite convinced. To fully explore the situation, he proposed a personal conference between himself and Beauregard. Before departing for the meeting, Beauregard wired Davis that to divide his small force to aid Lee would endanger the safety of Richmond. He used the same argument on Lee when he came to the latter's field headquarters on the evening of May 29. Although he admitted that probably four thousand of Butler's troops had gone to Grant, he insisted that he faced a superior enemy. He had only twelve thousand infantry, he said, and could spare none to Lee.[33] His attitude seems strangely inconsistent with the plan he had presented on the eighteenth. The explanation is, of course, that he did not want to unite with Lee unless Lee was committed to use Beauregard's strategy.

On the day after the conference Grant again extended his left,

[30] *Official Records,* XXXVI, Pt. 3, pp. 818–19, 826, LI, Pt. 2, pp. 953, 961.
[31] Freeman (ed.), *Lee's Dispatches,* 194–97, 199, 203.
[32] *Official Records,* XXXVI, Pt. 3, 842; Rowland (ed.), *Jefferson Davis,* VI, 262.
[33] *Official Records,* XXXVI, Pt. 3, p. 849; Freeman (ed.), *Lee's Dispatches,* 204–205, 208–209.

this time toward Cold Harbor, only about eight miles northeast of Richmond. Lee shifted to confront him. Again the Confederate line was lengthened and consequently thinned. Lee knew that without help from Beauregard he could not hold. Instead of appealing to the War Department, he called directly on Beauregard for reinforcements. Promptly Beauregard replied: "War Department must determine when and what troops to order from here." He added that he furnished the department with adequate information on which to make a decision. Lee, irritated by Beauregard's refusal to assume responsibility, then telegraphed Davis that unless he received part of Beauregard's troops the result would be disaster.[34]

This blunt warning stung the high command into action. If Beauregard had been evading responsibility, so had Davis and Bragg. In a hurried conference, the President and his adviser decided to reinforce Lee, against any objection Beauregard might make. Peremptory orders went to Beauregard to send Hoke's division immediately to Lee. After this sudden bracing of spines, an almost comic denouement followed. Shortly after the orders were dispatched and before they reached Beauregard, Bragg received a message from Beauregard stating that he had just sent Hoke to Lee and would furnish another division as soon as possible. What was behind Beauregard's abrupt reversal of attitude? Perhaps he foresaw the decision coming from Richmond and concluded it would be politic to anticipate it. More likely, he was moved by a soldierly realization that Lee was in real trouble. His signalmen had reported that seventeen Federal vessels laden with troops had left Bermuda Hundred, obviously carrying more of Butler's men to Grant.[35]

Lee was grateful for Beauregard's aid, but he wanted more. Again he suggested to Beauregard that the latter, with part of his remaining force, move north of the James. As before, Beauregard demurred. He said that although sixteen thousand Federals had gone to Grant eight thousand were still on his front. For him to leave would endanger the line of communications between Richmond and Petersburg. Lee made another try. He said he would like Beauregard to take command of the right wing of the Army of Northern Virginia. To which Beauregard replied: "I am willing to do anything for our

---

[34] Roman, *Beauregard*, II, 563; *Official Records*, XXXVI, Pt. 3, p. 850.
[35] *Official Records*, XXXVI, Pt. 3, p. 857, LI, Pt. 2, pp. 969, 971.

success, but cannot leave my Department without orders of War Department." [36]

The government continued to detach more of his troops for service north of the James. He protested the depletions. In arguing against the loss of one brigade, he said that it constituted one third of his force and would be only one twenty-fifth of Lee's. According to this unique doctrine, the component basis of an army should be mathematics instead of need. In nearly every case, the government first asked him to send troops and then ordered him.[37] Nothing illustrates better the fundamental weakness of the Confederate command system than the weary series of telegrams exchanged in May and early June between Davis, Bragg, Beauregard, and Lee. Beauregard evaded his responsibility for determining what help he could give Lee; Davis and Bragg shirked their responsibility to decide, when he refused. The strangest feature of the whole affair was that, in the face of Lee's repeated requests, nobody in the high command thought to *order* Beauregard to join Lee.

Beauregard realized that his co-operation with Lee was going to be a continuing issue; he also thought that his enemies were watching for him to make a mistake. To protect himself against future criticism and to set the record straight, he filed with Bragg on June 3, the day of the battle of Cold Harbor, copies of recent telegrams between Lee and himself. In clear, cold terms, he informed Bragg that he was always ready to co-operate with Lee and that he would obey any orders of the War Department. He could not, however, advise the withdrawal of more troops from his theater; even with his present force he might not be able to hold the Richmond–Petersburg line. It was a curious document, almost like a lawyer's brief, and it revealed that Beauregard was becoming increasingly conscious of his reputation, perhaps to a point where he shrank from risking it in action.[38]

Although Grant made no move for several days after Cold Harbor, the Federals launched several minor and obviously diversionary offensives at other points on the Virginia front. Lee and the high command were puzzled as to where Grant would strike next. Beauregard was not. As a general he had his defects—the penchant for grand

[36] *Ibid.*, Pt. 3, pp. 864–65; Roman, *Beauregard*, II, 563.
[37] *Official Records*, XXXVI, Pt. 3, pp. 868, 870–71; Roman, *Beauregard*, II, 565–66.
[38] *Official Records*, XXXVI, Pt. 3, pp. 871–72.

planning, the disregard of logistics, the exaggeration of results to be attained—but his general strategic sense was often sound, especially where enemy intentions were involved.

Among the Confederate leaders he alone now divined what Grant was going to do. On June 7 he warned Bragg that Grant would shift southward to the line of the James, probably operating on the south bank. Two days later he gave Bragg a more detailed analysis. He predicted that Grant would slide around Lee's flank to the James and advance on both sides of the river or, more probably, that the Federal commander would place all of his army below the James and operate against Richmond from the fortified base of Bermuda Hundred.[39] It was a grimly accurate forecast.

Hardly had he dispatched his second warning than he received news that seemed to confirm his views. A Federal force of infantry and cavalry from Bermuda Hundred had crossed the Appomattox on pontoon bridges and was attacking Petersburg. This thrust was one of Grant's diversionary offensives. Petersburg was defended by but one brigade. The Confederate commander, H. A. Wise, called for help from the home guards and all able-bodied males. A motley collection of old men, boys, hospital workers, and prison inmates joined Wise's regulars. They beat off the feebly delivered attack until troops sent by Beauregard arrived. The Federals then withdrew.[40]

During the course of the day Beauregard transmitted to Richmond a number of telegrams begging for the restoration of his troops which he had sent to Lee. He said that unless they were returned he could not hold the Richmond–Petersburg line; he would have to abandon his position at Bermuda Hundred or Petersburg. Although the government ordered two brigades to Drewry's Bluff, nobody in the high command took his fears very seriously. Lee assured him that the Federal movement was only a reconnaissance and that Grant had not reinforced Butler. That it was a reconnaissance Beauregard realized, but he judged it was a prelude to a larger offensive by Grant. In his soothing dispatch Lee said something that revealed much about his mental picture of the strategic situation, a picture that would pro-

[39] *Ibid.,* 878–79, 886.
[40] *Ibid.,* 884–85 Roman, *Beauregard,* II, 225–26; *Battles and Leaders,* IV, 534–37.

foundly influence his acts in the next few days. He said that Grant could not cross the James without his knowing it.[41]

On June 12 Grant started a movement that would test the accuracy of Lee's boast and prove Beauregard a prophet. Giving up hope of bringing Lee to a showdown battle north of Richmond and not wishing to drive his adversary into the city's defenses, he decided to shift his army south of the James and capture Petersburg. Holding that transportation center, he could force Lee to come out of Richmond and fight. As Grant's troops moved toward the James General W. F. Smith's Eighteenth Corps, part of the reinforcement from Butler, was in the lead, a circumstance that would give Beauregard a lot of trouble in the hours just ahead. By the evening of the thirteenth the army had reached the James; the next afternoon the van crossed the river and debarked at Bermuda Hundred. Almost fifty thousand Federals were at Bermuda the night of the fourteenth. Grant himself arrived, and directed Smith to cross the Appomattox and attack Petersburg.

The events of June 12–14 and of the following three days constitute one of the most complex and puzzling episodes of the war and one of the most argued about. Ever since, the partisans of Lee and of Beauregard have disputed over which general gauged the situation correctly. One thing is certain: for the entire day of the thirteenth and for part of the fourteenth Lee did not know where Grant had gone. He knew that the Federals had left his front but not what route they had taken. To guard the approaches to Richmond along the James, he moved his army south toward that stream; from his new position he could also co-operate more easily with Beauregard if Grant crossed the river. By the afternoon of the fourteenth Lee knew that the bulk of Grant's army was on the north side of the James. He did not know that the advance was at Bermuda.[42] At this point the complexities begin to operate. In an attempt to simplify them, the incidents of these days will be presented in a diary arrangement.

June 14: Lee was undecided as to whether Grant would advance along the north side of the James or cross to the south side. Beauregard informed Bragg that Grant's move toward the river and reinforcements to Butler made his position critical; he asked for the re-

---

[41] *Official Records,* XXXVI, Pt. 3, pp. 884–85; Rowland (ed.), *Jefferson Davis,* VI, 270; Roman, *Beauregard,* II, 566.

[42] Freeman (ed.), *Lee's Dispatches,* 227–32.

turn of his troops with Lee. To Lee he reported that transports were moving up the James and that deserters said that the Eighteenth Corps and part of the Tenth had joined Butler. These two units had originally been in Butler's army before being sent to Grant. Lee interpreted this intelligence to mean that Grant would operate on the north side and was reinforcing Butler for a simultaneous advance south. Nevertheless, he ordered Hoke's division to Drewry's Bluff. Later in the day Beauregard sent a staff officer, Colonel S. B. Paul, to Lee to explain his situation.[43]

June 15: Early in the morning Smith's corps, perhaps 18,000 strong, attacked Petersburg. Beauregard had under his command only about 5,400 troops, 3,200 on the Howlett line and 2,200 at Petersburg. Around Petersburg stretched a line of field fortifications known as the Dimmock line. Ten miles in length, it was too extended to be held by Beauregard's scanty force. Throughout the day the Federals hurled a series of attacks that carried part of the outer line. Fortunately for the Confederates, none of the assaults were delivered with much strength or determination. If Smith had not been so timid, he could have seized Petersburg. Beauregard directed the defense from his field headquarters north of Petersburg, not coming into the city until later in the day. In response to his urging, the high command ordered Hoke to march to Petersburg. Hoke's first units arrived at seven that night and were placed on a new line that Beauregard's engineers were building back of the captured works. Shortly Smith called off his attack, even though the Second Corps of Grant's army had joined him. That night Beauregard directed his one division at Bermuda, commanded by B. R. Johnson, to move to Petersburg. When this division arrived, he would have a force of about 14,000 to confront one of over 40,000.[44]

About the middle of the day Colonel Paul reached Lee's headquarters. He said that Beauregard was in danger and wanted his troops returned. Lee was not impressed by Paul's description of Beauregard's peril. He said that most of Beauregard's force had already been ordered south of the James. Telling Paul that if Beauregard became seriously threatened he would come to his aid, Lee sent

[43] *Official Records,* XL, Pt. 2, pp. 652–53, LI, Pt. 2, p. 1012; Roman, *Beauregard,* II, 567.

[44] Roman, *Beauregard,* II, 229–31, 567; *Battles and Leaders,* IV, 540–41; Hagood, *Memoirs,* 265–67; Fitzhugh Lee, *General Lee* (New York, 1894), 346–47; Alexander, *Military Memoirs,* 552–53.

the colonel on his way.[45] Shortly after Paul left, a messenger from Bragg delivered to Lee a sheaf of telegrams from Beauregard. In the latest one, dated 7 A. M., Beauregard informed Bragg that his position was critical: Butler's troops loaned to Grant had been returned and Grant was at Harrison's Landing on the north side of the James. From this dispatch Lee concluded that Beauregard was faced only by Butler's restored army. He overlooked the importance of Beauregard's reference to Grant's location. (Beauregard, of course, was wrong, Grant being at Bermuda.) Beauregard was saying, not too clearly, that if Grant was on the north side he was certain to cross. This fact seemed so obvious to Beauregard that he did not bother to enlarge on it. Besides, he had warned Bragg on the ninth that Grant would soon strike south of the James.[46]

During the day Beauregard sent other telegrams to Bragg. Apparently he did not communicate with Lee, although he asked Bragg to transmit copies of two of his dispatches to the commander of the Army of Northern Virginia. Bragg seems to have followed Beauregard's request literally. He sent Lee nothing that Beauregard did not ask him to, with the curious result that some of Beauregard's most vital information did not reach Lee. At 9 A. M. Beauregard reported that the Federal Ninth Corps was rumored to be on his front. This intelligence, even without verification, was obviously of great import; it indicated that part of Grant's army was south of the James. Shortly before noon he told Bragg that he might have to choose between holding the Bermuda line and Petersburg and asked for instructions. These dispatches Bragg seems to have kept on file. At one in the afternoon Beauregard informed Bragg that he might have to remove Johnson's division from the Bermuda line and send it to Petersburg; in such case, the Bermuda line would be lost. He asked that a copy of his telegram be transmitted to Lee. From Petersburg at a little after nine that night, he reported that the Federals had penetrated part of his lines and that he was ordering Johnson to Petersburg. Lee would have to look to the defense of Drewry's Bluff and the Howlett line. This ominous news he wished passed on to Lee.[47]

[45] Paul's account of the interview is in Roman, *Beauregard*, II, 579–81. It contains some inaccuracies. He inferred that Beauregard had told him Grant was over the James, a fact Beauregard could not have known when he sent Paul to Lee; Freeman, *R. E. Lee*, III, 558–59.

[46] *Official Records*, XL, Pt. 2, p. 655.

[47] *Ibid.*, 655–56.

These two messages had not reached Lee when he retired that night. At two in the morning a staff officer woke him and handed him a dispatch from Beauregard, sent at fifteen minutes before midnight. In it Beauregard said that he had abandoned his lines at Bermuda in order to concentrate at Petersburg. Could not these lines be occupied by Lee's troops, he asked.[48] Lee pondered the meaning of the dispatch. Beauregard seemed to be saying that he was threatened by a strong force, but he did not indicate that the force was Grant's. Although Lee ordered two divisions to Bermuda, he was still convinced that Beauregard confronted only Butler. At the moment almost half of Grant's army was across the James.

June 16: At an early hour the Federals renewed their attacks and continued them until after nightfall. When the day began, over 40,000 Federal soldiers were on the field; by late afternoon the number had increased to over 60,000. Beauregard fought with 14,000. Despite the odds in their favor the attackers gained little ground. They seized several points on the Confederate right but failed to break the main defensive line. When a part of the line gave way, Beauregard had new works constructed immediately in rear. His defense was bold and brilliant. At intervals he counterattacked as though he had a large force at his disposal. The Federal generals were impressed. A commander who held such an extended line and who could launch counterattacks must be present in strength. They conducted their assaults with needless caution.[49]

On the morning of this day Lee established his headquarters at Drewry's Bluff. With him on the south side of the river were approximately 21,000 of his troops; about 25,000 were still north. Anxiously Lee waited for intelligence from Beauregard. Beauregard's first dispatch, filed at 7:45 A. M., said that the Second Corps, of Grant's army, was among the force on his front and asked for reinforcements. This message did not reach Lee.

A second one, filed at 9:45, did. Lee read that a heavy force was pressing on Petersburg and that Beauregard needed help. Lee replied that he did not know the position of Grant's army and that until he did, he could not strip the north bank of the James. In a later telegram informing Beauregard that he was occupying the abandoned

---

[48] *Ibid.,* 657; Freeman (ed.), *Lee's Dispatches,* 244.

[49] Roman, *Beauregard,* II, 232; Hagood, *Memoirs,* 267–68; *Battles and Leaders,* IV, 541–42.

Bermuda Hundred line, Lee asked if Beauregard had heard of Grant's crossing the James. Before this query reached Beauregard a dispatch came in from Beauregard announcing that he might have sufficient force to hold Petersburg. Lee was reassured by this that only Butler menaced Petersburg. He found further comfort in Beauregard's answer to his inquiry about Grant. Beauregard said only that forty-two transports had passed up the James. Happily Lee told Beauregard that these vessels were merely returning Butler's troops.[50]

That night Beauregard sent Lee a more definite picture of the situation. He was shortening his lines, he said, and hoped to make them stronger. As yet he had received no satisfactory information of Grant's crossing, but he did know that the Second Corps was in his front.[51] Here was the first specific information that a unit from Grant's army was at Petersburg. Lee was puzzled but still not convinced that the bulk of the Union army was south of the James. The presence of this corps might be only an attempt by Grant to deceive while he struck on the north side. Actually, by midnight ninety thousand Federals had crossed the river.

June 17: The Federals began to attack at three in the morning and did not stop until eleven at night. Although the first assaults were repelled, Beauregard saw that his lines would soon break under the pounding. With his engineers he selected a new and shorter line, which he had marked with white stakes so the troops could retire to it at night. At dusk the Federals smashed one section of the original line. They would have broken through but for the arrival of a brigade from Lee which rushed into the gap. After the firing ceased, Beauregard directed that campfires be lit and sentinels thrown forward. Behind this deception the weary soldiers retired in the darkness to the new line. Before seeking rest, they scooped out trenches with their bayonets, knives, and tin food cans.[52]

Beauregard's descriptions of his situation continued to puzzle Lee. In the morning Beauregard telegraphed that two corps were in his front but that with reinforcements he could take the offensive. Lee replied that without more definite information of Grant's movement it would be imprudent for him to draw more men to the south side. As the afternoon wore on Beauregard's reports became more alarm-

---

[50] *Official Records,* XL, Pt. 2, p. 659, LI, Pt. 2, p. 1078.

[51] *Ibid.,* LI, Pt. 2, pp. 1078–79.

[52] *Battles and Leaders,* IV, 542–43; Roman, *Beauregard,* II, 233–34; Hagood, *Memoirs,* 268; Alexander, *Military Memoirs,* 554.

ing and more specific. At four-thirty he said that he had reliable information that Grant had crossed the James. Half an hour later he wired that prisoners had been taken from four corps in Grant's army. Checking this news with other intelligence, Lee was almost convinced. He prepared to cross the remainder of his army.

Then came a dispatch, about ten that night, that removed any last doubts Lee may have had. It also suggested that if Lee was coming he had better come fast. Beauregard said that increasing numbers of the enemy would compel him that night to withdraw to a shorter line. "This I shall hold as long as practicable," he wrote, "but without reinforcements, I may have to evacuate the city very shortly." Lee ordered all of his army to move to Petersburg at dawn.[53]

At seven-thirty in the morning on the eighteenth as Beauregard's exhausted troops braced for another attack, the vanguard of Lee's army reached the Petersburg lines. As other units arrived they replaced Beauregard's men. There would be no breaking of the lines now. Soon Lee rode in. Later he and Beauregard inspected the ground. Beauregard, all optimism again, proposed an attack on Grant's flank. Lee said that his troops were too weary for an offensive. It was enough for the moment to have saved Petersburg.[54]

Out of the tangled events of those June days emerged one of the great historical controversies of the war. Beauregard and his friends helped to incite it with their postwar writings. They claimed, or implied, that almost from the first Beauregard knew Grant had crossed the James and that he apprised Lee, who refused to believe. In their account Lee ignored repeated and clear warnings from Beauregard and left the latter to battle at Petersburg against great odds. At the last desperate minute Beauregard convinced Lee and saved the Confederacy. It was a pretty story and attracted many believers. Probably the case for Beauregard was more widely accepted in the history books than the case for Lee.

Although Lee always had his supporters, his side of the argument has been most fully presented in recent years. The Lee admirers point out that the records do not sustain Beauregard. Beauregard did not tell Lee that he faced Grant's troops; until almost the last he thought

---

[53] *Official Records*, XL, Pt. 2, pp. 664–65, LI, pp. 1079–80; Roman, *Beauregard*, II, 234–35.

[54] Roman, *Beauregard*, II, 246–47; *Battles and Leaders*, IV, 543–44.

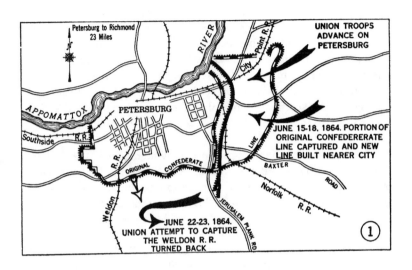

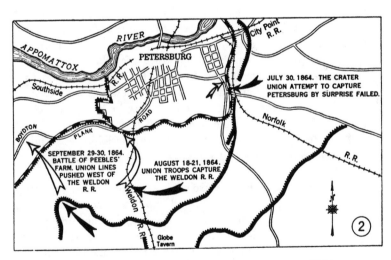

CONFEDERATE LINES AT PETERSBURG, SUMMER OF 1864

he confronted only Butler's restored army. He did not furnish Lee with clear, definite intelligence; his reports were vague and contradictory. Lee did not ignore Beauregard's warnings or leave the latter in peril at Petersburg; he complied with every request Beauregard made for reinforcements. Lee was charged with a large mission: the defense of Richmond. He could not abandon the James River line until he was certain the Federals had left it. When Beauregard provided satisfactory evidence that Grant was south of the river, Lee shifted to meet the threat. His every move was made at the right time.[55]

The Lee presentation seems more convincing than it is. It has a surface plausibility and a technical correctness that are deceptive. Lee's admirers assume that if they can show Beauregard was wrong— in his intelligence reports or in his understanding of the strategic situation—then Lee must have been right. Beauregard was wrong on a number of points. He did send in vague reports, for which he was not entirely to blame. He was served badly by a rudimentary intelligence system and could not quickly identify the enemy units in his front. But it was not Beauregard's reports that misled Lee—it was the fact that the first Federal troops to appear at Petersburg were Butler's troops returning from Grant. The story might have been different if a corps from Grant's army had led the attack. Beauregard did not at an early date inform Lee and the high command that Grant was over the James. He probably understood well enough what Grant was doing. Just a few days before he had predicted to Bragg that Grant would make precisely such a move. Having put himself on record, he seemed to feel his responsibility was ended. Let Lee and Bragg figure out the obvious. He had to take care of his own line.

But even when all of Beauregard's mistakes are written large they look small in comparison with the all-important fact that Robert E. Lee, from the beginning almost to the last, did not understand Grant's movement or his objective. Lee assumed, as most historians have since, that Grant was trying to get into Richmond. Attacking Lee near the strong defenses of the capital was the thing Grant was trying to avoid. His purpose was to draw Lee into battle in the

[55] Freeman, *R. E. Lee,* III, 442.

open country around Petersburg. Nothing that Beauregard did or failed to do caused Lee to misread the situation. The false picture was in Lee's mind.

Beauregard had no need to exaggerate his role in the campaign. In his defense of Petersburg was glory enough. Again he demonstrated that in a crisis he was a fine combat officer. He might be theatrical and theoretical before a fight, but when he went in he went hard. Seldom in war has a general contended successfully so long against such odds. It was his best battle of the war.

CHAPTER FIFTEEN

Commander of the West

G RANT'S PLAN to force a showdown decision at Petersburg had failed—foiled by Beauregard's stubborn defense and the
arrival of Lee's army. Reluctantly now the Federal commander
realized that he would have to dislodge Lee by siege operations.
From north of the James to below Petersburg the Federals constructed
an elaborate line of trenches from which to conduct their operations.
Opposite the Federal line the Confederates built equally elaborate
works. In the course of the long siege Grant would jab at any point
in the Confederate line that seemed weak, but he concentrated his
efforts on his extreme left. Here he aimed to slide around Lee's flank
and secure possession of all the railroads supplying Petersburg from
the south and west.

Beauregard was not very happy with his position in Lee's army
or with the kind of warfare in which that army now had to engage.
He was a full general serving under the command of another full
general. Before Lee crossed the James, Beauregard had commanded a
department and an army. Now he became, in effect, a corps commander in a larger organization. Because of his rank and reputation
Lee treated him with special deference, but the situation was un-
comfortable for both generals. Beauregard had been an independent
commander too long to be satisfied with a subordinate status.

In the siege operations Beauregard acted under Lee's direction. He
executed plans devised by Lee; if he formed a plan he had to secure
Lee's approval to carry it out. On the Confederate line Beauregard
commanded a section running from the Appomattox River to a
point east of Petersburg. Late in June Lee decided to hurl an attack at the extreme left of the Union line. As most of the troops to
be used in the movement were Beauregard's, Lee instructed him to
plan the offensive. The attack failed, partly because the Federals
fought well and partly because the Confederate subordinate generals
did not co-ordinate their advance. Although Lee blamed nobody,

there was some criticism of Beauregard, particularly from officers in Lee's army.[1]

Through the hot weeks of July the siege continued with deadly monotony. The Confederates on Beauregard's part of the line knew that the Federals were mining in their vicinity, but efforts to locate the tunnel failed. At an early hour on the morning of the thirtieth its location became ghastly clear. The Federals exploded a mine that blew a breach in the Confederate line one hundred and seventy feet long—the famous crater. Their plan was to pour a strong force through the opening and possibly capture Petersburg.

The sound of the explosion awoke Beauregard from sleep. Learning what had happened, he sent a courier to inform Lee and ask for reinforcements. Then he rode to the scene to survey the damage. Almost immediately Lee arrived and took over the direction of operations. After sharp fighting the Confederates drove the attacking force back and closed the gap.[2] Beauregard's role in the affair epitomized his position in Lee's army. He was somebody else's agent, in this case almost an onlooker.

Beauregard's next important participation in the siege, and his last one, occurred in mid-August. A strong Federal force moved below Petersburg and seized a point on the Weldon railroad. Of the several railways running into Petersburg, this line was closest to the Federal position and hence was the most difficult for the Confederates to defend. At the time, Lee was north of the James, where an enemy demonstration seemed to threaten the Richmond defenses. In Lee's absence Beauregard commanded at Petersburg.

Well aware of the importance of the Weldon road, he prepared an attack to dislodge the Federals, who after occupying a mile of track moved north toward the city. On the nineteenth he sent four brigades against them. The Confederates captured twenty-seven hundred prisoners and drove the Federals back to the railroad, but they could not drive them from it. Two days later, with Lee himself present, the Confederates tried again and failed. The Federals were too strong to be ejected by any force that Lee could dispose.[3]

The loss of a section of the railroad was a serious setback for the Confederates; Richmond's communications with the Deep South

[1] *Official Records,* XL, Pt. 1, pp. 799, 804–805; Hagood, *Memoirs,* 270–78.
[2] Roman, *Beauregard,* II, 259–64; Wise, *End of an Era,* 355–68.
[3] *Official Records,* XLII, Pt. 1, pp. 857–58; Hagood, *Memoirs,* 288–98; *Battles and Leaders,* IV, 568–71.

were partially cut. In the capital the high command inclined to the belief that Beauregard had erred in not using enough troops in his attack. Lee refused to join in any criticism of Beauregard. The attacking force had been small, the commanding general told the President, but more men could not have been spared. In the face of Grant's superior numbers all along the line, the fall of the Weldon road was inevitable.[4]

Lee's intervention prevented a quarrel between Beauregard and the administration, but two earlier brushes had left their scars. In June Bragg addressed a cold letter to Beauregard asking at what hour on the fifteenth he had ordered the evacuation of Bermuda Hundred and if he had informed Lee of his action. Recognizing the implied censure, Beauregard replied with a document of eight pages. His explanation did not satisfy Davis. In official comment on the general's letter Davis wrote that Beauregard's action had endangered Richmond and might become the subject of official inquiry.[5]

The administration did not pursue the matter, but in July Bragg raked up another issue. In a letter to General Cooper he complained that in May Beauregard without authority detained in North Carolina a regiment which had been ordered to Richmond and thereby placed the capital in peril. In due course Cooper sent the letter to Beauregard for comment. Beauregard was infuriated. Informing Cooper that he had documentary evidence to prove he was authorized to hold the regiment, he asked for a court of inquiry. A nasty situation was averted when Lee entered the controversy. He said that Beauregard's explanation was satisfactory and no court was necessary. Bragg then asked to withdraw his letter from the files, and Beauregard withdrew his request for a court.[6] But Beauregard never forgave Bragg. He told Congressman Miles that he had always considered Bragg his friend, but he knew now that he was an enemy. "I have nothing to ask of him or his 'Master,' " he said. "I defy them both." [7]

Twice that summer Beauregard thought he might be restored to independent command. Lee had sent a small army commanded by Jubal Early to hold the Shenandoah Valley. When this force was strength-

[4] *Official Records,* XLII, Pt. 2, p. 1198.

[5] Beauregard to Bragg, June 21, 1864, in Beauregard Papers (Duke University).

[6] *Official Records,* XL, Pt. 3, pp. 802–803, XLII, Pt. 2, p. 1179.

[7] Beauregard to Miles, August 30, 1864, in Beauregard Papers (Library of Congress), Letterbook, Letters, April 22–November 15, 1864.

ened for the purpose of threatening the approaches to Washington, Beauregard hoped that he would be chosen to lead it. But the command remained with Early, who had headed a brigade under Beauregard at Manassas. Beauregard did not blame Lee for passing him over but the administration.[8] An even bigger assignment opened when Davis removed Joe Johnston from the command of the army defending Atlanta against Sherman. This was Beauregard's old army, the one from whose command he had been removed in 1862 and the one to which he always wanted to return. He wanted to go now. Again he was disappointed. The President gave the post to John B. Hood. The antiadministation press shrieked that Davis' jealousy had deprived the Western army of the general best fitted to be its commander.[9]

Beauregard was willing now to accept almost any assignment if it would get him out of Virginia. He considered asking the government to return him to command at Charleston.[10] He heard that he might be sent to Wilmington to inspect the defenses there and possibly remain as commander. Wilmington would be all right, he told Miles, although he had hoped never again to be connected with a siege. "My greatest desire has always been to command a good army in the field," he added. "Will I never be gratified?" [11]

The man behind the Wilmington suggestion was Lee. Conscious of Beauregard's unhappy state and perhaps not quite satisfied with his generalship, Lee was prepared to shift the Creole to another theater. Early in September Lee asked Beauregard to examine the Wilmington defenses. After Beauregard arrived in North Carolina, Governor Z. B. Vance wrote Lee asking if Beauregard could not be given the Wilmington command. The opportunity seemed too good to lose. Lee submitted Vance's letter to Davis with the observation that he had told Beauregard he could go to Wilmington or Charles-

[8] Roman, *Beauregard*, II, 273–74.

[9] Jordan to Beauregard, July 21, 1864, in Henkel's Catalog, Beauregard *Papers*, Pt. I; Charleston *Courier*, July 29, 1864; Charleston *Mercury*, July 15, August 26, 1864; Richmond *Whig*, quoted in Eliot, *West Point in the Confederacy*, 184.

[10] Beauregard to Cooper, July 19, 1864, unsent letter, in Beauregard Papers (Library of Congress), Letterbook, Miscellaneous Book, January 23, 1861—April 27, 1865.

[11] Beauregard to Miles, August 30, 1864, *ibid.*, Letterbook, Letters, April 22—November 15, 1864.

ton. Either place would be an excellent assignment, Lee said invitingly.[12]

While Beauregard was at Wilmington, the country was shocked by the news that Atlanta had fallen to Sherman. Bitter criticism of Davis and Hood was coupled with demands that Johnston or Beauregard be given the command of the Western army. At Hood's camp many of his generals said openly that he should be replaced by Johnston or Beauregard; they saw to it that their feelings were known in Richmond. Observers in the capital predicted that Davis would never appoint Beauregard.[13]

The President was sometimes a smarter politician than his enemies credited him with being. He realized now that he would have to do something to allay the storm of criticism and raise popular morale. If he had to make use of a general he detested, he would do it. He asked Lee to find out if Beauregard would be willing to serve in Georgia. Lee apparently understood Davis to mean that Beauregard was being considered for the command of Hood's army, and so presented the question to Beauregard. Beauregard replied that he felt unequal to the responsibility but in his eagerness to aid the cause would obey any order of the government. Lee informed Davis of Beauregard's decision.[14]

The President had also decided that it would be a wise move for him to go to Georgia, speak to the people, and personally examine the situation in Hood's army. Lee's message arrived as he was getting ready to leave by train. To facilitate a meeting with Beauregard, Davis asked Lee to send the general on an inspection trip to Charleston. Beauregard could meet the train at a point along the way, Davis suggested, and they could confer at leisure. For some reason Beauregard was unable to join the President. He did not reach Charleston until September 25, at which time Davis was in Macon. At Charleston Beauregard received a telegram from Davis asking him to be at Augusta on October 2.[15]

The President proceeded to Hood's camp at Palmetto, southwest

[12] *Official Records,* XLII, Pt. 2, pp. 1235, 1242; Roman, *Beauregard,* II, 274.

[13] *Official Records,* XXXVIII, Pt. 5, p. 836; Johnston, *Narrative,* 368; Frank E. Vandiver (ed.), *The Civil War Diary of General Josiah Gorgas* (University, Ala., 1947), 140; Jones, *Rebel War Clerk's Diary,* II, 288.

[14] *Official Records,* XXXIX, Pt. 2, p. 846; Roman, *Beauregard,* II, 274–75.

[15] Rowland (ed.), *Jefferson Davis,* VI, 340; *Official Records,* XXXV, Pt. 2, pp. 630–31; Roman, *Beauregard,* II, 275–76.

of Atlanta. Here he talked to Hood and the generals and delivered speeches to the troops. Here too he resolved what to do about Hood. The records are not clear on whether or not he had decided to remove Hood before reaching Palmetto. He may have toyed with the idea of giving the command to Beauregard; it is more probable that from the beginning he had in mind the decision he announced to Hood. This decision was essentially a political device, designed to silence the critics of Hood, satisfy the friends of Beauregard, and save face for the administration. Davis proposed to leave Hood in command of his army and to appoint Beauregard commander of a new department to be called the Military Division of the West. Beauregard's command would extend from Georgia to the Mississippi, a vast region comprising all or parts of five states, and would include in addition to Hood's force General Richard Taylor's army in Alabama.[16]

Promptly on October 2 Beauregard arrived at Augusta. Davis briefed him on the situation in Georgia and said Hood was going to operate on Sherman's communications. Then Davis offered Beauregard the command of the new department. Although Beauregard must have been surprised and also disappointed that he was not to have a field command, he readily accepted the assignment. Either he was a great patriot or at this stage of the war he did not particularly care what kind of command he held. The post he agreed to take was as difficult and disagreeable a one as any general in the war was asked to assume.

Beauregard knew what he was getting into. The President put his instructions into writing. Beauregard was to establish his headquarters at a place where he would be in easy communication with Hood and Taylor. He was to repair in person to any part of his command whenever he judged that *for the time* his presence was necessary or desirable. Only when present with an army was he to exercise command of troops. Only in case of a crisis was he to interfere with the field generals, which meant specifically with Hood. In short, Davis provided that Beauregard should act as an adviser and not as a real

---

[16] Rowland (ed.), *Jefferson Davis*, VI, 344–45. Davis was at Palmetto from September 25–27. On the last day of his visit he discussed with Hood the appointment of Beauregard as departmental commander. The next day, in a letter from Opelika, Davis put his decision in writing.

commander.[17] This was not the first time that the Confederate high command had set up such a departmental system. Earlier in the war a similar arrangement had been created in the West for Joe Johnston. The experience with it should have warned Davis against a repetition. The commander of a department like this could exercise no direction over the forces under him unless he assumed command of an army, which he was not supposed to do. One wonders why the high command established these departments. Perhaps the reason was to lay on the shelf a general who was out of favor.

Beauregard understood his position and was not disposed to go beyond it. In fact, he showed a definite desire to avoid responsibility. He wrote a curious letter to Davis in which he said: Does my presence with an army *impose* on me the necessity of assuming command? Shouldn't my orders merely pass through the commanding general? Davis replied: You are right, you are not to assume command of an army. If you did you might not be able to leave it! [18]

Before Beauregard ever entered upon his duties, one of the field commanders in his department had started an important new operation. At Palmetto Hood had discussed with Davis the necessity of doing something to recoup the loss of Atlanta; he had proposed a movement which the President had approved. In briefest form, Hood's plan was to strike at the railroad north of Atlanta and entice Sherman back for a battle on his line of communications or near the Alabama border. If Sherman could be beaten decisively, the invasion road to Tennessee would be open. Davis understood, however, that if at any time Sherman moved south of Atlanta Hood would follow him.[19]

In their interview at Augusta the President had told Beauregard in general terms of Hood's plan. Beauregard now decided that he should confer personally with Hood, who had moved north of Atlanta, and find out exactly what Hood intended. Traveling partly by rail and partly on horseback, Beauregard overtook Hood on October 9 at Cave Spring, about seventy miles northwest of Atlanta and close to the Alabama line. Hood informed Beauregard that he

[17] *Ibid.*, 348–49; Roman, *Beauregard,* II, 277–79; *Official Records,* XXXIX, Pt. 2, p. 785; Thomas Robson Hay, *Hood's Tennessee Campaign* (New York, 1929), 28–29.
[18] *Official Records,* XXXIX, Pt. 3, p. 870; Rowland (ed.), *Jefferson Davis,* VI, 368.
[19] John B. Hood, *Advance and Retreat . . .* (New Orleans, 1880), 243–59.

was going to draw Sherman north by hitting the railroad around Resaca and Dalton; if a favorable opportunity presented itself he would give battle. Although Beauregard thought that Hood had not planned his moves very carefully and might place his army in peril, he gave his approval to the proposed operation. Then he proceeded to Jacksonville, Alabama, to confer with Taylor and to establish a supply depot for Hood.[20]

At Jacksonville Beauregard formally assumed command of the department and issued a rhetorical proclamation urging the people to support the armies with mass enlistments. After meeting Taylor, he started to rejoin Hood.[21] He expected to find Hood at Blue Pond, northeast of Jacksonville. When he reached there, he was surprised to learn that Hood had shifted to Gadsden, twenty-seven miles to the west. Puzzled by Hood's movement and irritated that he had not been informed of it, Beauregard went on to Gadsden, arriving on the twenty-first. Here he received astounding news. Hood announced that he was going to invade Tennessee.[22]

Since meeting Beauregard at Cave Spring the erratic Hood had decided upon a new plan. After maneuvering on the railroad, he concluded that he would not be able to bring Sherman to battle on ground favorable to the Confederates. He then fixed upon the bold expedient of an offensive into Tennessee. It is difficult to summarize Hood's design. Several times he changed details in it, and his descriptions of the scheme, written during and after the war, do not always agree. But the main outline seems reasonably clear. He would cross the Tennessee River at Guntersville and move rapidly toward Nashville. Sherman was known to have sent back a part of his army to defend Tennessee; Hood would defeat this force and move into Kentucky. If Sherman followed the Confederates, Hood would fight him in Tennessee. If Sherman marched south from Atlanta, Hood would cross the mountains and join Lee for a decisive blow against

[20] Roman, *Beauregard,* II, 280–81, 599–600; *Official Records,* XXXIX, Pt. 1, pp. 795–96.

[21] Roman, *Beauregard,* II, 281–85; Taylor, *Destruction and Reconstruction,* 206–208. Taylor's account of his conference with Beauregard is dramatic and highly improbable. Either he confused it with later events or his memory played him false.

[22] Roman, *Beauregard,* II, 286.

Grant! It was a desperate and dramatic project and had perhaps one chance in ten thousand of succeeding.[23]

At Gadsden Beauregard and Hood spent the better part of two days discussing the plan. Although Beauregard had some misgivings and some objections, he thought that Hood might succeed if he moved fast. He said that a new base would have to be set up, and advised that it be located at Tuscumbia, on the Memphis and Charleston Railroad in western Alabama. Before giving his final approval, he talked with the corps generals about the condition of the army. From them he gained the impression that a withdrawal south to confront Sherman around Atlanta would seem like a retreat and would wreck morale. Persuaded that the invasion scheme offered at least a promise of victory, Beauregard told Hood to start his movement.[24]

On October 22 Hood advanced to Guntersville. Beauregard stayed at Gadsden to superintend the shifting of supplies from Jacksonville to Tuscumbia. In a few days he left to join Hood. He had almost reached Guntersville when he heard that Hood was moving toward Decatur, fifty miles farther west on the Tennessee. Again Hood had failed to inform his superior of a change in plan. Now, as later in his campaign, he seemed to regard Beauregard almost as a figurehead. His important reports he sent to Richmond.[25]

Beauregard caught up to the army near Decatur. Angrily he rebuked Hood for not announcing his march change and for going so far west. Hood said that the approaches at Guntersville were too

[23] Hood, *Advance and Retreat*, 262–68; *Official Records*, XXXIX, Pt. 1, pp. 802–803.

[24] Hood, *Advance and Retreat*, 268–69; *Official Records*, XLV, Pt. 1, pp. 647–48; Roman, *Beauregard*, II, 287–88. After the war Davis charged that Beauregard originated the plan to invade Tennessee and forced it on Hood. See Rowland (ed.), *Jefferson Davis*, VIII, 376, 415–16; Davis, *Rise and Fall*, II, 567–69. Like many of Davis' postwar statements, this one is completely at variance with the documents. Beauregard, for his part, said after the war that he knew Hood's plan would fail and that he accepted it only because he understood Davis and Bragg were for it. The war records indicate that Beauregard believed Hood might succeed. In his report he wrote that the operation failed only because of delay in execution; *Official Records*, XLV, Pt. 1, pp. 650–51. Davis, as late as November 7, advised Hood to break Sherman's communications and to pursue Sherman if he moved south of Atlanta; Rowland (ed.), *Jefferson Davis*, VI, 398–99. There can be little doubt that the invasion scheme was Hood's alone.

[25] Roman, *Beauregard*, II, 289–92; Hay, *Hood's Tennessee Campaign*, 38–39.

heavily guarded for him to cross. He added that the same situation existed at Decatur and that he would have to move down the river to Courtland. He reached the latter place on October 30. Here he informed Beauregard that he did not have enough provisions to sustain his army in Tennessee. The troops were almost shoeless, Hood said, and he was going to Tuscumbia to collect supplies.[26] When he reached Tuscumbia, he had marched over almost the width of Alabama.

Beauregard was heartsick at Hood's delays and infuriated by his subordinate's refusal to take him into his confidence. Twice he asked Hood for a definite statement of his future plans; each time Hood replied vaguely and evasively. Nevertheless, Beauregard reported hopefully to Richmond that Hood would cross the Tennessee on November 9. Hood did cross, on the tenth, but he stopped at Florence on the opposite side. When he was still there a week later, Beauregard wrote him a sharp note saying he "desired" Hood would take the offensive at the earliest practicable moment. Not until the twenty-first did Hood advance into Tennessee. Five days earlier Sherman had started from Atlanta on the march that would gut the last vital resources of the Confederacy.[27]

Shortly before Hood moved to Tennessee Beauregard left Tuscumbia to inspect the Confederate defenses in northeast Mississippi. To the other generals in his department he addressed a communication advising them to husband their forces and employ against the enemy a Fabian strategy. He cited a historical example that was hardly cheering: "Hannibal held the heart of Italy sixteen years, and then was defeated." [28] At Corinth he received intelligence that Sherman was moving on Macon. Knowing that he could do nothing more to help Hood, he decided to return to Georgia to direct the resistance against Sherman. He reached Macon on November 24.[29]

For the remaining weeks of 1864 Beauregard would devote all his efforts to organizing a defense against the invaders. His efforts would fail; by the end of the year Sherman would be at Savannah on the

---

[26] *Official Records*, XXXIX, Pt. 1, pp. 796–98; Roman, *Beauregard*, II, 292–94.

[27] *Official Records*, XXXIX, Pt. 1, pp. 798–801; Roman, *Beauregard*, II, 295–298, 301.

[28] *Official Records*, XLV, Pt. 1, p. 1218.

[29] *Ibid.*, XLIV, 866, 869–70, XLV, Pt. 1, p. 1222; Roman, *Beauregard*, II, 301–302.

seacoast. Beauregard failed partly because of his own mistakes and partly because of factors in the situation over which he had no control. Both he and the high command did not understand for a time the nature of Sherman's movement. The Federal army, over sixty thousand strong, advanced on a broad front with the right wing directed at Macon and the left at Augusta, both of which were occupied by Confederate forces. The Confederates could not figure out which place Sherman intended to attack. Actually he was interested in neither. At the right moment he reunited his wings and continued his advance, leaving the towns and their garrisons in his rear.

This episode epitomizes the entire Georgia campaign and the fatal defect in Confederate strategy. Southern forces were scattered all over Beauregard's department—at Mobile, Montgomery, Macon, Augusta, Savannah—and in South Carolina as well. Only an immediate concentration of these troops could have stopped Sherman. Although Beauregard divined fairly soon that Sherman was heading for the coast and would not waste time attacking interior towns, he did not stress to Richmond the necessity of assembling the forces in his command. For the most part, he urged that he be given reinforcements from other areas.[30] One explanation of his course is that he knew Davis would object to endangering minor points by stripping them of troops. Another is that he undoubtedly realized the strained Confederate railway system could not rapidly bring together a large body of men. Whatever the reasons, the great advocate of concentration did not concentrate. He had to scurry from town to town evacuating dispersed garrisons while the massed Federal army rolled on in triumph.

Beauregard stayed at Macon about five days. Part of the force there he ordered to General Hardee, commanding at Savannah. To Hood he sent a telegram urging immediate action to counteract Sherman's offensive. He reported his presence to Richmond and outlined his actions. Then he left for Mobile, where another Federal attack was rumored. On the way he received an order extending his command eastward to the seacoast. He immediately turned back and headed for Augusta, near the Georgia–South Carolina border. En route he received a letter from Davis expressing the hope that Beauregard could defeat Sherman or reduce his army to ineffectiveness.

[30] *Official Records,* XLIV, 859; Roman, *Beauregard,* II, 610.

The President added that Hood could not change the plans of Sherman and Grant unless he succeeded in crossing the Ohio River.[31]

Beauregard reached Augusta on December 6. Almost the first thing he did was to answer Davis' letter. His reply shows that he did not as yet understand completely the nature of Sherman's movement. He thought Sherman was on a big raid with a force of thirty-six thousand. Sherman could be prevented from capturing Augusta, Savannah, and Charleston, he assured the President, and would suffer serious losses before reaching the coast. In Davis' remarks about Hood Beauregard saw an implied censure of himself. Defensively he listed his reasons for not countermanding Hood's offensive after Sherman struck: Hood could not return in time; a retrograde movement would impair army morale. If Hood could win, Beauregard concluded, Sherman would have to retreat.[32]

From Augusta Beauregard went to Charleston and then to Savannah. At the latter place he directed Hardee to hold out as long as possible but not to risk capture of the garrison. As preparation for a possible evacuation, Hardee was to begin construction of a pontoon bridge over the Savannah River. Beauregard informed the high command that he had ordered Hardee to yield the city rather than lose his force. Was his decision approved, he asked, and would the same principle apply to Charleston?[33]

Beauregard then returned to Charleston, which he intended to make his temporary headquarters. He was there but a few days when an urgent summons from Hardee called him back to Savannah. Sherman was approaching the city, and Hardee wanted to know when to evacuate. Traveling part of the way in a wagon, because the railroad between Charleston and Savannah was vulnerable to Federal fire, Beauregard arrived on December 16. The next day Sherman demanded that Hardee surrender the town. Beauregard directed Hardee to refuse, but he knew that he would have to get the garrison out fast. Taking complete charge of operations, he ordered an immediate evacuation and prepared the memoranda and instructions to govern the movement. The withdrawal was delayed by several factors, not the least of which was the necessity of completing the pon-

---

[31] Roman, *Beauregard*, II, 302–303, 610; *Official Records*, XLIV, 890, 905, 911.

[32] *Official Records*, XLIV, 931–33.

[33] Roman, *Beauregard*, II, 312–14; *Battles and Leaders*, IV, 679–80; *Official Records*, XLIV, 959.

toon bridge, but by the twentieth Hardee's force of ten thousand was safely over the river.[34]

While he was directing the evacuation, Beauregard was pleased to receive from Richmond approval of his policy of yielding threatened points. But he felt constrained to warn Davis that the abandonment of Savannah, as necessary as it was, would result in the loss of the railroad from Augusta to Charleston and soon of Charleston itself. Could not he be reinforced from Virginia, he asked, until Hood returned to Georgia? Davis replied that no troops from Lee could be spared; Beauregard would have to do with what he had even if Charleston was lost. The President seemed stunned by the situation. He told Lee that he could not realize the consequences portrayed by Beauregard.[35]

After the fall of Savannah Beauregard returned to Charleston. He instructed Hardee to form a defensive line behind the Combahee River. Although he knew now that Sherman was engaged in an invasion instead of a raid and would soon plunge into South Carolina, he made no attempt to concentrate his forces.[36] The Confederate line from Augusta to Charleston was thinly held. Around Charleston were perhaps sixteen thousand troops. The only possible chance of stopping Sherman was to unite them and other forces in the state with Hardee's little army and try to strike one column of the Federal army after it crossed the Savannah. This strategy was not adopted, probably because it would have meant the abandonment of Charleston. The result was that the South Carolina campaign was a repetition of the one in Georgia. When Sherman advanced, town after town went down before him like sitting ducks.

Shortly before Christmas Beauregard received from Hood a request for reinforcements. Since late November Beauregard had not had any definite news of Hood's movements. Suspecting now that Hood had not been able to accomplish anything in Tennessee, he replied that no reinforcements were available and that if the campaign was over Hood should retire behind the Tennessee River and send part of his force to Georgia. Actually Hood had suffered a

[34] Roman, *Beauregard*, II, 315–18, 618–19; *Southern Historical Society Papers*, VII (1879), 295–96; *Battles and Leaders*, IV, 679–80.

[35] Roman, *Beauregard*, II, 317; Rowland (ed.), *Jefferson Davis*, VI, 423; *Official Records*, XLII, Pt. 3, p. 1280.

[36] Roman, *Beauregard*, II, 319–20, 626; *Official Records*, XLIV, 970.

smashing defeat at Nashville on December 15-16 and was retreating with his broken army to Tupelo, Mississippi.[37] On Christmas Day Beauregard heard from an officer in Montgomery that there were vague reports Hood had met a reverse and that his army was moving southward. Then a dispatch came from Hood asking Beauregard to visit the army.[38]

Seriously concerned but not suspecting the extent of the disaster, Beauregard prepared to leave. He asked the War Department to relieve him of his coastal command so he could devote full attention to affairs in the West. He also requested authorization to replace Hood with Taylor if he judged a change in commanders was necessary. Before departing, he placed Hardee in command at Charleston and instructed him to abandon the city at Sherman's approach.[39]

As he traveled west Beauregard received a dispatch from Hood that stated the army had recrossed the Tennessee without material losses and was being assembled at Tupelo. Cheered by this information, Beauregard made plans to bring Hood's troops to Georgia. All the greater, therefore, was his shock when he reached Tupelo on January 15 and saw the shattered ranks of the once-proud Army of Tennessee, with only one corps fit for action. To his relief, he did not have to remove Hood. The general, as broken as his army, asked to be relieved. Beauregard gave the command to Taylor.[40]

Beauregard spent several days helping Taylor reorganize the army. Now that he was with the Army of Tennessee, he became more impressed with the dangers it faced and less concerned with the situation in South Carolina. He warned Davis that to divide Taylor's force to reinforce Hardee would expose Mobile and other points to capture. Already Taylor lacked enough troops to defend his department against a determined offensive.[41]

The government gave Beauregard little time to worry about affairs in the West. Sherman was advancing into South Carolina, and Beauregard was summoned back to meet the new threat. On February 1 he arrived at Augusta and for two days conferred with Hardee

[37] *Official Records,* XLIV, 984–85. Hood, on December 17, sent Beauregard a misleading account of his defeat. This dispatch, which minimized the disaster, was not received by Beauregard until later; Roman, *Beauregard,* II, 626.
[38] Roman, *Beauregard,* II, 627; *Official Records,* XLV, Pt. 2, p. 738.
[39] Roman, *Beauregard,* II, 322–24, 328.
[40] *Ibid.,* 328–33; *Official Records,* XLV, Pt. 2, pp. 757, 784–85.
[41] *Official Records,* XLV, Pt. 2, p. 789, XLIX, 1.

and his other generals. At the end of the meeting Beauregard's chief of staff drew up a memorandum of the course of action agreed upon. With a force of about thirty-three thousand, the Confederates would endeavor to hold a line from Augusta to Charleston of over a hundred miles in length. If the Federals broke over the Combahee, Hardee was to retire toward Charleston and the other forces toward Columbia, the capital. Should Charleston be threatened, Hardee was to go to Columbia. It was a gloomy document, and ended with the plaintive observation that the enemy had no line of communication which could be cut.[42]

A worse strategy could hardly have been devised. As he had done in Georgia, Sherman moved his army in two columns, one pointing at Augusta and one at Charleston. Again the Confederates were confused; they were convinced Sherman was going to Charleston. In the interior he pulled his wings together and advanced on Columbia. He did not have to attack Charleston. Once he reached Columbia he would flank the port city, and its garrison would have to evacuate to escape being caught in a pocket. Only a concentration and a rapid blow at one of Sherman's separated columns could have stopped the Federals.

Beauregard did not seem to have much faith in his own plan. On February 3 he wrote three despondent dispatches to the President. In the first he said that he would be unable to effect a concentration before Sherman reached Columbia. He was going to the capital and hoped the government could send reinforcements there. In the second he said that with additional troops from Virginia and North Carolina he could defeat and maybe destroy Sherman. In the third, as an exercise in futility, he detailed how he would have fought Sherman if he had twenty-five thousand men.[43]

On the tenth Beauregard arrived at Columbia. Here he received several dispatches from Hardee begging his presence at Charleston. Hardee, in ill health and as confused as everybody else by Sherman's movements, was having evacuation troubles. Would Beauregard come and tell him whether to withdraw and if so, when? With some sharpness Beauregard replied that, as previously agreed upon, Hardee was to evacuate when he judged the town was in danger of capture. Beauregard said that he could not determine the precise time but

[42] Roman, *Beauregard*, II, 336–39.
[43] *Ibid.*, 342–43.

that any needless delay would be fatal. Although Beauregard did not know it, Hardee's indecision had been intensified by the receipt of a dispatch from Davis urging him to hold the city until it could be determined if Beauregard could halt the enemy in the field.[44]

When Hardee still hesitated to act, Beauregard decided he had better go to Charleston. He arrived on the morning of the fourteenth and left that night. In the space of a few hours he convinced Hardee that he must withdraw, prepared written orders to execute the evacuation, and arranged for the garrison to move to Chesterville, about fifty miles north of Columbia.

The next day, from Sumterville, he telegraphed Hardee to begin his movement. Again Hardee delayed. He sent Beauregard a second message he had received from Davis. The President thought that evacuation should be postponed. Beauregard might be able to halt Sherman, and in that case the city would be saved and the pain of seeing it pass into enemy hands averted. Davis was mixing sentimentality with his fixation for holding doomed places. Beauregard's temper flamed when he read the President's dispatch. What did the man in Richmond know of conditions in the field? He telegraphed Hardee: I don't have even enough troops to hold Columbia; instead of changing our plan carry it out immediately—in short, pay no attention to Davis. Hardee could not disregard this order. On the night of February 17-18 he left Charleston.[45]

On his way back to Columbia Beauregard heard that Sherman was moving on the city. He informed Lee, who had just been made general in chief of all Confederate armies, that he would hold Columbia as long as he could with his limited means. Reaching the capital on the night of February 15, he found the situation worse than he had expected. Sherman was close and moving fast. The next day Beauregard telegraphed Lee that he would have to evacuate Columbia and that he would try to concentrate at Chesterville. On the seventeenth the Confederates withdrew and moved northward.[46] Before reaching Chesterville, Beauregard decided that he would have to assemble his forces at another point; Sherman would be at Chesterville before Hardee could get there. In two telegrams to Lee on the

[44] *Ibid.*, 345, 637–38; Rowland (ed.), *Jefferson Davis*, VI, 479–80.

[45] Roman, *Beauregard*, II, 346–50; *Official Records*, XLVII, Pt. 2, pp. 1179–80, 1194.

[46] *Official Records*, XLVII, Pt. 2, pp. 1192–93; Roman, *Beauregard*, II, 350–53.

nineteenth Beauregard announced that he would have to retire to Greensboro, North Carolina.[47]

His dispatches were received by the high command with bewildered incredulity. Davis, who had asked Lee to go to South Carolina to confer with Beauregard, endorsed on one of the messages that the rapidity with which the Federals were expected to move indicated that little effort was being made to stop them.[48] Something entirely different was indicated, which the President failed to grasp. Sherman, the master of logistics, was introducing a new element in war. Nothing like his great march through an enemy country had occurred in modern times. The Confederate leaders had not believed at the first that any general could make such a march. Despite the evidence they did not quite believe it now.

Lee was as skeptical as Davis. He wrote the President that he did not see how Sherman could execute the movement anticipated by Beauregard. Noting that Beauregard was vague as to his own purposes (in the face of Sherman's rapid advance he had to be vague), Lee said: "He does not appear . . . to be able to do much." Lee was convinced that Beauregard did not understand the situation in South Carolina and would have to be relieved. To Secretary of War John C. Breckinridge the general in chief wrote that he had heard Beauregard's health was feeble. Should Beauregard's strength give way, Lee said, there was no one in the department to replace him. He suggested that Joe Johnston be assigned to the Carolina command.[49]

Davis did not like Johnston any better than he did Beauregard, but under continued pressure from Lee he made the appointment. On February 22 Johnston was named commander of the forces opposing Sherman; Beauregard was assigned to duty with Johnston.[50] Before accepting, Johnston visited Beauregard at Charlotte to ask if Beauregard was willing to serve under him. Beauregard was all courtesy and dignity. In defense of the cause, he replied, he would be happy to work with Johnston. He said the same thing in a note to Lee. But below the surface he was hurt. He had not expected to be

[47] Roman, *Beauregard*, II, 354; *Official Records*, XLVII, Pt. 2, p. 1222.

[48] Rowland (ed.), *Jefferson Davis*, VI, 481; *Official Records*, XLVII, Pt. 2, p. 1222.

[49] Robert E. Lee to Davis, February 19, 1865, in *Official Records*, LIII, 412–13; Lee to John C. Breckinridge, February 19, 1865, *ibid.*, XLVII, Pt. 1, p. 1044.

[50] *Ibid.*, XLVI, Pt. 2, pp. 1244–45; Roman, *Beauregard*, II, 357, 644–45.

removed. He had done well with his limited resources, he thought, and he had not complained about his health. Bitterly he reflected that it was his fate to be a second in command—under Joe Johnston at Manassas, under Albert Sidney Johnston at Shiloh, under Lee at Petersburg, and now again.[51]

After Johnston assumed command, Beauregard's duties became routine. Johnston took over the direction of the troops in the field. To Beauregard he assigned the tasks of ordering movements in rear areas and guarding the army's line of communications. Necessarily Beauregard moved about a lot, but most of the time his headquarters were at Raleigh. He accepted his subordinate position loyally. Only once or twice did he suggest a plan of strategy to Johnston, who rejected his suggestions. On one occasion he came to Johnston in the field to ask if he could help with the troops. Johnston told him he was more useful at Raleigh. When he was offered a small command in western Virginia and eastern Tennessee, he said that he preferred to stay with Johnston. It is probable that at this stage he had no real hope that the war could be won. Contemplating the vast forces the Federal government was bringing against the Confederacy, he exclaimed: "I wonder if Minerva has stamped on the earth for our foes?" [52]

The change in commanders did not change the dark military situation. Johnston was no more successful than Beauregard in halting or hurting Sherman. Johnston was not to blame. He had about thirty thousand men, while Sherman had been reinforced to ninety thousand. Like Beauregard, Johnston found that he could not effect a concentration before Sherman's onward rush. By April, the Federal host was at Goldsboro, with raiding parties sweeping widely to the north. The Virginia border and Grant's army were not far away.

Crowding disasters now struck the Confederacy on the Virginia and North Carolina fronts. On April 2 Richmond and Petersburg fell. While Lee fled to the west, Davis and his Cabinet took the road south to Johnston's army. On the fifth the President reached Danville, Virginia, where Beauregard sent a cavalry force to guard the official party. A few days later Davis informed Beauregard that the commander at Danville feared an attack; the President suggested

[51] Johnston, *Narrative*, 371–72; Roman, *Beauregard*, II, 361–62; *Official Records*, XLVII, Pt. 2, p. 1248.

[52] Roman, *Beauregard*, II, 377, 380, 381–83.

that Beauregard come to Danville.[53] Although Beauregard thought there was no danger, he obeyed the summons. As he left Raleigh by train he learned that Lee had surrendered to Grant. He knew the end had come. At Greensboro he telegraphed to Danville asking if his presence was still required. One of Davis' aides replied that the President had started for Greensboro and would see Beauregard there.[54]

Beauregard's headquarters were in three boxcars in which he and his staff had traveled to Greensboro. Early in the morning on April 11 he was told that Davis' train had arrived. Crossing the tracks, he went to the President's car. Davis greeted him cordially and then took him aside to discuss the military situation. Beauregard said that it was hopeless. To the general's amazement, Davis disagreed. The President said that Lee's surrender had not been confirmed and that it might be yet possible to concentrate the forces of Lee and Johnston. Besides, if it came to the worst, resistance could be carried on west of the Mississippi. The President summoned Johnston from the field to learn his opinions.[55]

Johnston arrived the next morning. He established quarters in one of Beauregard's boxcars. Shortly the generals were told that Davis wanted to see them. Going to the official car, they found the President and several Cabinet members waiting. Johnston and Beauregard had thought they would be asked about their resourcces. Instead Davis opened the session with a speech to the effect that he would raise a large army by bringing in deserters and conscripting enrolled men on the draft lists. The generals said that men who had deserted or avoided service when the situation was less critical would not fight now. After this sharp exchange of opinion, Davis adjourned the conference. He said he would delay a decision until Secretary of War Breckinridge arrived from Virginia with more definite news about Lee.

Breckinridge reached Greensboro that night and confirmed Lee's surrender. Johnston and Beauregard talked together. They agreed that the cause was lost and that the only recourse was to make peace. Johnston then went to Breckinridge and said that he and Beauregard had decided the war must be ended. He was willing to say the same

[53] *Official Records,* XLVII, Pt. 3, pp. 774–76.
[54] Roman, *Beauregard,* II, 389, 662.
[55] *Ibid.,* 390–93.

thing to Davis, Johnston added. Breckinridge replied that he would get Johnston a chance to speak his views.

On April 13 Johnston and Beauregard received word that the President wished to see them. Davis had moved his quarters to a private home in Greensboro. In a small upstairs room Davis and the Cabinet received the generals. After making some general remarks, Davis turned to Johnston and said that he wished to hear what Johnston and Beauregard thought about the Confederacy's situation. The President added: "Our late disasters are terrible; but I do not think we should regard them as fatal. I think we can whip the enemy yet, if our people will turn out."

Johnston arose. Perhaps through his mind there flashed a thought of his numerous past differences with Davis and of the many times the President had put him in his place. It was his turn now. A Cabinet member noted that his tone and manner were almost spiteful. He whipped the sentences out. "My views are, sir, that our people are tired of the war, feel themselves whipped, and will not fight. . . . We cannot place another large army in the field. . . . My small force is melting away like snow before the sun, and I am hopeless of recruiting it."

A silence of several minutes followed. Davis stared at a piece of paper which he kept folding and unfolding. In a low even tone the President said: "What do you say, General Beauregard?" "I concur in all General Johnston has said," came the reply. Perhaps Beauregard was having his own moment of satisfaction. After another silence Davis asked Johnston what he proposed to do. Johnston replied that he would like to approach Sherman and try to negotiate a general peace. At the suggestion of a Cabinet member Davis dictated a letter to Sherman which Johnston signed. This was as much authorization as the President would give. Others must treat for peace. He prepared to continue his flight southward.[56]

Johnston found Sherman eager to conclude a compact that would provide for the surrender of all Southern armies. The two com-

[56] The events and conferences of April 12–13 are described in the following sources: Stephen R. Mallory, "Last Days of the Confederate Government," in *McClure's Magazine,* XVI (1901), 240–42; Reagan, *Memoirs,* 199–200; Roman, *Beauregard,* II, 394–95, 664–66; Johnston, *Narrative,* 396–400; Davis, *Rise and Fall,* II, 678–81. These accounts differ in minor details. Some state that the last meeting was held in the day, others say that it was at night. Mallory erroneously dated this session April 15. The quoted statements in the narrative are from Mallory's article.

manders signed a document that became famous as "the Sherman–
Johnston treaty." Davis, after some urging by Breckinridge, approved
it, but the Federal government repudiated Sherman's action. Sherman was instructed to negotiate a strictly military convention for the
capitulation of Johnston's army. Johnston, determined to stop further
bloodshed, met Sherman again and arranged for his troops to lay
down their arms. While Johnston was treating with Sherman, news
reached the Confederate camp that President Lincoln had been as-
sassinated. Many of the soldiers started to celebrate. In front of Beauregard's tent some drunk men were singing. A staff officer said this
was the only time in the war he saw Beauregard completely lose his
temper. "Shut those men up," he snapped. "If they won't shut up,
have them arrested. Those are my orders." [57]

After the surrender Beauregard prepared to leave for home. In a
sad farewell note to his staff he said: "The day was, when I was
confident that this parting would be under far different and the most
auspicious circumstances—at a moment when a happy and independent people would be ready . . . to welcome you to your re-
spective communities—but circumstances, which neither the courage,
the endurance, nor the patriotism of our armies could overcome,
have turned my brightest anticipations, my highest hopes, into bitter
disappointment, in which you must all share." [58]

On May 1, accompanied by his staff and Louisiana officers whom
he had invited to join him, Beauregard started south. Part of the way
the group traveled in army wagons and traded army provisions for
food. In South Carolina those of his staff who were from that state
took their leave. After a visit with Governor Pickens at Edgefield,
he went on to Augusta and then to Mobile. At Mobile he booked
passage in a United States naval transport bound for New Orleans.
On the twenty-first he stepped ashore in his city. He was home for
the first time in four years.[59]

[57] Basso, *Beauregard,* 282.
[58] Roman, *Beauregard,* I, 9.
[59] *Ibid.,* II, 410–15; Basso, *Beauregard,* 282–83; New Orleans *Times,* May
22, 1865. In Roman, the day of his arrival is wrongly given as May 20.

CHAPTER SIXTEEN

Reconstruction

A<small>BOUT A WEEK</small> after his return, Beauregard went to his mother's home. As he rode through the streets of Algiers, a settlement across the river from New Orleans, a man stopped him and asked, "Are you Beauregard?" In his grave manner Beauregard replied that he was. The man, who was probably drunk, screamed, "I believe you are a damn nigger. I always did believe you were a nigger. Tell me if you are a nigger or not." Followed by a stream of abuse, the hero of Manassas proceeded hurriedly on his way.[1]

In the first days of Reconstruction Confederate generals were not safe from insult and ridicule, even in their own communities. They were liable to other and more severe penalties as well. Generals, like Beauregard, were excluded from the amnesty proclamations of Presidents Lincoln and Andrew Johnson. They could not vote or hold office and had no clearly defined political or civil status. Furthermore, they could not be certain that the paroles they had signed on surrendering would protect them from prosecution as rebels. Beauregard's family worried that he would be arrested, charged with deserting his post at West Point to join the Confederacy, and exiled or executed.[2]

Beauregard himself had little fear that he would be brought to trial. He was chiefly concerned with whether he should take an oath of loyalty and apply for a pardon. He thought that he should not, until Lee and Johnston, who ranked him, had been cleared. He wrote those generals asking their advice. To Lee he observed: "It is hard to ask pardon of an adversary you despise."[3]

Both Lee and Johnston replied that patriotism and duty required

[1] Report by Lieutenant William Dougherty to Lieutenant Lucius Croker, in Confederate Records of Military Service of Adjutant General's Office (National Archives).
[2] René Beauregard, "Magnolia."
[3] Beauregard to Lee, September 1, 1865, in Robert E. Lee Papers (Confederate Memorial Institute, Richmond).

submission to the victors; they counseled him to seek amnesty.[4] Before their letters reached New Orleans, Beauregard had decided for reasons of his own to make his peace with the government. He had a natural desire to recover citizenship so that he could move about freely and as an engineer secure a job that would enable him to support his family. He was told that many young ex-Confederates were flocking to New Orleans and that they could not get employment because they would not take an oath of loyalty. If he led the way, they would follow his example. On September 16 he appeared at the City Hall and before the mayor swore fealty to the United States.[5]

After subscribing to the oath, Beauregard wrote President Johnson applying for the benefits of the amnesty proclamation, that is, for a pardon. Briefly he described his reasons for supporting the Confederacy and for now seeking absolution:

> In taking up arms during the late struggle (after my native State, Louisiana, had seceded) I believed, in good faith, that I was defending the constitutional rights of the South against the encroachments of the North. Having appealed to the arbitration of the Sword, which has gone against us, I accept the decision as settling finally the questions of secession & slavery—& I offer now my allegiance to the Govt. of the United States, which I promise, truly and faithfully, to serve & uphold hereafter, against all external or internal foes.

It was a good letter, short and to the point and devoid of his usual rhetoric. He admitted defeat without crawling for forgiveness. With a touch of pride he added to his signature, "late Genl. C. S. A." [6]

He had not easily arrived at his decision to seek a pardon. Several times he had considered leaving the country to take service with a foreign army. Nor was all the bitterness of defeat gone from his heart.

[4] Lee to Beauregard, October 3, 1865, in Robert E. Lee Papers in De Butts–Ely Collection (Division of Manuscripts, Library of Congress) ; Johnston to Beauregard, October, 1865, in Henkels' Catalog, *Beauregard Papers,* Pt. I. Beauregard's letter to Johnston has not been located, but its contents are indicated in Johnston's reply.

[5] Maury, *Recollections,* 236; New Orleans *Picayune,* September 19, 1865; New Orleans *Times,* September 18, 1865.

[6] Beauregard's oath, his letter of September 16, 1865, to Johnson, and a document approving his application signed by the governor of Louisiana and the mayor of New Orleans are in the Amnesty Papers in the Records of the War Department (National Archives). I am indebted to the staff of the National Archives for locating these items and for furnishing photostats of them.

He wrote Augusta J. Evans: "I shall abide my fate here. I defy them now, altho defenceless as I did formerly at the head of my troops— my imprisonment or death would only add to their disgrace." [7]

At one time it seemed that Beauregard might be subjected to a trial. In the confusion following the surrender of the armies, the baggage and papers of several Confederate leaders, Beauregard's among them, were captured. The government brought the papers to Washington for the purpose of examining them for evidence of treason. A staff of researchers headed by Francis Lieber, the noted political scientist, began to comb the documents for information upon which to base suits against Davis, Beauregard, and others. Sensational reports leaked out to the press that damning proof against Beauregard had been discovered.[8] Actually Lieber and his assistants, after going through thousands of letters, could not find any evidence against anybody. Lieber was particularly disgusted with Beauregard's papers. He reported that they consisted mainly of mash notes from the general's female admirers. "Beauregard," wrote Lieber, "is the veriest coxcomb, corresponding with scores of Misses and receiving information about the *noblesse* in his occus." [9]

Beauregard later tried to induce the government to return his papers. He argued that they were private property accidentally captured after the war had ended. He wrote to Johnson and Grant on the subject and interviewed those dignitaries in Washington. All he got back was his baggage and books. Fortunately for history the government retained the letters for future publication in the *Official Records*.[10]

[7] Beauregard to Augusta J. Evans, December 16, 21, 1865, in Beauregard Papers (Library of Congress), Letterbook, Private Letters, December 16, 1865–April 18, 1867.

[8] Dallas Irvin, "The Archive Office of the War Department: Repository of Captured Confederate Archives, 1865–1881," in *Military Affairs*, X (1946), 93–111; New York *Herald*, quoted in New Orleans *Times*, July 4, 1865; New Orleans *Times*, July 10, 1865; New Orleans *Picayune*, July 7, 1865.

[9] Francis Lieber to H. W. Halleck, September 10, 1865, in Francis Lieber Papers (Huntington Library, San Marino, Calif.). A copy of Lieber's letter was furnished me through the kindness of Professor Frank Freidel, Stanford University.

[10] Beauregard to Ulysses S. Grant, October 15, 1866, Grant to Beauregard, October 22, 1867, Beauregard to E. D. Townsend, November 25, 1867, Townsend to Beauregard, December 3, 1867, in Adjutant General's Office files (National Archives); Beauregard to Grant, October 12, 1866, in Beauregard Papers (Library of Congress), Letterbook, Private Letter, December 16, 1865—April 18, 1867.

It was one thing to ask for a pardon and another to get it. Johnson took no action on Beauregard's application, probably feeling that it was impolitic to absolve such a prominent Confederate. Among the friends who interested themselves in Beauregard's behalf was Madame Octavia Walton Le Vert of Mobile, authoress and world traveler. She went to Washington to request Johnson to pardon Beauregard and other leaders. The President was supposed to have told her that he could not exonerate Beauregard at present but that he hoped the general would not go abroad, as the country needed such men.[11]

In 1866 Beauregard went to Europe on business for a railroad corporation with which he had become associated. On his return he stopped over several days in New York, where Madame Le Vert was then holding court. She gave a dinner for him at the Fifth Avenue Hotel. When the party retired to the drawing room, the corridor was packed with spectators eager to catch a glimpse of Beauregard; many pressed forward to seek an introduction. From New York Beauregard went to Washington, where he secured interviews with Johnson and Grant to discuss his pardon and the return of his papers. What transpired at these meetings is not known, but the general returned to New Orleans without winning either of his objectives.[12]

Beauregard had acquired a new reason for wishing to clear his name. Before the war he had owned four squares of land in Memphis, just outside of the city limits. The Freedmen's Bureau had taken over three of them as abandoned property and erected a schoolhouse on one; Negroes had built huts on the others. When Beauregard sought restoration of his property, he was told that he could not get it as long as there was a possibility the government might bring court proceedings against him. Long months of fruitless effort followed. Beauregard hired attorneys and made several trips to Washington to see Johnson, Grant, and the attorney general. Not until 1868 was the land returned, after Johnson had removed his disabilities. On July 4 of that year the President by proclamation extended amnesty to a

[11] New Orleans *Times,* October 13, 1865; Baltimore *Gazette,* quoted *ibid.,* November 4, 1865; Mrs. Clay, *Belle of the Fifties,* 368.

[12] New Orleans *Times,* September 28, 1866; New York *Express,* quoted *ibid.,* October 10, 1866; Louisville *Democrat,* quoted *ibid.,* October 15, 1866; *ibid.,* October 18, 20, 1866; Beauregard to Andrew Johnson, October 12, 1866, in Andrew Johnson Papers (Division of Manuscripts, Library of Congress).

new group of former Confederates. Beauregard was included in this mass pardon.[13]

Even now he was not a complete citizen. By the terms of the Fourteenth Amendment, which the Radical Republicans pushed to ratification, he was one of the ex-Confederates who were denied the right to hold office. This disability could be removed only by action of both houses of Congress. In 1874, when Beauregard was considering going abroad for a period of years to assume a foreign command, he asked Senator John B. Gordon of Georgia, a former Confederate general, to introduce a bill annulling the penalty. He said that he wanted to go as an American citizen and "to be treated and respected as such." Later he decided not to leave, and requested Gordon not to act.[14]

Two years later the urge to remove the last stigma was too strong to resist. He was resolved now to put aside the idea of foreign service and stay with the South. Again he wrote to Gordon. He had a chance to help his state by becoming a levee commissioner, he said. Would Gordon get his disabilities removed so he could accept the position? Gordon presented the letter to the Senate as a petition. Several months later Beauregard submitted a formal petition to the Congress, which was presented by Senator W. C. Whyte of Maryland.[15] A bill rescinding Beauregard's disabilities was passed by both houses in the summer and signed by the President on July 24, 1876. Writing to thank Whyte, Beauregard said: "It is a satisfaction to know that I am once more entitled to all the rights & privileges of an American citizen." [16]

[13] Beauregard to A. H. Markland, February 10, 1867, in Beauregard Papers (Library of Congress), Letterbook, Private Letters, December 16, 1865—April 18, 1867; Beauregard to Gantt and Waddell, attorneys of Memphis, June 3, 1867, December 29, 1868, and to B. B. Waddell, November 19, 1867, *ibid.*, Letterbook, Private Letters, April 19, 1867—February 4, 1869; Beauregard to Mrs. D. B. Harris, December 12, 1867, in Harris Papers; David Macrae, *The Americans at Home* . . . (Glasgow, 1885), 312; J. T. Dorris, *Pardon and Amnesty under Lincoln and Johnson* (Chapel Hill, 1953), 352–56.

[14] Beauregard to Gordon, June 22, November 22, 1874, in Beauregard Papers (Library of Congress), Letterbook, Private Letters, February 28, 1872—December 1, 1875.

[15] Beauregard to Gordon, January 9, 1876, and Beauregard to the Congress, May 23, 1876, in Records of the United States Senate (National Archives). Again I am grateful to the staff of the National Archives for finding these documents and providing photostats.

[16] *Statutes at Large of the United States,* IX (Washington, 1877), 467; Beauregard to W. C. Whyte, July 24, 1876, in Beauregard Papers (Library of Congress), Letterbook, Private Letters, December 4, 1875—March 24, 1880.

In the Reconstruction period a number of Confederate officers, embittered by defeat or disgusted by conditions in the South, left the country to take appointments in foreign armies. Several times Beauregard considered leaving Louisiana and living out his days abroad. Not until 1875 did he definitely decide to remain in the United States.

Only a few months after Beauregard had returned from the war rumors circulated in New Orleans that he was going to accept a foreign command. It was said that he had been offered a general's commission in the French army, that he had been invited to take the command of Emperor Maximilian's troops in Mexico, and that he had applied for the command of the Papal army in Rome.[17]

These reports seem to have been pure speculation, but in 1865 he did try to secure a post in the Brazilian army. He made his application through his former chief of staff, Jordan.[18] He told a friend that if the Emperor of Brazil came through with a favorable offer he would transfer his home to that country. His heart would bleed to bid farewell to Louisiana, he said, but if he could not help his state or himself by staying he would have to go elsewhere.[19] The Brazilian government made some kind of offer, but he declined it. He explained his reasons in a public letter to counteract charges being made in Europe that he was a mere soldier of fortunte seeking a job. Yes, he said, he had thought of seeking refuge in Brazil from the hatred of Northern fanatics. But the generous sentiments for the South expressed by President Johnson had decided him to stay with his section. "I prefer to live here, poor and forgotten," he said, "than to be endowed with honor and riches in a foreign country." [20]

In 1866 when Beauregard was in Europe on his railroad business, the rumors started again. He was supposed to have offered his services to the King of Italy and to have sought a position as military adviser to Louis Napoleon of France. The basis for the latter report probably was that he asked the French Emperor for an interview so that he could tell him about the latest advances in the use of naval mines and small arms. He told Louis Napoleon that he wanted to

[17] New Orleans *Times*, August 13, 1865; Paris *L' Avenir Nationale*, quoted *ibid.*, November 4, 1865; *ibid.*, November 13, 1865; New Orleans *Picayune*, September 6, 1865.

[18] Jordan to Beauregard, August 12, 1865, in Thomas Jordan Papers (Duke University Library).

[19] Beauregard to E. P. Alexander, August 27, 1865, in Alexander Papers.

[20] New Orleans *Times*, December 5, 1865.

help France because the Emperor had sympathized with the Confederacy.[21]

Actually at this time Beauregard was not interested in a foreign command. He was fairly satisfied with his position in Louisiana and hopeful that Radical Republican rule would soon be overthrown. But without seeking an offer, he got one. Rumania, a principality of Turkey's which was rising in strength, wanted to build up its military force. The Rumanian government sent commissioners to Paris to proffer Beauregard the post of general in chief. According to newspaper reports the bid included a huge cash payment and the title of prince. Beauregard seriously considered taking the post. One of the conditions he laid down for acceptance was that he could bring a certain number of former Confederate officers with him. But in the end he decided that his place was in the South.[22]

After the election of 1868, in which the Republicans carried the nation and Louisiana, Beauregard again thought of leaving the country. He tried, unsuccessfully, to induce the Brazilian government to make him another offer.[23] His old friend Jordan was in command of an army of Cuban rebels fighting to throw off the rule of Spain. Beauregard suggested to the Spanish government that if he were given a post in the army of Spain he could use his influence with Jordan to settle the revolt. The Spaniards refused the bait.[24]

Early in 1870 General Dan Adams, formerly of the Confederate army, approached Beauregard with a proposition to become commander of the Egyptian army. The Khedive of Egypt, Ismail Pasha, ambitious to extend his territory and to free himself from the overlordship of Turkey, was building a strong army. To strengthen his

[21] *Ibid.,* July 14, 19, 23, 27, August 8, 1866; Basso, *Beauregard,* 295–96; Beauregard to Louis Napoleon, July 20, 1866, in Beauregard Papers (Library of Congress), Letterbook, Private Letters, December 16, 1865—April 18, 1867.

[22] New Orleans *Times,* July 27, August 1, 1866; Wade Hampton to Beauregard, July 21, 1866, in Beauregard Papers (The Cabildo, New Orleans); Beauregard to R. J. Walker, November 23, 1868, in Beauregard Papers (Library of Congress), Letterbook, Private Letters, April 19, 1867—February 4, 1869. In Henkels' Catalog, *Beauregard Papers,* Pt. II, p. 38, is a document by Beauregard listing the conditions on which he would go to Rumania.

[23] Beauregard to Jordan, November 23, 1868, and to R. J. Walker, November 23, 1868, in Beauregard Papers (Library of Congress), Letterbook, Private Letters, April 19, 1867—February 4, 1869.

[24] Beauregard to F. N. Casada, September 6, 1869, *ibid.,* Letterbook, Private Letters, February 6, 1869—February 5, 1872.

officer corps he invited ex-Confederate officers to take service with him. Now he wanted a general of reputation to command his forces. Adams acted as his intermediary.

Beauregard saw money and security in the Egyptian situation. He told Adams that he would accept an offer if the Khedive would let him select his own staff, pay him the salary of the general in chief of the United States army and transportation expenses, deposit a bonus to his credit in America before he sailed, and provide half pay to his family for fifteen years in case of his death. Whether the Khedive met these terms is not known, but he did offer Beauregard the command, at a reported salary of $12,000 a year plus rations.[25]

The events that followed are shrouded in mystery and contradiction. Beauregard claimed later that he declined the offer. Actually he tentatively accepted it. At least he wrote to a number of his friends proffering them positions in the Egyptian army.[26] Then something happened. The Khedive withdrew his proposal. A fascinating story appeared to account for his action. In Egypt as a consul general in the United States diplomatic corps was George H. Butler, a nephew of the Union general whom Beauregard had denounced bitterly in the war for his administration of occupied New Orleans. According to press reports, Butler went to Ismail and protested that to hire more Confederates, and especially Beauregard, would be an insult to the United States.[27]

Years later George Butler confirmed the newspaper stories. He said that he told the Khedive Beauregard was treacherous and would betray him. Some Confederates he would not have opposed, said Butler: "But, frankly, there wasn't room in Egypt for Beauregard and myself at the same time. . . . I kept Gen. Beauregard out of Egyptian gold lace and piastres purely because I considered him an eminent mistake." [28]

[25] Beauregard to Adams, March 25, April 23, May 14, July 19, 1870, *ibid.* The manuscript letter of April 23 is in the Beauregard Papers (Tulane University), with an attached note by Adams saying Beauregard could be "secured." See also Pierre Crabitès, *Americans in the Egyptian Army* (London, 1938), 7–8.

[26] Roman, *Beauregard,* I, 10; Beauregard to Wade Hampton and John B. Gordon, June 16, 1870, in Beauregard Papers (Library of Congress), Letterbook, Private Letters, February 6, 1869—February 5, 1872; Beauregard to E. P. Alexander, June 17, 1870, in Alexander Papers.

[27] Dan Adams to Beauregard, July 14, 1870, in Henkels' Catalog, *Beauregard Papers,* Pt. II; Basso, *Beauregard,* 296–97.

[28] Interview with Butler in New York *World,* reprinted in New Orleans *Times-Democrat,* July 21, 1882.

Butler's story has qualities of high drama—an old feud and an old score at last repaid. Unfortunately it also contains an element of exaggeration. He undoubtedly talked to the Khedive, but it is unlikely that the ruler changed his decision merely because a young diplomat said Beauregard was dangerous. Beauregard himself did not think that Butler had swayed Ismail, saying that the Khedive would not have been influenced by "the slimy emanations of so vile a reptile." His own explanation was probably nearer the truth: the Sultan of Turkey had called Ismail in and told him to cut down on his military preparations.[29]

Beauregard was deeply disappointed by the collapse of the Egyptian negotiations. Still disgusted with conditions in Louisiana and still determined to leave the country, he wrote to friends in Paris and Washington offering his services to France in her war against Prussia. He said that he wanted to come and defend the land of his ancestors. If he came, "thousands upon thousands" of Southerners would follow him. To defend France he asked for a general's commission and $500 a month.[30] If his application was placed before the French government, it was never acted upon.

Beauregard's last attempts to secure a foreign command were made in 1873–75. In these years he seemed willing to take anything that would get him out of reconstructed Louisiana. He tried to interest the Khedive in making another offer.[31] Nothing came of this effort, but the government of Argentina proffered him the command of its army. The negotiations were conducted by an American named Hunter Davidson, who held a post in the Argentine military organization. Beauregard told Davidson he would accept if the government would deposit $50,000 to his credit in a London or Paris bank and pay him $20,000 a year and traveling expenses. Davidson was aghast at Beauregard's conditions. He informed the general that the requirement of a deposit would wound the feelings of a sensitive people.

Beauregard then reversed his stipulations. He would go for $25,000 a year and $40,000 to be paid him when his duties were completed. Davidson thought the government would agree, but no offer ever

[29] Beauregard to Adams, July 19, 1870, in Beauregard Papers (Library of Congress), Letterbook, Private Letters, February 6, 1869—February 5, 1872.
[30] Beauregard to John Slidell, July 28, 1870, to Adams, November 24, 1870, to W. W. Corcoran, January 10, 1871, ibid.
[31] Beauregard to W. W. Loring, March 22, 1873, ibid., Letterbook, Private Letters, February 28, 1872—December 1, 1875.

came. As Beauregard observed, Argentina could not afford him. In his disappointment he even thought of accepting a position in the army of Japan and fighting the Chinese.[32] By 1876 he had abandoned any idea of foreign service. His economic situation had improved, and Louisiana seemed about to be redeemed from Reconstruction.

In the reconstruction of his state Beauregard played a prominent and vocal if not a dominating role. He spoke out, not always wisely, in letters, interviews, and speeches on almost every issue of the times. He headed one important movement that, had it succeeded, would have changed the course of Reconstruction. He spoke and acted as a Southerner, a war hero, and an industrialist of the New South. Besides, he had become accustomed to pronouncing opinions in the war, and it was hard to break the habit.

A basic factor in Beauregard's thinking about Reconstruction was his opinion of the Negro population of the South, now free as a result of the war. He believed that the Negroes were naturally inferior, ignorant, and indolent. In one dazzling prediction, he said that in seventy-five years the colored race would disappear from America along with the Indians and the buffalo.[33] Holding these views, he was convinced that the whites could manage the Negroes politically as they had controlled them economically when slaves.

His racial notions appeared to the fullest in the first important pronouncement he made on Reconstruction. In March, 1867, the Radical Republicans passed through Congress their final Reconstruction plan, the core of which was enforced Negro suffrage. Excitement ran through the South, as many people advocated resisting the radicals. Beauregard wrote a public letter, which was widely printed in newspapers in all sections, advising Southerners to accept the situation. We must submit or resist, he said sensibly, and resistance is futile. In Negro suffrage he saw an element of strength for the South in the future and a possibility of defeating the radicals with their own weapon. "The Negro is Southern born; with a little education and

[32] Beauregard to Davidson, June 2, July 1, 1874, to John B. Gordon, November 22, 1874, February 8, 1875, to Camille de Polignac, May 26, 1875, to W. W. Corcoran, June 12, 1875, *ibid.;* Davidson to Beauregard, June 16, 25, August 11, 1874, January 18, 1875, in Beauregard Papers (Tulane); Beauregard to E. P. Alexander, July 2, 1874, in Alexander Papers.

[33] Beauregard to John Laird, May 24, 1867, and to Edward Macrae, April 11, 1868, in Beauregard Papers (Library of Congress), Letterbook, Private Letters, April 19, 1867—February 4, 1869; Macrae, *Americans at Home,* 232; Beauregard to Early, November 27, 1874, in Early Papers.

some property qualifications he can be made to take sufficient interest in the affairs and prosperity of the South to insure an intelligent vote," he wrote. Negro voters thus managed would restore to the South its former influence in the national government.[34]

He was being completely pragmatic and knew it. He told Augusta J. Evans that he wished he could have said something else: "Would that I could have said to [my soldiers], resist, and 'hang out our banners on the outer wall etc'! but the day of retribution has not yet come when we shall be able to satiate our spirit of revenge on those fanatics and radicals of the North. Whenever it does, we shall make them drink of the poisoned chalice to the very dregs!" Nor was he as hopeful of the South's future as he had written. He observed to Lee that maybe a counterrevolution would be necessary to overthrow the radicals. What the country needed, he declared, was a Washington or a Louis Napoleon! [35]

In the summer of 1868 Beauregard was vacationing at White Sulphur Springs. Here also were Lee, Alexander H. Stephens, and a number of other former Confederate military and civil officials. To the resort came William S. Rosecrans, once a Union general and now a politician helping to manage the Presidential campaign of Horatio Seymour, the Democratic candidate. He came to get the Southerners to sign a statement designed to aid Seymour's cause. The Republicans were charging that Southerners, most of whom were Democrats, could not be trusted to deal justly with Negroes. Rosecrans wanted the ex-Confederates to say this was not so. He placed his idea before Lee, who called the Southerners to his cottage to confer with Rosecrans. The result of the meeting was a document signed by Lee, Beauregard, and approximately thirty others, saying that the South accepted the results of the war and emancipation and that it felt kindly toward the Negro but was opposed to his exercising political power.[36]

Beauregard was happy to strike a blow against the Republicans, but he must have been enraged by an interview Rosecrans gave out after returning north. A reporter asked Rosecrans if Lee's answer

[34] New York *Tribune,* April 1, 1867.

[35] Beauregard to Augusta J. Evans, March 27, 1867, in Beauregard Papers (Library of Congress), Letterbook, Private Letters, December 16, 1865— April 18, 1867; Beauregard to Lee, July 30, 1867, in Beauregard Papers (Duke University).

[36] New Orleans *Picayune,* September 4, 6, 8, 1867; Freeman, *R. E. Lee,* IV, 373–77.

to his request had not been weak. Rosecrans replied that in some ways Lee was weak, although on the whole a sincere man. What about Beauregard, said the journalist; wasn't he weak? "By the side of Lee, certainly," said Rosecrans. "Take him alone, however, and he strikes you as quick, ready and incisive—well, a man of the world, a good business character, a smart active Frenchman. But with Lee he dwindles. Lee says shut the door, and Beauregard shuts the door." The reporter asked if the Southern generals would let the Negro vote. Rosecrans answered: "Lee will not, probably, but Beauregard will. He is in favor of it and so expressed himself to me." [37]

The Republicans carried the election of 1868. U. S. Grant was elected President, and the Republicans won control of the government of Louisiana. Beauregard predicted that Grant would become the tool of designing politicians,[38] and then relapsed into comparative silence for four years. In this period he was absorbed first in his railroad activities and later in his attempt to secure the Egyptian command.

Not until 1872 did Beauregard resume interest in poltics. In that year and the next he would make his most significant contribution to the Reconstruction story. A new party appeared in Louisiana in 1872, the Reform party. Composed of conservative New Orleans businessmen, the party advocated economical state government and recognition of the Negro's civil and political rights. Beauregard was one of the guiding spirits in the group. In 1872 the Reformers took no stand on national issues. On the state level they fused with the Democrats in an unsuccessful attempt to elect a non-Republican governor. Some of the leaders, however, stated their preference as to Presidential candidates. Beauregard, in a public letter, endorsed Horace Greeley, the Liberal Republican nominee running against Grant. He called for peace, reconciliation, a forgetting of old issues, and a union of conservative–minded people to remove corruption and extravagance from government.[39]

Beauregard's candidates were defeated in 1872. Grant was elected to a second term, and the Republicans retained control of the state

[37] Interview with Rosecrans, in Cincinnati *Commercial,* reprinted in New Orleans *Picayune,* October 15, 1868.

[38] Beauregard to A. H. Stephens, November 2, 1868, in Stephens Papers.

[39] T. Harry Williams, "The Louisiana Unification Movement," in *Journal of Southern History,* XI (1945), 350–51; New Orleans *Times,* May 29, 1872.

government. But in the campaign Beauregard and the other Reform leaders had glimpsed a hope for the future; they discerned a method by which Republican rule in Louisiana might be overthrown. The Reformers had taken the position that Negro political power was a reality and might as well be accepted. Recognize this fact, they said, and induce the Negroes to vote with the right white people. In other words, if you can't lick them, get them to join you. The Reformers did not attract many Negro votes, mainly because their platform on Negro rights was vague and general. They were convinced, however, that the salvation of the state lay in persuading the colored voters to leave the Republicans and unite with the whites in a new political organization. In 1873 they brought forth a detailed and specific plan to combine the races in a political union. This was the "Louisiana Unification Movement," one of the most unusual and important phenomena of the Reconstruction period.

The first news that a Unification party was being formed appeared in the New Orleans press in the spring of 1873. Immediately approving letters and interviews flooded the newspapers, especially the *Times,* conservative organ of the business interests and leading journalistic champion of the proposed party. Most of the communications were from businessmen, who declared that they were willing to cooperate with Negroes and recognize their political and civil equality if only the Negroes would agree to work for lower taxes. While the press discussed unification, the sponsors of the movement were holding a series of secret meetings. Their identity was for the moment unknown, but it was revealed that a committee of one hundred, fifty from each race, was perfecting an organization and drawing up a statement of beliefs. Then it was announced that on June 16 the committee would hold a public session to hear a report from its committee on resolutions, a report that would be the platform of the party.[40]

At the meeting on the sixteenth New Orleans saw the men who were backing the Unification movement and read their plan to save Louisiana. The fifty white sponsors were the business, legal, and journalistic leaders of the community; included in the group were the presidents of practically every corporation and bank in the city. The Negro sponsors were the wealthy, cultured aristocracy of the race; many of them were the so-called "Creole Negroes" who had

---

[40] Williams, "Louisiana Unification Movement," *loc. cit.,* 352–56.

been free before the war. The chairman of the important resolutions committee was Beauregard.[41]

Speaking for his committee, Beauregard presented to the meeting a report that was unanimously adopted. This report is a significant document in the history of Reconstruction. It represented the efforts of conservative businessmen to meet and solve the problem of carpet-bag government forced on the South from the outside. The business classes and their allies, the planters, bore the brunt of the heavy taxation levied by the Republican governments. More than anything, the propertied groups wanted taxes lowered. They knew that to realize their objective they had to have the political support of the colored voters. Negro votes had imposed the tax burden, Negro votes could lift it. If in order to persuade the Negroes to do so it was necessary to grant them political and civil equality, then the equality would have to come.[42]

This is precisely what Beauregard and the Unifiers proposed. Their report advocated complete political equality for the Negro, an equal division of state offices between the races, and a plan whereby Negroes would become landowners. It denounced discrimination because of color in hiring laborers or in selecting directors of corporations, and called for the abandonment of segregation in public conveyances, public places, railroads, steamboats, and public schools.[43] After adopting the report the Unifiers appointed a committee to arrange a great mass meeting in New Orleans to ratify publicly the co-operation platform.

Beauregard issued a public statement defending his reasons for supporting unification. Pragmatic as always, he argued that the Negroes already had equality and the whites had to accept that hard fact. Continued Negro co-operation with the carpetbaggers would ruin the state. Therefore the whites must persuade the Negroes to leave the Republicans. The recipe was simple—let the whites recognize the Negroes' rights. Once this was done, the Negro would desert the alien carpetbagger and join his natural friend, the Southern white man. Presumably he would also let the white man direct his vote.[44]

[41] *Ibid.*, 356–58.

[42] T. Harry Williams, "An Analysis of Some Reconstruction Attitudes," in *Journal of Southern History,* XII (1946), 479–82.

[43] New Orleans *Times,* June 17, 1873; New Orleans *Picayune,* June 17, 1873.

[44] New Orleans *Times,* July 1, 1873. For a similar defense of his motives, see Beauregard to Early, *ibid.*, August 8, 1873.

The Unification program secured wide approval in New Orleans and the plantation belt of south Louisiana, but in the country parishes it was received with loathing and execration. The white masses simply would not accord such concessions to Negroes.[45] Without their support the movement was doomed to failure. Nor were the Negro masses greatly stirred by Unification. They viewed the promises of the whites with suspicion and were not inclined to follow the leadership of the Negro intellectuals in New Orleans.

The mass meeting on July 15 witnessed the death of the movement. Most of the crowd were Negroes. For some reason Beauregard was not present; maybe he sensed the outcome. A parade of speakers, white and colored, mounted the platform to air their views. The Negro orators, in a patronizing manner, congratulated the whites on giving up their prejudices and promised to guide them on the upward path to complete tolerance. A Negro politician, one of the class that had an interest in killing Unification, really ruined the meeting. He said that when the Negroes received full recognition of their rights, then, but not until then, would they unite with the whites to overthrow the Republicans and give Louisiana honest and economical government.[46]

Even the leaders of Unification had to admit that the meeting and the movement had failed. The white and colored masses were not ready for political union. Sadly the New Orleans *Times* observed that Beauregard had made the mistake of appealing "to a sense of kindness and justice and magnanimity that was slightly inaccessible." [47]

After the collapse of Unification Beauregard played no further part in Reconstruction except to occasionally denounce the Republicans in a letter or interview. Like most Southerners, he rejoiced when Republican President R. B. Hayes withdrew Federal troops from the South after the disputed election of 1876 and Republican rule in Louisiana disappeared.[48] Also like most Southerners, he hoped

[45] Williams, "Louisiana Unification Movement," *loc. cit.*, 362–64.

[46] *Ibid.*, 364–66.

[47] New Orleans *Times,* July 22, 1873.

[48] Beauregard to Early, May 12, 1874 (MS. in Confederate Museum, Richmond); Richmond *Enquirer,* October 8, 1874, clipping in Beauregard Papers (Louisiana State University); Beauregard to R. N. Gourdin, June 1, 1875, in Gourdin–Young Papers; Beauregard to Paul Hamilton Hayne, March 6, 1877, in Paul Hamilton Hayne Papers (Duke University Library); Beauregard to Miles, January 11, 1875, in Miles Papers; Chicago *Times,* April 10, 1879, clipping in Beauregard Papers (Louisiana State University).

for a Democratic victory nationally. In 1880 he thought that the Democratic candidate, W. S. Hancock, an old friend, might be elected. He laid plans to persuade Hancock to appoint him ambassador to France. To increase his chances he asked the governor of Louisiana to name him to the United States Senate to fill a vacancy caused by death. Beauregard's political adventures always failed. The governor selected another person, and Hancock was defeated.[49]

Before his death Beauregard had mellowed greatly in his attitudes toward Reconstruction and Republicans. But on occasion the old resentments and hatreds could flare forth. In 1885, when General Grant was dying of cancer, a Chicago journal asked Beauregard to write a five-hundred-word expression on Grant for use in its next issue if the former President died. On the back of the telegram Beauregard wrote: "Answer: Let him die in peace, & may God have mercy on his soul. G. T. Beauregard cannot comply with your request, but regret to hear of his great sufferings."[50]

For one Republican he always manifested great respect. In 1889 the president of the Lincoln Memorial League invited him to Springfield to participate in ceremonies honoring Abraham Lincoln. Beauregard wanted to go, but he was unable to make the trip. Regretfully he replied that he would be present in spirit to pay homage "to the memory of a great & a good man." He continued: "At his untimely taking off, his life was invaluable; a proud people had suffered humiliation. His life was of extraordinary importance to the country he served so well, with a clear intellect—and loved so profoundly, with a big & guileless heart."[51]

[49] Beauregard to Miles, July 27, 1880, in Miles Papers; Beauregard to Samuel McEnery, August 23, 1880, in Beauregard Papers (Library of Congress), Letterbook, Letters, March 9, 1880—December 5, 1883.
[50] Editor of Chicago *Current* to Beauregard, April 4, 1885, in Henkels' Catalog, *Beauregard Papers*, Pt. II.
[51] Beauregard to R. B. Hoover, April 5, 1889, in Lincoln Memorial League Papers (Illinois State Historical Library, Springfield). I am indebted to Miss Hazel Wolf, Peoria, Illinois, for providing me with a copy of this letter.

CHAPTER SEVENTEEN

Painting the Monkey's Tail

GENERAL GEORGE PICKETT, the hero of Gettysburg, tried to sell insurance after the war. He was a poor agent. He felt that there was something vulgar and unseemly in asking a man to buy a policy. His company's representative in Petersburg told him, in the expressive new language of business, that he would have to unbuckle a few holes and thaw out if he wanted to paint the monkey's tail sky-blue. Sadly Pickett reflected that he could not paint and hated to associate with artists who could. He was nothing but a soldier. The war was over, and he was of no more account.[1]

The professional soldiers of the Confederacy faced a bleak situation at the war's end. Trained for one profession, they could not exercise their trade in the United States. Unless they had graduated from the engineer corps at West Point, their education did not fit them for employment in civilian society. Nor did the habits acquired during long years in the army prepare them to hold positions where they had to deal with civilians as equals or superiors.

Many of the Southern generals had to work at anything that would afford them a living. In some cases jobs were created for them. Insurance companies and other concerns, anxious to honor a war hero or to capitalize on his name, would appoint a general to a purely honorary or titular office. Most of the generals lived and died in modest economic circumstances; a few were almost penniless at their death. Of the prominent officers Beauregard was the only one to accumulate much property, the only one to become, by Southern standards, wealthy. As an engineer of reputation he found quick employment with railroad corporations. As a man of the world he was not embarrassed to associate with the artists who were painting the monkey's tail. He was a pretty fair man with a brush himself.

[1] A. C. Inman (ed.), *Soldier of the South: General Pickett's War Letters to his Wife* (Boston, 1928), 152–54.

For a few months after his return from the war Beauregard was without income and without employment. He brought home with him only his personal effects and a five-dollar gold piece. Living with his son René, he wondered bitterly what would become of him.[2] This grim period ended in October, when he accepted a position with the New Orleans, Jackson, and Great Northern Railroad as chief engineer and general superintendent at a salary of $3,500 a year. A month later his remuneration was increased to $5,000.[3]

The Jackson Railroad, as it was familiarly known, ran for 206 miles (on the present Illinois Central line) from New Orleans to Canton, Mississippi. Built in the 1850's, its promoters had planned, before the war interrupted their work, to extend it to Nashville or a point on the Tennessee River. Their motive was to connect New Orleans with the Ohio Valley and to connect the cotton planters of the interior with New Orleans. Because the road seemed of vital importance to the lower Mississippi Valley, the states of Louisiana and Mississippi and the city of New Orleans furnished financial aid by buying stock. Potentially the Jackson line was a valuable property. In 1860 its gross earnings were $1,272,682 and its net profit was $556,700. It had liabilities of over $4,000,000, which the owners confidently expected to pay out of current revenues.[4]

During the war the Federal government seized possession of the railroad. When the line was returned to the owners in 1865, it was in a state of near ruin. Ninety per cent of the rolling stock had been destroyed or damaged. In 1860 the company had owned forty-five locomotives, thirty-seven passenger cars, nine baggage and express cars, and about five hundred freight cars. It received back four locomotives, four passenger cars, and thirty-six assorted freight and baggage cars. Most of the depots had disappeared, most of the bridges had been destroyed, half of the crossties had rotted, and thirty miles of rail had been bent and twisted by Union marauders.[5]

[2] René Beauregard, "Magnolia"; Basso, *Beauregard,* 292; King, *Creole Families,* 456.

[3] John F. Stover, "The Development of Northern Financial Control over Southern Railroads, 1865–1900" (Ph.D. dissertation, University of Wisconsin, 1951), 202–204.

[4] New Orleans *Picayune,* January 30, 1866; article by G. W. R. Bayley, *ibid.,* March 23, 1873; New Orleans *Times,* January 27, 1866. The history of the railroad is extensively treated in Thomas D. Clark, *A Pioneer Southern Railroad From New Orleans to Cairo* (Chapel Hill, N. C., 1936).

[5] Stover, "Northern Control over Southern Railroads," 202; Clark, *Pioneer Southern Railroad,* 120; New Orleans *Picayune,* January 30, 1866; article by G. W. R. Bayley, *ibid.,* March 23, 1873.

Obviously the Jackson line needed many improvements before it would be a railroad again. Its greatest and most immediate need was the services of a skilled engineer who could repair the war damages and put the road in running condition. If the route to Canton could be reopened, revenue would flow in and the company could proceed on a firmer financial basis. The directors were convinced that in Beauregard they had found the man for the job. New Orleans, proud of her distinguished son and relieved to see him employed, agreed.[6]

The directors chose wisely. Beauregard took his duties seriously and performed a remarkable job of rehabilitation. In a relatively short time the rolling stock was replaced, the track was repaired, and cars were rolling between New Orleans and Canton on a regular schedule.[7] In his annual report of April, 1866, Beauregard could boast that since June of 1865 the road had earned $760,319. Most of the revenue had been plowed back into improvements, leaving a net profit which he estimated to be $175,000. He predicted that earnings would soon soar to $1,500,000 a year and that the annual net would be $500,000.[8]

His optimism about the railroad's earning powers was soundly based, but the financial situation was not as bright as he pictured it. The company had large liabilities which sometime would have to be met. The fixed or bonded debt, held by Northern and European capitalists, was almost three million dollars; the unpaid interest on the bonds amounted to probably a million dollars. Obviously the company could not pay the interest on the mortgage bonds, meet its debts to general creditors, and at the same time continue to expand its services.[9]

The directors became painfully aware of the threat to the road's future posed by the liabilities when some local bondholders threatened a lawsuit to foreclose the mortgage. They decided that some kind of deal would have to be made with the Northern and European creditors about the overdue interest coupons. Somebody in the com-

[6] New Orleans *Picayune,* October 18, November 1, 1865; New Orleans *Times,* October 18, 24, 25, 1865.

[7] New Orleans *Times,* January 27, April 13, June 21, 1866; New Orleans *Picayune,* February 3, March 7, 1866; article by G. W. R. Bayley, *ibid.,* March 30, 1873.

[8] New Orleans *Picayune,* April 12, 1866.

[9] *Ibid.,* April 12, 1866; article by G. W. R. Bayley, *ibid.,* March 30, 1873.

pany who knew its problems and who was a man of reputation would have to meet with these men and convince them that the road could honor its obligations. Beauregard was the only one who could do the job, the directors concluded, and he should go as president of the company. In April, 1866, he was elevated to that office. He was instructed to persuade the bondholders to exchange their coupons for second mortgage bonds. In May he left for the Northeast and Europe.[10]

On the eve of his departure a New Orleans newspaper warned the North not to try to claim him as a national hero. The editor had noted a tendency in Northern journals to appropriate things peculiarly Southern—the valor of Southern arms, the skill of Southern generals, the vastness of the Southern rebellion—and boastfully credit them to "the national account." As Beauregard was the greatest engineer of the age, said the editor, "we wish it to be distinctly understood by our Northern friends . . . that Gen. Beauregard is our Gen. Beauregard. And though we have no objection to their doing everything they can for him in a business way, we do object to their claiming him as theirs and passing the credit of his genius to their little national account." [11]

They did claim him though. In Baltimore huge crowds pressed around his hotel to catch a glimpse of him. Prominent citizens and former friends, including army officers who had known him before the war, called to pay their respects. Joe Johnston was in town, and he and Beauregard met for the first time since the war.[12] Similar scenes occurred in New York. The reporters of the metropolitan journals sought him out for interviews and got him to talking about his campaigns. Most of them were highly impressed and described him as one of the great captains of the war. One reporter had an interesting reservation. He said that Beauregard was not a first-class military man but was a first-rate second-class man.[13]

After conferring with the Eastern bondholders, who said they

[10] *Ibid.,* April 17, 18, 1866; article by G. W. R. Bayley, *ibid.,* March 30, 1873; New Orleans *Times,* May 5, 8, 1866.

[11] New Orleans *Picayune,* May 6, 1866.

[12] Baltimore *Sun,* quoted in New Orleans *Crescent,* May 22, 1866; New Orleans *Picayune,* May 20, 1866.

[13] New York *Times,* quoted in New Orleans *Times,* May 16, 1866; New Orleans *Picayune,* May 21, 1866; New York *Times,* quoted *ibid.,* May 23, 1866.

were quite willing to accept the arrangement proposed by the company, Beauregard sailed for England, arriving on May 26.[14] In England he was lionized even more than he had been in the North. Crowds followed him on the streets, receptions were given in his honor, and members of the nobility invited him to visit them. He made a brief visit to Paris, where he talked to the French creditors and was received by the Emperor in a private audience.[15]

The social affairs were pleasant and flattering, but Beauregard was chiefly interested in convincing the bondholders that the Jackson road had a future. On this project he worked hard and succeeded brilliantly. At a meeting of the European creditors in London he presented the company's proposal to exchange interest coupons for second mortgage bonds. His audience was persuaded and endorsed the arrangement. Beauregard returned home with precisely the agreement the directors had asked him to secure.[16]

The next few years were prosperous ones for the Jackson road. Its rolling stock was increased and its services expanded. The annual gross income averaged a million and a half dollars. Almost a million dollars in overdue interest was funded. Although the total debt was still huge and the company was unable to pay any stock dividends, the directors felt that the road was at last on a sound basis.[17] For the progress that had been made Beauregard could claim most of the credit. In a real sense it was his railroad. When the company needed money in 1868, he was the man who went to New York and raised the required sum.[18] He was happy in his work and proud of what he had accomplished. Writing to Lee, he said: "I have become such a 'Railroad man' that you wd. supposed if you were to see me

[14] Beauregard kept a brief journal of his trip, which is in the Beauregard Papers (Cabildo); it is extremely sketchy and contains no entries after his arrival in England. Two directors accompanied Beauregard.

[15] See the following letters in the Beauregard Papers (Louisiana State University): W. H. Chadwick to Beauregard, May 31, 1866; ———— Townsend to Beauregard, June 10, 1866; William Busby to Beauregard, June 11, 1866; James Smith to Beauregard, June 12, 22, 1866; F. W. Hewlett to Beauregard, n. d. 1866. See also Liverpool *Daily Post,* quoted in New Orleans *Picayune,* June 19, 1866; New Orleans *Times,* June 16, July 14, 19, 1866.

[16] New Orleans *Times,* July 15, 16, 1866; article by G. W. R. Bayley, in New Orleans *Picayune,* March 30, 1873.

[17] New Orleans *Times,* January 19, April 14, 1867, January 25, 1868; New Orleans *Picayune,* January 24, April 29, 1868, April 10, 1870; article by G. W. R. Bayley, *ibid.,* March 30, 1873.

[18] New Orleans *Picayune,* May 26, 1868.

in my office or at work, that I had never done anything else all my life—indeed I took to it quite naturally."[19] He was not permitted to stay at it very long. Just when he had achieved his greatest success in the postwar world and was making a name as a railroad man, his road and his job were cruelly wrenched from him by the politicians.

Well over half of the stock in the company was owned by the state of Louisiana and the city of New Orleans. In this situation lay a great potential danger for Beauregard and the directors. The politicians, in this case the Republican rulers of the state, could, if they desired, take over the control of the company. Beauregard recognized the threat, and several times he tried, without success, to interest capitalist friends in buying a controlling share of the public stock.[20]

Early in 1870 the danger suddenly became real. Governor Henry Clay Warmoth and his Republican followers announced that they intended to secure control of the Jackson road.[21] At Warmoth's direction, the legislature passed on April 1 a bill directing the governor to sell the state's stock within ten days and authorizing the city government to sell its stock. Immediately Warmoth published a notice that he would receive bids at his office. At the same time the city council proclaimed that it was open to offers.[22] All that was needed now was a buyer, and he was already on hand. In fact, he had conceived and directed the actions of the politicians.

Henry C. McComb, from Wilmington, Delaware, was a typical speculator of the new industrial age. Backed by Northeastern financial interests, he had secured control of a number of railroads in Mississippi and Tennessee and combined them into what he called the Southern Railroad Association.[23] Now he had decided to add the

[19] Beauregard to Lee, January 21, 1868, in Beauregard Papers (Duke University).

[20] Beauregard to Émile Erlanger, December 27, 1869, and to Sam Jones, February 3, 1870, in Beauregard Papers (Library of Congress), Letterbook, Private Letters, February 6, 1869—February 5, 1872. Beauregard himself owned thirty-five shares; New Orleans *Picayune,* June 2, 1870.

[21] Beauregard to Isaac Sherman, February 4, 1870, and to the New Orleans *Bee,* March 11, 1870, in Beauregard Papers (Library of Congress), Letterbook, Private Letters, February 6, 1869—February 5, 1872.

[22] New Orleans *Picayune,* March 30, 1873; Frances Byers Harris, "Henry Clay Warmoth, Reconstruction Governor of Louisiana" (M.A. dissertation, Louisiana State University, 1943), 82.

[23] Clark, *Pioneer Southern Railroad,* 124–25; Stover, "Northern Control over Southern Railroads," 205-206, New Orleans *Times,* June 12, 1873.

Jackson road to his system, and was in New Orleans carrying on hush-hush negotiations with Warmoth.[24]

First to accept McComb's money was the city government, which sold its investment, extravagantly valued at $2,000,000, for $320,000. On April 4 McComb and the mayor appeared at the offices of the Jackson road and directed Beauregard to enter the transfer on his stock book. Beauregard, saying the sale had been illegal, refused. McComb then induced a pliant Federal judge to order Beauregard to act.[25]

On the ninth Warmoth sold the state stock, valued at $884,000, for $141,400. That afternoon the governor and McComb went to Beauregard's office and demanded that the stock be transferred to McComb on the books. Again Beauregard refused. He took the position that as the state had originally paid cash for only half of its stock, it had no fully paid shares to sell; he also contended that the city and state could not vote their shares as individuals did and hence that McComb had no real control.[26]

McComb's next step was to get his judge to issue an injunction forbidding the Jackson stockholders to meet to elect a board of directors without including McComb. They met unofficially to protest the order at a dinner session, with a huge nougat pyramid as the centerpiece and bottles of rare old wine throwing a rosy light on the feast.[27] All was not cheer, however, in Beauregard's camp. His ranks were breaking; some of the directors had gone over to McComb. One of them came to Beauregard with a proposal to compromise the fight. He said that the only reason the governor and the mayor were hostile to the railroad was because Beauregard was president. If Beauregard would resign his office, McComb would agree to appoint him traveling financial secretary and he could spend most of his time in Europe! Indignantly Beauregard told the man to get out. He had lost his outer

[24] H. C. McComb to Henry Clay Warmoth, April 8, 1870, in Henry Clay Warmoth Papers (Southern Historical Collection, University of North Carolina Library).

[25] New Orleans *Picayune*, April 5, 6, 7, 1870; New Orleans *Times*, April 5, 6, 1870.

[26] New Orleans *Picayune*, April 10, 1870; article by G. W. R. Bayley, *ibid.*, March 30, 1873; Stover, "Northern Control over Southern Railroads," 206–209.

[27] New Orleans *Picayune*, April 19, 1870; New Orleans *Times*, April 20, 1870.

works on Morris Island, and now he was at Sumter determined to battle to the last.[28]

Beauregard obeyed the court order and did not try to convoke a meeting to choose a board of directors. But on April 25 McComb and his supporters invaded the company offices and announced they had come to elect a new board. Beauregard said, "This is an illegal election. I order you out." When they refused to leave, some of Beauregard's friends present offered to throw them out by force. Beauregard said he wanted no violence. He had the gas turned off and departed to swear a complaint of trespass against the McComb group. They were arrested and immediately freed on bail.[29]

The railroad now had two boards of directors, with some men on both boards. The question of which one was the governing body was decided by the same judge who had issued the injunctions for McComb. To nobody's surprise he handed down a decision saying that the McComb board was legal and that the old or Beauregard directors were usurpers and were to be ousted.[30]

On June 17 the parish sheriff served the court order on Beauregard. McComb and his directors were present. Beauregard read the order and said he would have to obey it. He asked McComb to retain the road's employees. McComb said that he had no hard feelings against Beauregard, and offered his hand. Taking it, Beauregard said, "I wish you success, sir, in your management of the road. We took it when it was in ruin, and turn it over to you now in pretty good condition." McComb observed that had there been no opposition to his securing control Beauregard would have been continued as president. Grave as always when administering a rebuke, Beauregard replied that he had done only his duty to the stockholders.[31]

Beauregard had been sold out, in a deal that reeked of fraud and corruption. The money that McComb paid the state was supposedly

[28] Memorandum by Beauregard of an interview with C. Fellowes on April 19, 1870, in Beauregard Papers (Library of Congress), Letterbook, Private Letters, February 9, 1869—February 5, 1872; Beauregard to Dan Adams, April 23, 1870, in Beauregard Papers (Tulane University).

[29] New Orleans *Picayune,* April 26, May 4, June 1, 2, 1870.

[30] *Ibid.,* June 14, 1870.

[31] *Ibid.,* June 18, 1870. Beauregard said later that McComb at one time had offered him the presidency and a salary of $10,000 if he would support the sale of the government stock; New Orleans *Times,* June 15, 1873. McComb's remark at the meeting described above seems to bear the charge out.

split among Warmoth and his cronies, with the governor taking $73,437.[32] It was all you could expect from carpetbaggers, said New Orleans. But in the Gilded Age nothing succeeded like success, no matter how achieved—and in New Orleans as well as in Northern urban centers. Four years after the big sellout a delegation of the city's leading businessmen called on McComb in his rooms at the St. Charles Hotel and presented him with a written testimonial in a box inlaid with silver. The testimonial read: "When you came you found that road with broken and disordered connections. Practically you have rebuilt it. . . ." [33]

New Orleans was one of the first American cities to have a street railroad system or, to use modern terms, a bus system. By 1865 approximately six companies served the transportation needs of the community, each one operating in a designated area. Largest of the six was the City Railroad Company and the oldest was the New Orleans and Carrollton Railroad Company, which was chartered in 1833 to connect the city with the resort village of "Carlton" just up the river. The Carrollton road was the only one to employ locomotives, the cars on the others being drawn by horses or mules, with one animal to a car.[34]

The street railroads, providing cheap and ready transportation to the city's masses, played an important part in the economic life of New Orleans. The companies cut expenses by not employing conductors. As a passenger entered a car, he dropped his fare in a box with glass sides at the driver's back; if the fare was correct the driver touched a spring which dropped the money into a receptacle below.[35] The seats were on the sides of the car, with eight people supposed to be seated to a side. From the roof dangled straps for the use of passengers who had to stand. The rule on the number of riders to a side was freely ignored on all the lines, and passengers were always complaining about the crowded conditions.[36] Male riders grumbled that

[32] New Orleans *Times,* August 17, 1873.
[33] *Ibid.,* March 7, 1874.
[34] *Ibid.,* May 24, 1866, July 26, 1873; New Orleans *Picayune,* July 26, 1873.
[35] Macrae, *Americans at Home,* 308–309; New Orleans *Times,* October 17, 1866; New Orleans *Picayune,* May 8, 1866.
[36] New Orleans *Times,* December 17, 1865; New Orleans *Picayune,* February 4, 1868, August 18, 1873.

women took too much space because of their dresses, which, said one indignant editor, were expanded with "whalebone and wire" to a size where men were being pushed out of the car.[37]

Horses and mules were used to draw the cars because they were considered safer than locomotives, which, it was believed, were likely to get out of control or explode. Besides, city residents disliked the noise made by the engines. Animal locomotion might be secure, but it was also slow. Many of the mules were old and feeble and moved according to their condition. A reporter described a mule pulling a car he was in as "a perfect curiosity of slowness. A respectable sloth would beat him in a race, and before a mud turtle he would be nowhere." [38] Although the leisurely progress of the cars maddened people in a hurry, lovers found the pace a delight. They would settle in an obscure corner and enjoy "the blessings and beatitudes of a requited love." These "amatory couples" favored especially the long ride to Carrollton and back, which they "regarded almost in the light of a honeymoon." [39]

By anybody's standards the Carrollton line was the most romantic of the street railroads. As the cars crept along, the city dweller could feast his eyes on green fields and grazing cattle. At Carrollton he could feast on some of the best food in the region at the Carrollton House and later admire the flowers and shrubs in the famous Carrollton Gardens. Before the war hundreds of New Orleans people went to Carrollton every Sunday in the summer. The village was even more popular in the postwar years. After 1865 the favorite eating place was Victor's, where dinner was served on a veranda overlooking the river. The ride to this center of beauty cost only ten cents.[40]

With all its romance and charm, the Carrollton road failed to make money. The management seemed to be under the impression that the line should be run primarily for the benefit of the employees and secondarily for the convenience of the public. Only a few cars were in service, and the daily revenue in 1866 was only $350. The stockholders had not received a dividend for ten years.[41]

[37] New Orleans *Picayune,* June 1, 1866.
[38] New Orleans *Times,* January 16, July 10, 1866.
[39] New Orleans *Picayune,* April 25, 1874.
[40] Eliza Ripley, *Social Life in Old New Orleans* (New York, 1912), 63–64; New Orleans *Times,* June 17, August 16, 1866; New Orleans *Picayune,* June 17, 1866; New Orleans *Times-Picayune,* February 4, 1945.
[41] New Orleans *Times,* October 3, 1865, April 21, 1866; article by G. W. R. Bayley, in New Orleans *Picayune,* March 16, 1873.

Some of the stockholders decided that the road could be made into a paying property if placed under the management of an experienced engineer. In April, 1866, they offered to lease it to Beauregard, then becoming known as the savior of the Jackson road. Beauregard agreed to lease the line for twenty-five years and pay the stockholders a guaranteed annual income. New Orleans was pleased to hear that the new management planned to substitute horsecars for its screaming locomotives and to replace its cars, the most antique in the city, with the latest Northern models. Other future improvements were announced. When the new rolling stock arrived, cars would leave Canal and Baronne streets for Carrollton every five minutes instead of every fifteen as at present. Eventually the company hoped to lay a double line of track in the upper part of the city.[42]

By himself Beauregard did not have the financial resources to lease the road and make the contemplated improvements. He looked around for some capitalists to associate with him as lessees. He found two willing backers in Thomas P. May and A. C. Graham. Both men were stockholders in the First National Bank and alternated as president, Graham holding the office in 1866 and May taking over in January, 1867. In April, 1866, the three entered into an act of partnership. May and Graham agreed to advance capital for the road to an amount not to exceed $150,000 each; they were to be repaid from the net profits with eight per cent interest. Beauregard was to serve as manager at a salary of $5,000 (giving him, with his Jackson salary, an annual income of $10,000). It was understood that Beauregard was to concentrate on running the railroad while his partners took care of financial matters. To .this end Beauregard gave May a power of attorney.[43]

Thus began a business arrangement that was to cause Beauregard untold embarrassment. Impressed by the reputation of his associates, he did not think to inquire if their resources were what they represented. Nor did he become suspicious when they were unable to ad-

[42] New Orleans *Picayune,* April 10, 1866; New Orleans *Times,* May 11, 1866; Beauregard to board of aldermen of New Orleans, n. d., in Beauregard Papers (Library of Congress), Letterbook, Private Letters, December 16, 1865—April 18, 1867.

[43] Beauregard to New Orleans *Times,* December 4, 1871, reprinted in New Orleans *Picayune,* August 7, 1863; Beauregard to R. J. Walker, June 5, 1867, in Beauregard Papers (Library of Congress), Letterbook, Private Letters, April 19, 1867—February 4, 1869.

vance the sums they had promised. They suggested to him that expenses could be reduced, meaning they would have to put up less money, if the lessees and the stockholders united their interests. Beauregard obligingly negotiated with the stockholders a fusion agreement which canceled the lease and increased the capital stock by $400,000. The new stock was to be divided between the lessees and the old stockholders. Beauregard was to be the president of the reorganized company.[44]

With full faith in the substance of his partners, Beauregard set to work to improve the road. New cars were installed, old equipment was refurbished, and construction of new tracks was started.[45] While Beauregard watched the road grow, May and Graham were playing a numbers game at the First National. The money for the expansion was supposed to come from the bank. May and Graham opened an account in Beauregard's name. Unknown to Beauregard, they wrote checks drawn against the account and signed his name. Many of the checks were written when Beauregard was in Europe for the Jackson company, at which time they bought, among other things a hotel. By March, 1867, the account was overdrawn by $123,210. Some of the money was expended on the railroad, and some, it was later charged, went into speculation in cotton and gold. For a time May was able to conceal the deficiency. Once he drew a promissory note in Beauregard's name for $40,000 and later he drew a bill of exchange on Graham, who had gone to New York, for $125,000.[46]

Eventually the economic realities caught up with May and Graham. In May, 1867, they failed, and the bank went into receivership. As the First National was a national bank, their assets, including the lease in the Carrollton road, were transferred to the Federal government. For the first time Beauregard learned what his partners had been doing. He was profoundly shocked. He was also alarmed because the government had May and Graham's interest in the lease. As the fusion agreement of 1866 had not been completely executed,

---

[44] A copy of this agreement of November 23, 1866, is in the Beauregard Papers (Louisiana State University).

[45] New Orleans *Times,* June 17, September 16, 1866, May 28, 1867.

[46] New Orleans *Picayune,* August 3, 1873; answers filed by Beauregard in bankruptcy proceedings against bank, MS. dated December 24, 1868, in Beauregard Papers (Louisiana State University).

Beauregard claimed that the partnership was dissolved and that he had the right to purchase the lease from the government.[47]

The government was willing to sell if Beauregard could raise the money. Three friends of his—Joseph Hernandez, G. W. Binder, and Alex Bonneval—offered to buy the interest of May and Graham. After the sale was made, the three benefactors became copartners in the lease. The four lessees then concluded a fusion agreement with the stockholders similar to the one of 1866. Beauregard continued to serve as president at a salary of $5,000.[48]

Several years later the receiver for the First National, Charles Case, sued Beauregard, May, and Graham for certain sums allegedly owed the bank. The United States Circuit Court handed down a judgment assessing the defendants $79,000 each. No money was obtained from them. The partnership had been dissolved, Graham had left the state, and Beauregard and May had no property on which to levy.[49]

Nobody blamed Beauregard for what had happened. His only wrong was that of being too trusting and too gullible. Even Case was careful to point out that Beauregard was innocent of any involvement in his partner's deals. Nevertheless, Beauregard was deeply wounded. A man's reputation was always precious, he said, and doubly so after he had emerged from a war which left him little else.[50]

Other troubles than financial ones harrassed the road. In 1871 and again in 1874 the Republican legislature, in moves reminiscent of the plot against the Jackson line, threatened to investigate the company to determine if the charter was being complied with and the public interest being protected. The city council, responding to complaints that the high tracks interfered with street hauling, forced Beauregard to lower the grades. As the population of the city grew, a greater traffic burden was placed on the road, especially on St.

[47] Beauregard to R. J. Walker, June 5, 1867, in Beauregard Papers (Library of Congress), Letterbook, Private Letters, April 19, 1867—February 4, 1869; sworn statement by Beauregard before notary public A. Ducatel, August 6, 1867, in Beauregard Papers (Louisiana State University).

[48] Copy of agreement between Beauregard and Joseph Hernandez, G. W. Binder, and Alex Bonneval, August 23, 1867, in Beauregard Papers (Louisiana State University); New Orleans *Picayune,* August 3, 1873.

[49] New Orleans *Republican,* February 20, 27, 1873; New Orleans *Picayune,* August 3, 1873.

[50] Charles Case to Beauregard, December 15, 1871, and Beauregard to Case, December 17, 1871, in Beauregard Papers (Louisiana State University).

Charles Street. Citizens on the Carrollton route held indignation meetings to protest that not enough cars were in service and those being used were too crowded.[51]

No criticism, however, could negate the fact that Beauregard was making a railroad out of the line and making it pay. In 1873 the company owned 59 cars and 249 horses and mules. That year 4,863,354 passengers traveled on the road; the average daily receipts were $668. In 1866 the stock sold for $7.50 a share: it was now worth $115. Dividends of from six to ten per cent were regularly declared. A double track ran from Canal Street to Carrollton, and a double track branch had been constructed on Jackson Street to connect with the river. Beauregard was full of plans for more improvements in the future.[52]

Beauregard's first railroad had been taken away from him after he had built it into a paying property. Ironically, the same thing was to happen with his second line. His very success helped to bring about his undoing. The biggest stockholders, dazzled by their prosperity, decided that the road would produce even more revenue if they could get their hands on the management. To accomplish their objective, they had to unseat Beauregard as president. This was not hard to do. Of the two hundred stockholders, fifty owned a controlling share and and by combining could elect a new slate of officers. They were quickly organized by a tobacco commission merchant, W. Van Benthuysen, who announced as a candidate for president. He and his followers charged that Beauregard had mismanaged the company and that a new president and board of directors should be chosen at the annual meeting in January, 1876.

Beauregard fought back valiantly, trying to rally the smaller stockholders, but his cause was hopeless. He simply did not have the votes. At the January meeting Van Benthuysen and his ticket won by a majority of two to one.[53]

[51] Committee on Railroads of the House of Representatives to Beauregard, February 8, 1871, in Beauregard Papers, *ibid.;* New Orleans *Times,* February 4, 1874; New Orleans *Republican,* January 21, 23, 30, February 18, May 31, June 14, July 9, October 30, December 24, 1873.

[52] New Orleans *Times,* July 26, 1873; article by G. W. R. Bayley, in New Orleans *Picayune,* March 16, 1873.

[53] New Orleans *Picayune,* December 29, 1875, January 4, 18, 1876; New Orleans *Times,* January 4, 1876; printed circular issued by Beauregard and his supporters, dated December 29, 1875, in Beauregard Papers (Louisiana State Uniyersity); MS. memorandum by Beauregard, January 4, 1876, *ibid.* Beauregard himself owned eighty shares.

In devising schemes to make money Beauregard displayed the same fertility of imagination and sometimes the same lack of judgment that had marked his formulation of strategic plans during the war. He was willing to try anything. He applied for the post of chief engineer with the New Orleans, Mobile, and Texas Railroad, and did not get it; he offered to become president of the Texas Pacific Railroad, and was not accepted.[54] He took a position as financial agent of the Calcasieu Sulphur and Mining Company, charged with the function of raising capital for the corporation.[55] He proffered his services to a company trying to secure capital to dig a canal across the isthmus of Central America, and he attempted to interest the Mexican government to pay him to build bridges.[57]

New corporations with new ideas always fascinated him. He could not resist joining them and championing their products. Nearly always he got his fingers burned. One such company was the Ammonia Thermo-Specific Propelling Company, of which he became a member of the board of directors. It was organized to manufacture a new type of engine for use on street-railway locomotives. Beauregard was drawn to the company by his interest in the engines, which he hoped to install on the Carrollton road. The other directors were interested in nothing but speculation. They would drive the price of their stock down, buy up large amounts, and then let the price rise. Engrossed with the engines, Beauregard did not know what his associates were doing and could not understand why so few machines were manufactured.[58]

Another of his corporation adventures was the Steiner Gas Company. Beauregard and twenty others purchased a patent on an invention to furnish light by gas. He could not raise enough capital to put

[54] Beauregard to J. G. Walker, July 6, 1873, in Beauregard Papers (Library of Congress), Letterbook, Private Letters, February 28, 1872—December 1, 1875.

[55] Letters from Beauregard to V. A. Belaune, July 13, 1874, to C. R. Griffing, July 13, 1874, to W. J. Marrin, August 12, 1874, *ibid.*

[57] Beauregard to C. K. Garrison, November 3, 1868, and to Erlanger, November 27, 1868, in Beauregard Papers (Library of Congress), Letterbook, Private Letters, April 19, 1867—February 4, 1869; Beauregard to Porfirio Diaz, November 26, 1881, April 17, 1882, *ibid.*, Letterbook, Letters, March 9, 1880—December 5, 1883; Diaz to Beauregard, March 27, 1882, in Beauregard Papers (Cabildo).

[58] New Orleans *Times,* July 12, 1873; New Orleans *Republican,* May 11, 25, 1873.

the company in operation.[59] In 1879 he organized the Municipal Gas Company to supply gas to homes for heating and cooking purposes. The city council granted the company the right to lay down pipes and mains. Two years later Beauregard had to admit that financial aid he had been promised from New York capitalists was not forthcoming and that he could not complete the project.[60]

One enterprise that Beauregard was a part of succeeded. He played a role, not a big one, in solving the old problem of keeping the mouths of the Mississippi open to ocean-going commerce. The clogged passes had challenged his interest ever since he and John Barnard as young officers had investigated the mystery of the sandbars and the mud lumps and he had invented his bar-excavator. Immediately after the war ended, he had toyed with the idea of forming a company to deepen the channel by dredging.[61]

Nothing came of his project or of similar plans by others, for the simple reason that the cost was too great. Only the national government had the resources to open the passes and keep them open. And it was to the government that New Orleans turned in the 1870's when the piled-up silt and sand seemed to threaten the destruction of the port's trade. The engineer corps of the army sent boats to dredge the channel, but this scooping freed the passes only temporarily. The officer in charge of the dredging reported that there was no way of maintaining a depth sufficient to float large vessels; he recommended that the government construct a ship canal from Fort St. Philip to the gulf. The canal solution appealed to New Orleans, although some professed experts continued to advocate deepening the mouths. Beauregard took advantage of all the interest in the subject to advertise his bar-excavator to the public.[62]

Congress appointed a military commission to study the proposed

[59] Beauregard to W. M. Gwin, April 7, 1871, and to John Claiborne, May 9, 1871, in Beauregard Papers (Library of Congress), Letterbook, Private Letters, February 6, 1869—February 5, 1872.

[60] Beauregard to J. W. Patton, December 22, 1879, ibid., Letterbook, Private Letters, December 4, 1875—March 24, 1880; Beauregard to the mayor and city council, January 10, 1881, ibid., Letterbook, Letters, March 9, 1880—December 5, 1883; New Orleans Democrat, May 30, 1879.

[61] Beauregard to S. P. Griffin, January 31, 1866, and to J. B. Eustis, February 3, 1866, in Beauregard Papers (Library of Congress), Letterbook, Private Letters, December 16, 1865—April 18, 1867; Beauregard to George Williamson, February 22, 1866, in New Orleans Times, March 5, 1866.

[62] New Orleans Republican, February 4, 5, April 16, 1873; New Orleans Picayune, April 1, 12, 24, May 6, 10, 1873; New Orleans Times, April 3, 1873.

canal and other recommended ways of improving navigation at the mouths of the river. This body, headed by Beauregard's old friend Barnard, held sessions in New York during the summer of 1873 and in the autumn came to New Orleans. Among the witnesses heard in New Orleans was Beauregard. He came out flatly for the canal in preference to any other plan. By the end of the year the commission had completed its work; the members recommended to Congress that the canal be built.[63]

At this point a new figure stepped into the picture. James B. Eads, the famous St. Louis bridge builder, announced that he could open a pass and maintain a channel depth of at least twenty-eight feet in far less time and for far less money than the canal would require. Eads believed that if a river could be narrowed at its mouth the current would flow faster and the stream would scour its own bottom. He proposed to constrict the Mississippi by extending its banks with jetties—piers or ramparts built over the bar. So confident was Eads in his plan that he told Congress he would erect jetties at any pass it selected and not accept any money unless his barriers worked.[64]

Almost everybody jeered at Eads's scheme—the army engineers, the river experts, and the canal supporters. New Orleans, obsessed with the canal idea, was almost solidly opposed. The Chamber of Commerce adopted ringing resolutions condemning jetties as impractical and demanding the canal. Twenty-seven leading businessmen, of whom Beauregard was one, signed an appeal to Eads begging him to withdraw his proposition.[65] When Eads wrote a powerful reply to the Chamber's resolutions, Beauregard decided to answer Eads in the newspapers. Perhaps remembering that he had endorsed jetties before the war, he was careful to say that he was not now against them per se. He merely believed the canal would be cheaper and more permanent. Then, as if to protect himself if Eads turned out to be right, he said: "I know not what your plan of jetties may be, but I agree with you in the opinion that there are few obstacles in engineering that 'dollars and *sense*' cannot overcome." Now, if

[56] Beauregard to Hunter Davidson, June 2, 1874, *ibid.;* Beauregard to H. B. Wright, December 14, 1874, in Beauregard Papers (Tulane University); New Orleans *Times,* April 8, 1874.

[63] New Orleans *Republican,* July 20, August 7, November 12, 29, 1873; New Orleans *Times,* November 23, December 1, 25, 1873, January 23, 1874.

[64] Louis How, *James B. Eads* (Boston, 1900), 81–87.

[65] New Orleans *Times,* January 17, February 15, March 3, 27, 1874.

Eads would care to use Beauregard's bar-excavator, he might accomplish something.[66]

A somewhat skeptical Congress finally authorized Eads to construct jetties at South Pass, the smallest of the river's three mouths. Eads feared that his enemies would try to discredit him and influence Congress to cancel the agreement before the project was completed. To counteract them he decided to bring some of his New Orleans opponents into his camp. The man he wanted most was Beauregard. He told Beauregard he wanted to employ his "professional advice and personal influence," which meant that he wished Beauregard to lobby in Washington and elsewhere for Eads's interests. For this service he offered to pay Beauregard $5,000. Beauregard accepted, and supported the jetties as energetically as he had previously criticized them.[67]

The jetties succeeded magnificently. After they proved themselves, Beauregard acted as though he had always favored them. In a newspaper interview he said that he and Eads had to overcome terrific opposition to convince Congress the ramparts were practical. But they had done it; the jetties were completed; and New Orleans could now fulfill her manifest destiny.[68]

Beauregard made money in the 1860's and early 1870's. His combined salary of $10,000 from the Jackson and Carrollton lines was equal to perhaps three times that amount in the inflated currency of a more modern period. How much he saved is a question. At one time he owned eighty shares of stock in the Carrollton road and thirty-five in the Jackson; these assets were not in his possession at his death. It is probable that Beauregard sank some of his capital in his speculative enterprises.

But his years of greatest prosperity were yet to come. He would become a man of substance finally, not by running railroads or forming corporations, but by lending his name and reputation to a gigantic gambling combination.

[66] *Ibid.*, May 2, 1874.

[67] James B. Eads to Beauregard, January 2, 1877, in Beauregard Papers (Louisiana State University); Beauregard to Eads, January 16, 1877, and to R. L. Gibson, February 7, 10, 1878, in Beauregard Papers (Library of Congress), Letterbook, Private Letters, December 4, 1875—March 24, 1880; Eads to Beauregard, November 5, 1877, in Beauregard Papers (Tulane).

[68] St. Louis *Post-Dispatch*, quoted in Chicago *Times*, April 10, 1879, clipping in Beauregard Papers (Louisiana State University).

CHAPTER EIGHTEEN

The Louisiana Lottery

T HE NEW YORK lottery syndicate of C. H. Murray and Company was intrigued by the reports of its Louisiana agent, Charles T. Howard. People in New Orleans had a mania for gambling, he said; they bought up the company's tickets as fast as they went on sale. Maybe, suggested Howard, the syndicate should transfer its interests to New Orleans and seek a charter from the legislature. He was sure that the legislature was the kind of body that would grant the kind of charter that syndicates liked to have. His associates were impressed. In many states sentiment against gambling was rising; restrictive laws were making it increasingly difficult to operate games of chance. They told Howard to approach the legislature.

Howard was a superb approacher. Born in Baltimore, he had come to New Orleans in 1852. For years he acted as the agent of the Alabama Lottery Company. Supposedly he had served in the Confederate army and navy; his enemies claimed that he had concocted a war record out of his imagination. After the war he reappeared in New Orleans as the agent of the Murray company. Burly, bluff, flashy, he was the epitome of the Gilded Age speculator. Like others of his kind he knew what he wanted and used whatever methods were necessary to reach his goals. He believed greatly in the persuasive power of money. He could be affable and generous or domineering and tight-fisted. When crossed, he was ruthless. Seeking social prestige in New Orleans, he applied for membership in the exclusive Metairie Racing Club. When he was rejected, he told the directors that he would ruin their organization. In fact, he said, he would turn their site into a cemetery—which is exactly what he did. Beauregard, who took his money and was a little sensitive about the association, said after his death that he was "rough but had a very good heart." [1]

---

[1] Hodding Carter, *Lower Mississippi* (New York, 1942), 328–29; Alexander K. McClure, *Recollections of Half a Century* (Salem, Mass., 1902), 173–74; Beauregard to Early, June 1, 1885, in Early Papers.

Howard knew what he was talking about when he advised his colleagues to center their business in Louisiana. The moral climate of the southern part of the state was favorable to gambling; churches and schools in New Orleans had conducted lotteries since territorial days. For a time before the war lotteries were forbidden by state law, but the legislature of 1866 had made them legal again. And the Reconstruction legislature of 1868 was painfully eager to charter a lottery company—if the company was willing to be generous with money in the right places.

Howard had the money. According to report, he handed out $300,000 to get his bill. The charter was worth the expense. The legislature granted to a corporation to be known as the Louisiana State Lottery Company the right to operate a lottery for twenty-five years. For that period the company was to have sole rights; no other lottery company could be authorized by the state. The company was tax exempt, but was to pay the state $40,000 a year for the support of Charity Hospital in New Orleans.

Five of the seven incorporators were dummy figures; only Howard and Murray represented the syndicate. Nine days after the charter was granted the incorporators signed away their rights to Murray, Zachariah E. Simmons, and John A. Morris—the owners of the syndicate—and Howard was installed as president. A few years later Murray and Simmons withdrew or were bought out, and Morris and Howard assumed full control.[2]

Thus was created what was undoubtedly the largest gambling organization to exist in the United States before the twentieth century, an organization that at the height of its power had an annual gross income of almost $29,000,000. For over twenty years the lottery company dominated the political, economic, and social life of New Orleans and the state. It controlled nearly every legislature from 1868 to 1890. It controlled all of the newspapers in New Orleans and most of those in the state. By allying its interests with the four largest banks in the city, it controlled the sources of credit. The basis of the lottery's rule was money. It spent part of its huge revenue to buy support. The lottery provided cash to the politicians; it con-

[2] Carter, *Lower Mississippi*, 328–30; McClure, *Recollections*, 174; Berthold C. Alwes, "The History of the Louisiana State Lottery Company," in *Louisiana Historical Quarterly*, XXVII (1944), 7–14; Clarence C. Buel, "The Degradation of a State," in *Century Illustrated Monthly*, XLIII (1892), 622–23.

tributed to education and charity; it helped distressed people like flood sufferers. If a worthy cause needed aid, the lottery always came forward with a donation. It maintained the French Opera House; it financed the construction of cotton mills; and it built a sugar–manufacturing plant for the sugar planters. Such favors were excellent investments in public relations; they made the lottery seem like a benevolent institution. Gambling couldn't be wrong, people said, when the money was put to good purposes. Besides, look at the savings to the taxpayers.[3]

In buying its charter the lottery dealt with Republicans. It was equally ready to deal with Democrats—when the Democrats were in a position to help the lottery. The Democrats were as ready as Republicans to take the company's money. In 1876 there was a disputed election in Louisiana. Both sides claimed victory, and two governors and two legislatures appeared in New Orleans. Eventually, with the acquiescence of the national government, a compromise was arranged by which the Democrat, Francis T. Nicholls, became governor and a majority of the seats in the legislature went to the Democrats. In order to make the compromise work, a number of Republicans had to join the Nicholls legislature to give it a quorum. The lottery provided the money to carry out the deal, putting up a sum estimated to have been either $43,000 or $60,000.[4]

Having helped to create the Nicholls government, the lottery owners were naturally embittered when the legislature passed and the governor signed a bill revoking the charter and declaring lotteries illegal. They claimed that this action violated a pledge by the Democratic managers to let the lottery alone. Determined to fight back, they tested the legality of the legislative act in the Federal courts and won a decision that the legislature could not alter the nature of a contract. A constitutional convention was scheduled to meet soon, however, and it could change anything, including a charter. The lottery went to work on the convention; according to reports it promised the Democrats $250,000 in return for favorable treatment. The results were highly favorable. The convention adopted a provi-

[3] Carter, *Lower Mississippi*, 333–37; Alwes, "Louisiana State Lottery Company," *loc. cit.*, 63–67; A Louisianian, *The Cornucopia of Old: The Lottery Wheel of the New* (New Orleans, 1877), 11–12. The last item is a pamphlet published to defend the lottery when it was under attack.
[4] Henry Clay Warmoth, *War, Politics and Reconstruction* (New York, 1930), 239; Ella Lonn, *Reconstruction in Louisiana After 1868* (New York, 1918), 523; New Orleans *Times,* March 28, 1879.

sion declaring lotteries to be legal until 1895 but requiring the company to surrender its monopoly.[5]

The next ten years, from 1880–90, were the most prosperous in the lottery's history. They were also the most secure. The lottery's power in politics was almost absolute. No competing companies were chartered, and attacks on the company were fought off or, as was usually the case, shrugged off. The best and richest people in New Orleans associated with the company's owners and praised the lottery as a beneficent organization. They also bought its tickets.[6]

All kinds of people—rich, average, poor—bought tickets, and from all over the country. Over ninety per cent of the company's business came from outside the state; it had branch offices in New York, Chicago, Washington, Kansas City, and other places. The profits of the owners soared to almost incredible heights. The value of the stock rose from $35 a share to $1,200; dividends of over 100 per cent were regularly declàred. Each year the company held ten "regular" drawings and two semiannual drawings. The revenue from tickets for the regular sessions usually came to $20,000,000; the semiannual drawings produced $8,000,000. In addition, there were daily drawings that grossed $800,000. Thus in an average year the company would take in $28,800,000. In prizes it would pay out approximately $15,000,000. Other expenses, including $2,000,000 for advertising and a like sum for commissions, brought the total outlay to around $20,000,000, leaving a net profit of about $8,500,000. In exceptional years the profit was reported as high as $13,000,000.[7]

The man who devised the system of prizes and who was the real brains of the lottery was an Alsatian named Maximilian Dauphin. Brought in to serve as manager, he became president after Howard died in 1885. He installed the method used in the Venice lottery, whereby the company paid out in prizes only 52 per cent of its intake. That is, of every $100 received the lottery kept $48. Sometimes the company won its own prizes by splitting tickets into fractions. Thus, a twenty–dollar ticket would be divided into twenty one–dollar frac-

---

[5] Alwes, "Louisiana State Lottery Company," *loc. cit.*, 32–39; New Orleans *Times*, March 28, 1879; Carter, *Lower Mississippi*, 330–31.

[6] Alwes, "Louisiana State Lottery Company," *loc. cit.*, 41–52; New York *World*, March 16, 1879.

[7] Letter with signature torn off to Postmaster General John Wanamaker, May 4, 1889, in Benjamin F. Flanders Papers (Department of Archives, Louisiana State University); Carter, *Lower Mississippi*, 332–33.

tions, and the company would withhold parts of the ticket from sale.[8]

The price of the tickets was small enough and the prizes large enough to keep buyers in a constant state of temptation. A fifty–cent ticket stood a chance of winning its holder $7,500, and a dollar ticket twice that amount. For $20 a man might get $300,000. A forty–dollar ticket at a semiannual drawing might win the grand prize of $600,-000. This prize was never drawn, but a New Orleans barber won $300,000. The newspapers, prospering from the lottery's advertising, reported many cases of sensational winnings. A resident of Louisville invested $100 and received $25,000; a lady purchased for twenty-five cents a fourth of a ticket that drew $6,000. They rarely mentioned the hundreds and hundreds of people, many of them poor, who bought chances month after month without receiving a cent.[9] One journalistic critic of the lottery estimated that a man who purchased a daily ticket would have one chance in eighty-four years to get a prize of $243.35. Had Methusalah bought a daily ticket, said this editor, he would have spent $250,000 and won $2,678.85.[10]

A whole folklore grew up about the lottery and its prizes. If you saw a stray dog, you should play number six; a drunk man, fourteen; a dead woman with gray hair, forty-nine; and a naked female leg belonging neither to your wife or your mistress, eleven.[11] In its advertising, the company told of invalids who had become well, weaklings who had become men, unsuccessful lovers who had gained their hearts' desire—all by drawing a lottery prize. One ad advised young couples to marry so they could share their prizes "in mutual ecstacy." Another exhorted young men to buy a ticket, to "go to the nearest office and step up like a chicken to the dough pile and ask for the article like a man."[12]

Many of the lottery ads were in doggerel. One such effusion ran as follows:

[8] Buel, "Degradation of a State," *loc. cit.*, 619; Carter, *Lower Mississippi*, 332.

[9] New Orleans *Republican*, April 5, August 27, 1873; New Orleans *Picayune*, July 12, 1873; New Orleans *Times*, April 1, 1874; Carter, *Lower Mississippi*, 332.

[10] New Orleans *Democrat*, June 2, 6, 1878.

[11] Carter, *Lower Mississippi*, 332.

[12] New Orleans *Times*, May 9, 1873, January 21, 1874. For other ads, see *ibid.*, December 27, 1873, May 4, 1874, July 22, 1882; New Orleans *Republican*, January 1, 5, December 27, 1873.

A soldier of the Legion lay dying in Algiers;
His nose it wanted wiping and his eyes were filled with tears;
But a comrade came to feed him with tripe and chicken tea,
Who had drawn $5,000 in the State Lottere-e.
So he grew well and jolly, and not another line
Should ever have been written of Bingen on the Rhine.

A poem designed to interest courting males proclaimed:

Huzzah! At last the word is spoken,
And I can wed where I adore;
The spell of poverty is broken
By 4-11-44.

Following the verse was this statement: "The accomplished author of the above, who parts his hair in the middle, was safely launched upon the sea of matrimony, and the next drawing of the Louisiana State Lottery comes off Saturday, May 9. 'Tickets, gentlemen, tickets.' "

A more classical attempt was this parody of Fitz-Greene Halleck's "Marco Bozzaris":

At midnight in his guarded tent,
The Turk lay dreaming of the hour,
When creditors in suppliance bent,
Should tremble at his power.
In dreams his hands a ticket bore
Marked 4-11-64.
He woke to hear his sentries' cries.
"Great God, the Pasha's drawn a prize."
He woke to play those numbers straight.
Bozzaris met no nobler fate.[13]

The drawings took place in the lottery's hall at St. Charles and Union streets. At one end of a large room was a raised platform on which were placed two large glass wheels, one bigger than the other. Each ticket was rolled into the size of a man's finger and inserted into a brass tube; the tubes were put in the large wheel. The prizes, represented on cards, were prepared in a similar manner and put in the small wheel. At a regular drawing there would be 10,000 tickets and

[13] New Orleans *Times,* April 30, May 1, 1874. For other poetic ads, see *ibid.,* April 24, 26, 27, 28, 29, May 5, 6, 1874.

243 prizes. Two little boys were blindfolded and placed at each wheel. After lottery employees had spun the wheels vigorously to mix the tubes, the boy at the big wheel drew out a ticket. Its number was read and then registered on a blackboard. The boy at the little wheel then drew a card which designated the prize of the ticket just drawn. This process was repeated until all the tubes in the small wheel had been withdrawn. Often the process lasted ten hours.

The company took elaborate precautions to invest a drawing with the appearance of honesty. The tickets were held up so that the audience could see the numbers. At frequent intervals the wheels were revolved to demonstrate that the tickets were not rigged and that fate alone determined which ones were drawn. Prominent citizens sat on the platform to "supervise" the proceedings.[14] In a technical sense, everything was honest. There was no way in which the company could give a prize to a selected individual. The dishonesty lay in the slim chance a buyer had to win a prize and in the fact that the company could win its own awards.

Despite the precautions, there was criticism that the drawings were fraudulent. Disappointed buyers inevitably charged that the lottery stacked the tickets to throw prizes to its friends or to itself. Dauphin realized that such accusations could seriously damage the lottery and that they must be stopped. Studying ways to place the drawings above suspicion, he hit upon the idea of hiring two Confederate generals to sit on the platform and supervise the wheels. Who could even think there was anything crooked in an enterprise vouched for by heroes who had worn the gray?

Naturally Dauphin thought first of Louisiana's foremost warrior. He offered one of the posts to Beauregard and gave Beauregard the privilege of choosing his colleague. Beauregard had no reason to like the lottery. He must have known that it had put up money to help pass the bill authorizing the sale of the state stock in the Jackson railroad. He believed that it had secured its charter by corrupt methods.[15] Still, he was without employment, and the salary was tempting. According to family tradition, he hesitated to accept for fear a lottery connection would injure his reputation. His friends and

[14] *Ibid.,* February 15, 1874; New Orleans *Picayune,* July 12, December 18, 19, 28, 1875.

[15] Lonn, *Reconstruction in Louisiana,* 92; Beauregard to David F. Boyd, November 27, 1873, in Boyd Papers.

family convinced him that the lottery was respectable and that his fame could not be tarnished.[16]

He may well have had a few qualms, although in New Orleans there was no particular feeling against gambling and many of the best people were associated in some way with the lottery. Rather defensively, he announced he was accepting the position because the company was licensed by law and he would be performing a public service by guaranteeing honest operations.[17]

Certainly there was no hint of any embarrassment in the letters he wrote to former comrades concerning the second supervisorship. He first offered the post to Wade Hampton, the famous South Carolina cavalry leader. Hampton said he would take it if he failed to be elected governor. When he won the office, Beauregard approached Jubal A. Early of Virginia. Early said he was interested, but he wanted to know if the lottery was controlled by Republicans. Certainly not, Beauregard replied; he would have nothing to do with it if it was. Howard was a former Confederate soldier and a member of some of the most exclusive organizations in New Orleans. Morris was a Yankee but a Democrat and a gentleman; he was even the uncle of General Hood's daughter! Early was persuaded.[18]

Beauregard and Early would hold their positions from February, 1877, to 1893, when the lottery ceased operations. The salaries they received caused much speculation then and later. Beauregard supposedly was paid $30,000 a year and Early somewhat less, on the theory that a full general was more valuable than a lieutenant general. These reports were exaggerated, but the actual remuneration is difficult to determine. In 1877 and for several years thereafter Beauregard and Early each received $2,500 a drawing, with two appearances guaranteed—that is, a base salary of $5,000.[19] Beauregard could have made $30,000 only by serving as supervisor at the ten regular drawings and the two semiannual affairs. It is unlikely that he did so, because the company would not have needed his presence

[16] René Beauregard, "Magnolia."

[17] Alwes, "Louisiana State Lottery Company," *loc. cit.*, 17.

[18] Beauregard to Wade Hampton, June 27, 1876, and to Early, December 10, 1876, in Beauregard Papers (Library of Congress), Letterbook, Private Letters, December 4, 1875—March 24, 1880; Beauregard to Early, January 3, 1877, in Early Papers.

[19] Memorandum of agreement between Beauregard and Early and C. T. Howard and M. H. Dauphin, February 17, 1877, in Early Papers.

at some of the smaller drawings, and he took frequent and long vacations in the summers.

As the income of the company increased, the pay of the supervisors went up. In 1881 Early received a base salary of $10,000 and $150 a month for expenses. Two years later Beauregard told Morris that he would resign if his salary of $10,000 was not raised. He said that the stipend was not enough to compensate for the vilification he had to endure.[20] A safe estimate would seem to be that the two supervisors or commissioners were paid a minimum salary of $10,000 and that in some years extra appearances brought their remuneration up to $15,000 or even $20,000.[21]

The duties of Beauregard and Early were not heavy. Before a drawing they counted the tickets in the large wheel and vouched that all were there. Then they had a statement read that the drawing would be conducted honestly. On the back of each ticket was a printed declaration with the names of the commissioners affixed: "We will personally supervise, manage and control the Drawing, and all the arrangements therefor, wherein the number representing this ticket . . . may be drawn, and see that it is conducted honestly, fairly, and in good faith; and we authorize the use of this certificate in this ticket." After a drawing Beauregard and Early would announce the results in the newspapers. If most of the large prizes were won by the company, as frequently happened, they would explain that this was because not all the tickets had been sold.[22]

Beauregard and Early were also expected to defend the lottery against attacks and to lobby for its interests in Louisiana and the national capital. They obediently performed their duties when required. In 1878, when the company was having trouble with the Nicholls legislature, there was some criticism of the lottery's mono-

[20] Early to J. C. Early, December 23, 1881, *ibid.;* Beauregard to John A. Morris, September 11, 1883, in Beauregard Papers (Library of Congress), Letterbook, Letters, March 9, 1880—December 5, 1883.

[21] In 1893 the lottery moved to Honduras and hired new commissioners. A friend wrote Early that he had heard one of these men was to be paid $30,000 a year. Early replied that the report was false and that the man in question was not going to be paid anything like $30,000 or anything like the amount paid himself or Beauregard; Early to B. T. Johnson, July 1, 1893. A photostat of this letter was kindly furnished me by Forest H. Sweet, autograph dealer of Battle Creek, Michigan.

[22] New Orleans *Picayune,* June 13, 1877; New York *World,* March 16, 1879; lottery ticket for drawing of October 11, 1887, in Beauregard Papers (Duke University).

poly. The commissioners issued a statement saying that the monopoly charge was pointless. They offered the interesting argument that if lotteries were great evils it was better that they should be monopolies and under government license.[23] In 1879–80 the national government threatened to revoke the company's rights to use the mails, an action which would have been a deathblow. Beauregard and Early prepared a statement denouncing the proposed move.[24] Then Beauregard rushed to Washington to testify for the lottery before Congressional committees. He also collected testimonials from several members of Congress that he had done effective work. He wanted documentary evidence when he presented his bill to Howard.[25]

The drama and suspense of a lottery drawing were heightened by the presence of Beauregard and Early. One observer left a sensitive description of the two generals at work. Early came in first, dressed in Confederate gray, and stood by the large ticket wheel. Then Beauregard, wearing a black suit, appeared. With his handsome face, snow-white hair, and dignified form, he was undeniably a figure of distinction. As he took his place by the prize wheel and looked out over the crowd, his countenance was cold and impassive. Even in civilian clothes he looked military in the Gallic manner. Immediately this witness could imagine him reviewing massive battalions marching on the plains of Chalons.

Soon employees came in with sacks containing the tubes with the tickets and the prize numbers. Early dumped one sack into his wheel while two Negroes revolved the drums. Beauregard poured his smaller sack into the prize wheel, which he spun himself. Two blindfolded boys were brought on the platform to draw out the tubes. The commissioners consulted their watches, and announced that the game was open. The boy at Early's wheel drew a tube and handed it to Early, who opened it and read the number on the ticket—48,186. Beauregard's boy gave him a tube, and Beauregard read out "200." Ticket 48,186 had won a prize of $200. And so it went on until the 840 tubes in Beauregard's wheel had disappeared.[26] One wonders

[23] New Orleans *Picayune,* March 10, 1878.
[24] Beauregard to Early, November 17, 1879, in Early Papers.
[25] Beauregard to R. L. Gibson, March 17, 1880, to A. R. Shepherd, March 23, 1880, to G. A. Hanson, March 23, 1880, to Casey Young, April 7, 1880, in Beauregard Papers (Library of Congress), Letterbook, Private Letters, December 4, 1875—March 24, 1880.
[26] Marshall Cushing, *The Story of Our Post Office* (Boston, 1893), 512–15; Buel, "Degradation of a State," *loc. cit.,* 620.

if in the dreary hours of a drawing Beauregard thought of how different it might have been—if after Manassas his army had advanced on Washington . . . if the last attack at Shiloh had pushed the Federals into the river.

Beauregard realized that he was getting old and that his lottery salary was the last big money he could hope to make. He determined to be careful with his investments and save all he could. When his friend and literary collaborator, Alfred Roman, needed money Beauregard had to tell him he would be able to give little help. "I wish I could do more for you," he wrote, "but my obligations to those dependent on me & to myself, render it *impossible*. My salary as Com^{er} of the 'La. S. Lot Co'—will end with its charter, in about six years, hence I have to economize & save *all* I can to provide for that unwelcome period. I will then be too old to aspire to a lucrative position, & the fable of the invalid old lion cannot be forgotten by me." [27]

He declined to risk his capital even to aid his son-in-law, Charles Larendon, who had married his beloved daughter Laure. Larendon suggested that Beauregard sell some properties and join him in purchasing a plantation. Beauregard would have nothing to do with the proposition. Sternly he wrote Larendon: "In a matter of 'bread and Meat' there should be no *sentiment!* Altho I have not, unfortunately, always *acted* up to this doctrine, but now I am determined, if I can, to leave something to my children to live upon—which I will do if I can 'outlive' the charter of the 'L. S. L. Co.'—hence I must be prudent and careful." When Larendon persisted in his request, saying that he lacked money because he had made loans to friends who had not repaid, Beauregard again refused. Referring to Larendon's loans, Beauregard said he had made the same kind of mistake: "Those are the ordeals through which men of some means have to pass." [28]

Beauregard was not talking for effect when he hinted that he had sometimes let sentiment influence his judgment in financial matters.

[27] Beauregard to Roman, November 30, 1887, in Beauregard file of the Yates Snowden Papers (South Caroliniana Library, University of South Carolina).

[28] Beauregard to Charles Larendon, July 25, August 7, 1888, in Miss Laure Beauregard Larendon Papers. Miss Larendon, of Atlanta, Georgia, Beauregard's granddaughter, graciously permitted me to examine her collection of family papers.

He seems to have had a genuine weakness for signing notes for friends and lending money without security. To protect himself he finally signed a written promise to his children before witnesses that he would never endorse another note or make a loan that did not contain a guarantee and bear a legal interest rate.[29]

When he predicted that the lottery would not outlive the expiration of its charter, Beauregard knew what he was saying. Opposition to the company's power and wealth was steadily rising as the decade of the 1880's came to an end. Every year more and more people came to feel that it was wrong for the state to sponsor a gambling organization. The lottery managers, however, were as confident as ever that they could buy anything they wanted. In 1890 Morris announced that he would seek from the legislature a renewal of the charter for twenty-five years. He offered to pay the state an annual fee of $500,-000. Somebody asked him why he didn't make it a million. All right, said Morris grandly, he would, and upped his bid to $1,250,000. At the same time the lottery gave $65,000 to New Orleans for public works and disbursed $200,000 in parishes that had recently suffered from floods.

A majority of the legislators had signed a pledge not to renew the charter. But when the legislature met, the lottery was able to push through a bill in the form of a constitutional amendment extending the charter for twenty years.[30] Nicholls, who was governor again, vetoed the measure. Lacking the votes to override the veto, the legislature adopted a resolution stating that the governor had no right to disapprove an amendment and adjourned. Later the state supreme court decided, in a case brought by the company, that the amendment would have to be submitted to the people for a decision. The issue was to be settled in the election of 1892. Both sides girded for battle. There were lottery and antilottery candidates for governor and for all state offices and the legislature.

Before Louisiana voted, the Federal government swung a deadly blow at the lottery. Congress passed a law forbidding the sending of tickets through the mails and closing the mails to newspapers which

[29] Beauregard to Roman, August 6, 1888, in Roman Papers (Library of Congress).

[30] Terrific pressures were exerted upon members to induce them to depart from their pledge. One man was offered $75,000, but refused. Statement to the author by Mrs. Molly Banks Curry Gray of Plain Dealing, Louisiana, whose husband, Robert H. Curry, was a legislator.

contained lottery ads or prize lists. The company tried to conduct business by express, but the three principal express companies refused the use of their facilities. The lottery was out of business, and its owners knew it. The victory of the antilottery forces in the election was, in a sense, an anticlimax.

Quietly the company wound up its business and looked for other fields. In 1894 it removed headquarters to Honduras and became the Honduras National Lottery Company. There it struggled on for years with small success. The roaring, prosperous Louisiana days were gone forever. In Honduras two new commissioners sat on the platform. One was General W. L. Cabell, an old friend of Beauregard's. The other was his brother-in-law, Charles J. Villeré.[31]

[31] Carter, *Lower Mississippi*, 336–45; Alwes, "Louisiana State Lottery Company," *loc. cit.*, 68–70, 82–84, 89–98, 114–20, 131–37.

CHAPTER NINETEEN

Ghosts and Ghostwriters

THOMAS JORDAN, Beauregard's former chief of staff, had literary ambitions. He saw himself as the Thucydides of the Confederacy, writing its tragic history and encouraging generals—the ones he liked—to compose their personal source accounts. Hardly had the war ended when he commenced his historical activities. Living in New York, he approached the editor of *Harper's Magazine* proposing to do an article on Jefferson Davis, then a captive in a Federal prison. The editor liked the idea, and Jordan wrote the piece, a blistering attack on Davis' war leadership. He sent the proofsheets to Beauregard.[1]

In an accompanying letter Jordan said that he knew he would be accused of kicking Davis when he was down. He had considered the validity of this criticism and rejected it. Whatever Davis' situation, it was the duty of Jordan and others to proclaim the great truth that the former President had brought his country to ruin. He expected to write more articles, Jordan added, and in all of them he would demonstrate that Beauregard was the real genius of the South. He suggested that Beauregard himself do a review of the strategy of the war.[2]

Beauregard was horrified when he read the paper. He realized that the Southern people would naturally think he had inspired Jordan to write it. Immediately he dashed off letters to Jordan and to *Harper's* begging that the article not be published at the present. In his communication to the magazine he said that he had no objection to assailing Davis; in fact, he could speak a few words on that subject himself. But he did not think it was fair to criticize a prisoner who could not reply. His request was refused. *Harper's* answered that the article was in print and that being considered an appropriate

---

[1] Thomas Jordan, "Jefferson Davis," in *Harper's New Monthly Magazine,* XXXI (1865), 610–20.

[2] Jordan to Beauregard, August 12, 1865, in Jordan Papers (Duke University).

commentary, it would have been published even had Beauregard written sooner.[3]

Jordan was not the only person who urged Beauregard to write something about the war. Another was William J. Marrin, a New York lawyer who was a friend of Jordan's and who admired Beauregard tremendously.[4] In North Carolina General Daniel Harvey Hill had started a magazine devoted to Confederate history, *The Land We Love,* and he pressed Beauregard for contributions. Lee urged Beauregard to write the record of his campaigns for the guidance of future historians.[5] Lee and Hill were concerned with preserving the Confederacy's history, and they had some standards of objectivity. Jordan and Marrin were zealous and violent controversialists who were primarily interested in proving that Beauregard had been right on every issue and everybody else wrong. They were to have an unfortunate influence on Beauregard when he came to write about his military experiences.

Lee might not have been so quick to advise Beauregard to describe his campaigns if he had known Beauregard's opinion of his own generalship, an opinion which Beauregard might reflect in what he wrote. Beauregard gave Jordan his evaluation of the hero of the South: "I don't think he has much Milty foresight or pre-science or great powers of deduction . . . but he had great nerve, coolness, & determination—the greater the danger the greater was his presence of mind, although not very fertile in resources or expedients. . . . He is perhaps a little too cautious in civil as well as Milty matters—but he has a noble & high toned character. . . . But I don't think him capable of much generous friendship."[6]

---

[3] Beauregard to *Harper's Magazine,* September 2, 1865, and the magazine's reply, September 11, 1865, in Beauregard Papers (Missouri Historical Society); New Orleans *Picayune,* October 10, 15, 1865. Beauregard's letter to Jordan has not been located, but he refers to it in his communication to *Harper's.*

[4] The C. McC. Reeve Papers (Confederate Museum, Richmond) contain over sixty letters which Marrin wrote to Beauregard from 1865–86. Nearly all of them are concerned with historical writing of both men.

[5] J. William Jones, *Reminiscences, Anecdotes and Letters of General Robert E. Lee* (New York, 1874), 207; Daniel Harvey Hill to Beauregard, June 24, 1867, in Beauregard Papers (North Carolina State Department of Archives and History, Raleigh).

[6] Beauregard to Jordan, December [n. d.], 1868, in Beauregard Papers (Library of Congress), Letterbook, Private Letters, April 19, 1867—February 4, 1869.

The idea of writing about his battles appealed to Beauregard. It was natural that he would want to place on record his own account of his participation in the war. The same motive moved leading generals on both sides. Besides, for years after 1865 there was a market for war books. Southerners had an additional reason for producing memoirs. They wanted to consecrate the Lost Cause and to show that it would not have been lost if their advice had been followed. And so the generals and the civil officials wrote their books and articles and charged each other with losing the war. They called forth the ghosts of Manassas and Shiloh and many another battle to witness the correctness of their views. For years the South was convulsed by these literary brawls, which were always furious, sometimes comic, and often undignified. Some of the controversies were important, some were entirely trivial and needless. But the end result was to enrich the archives of history.

In 1868 Beauregard started work on a book which he tentatively entitled "My Reminiscences of the War." For several years he could find time only to collect documents on his campaigns. Finally he began to write brief descriptions, which he called "notes" or "narratives," of the principal episodes in his war career. It is evident that he planned a volume which would consist of short chapters written by himself, with a series of documents appended to each chapter. Busy as he was with his railroads, the composition went slowly. As late as 1872 he had written almost nothing.[7]

In the meantime Marrin decided to write, with Jordan's aid, a biography of Beauregard. Beauregard was pleased. He could rely on Marrin to do justice to his reputation, and he would be saved the labors of literary creation. He sent to the lawyer all the documents he had gathered and collected new ones for him. Marrin worked at the project for years. His dreams of being a Boswell ended in failure.

[7] Beauregard to Jordan, November 23, December [n. d.], 1868, *ibid.;* Beauregard to Hill, July 1, 1869, to Mason Monfitt and H. C. Turnbull, September 18, 1869, to J. C. Nott, October 30, 1869, to Johnson Hagood, August 1, 1870, *ibid.,* Letterbook, Private Letters, February 6, 1869—February 5, 1872; Beauregard to Jordan, May 14, 1872, *ibid.,* Letterbook, Private Letters, February 28, 1872—December 1, 1875; Beauregard to Miles, July 26, 1869, in Miles Papers. In the Beauregard Papers at the Library of Congress are many packs of foolscap paper on which Beauregard copied documents and wrote his "notes."

He had to inform Beauregard that although he had written several chapters he could not spare enough time to finish the book.[8]

Beauregard's interest in completing his own volume was quickened in 1874 when Joe Johnston's *Narrative of Military Operations* was published. Although Johnston spoke highly of Beauregard in several places, he described Manassas as though he was responsible for the victory. Beauregard was enraged. He said that after reading the *Narrative* he had doubts that he was present at the battle. Johnston, he thought, had stamped himself as "a dissatisfied and disappointed Officer." [9]

Also angry was the ever-watchful Marrin. He advised Beauregard to reply publicly to Johnston. Beauregard was willing but said that because of the press of other work he would need help. He asked Marrin to prepare notes to form the basis of his answer. "Refer to my natural disposition to concentrate and attack," he instructed. Marrin and Jordan, on their own, assailed Johnston in the newspapers. One of the first of the postwar controversies had started, and one of the firmest friendships of the war was broken.[10]

With an added incentive now to present his case and story to the public, Beauregard redoubled his activities. He continued to search for documents, writing to officers who had served with him to ask for reports and letters. The documents, however, were now secondary in his interest. Reversing his original plan of organization, he planned to write long chapters and use the documents merely as supporting evidence. After finishing several chapters, he would mail them to Jordan and Marrin for checking and revising. With all his efforts he

[8] Marrin to Beauregard, January 4, October 8, 20, 24, November 18, December 10, 1872, May 26, June 9, 19, 1873, January 1, 1874, in Reeve Papers; Marrin to Manning, February 8, 1873, in Williams-Chesnut-Manning Papers; Beauregard to Marrin, November 5, 12, 1872, May 31, 1873, in Beauregard Papers (Library of Congress), Letterbook, Private Letters, February 28, 1872—December 1, 1875; Beauregard to Early, August 3, 1881, in Early Papers.

[9] Beauregard to Early, May 12, 1874, in Beauregard Papers (Confederate Museum, Richmond); Beauregard to Miles, July 8, 1874, in Miles Papers; Beauregard to Alexander, July 8, 1874, in Alexander Papers.

[10] Beauregard to Marrin, April 12, 1874, in Beauregard Papers (Library of Congress), Letterbook, Private Letters, February 28, 1872—December 1, 1875; Marrin to Beauregard, May 19, July 16, 1874, in Reeve Papers.

made slow progress. By the summer of 1881 the manuscript was only two thirds finished.[11]

While Beauregard plugged away at his writing, a new enemy appeared in print. William Preston Johnston, the son of Albert Sidney, had been working for years on a biography of his father. Among those whom he asked for information on the Shiloh campaign was Beauregard, who referred the query to Jordan. Obligingly Jordan replied that Beauregard had been the actual commander before Shiloh and had planned the battle. Naturally incensed, Johnston told Davis, whose opinion he had frequently sought as he wrote his book, that he expected a controversy with Beauregard when his book came out.[12]

Johnston then wrote to Beauregard questioning Jordan's account and intimating that his version of who had planned and fought Shiloh would be very different. Beauregard knew what this meant—Albert Sidney was to receive all the credit and he was to be relegated to a secondary role. He replied that when he wrote of Shiloh in his book he would be fair. But, he warned Johnston, he would also defend himself: "While doing justice to the memory of the dead one should not be unjust to the reputation of the living." [13]

Johnston's biography appeared in 1878. It was worse than Beauregard had expected. Not only did the son claim that his father had planned Shiloh; he charged that Beauregard had thrown away the victory Albert Sidney had won by not ordering one more charge at the end of the first day's battle. As the book was released, Davis made a speech in Mississippi repeating Johnston's statements. One of Beauregard's friends, Alfred Roman, wrote an angry reply in a New Orleans newspaper.[14] The seeds for another controversy were sown.

[11] Beauregard to Robert F. Hoke, December 2, 1874, in Robert F. Hoke Papers (North Carolina State Department of Archives and History, Raleigh); Marrin to Beauregard, December 11, 1875, August 21, 1876, in Reeve Papers; Beauregard to Edward Willis, May 20, 1878, June 19, 1880, in Beauregard Papers (South Carolina Historical Society, Charleston); Beauregard to J. F. H. Claiborne, July 9, 1878, in J. F. H. Claiborne Papers (Southern Historical Collection, University of North Carolina Library); Beauregard to Gibson, January 22, 1878, in Beauregard Papers (Library of Congress), Letterbook, Private Letters, December 4, 1875—March 24, 1880; Beauregard to Jacob Thompson, May 29, 1880, to L. A. Wiltz, September 10, 1880, to Hagood, July 2, 1881, *ibid.*, Letterbook, Letters, March 9, 1880—December 5, 1883.

[12] Rowland (ed.), *Jefferson Davis*, VIII, 37–38.

[13] Beauregard to W. J. Johnston, November 30, 1877, in Barret Papers.

[14] New Orleans *Democrat*, July 14, 1878. Roman pursued the subject in the issues of July 28, August 11, 1878. His letters were signed "Cy."

Beauregard believed that Davis and Johnston had conspired to rob him of his laurels. In a private letter which found its way into the newspapers, as he probably meant it to, he characterized Johnston's book as "shallow, confused and wrongful." Johnston, waiting for Beauregard to publish, prepared a written answer to what he thought Beauregard's case would be.[15]

After the publication of Johnston's book, Beauregard concluded that unless he could speed up his writing he would be left at the post in the literary race. He decided to employ the services of a collaborator. The man he selected was Alfred Roman, a longtime friend and a member of an old Creole family. Roman was a lawyer and had a reputation as a facile writer. Other points in his favor were that he admired Beauregard fanatically and he needed money.

Roman accepted the assignment readily and gratefully. He wrote Beauregard: "I shall put into it all the zeal and energy of which I am capable; to which I shall add the cordial affection and the well known admiration which I profess toward you as a man, as a Captain and as a strategist; and I dare say that . . . I shall succeed in making of your book, a work worthy of you, and worthy to serve as a solid base for the future History of the great fight, begun, carried on and, so to speak, ended by you. . . . Heavens! How I should like to be stronger, more sure of myself." [16]

For his labors Roman was to receive half of the royalties from sales of the book. But with a large family to support on a small income Roman would need money before the book appeared. Beauregard agreed to lend him money without interest, which Roman was to repay out of his share of the royalties. By the spring of 1882 Beauregard had advanced to his colleague the sum of $3,700.[17]

Roman's part in the collaboration was to take Beauregard's notes and smooth out the writing, insert eulogies of Beauregard's generalship at appropriate points, and prepare attacks on Davis and other enemies of Beauregard. The nature of the book was to be entirely

---

[15] Beauregard to Claiborne, July 23, 27, 1878, in Claiborne Papers; Rowland (ed.), *Jefferson Davis*, VIII, 276–77, 345–46.

[16] Roman to Beauregard, July 30, 1879, in Roman Papers (Duke University). Photostats of the Roman Papers at Duke and the Library of Congress were furnished me by the staffs of those institutions. Most of the letters in both collections are in French; these were translated for me by Philip D. Uzee, Thibodaux, Louisiana.

[17] Beauregard to Roman, May 23, 1882, in Roman Papers (Library of Congress).

changed. Instead of writing in the first person Beauregard was now going to write in the third. Instead of being called "My Reminiscences" the book was to be given a title like the one it eventually received, *Military Operations of General Beauregard*. Roman's name was to appear on the title page as author. The reasons for the altered organization are obvious: "Author" Roman could praise Beauregard more lavishly than Beauregard could under his own name, and he could assail Beauregard's foes more bitterly than Beauregard might wish to.

The real author of the two-volume work which the two men produced and which is always referred to as "Roman's *Beauregard*" was Beauregard. Most of the writing was his. Roman always conceded that his role had been minor and technical. In what I wrote, he once told Beauregard, I was "following the landmarks indicated by your notes; developing the points which you asked me to develop; refuting the slander which you wanted me to refute. . . . I did all I could, in duty and conscience, to make of you a great Captain and at the same time a great man and a great patriot." [18] In his correspondence with Beauregard he always referred to the manuscript as Beauregard's book: "I say *yours* and not *mine,* because that is the pure truth. It is your book and not mine. It was from your notes that I wrote it." [19] Roman's role in this queer collaboration might be described as that of a ghostwriter in reverse.

One factor inspiring Beauregard and Roman to haste was their knowledge that Davis was preparing his memoirs. They wanted, almost literally, to beat him to the punch. For years the former President had been collecting material, writing to friends and associates to furnish him with reports and recollections. He intended his work to be a justification of Jefferson Davis and the Confederates States, two institutions which he seemed to confuse, and an absolute demolition of his enemies, who were legion. Among those to whom he planned to devote particular attention was Beauregard.[20]

He saw fit, however, to ask Beauregard if he could provide any documents. From Beauregard's reply Davis got the impression that

[18] Roman to Beauregard, February 25, 1883, in Roman Papers (Duke University).

[19] Roman to Beauregard, March 1, 1883, February 1, 1885, *ibid.*

[20] Rowland (ed.), *Jefferson Davis*, VII, 507–508; VIII, 145–47, 337–38, 377–86; Davis to L. B. Northrop, April 9, 1879, in Davis Papers (Duke University).

the general was willing to open his files. Beauregard meant only that he would furnish his recollections of particular events. He was probably trying to find out what Davis was up to. Realizing that he was dealing with a crafty foe, he then asked Jordan and Marrin for advice. Jordan, belligerent as always, was eager to conduct an epistolatory quarrel with Davis, but Marrin counseled giving the former President as little as possible. Davis, said Marrin, would twist any facts to his advantage.[21]

Davis beat Beauregard to publication by a margin of three years. The ex-President's memoirs, *Rise and Fall of the Confederate Government,* appeared in 1881. The thick two-volume work bristled with attacks on and criticisms of Beauregard. As he read its rancorous pages, Beauregard burned with fury; when he finished he was angrier than he had ever been in his whole life. Davis had set out deliberately to destroy his reputation, he believed. He unleashed his bitterness in a letter to one of his former officers: "His book is an outrage on truth & history. It is a fiction, a romance which should have been called 'The Rise & Fall of Jeff. Davis' by himself. . . . What a fall from the honored Presidency of the late glorious Confederacy to being a defamer of his former co-associates! Pooh! he stinks in my nostrils." [22]

Immediately he decided to revise his manuscript, then two thirds completed, by having Roman rewrite the sections dealing with Davis. He had let Davis off lightly in the first draft, he told Early, but now he was really going to hit him.[23] Carefully he instructed Roman on how the references to Davis should be changed, even suggesting specific phrases which he thought would be effective. The important thing to do, he said, was to call attention to Davis' loss of memory and illustrate this with instances from his volumes. "He prides himself greatly, I am told," Beauregard wrote, "on his good & retentive memory! The loss of it is a very sore point with him—hence we must

[21] Davis to Beauregard, April 1, 1878, in Henkels' Catalog, *Beauregard Papers,* Pt. II; Davis to Beauregard, April 27, 1878, in Rowland (ed.), *Jefferson Davis,* VIII, 185–86; Marrin to Beauregard, May 5, 1878, in Reeve Papers.
[22] Beauregard to Hagood, July 2, 1881, in Beauregard Papers (Library of Congress), Letterbook, Letters, March 9, 1880—December 5, 1883.
[23] Beauregard to Early, August 18, 1881, in Early Papers. See also Beauregard to Roman, July 6, 1881, in Roman Papers (Library of Congress); Beauregard to Marcus J. Wright, August 17, 1881, in Marcus J. Wright Papers (Southern Historical Collection, University of North Carolina Library).

'rub it in' right there—& to appear charitable we might attribute it to the 'infirmities of age' & the severe trials of his prison life." [24]

By the end of 1881 the collaborators had almost finished their narrative and were looking for a publisher. Two companies, the National Publishing Company of Philadelphia and the American Publishing Company of Hartford, Connecticut, refused to even consider the manuscript on the ground that a market for war books no longer existed. Beauregard then submitted the manuscript to the Houghton, Mifflin Company in New York, getting Marrin and J. C. Derby, a literary agent and littérateur, to act as his intermediaries. [25]

Marrin and Derby liked the book, and Houghton, Mifflin expressed a definite interest. The two critics and the company thought, however, that certain changes should be made, notably that a number of slighting references to the North and the Republican party should be eliminated. In November, 1882, Beauregard went to New York to discuss these matters directly with the company and with Marrin and Derby. After talking with all three, he wrote Roman that for the purpose of increasing Northern sales he had agreed to delete the political statements. A co-operative attitude, he said, would secure for them a larger advance and better royalty terms. He also suggested that the book should be dedicated to "the memory of the gallant dead of both sides," a gesture which would please everybody and help sales in the North. [26]

Roman objected vehemently to making any changes, and he rejected absolutely the proposed dedication. Beauregard attempted to soothe him by saying it was pointless to hurt sales by discussing political matters in a military book. With all his concessions, Beauregard failed to get a contract. The company refused to make an offer until the completed manuscript was delivered. [27]

[24] Beauregard to Roman, July 28, 1881, in Roman Papers (Library of Congress). See also Beauregard to Roman, September 2, 1881, *ibid.;* Beauregard to Roman, April 18, 1882, in Beauregard file, Snowden Papers.

[25] Beauregard to Roman, January 4, 1882, in Roman Papers (Library of Congress); Beauregard to J. C. Derby, July 18, 1882, and to Marrin, October 10, 1882, in Beauregard Papers (Library of Congress), Letterbook, Letters, March 9, 1880—December 5, 1883; Derby, *Fifty Years Among Authors,* 713; Marrin to Beauregard, October 10, 1882, in Reeve Papers.

[26] Beauregard to Roman, November 26, 1862, in Roman Papers (Library of Congress).

[27] Beauregard to Roman, December 5, 7, 1882, *ibid.* The nature of Roman's objections is apparent from Beauregard's letter of the fifth. When the book was published, it contained no dedication.

In a few months Beauregard and Roman finished the book. But now Houghton, Mifflin and Marrin and Derby wanted more changes. They thought there was too much praise of Beauregard and too much controversy with Davis and others. Also, they wished Beauregard to sign his name as author. Beauregard said that he could not consent to any further modifications. As for appearing as author, why, he had not written the book! [28]

Although Beauregard had refused to make the suggested alterations, he was shaken by the criticisms. He decided that perhaps he should let Marrin revise the manuscript. Roman, who was intensely jealous of Marrin, exploded. Why should Beauregard let "a Northern man" correct his work? Marrin would do just what the Houghtons wanted—remove the eulogies of Beauregard. And why should they be removed? Were they not deserved? "Let them show me where . . . I have said something exaggerated about you," Roman demanded. "Your book was written to say fine things about you." [29] This was the kind of argument Beauregard could not withstand. He agreed to submit the manuscript to another publisher.

He next offered it to Appleton's, who refused consideration because war books no longer sold. Then through Derby he submitted it to Scribner's, who admitted an interest. Again Beauregard traveled to New York, this time to see Charles Scribner. The publisher told him that the book had possibilities but that it was too Southern, too controversial, and too laudatory of the subject. Sadly Beauregard informed Roman that he was going to confer with Harper's. If he failed with them, he would offer the manuscript to Lippincott's in Philadelphia. If they turned him down, he did not know what he would do. [30]

Harper's relieved the strain by accepting the manuscript. The company suggested a number of revisions but did not press them when Beauregard and Roman insisted on keeping most of the material as it was. In September, 1883, Roman, as the author, went to New York to sign a contract. He reported to Beauregard that the Yankee

[28] Beauregard to Mrs. Emily Battey, February 6, 1883, and to Derby, February 13, 1883, in Beauregard Papers (Library of Congress), Letterbook, Letters, March 9, 1880—December 5, 1883.

[29] Roman to Beauregard, February 25, 1883, in Roman Papers (Duke University).

[30] Beauregard to Roman, April 17, May 27, 1883, in Roman Papers (Library of Congress).

publishers were very sharp and fixed up an agreement very much in their own favor.[31]

The book was published early in 1884, two large, handsome volumes—*The Military Operations of General Beauregard*. In the preface the subject assured the public that the work furnished a correct account of his military service. He said also that he wished to commend the author for the able and judicious manner in which he had written his narrative and that he endorsed every statement except the encomiums bestowed upon himself![32]

In many ways it was a valuable work. Although it contained very little about Beauregard that was personal, it presented his views of himself as a general and his opinions of the military events of which he had been a part. It contained a large number of documents which were not included in the *Official Records*. The most unfortunate feature of the book was its controversial nature. It criticized nearly every important Confederate civil and military official, with Davis and his advisers getting the heaviest blows, followed closely by Joe Johnston and Albert Sidney Johnston. Even Lee received a few mild taps. Southern reviewers, most of whom praised the book, regretted its quarrelsome tone. One commentator said that it seemed to have been Beauregard's misfortune to fall out with everybody he was associated with.[33]

Beauregard and Roman expected the book to sell well. In this they were disappointed. Harper's offered the set in four bindings at the following prices: cloth, $3.50; sheep, $4.50; half-morocco, $5.50; and full-morocco, $7.50. As was customary publishing practice at that time, the volumes were sold only by subscription; agents toured the country seeking orders.[34] Not many orders were secured. The market for war books had passed its peak. Beauregard thought that the company was either inefficient in its sales methods or was not trying to sell the book. Over a year after the book appeared, he complained that he had yet to see "the *color* of one of the Messrs Harpers'

[31] Beauregard to Harper and Brothers, June 5, July 16, August 24, 1883, in Beauregard Papers (Library of Congress), Letterbook, Letters, March 9, 1880—December 5, 1883; Roman to Beauregard, September 16, 1883, in Beauregard Papers (Tulane University).

[32] Roman, *Beauregard*, I, "Preface," n. p.

[33] *Southern Historical Society Papers*, XII (1884), 144, 258–66, 402–16, 433–47; New Orleans *Times-Democrat*, March 9, 16, 1884.

[34] Printed pamphlet issued by Harper's to advertise the book, in Roman Papers (Library of Congress).

checks." Hit especially hard by the scanty sales was Roman, who had looked forward to pocketing half the royalties. To aid his pinched collaborator, Beauregard canceled notes which he held on Roman amounting to $3,900. He also agreed to pay a note for $1,682, which represented expenses incurred in preparing the manuscript and half of which was chargeable to Roman.[35]

The exact number of copies sold is impossible to determine. The records of the company for those years were destroyed by fire. By 1887 it would seem that something over six thousand sets had been sold; in royalties Beauregard and Roman had received perhaps $2,500, although the sum was probably smaller. Whatever the amount, Beauregard had lost money by his effort to place his record in the files of history. In 1887 he conveyed to Roman his rights and interests in the sale and the profits of the book.[36]

War books might not sell, but the editors of the *Century Magazine* and of the *North American Review* were convinced that war articles would increase their circulation. In the 1880's they asked a number of leading Northern and Southern generals to write accounts of their important battles. These articles later formed the basis of the great four-volume source work, *Battles and Leaders of the Civil War.*

In 1884 the *Century* requested Beauregard to do an article on the battle of Bull Run. After first refusing on the grounds that he was too busy, he agreed.[37] Apparently Beauregard prepared the piece in the same way he had written his book. He wrote notes which Marrin and Jordan revised.[38] After the article was in proof he showed it to Roman, who did not like it. Roman said it was too long, too digressive, and too aggressive. "Why attack, always attack Mr. Davis?" he asked.

[35] Beauregard to Roman, October 11, 1884, July 17, December 31, 1885, February 24, 1887, *ibid.*

[36] Harry Shaw, Harper and Brothers, to the author, December 14, 1951. The estimate on the sales and royalties is based on a memorandum, August 3, 1887, in the Beauregard file, Snowden Papers. See also Beauregard to Roman, November 30, 1887, *ibid.* In 1906 Harper's had less than a hundred sets left; *Publications of the Southern History Association,* X (1906) 185–86. According to Mr. Shaw the book was carried in Harper's catalog until 1911.

[37] R. U. Johnson to George W. Cable, May 13, June 11, 1884, in George W. Cable Papers (Howard-Tilton Memorial Library, Tulane University). Apparently Johnson approached Beauregard through an intermediary. These letters were called to my attention by Professor Arlin Turner, Duke University.

[38] Marrin to Beauregard, August 29, September 10, 12, 1884, in Reeve Papers.

"You have already defended yourself in your book. Why come back to the accusations . . . ?" Everything that needed to be said had been said in the book, Roman insisted, and Beauregard should not write anything more. Roman, who usually disclaimed authorship of the *Operations*, was beginning to take an author's pride in his work.[39]

The article appeared in the November issue. It dealt as much with Beauregard's enemies in the Confederacy as with the ones in Yankee uniforms. Davis was criticized for not permitting a concentration before the battle, Joe Johnston for having said in his book that he had commanded during the engagement, and General Ewell for not obeying an order to cross Bull Run.[40] These accusations enraged Davis, Johnston, and Ewell's family. Johnston observed that Beauregard had not been prompted in this case by his usual malice "but by his inordinate vanity and disposition to write himself up as a strategist." [41]

Beauregard was not the only one who could deal out charges in magazines. In February, 1885, the *Century* carried an article by William Preston Johnston on Shiloh, which was a condensed repetition of the earlier account in his book.[42] Egged on by Marrin, Beauregard decided to write a reply in the *North American Review*. Roman begged him to avoid further controversy, but he said that when his detractors were flooding the country with lies he had to defend himself.[43]

Beauregard commenced work on the Shiloh article but soon found he would not have enough time to do it. He asked Roman if he would

[39] Roman to Beauregard, September 11, 1884, in Roman Papers (Duke University).

[40] P. G. T. Beauregard, "The Battle of Bull Run," *Century Illustrated Monthly Magazine*, XXIX (1884), 80–106.

[41] Davis to Early, November 20, 1884, in Davis Papers (Duke University); Johnston to Campbell Brown, November 6, 1864, in Polk-Brown-Ewell Papers. Campbell Brown, Ewell's stepson, wrote a rejoinder, "General Beauregard's Courier at Bull Run," *Century Illustrated Monthly Magazine*, XXX (1885), 478–79. Johnston also wrote a reply, "Manassas to Seven Pines," *ibid.*, XXX (1885), 99–120. Beauregard started an article to reply to Johnston. The article grew into a small book, published in 1891, *A Commentary on the Campaign and Battle of Manassas. . . .*

[42] William Preston Johnston, "Albert Sidney Johnston and the Shiloh Campaign," in *Century Illustrated Monthly Magazine*, XXIX (1885), 614–28.

[43] Marrin to Beauregard, January 26, 1885, in Reeve Papers; Roman to Beauregard, February 1, 1885, in Roman Papers (Duke University); Beauregard to Roman, February 3, 1885, in Roman Papers (Library of Congress); Beauregard to Wright, April 11, 1885, in Wright Papers.

like to ghostwrite the piece for the fee the magazine would pay. He was sure that the *Review* would offer $500; if the fee was less he would make up the difference. Roman, always in need of money, accepted the proposition. Beauregard then coached Roman on what to put in the article and on what points to criticize Albert Sidney Johnston. In particular he desired Roman to say in the beginning that "I" had always hesitated to write about Shiloh "because I did not wish to appear too egotistical by telling the whole truth." [44]

Roman plunged enthusiastically into the job. Now that he was doing the writing, he was not so cautious about provoking controversy. He told Beauregard that he would like to attack Johnston more vehemently but that writing in the first person cramped his denunciatory style: ". . . as it is you who is speaking, I have to exercise more restraint, more reserve." [45] He soon had the article finished, and Beauregard sent it to the editors of the *Review*. They accepted it, and asked Beauregard to write several more pieces, suggesting specifically the Charleston and Petersburg campaigns. Beauregard asked Roman if he would like to continue his ghostwriting career. Roman said he would, particularly if Beauregard could pay him in advance for the articles. [46]

Roman wrote the articles on Charleston in the latter part of 1885 and the ones on Petersburg early in the next year.[47] He approached the Virginia pieces with glee, because in them he would be able to dispose of Lee, the man who in his opinion and Beauregard's was wrongly held up as the greatest Southern general. He wrote Beauregard: "I am slowly getting ready for the third article—this one will be the bouquet! since we shall have for ourselves the free candy. Free candy—during the writing of the article—but afterwards? Be-

[44] Beauregard to Roman, July 17, 23, 1885, in Roman Papers (Library of Congress); Roman to Beauregard, July 21, 1885, in Roman Papers (Duke University).

[45] Roman to Beauregard, August 2, 1885, in Roman Papers (Duke University).

[46] Beauregard to Roman, August 5, 14, September 12, 1885, in Roman Papers (Library of Congress); Roman to Beauregard, August 8, September 9, 13, December 1, 1885, in Roman Papers (Duke University). The Shiloh article, "The Shiloh Campaign," appeared in *North American Review*, CXLII (1886), 1–24, 159–84.

[47] The articles were published in 1886 and 1887: "Defence of Charleston, South Carolina," *North American Review*, CXLII (1886), 419–36, 564–71, CXLIII (1886), 42–53; "Drewry's Bluff and Petersburg," *ibid.*, CXLIV (1887), 244–60; "The Battle of Petersburg," *ibid.*, CXLV (1887), 67–77, 506–15.

cause, shall we not forcefully touch upon the anointed of the Lord—the immortal Virginian—the greatest warrior of all the centuries next to Grant? You shall be mauled! Happily it will be you, not I." [48] Ghostwriting had other compensations than money.

After all his writing, his enemies would not down. They continued to raise their voices even in his own city. In 1887 New Orleans was making plans to unveil a monument of Albert Sidney Johnston at the Army of Tennessee tomb in Metairie Cemetery. At the solemn ceremonies Jefferson Davis was to be the principal speaker. Beauregard was naturally invited to attend. He told Roman that he did not think he would go. He doubted that he could sit quietly and listen to the lies of Davis and the other orators: "I wd. cry out—'You are all a set of d. Liars—& you have erected, here, a monument to the wrong man.'" [49]

He went, nevertheless, and regretted it. Davis delivered a eulogy of Johnston in which he said that that general planned the concentration at Corinth and the movement on Pittsburg Landing. In the entire Shiloh campaign, Davis continued, Johnston made only one mistake—he let another officer direct the march to the battlefield. Because of this the march was delayed and the battle was lost. [50]

These were cruel words to fling in Beauregard's face, and he struck back savagely. In a long letter to the newspapers, which Roman helped him prepare, he gave his version of Shiloh and denounced Davis for doing injustice to the living while pretending to honor the dead. Davis replied, and the bitter controversy was in full swing again. Apparently it would have to continue to the last. [51]

The last for Davis was not long in coming. He died in 1889. Beauregard, as one of the few surviving full generals of the Confederacy, was invited to ride in a carriage at the head of the procession in the funeral. He refused. He said to his family: "I told them I would not do it. We have always been enemies. I cannot pretend I am sorry he is gone. I am no hypocrite." [52]

[48] Roman to Beauregard, January 14, 1886, in Roman Papers (Duke University). See also Roman to Beauregard, January 25, February 9, 1886, *ibid.;* Beauregard to Roman, December 31, 1885, June 30, 1886, in Roman Papers (Library of Congress).

[49] Beauregard to Roman, March 2, 1887, in Roman Papers (Library of Congress).

[50] New Orleans *Picayune,* April 7, 1887.

[51] Beauregard to Roman, April 7, 25, 1887, in Roman Papers (Library of Congress); Rowland (ed.), *Jefferson Davis,* IX, 537–39; New Orleans *Picayune,* April 17, 24, 1887.

[52] Basso, *Beauregard,* 309–10.

CHAPTER TWENTY

Death of a Hero

THE OLD MAN was one of the sights of New Orleans. On the streets parents pointed him out to their children, and natives whispered to awed tourists that "le general" was passing. The erect, compact body, the handsome face crowned by luxuriant white hair, and the soldierly bearing would have attracted attention in any assemblage.[1] New Orleans was always convinced that at least in looks Beauregard was the beau ideal of a soldier—a Creole incarnation of Napoleon. Outside observers were not so easily impressed. When he visited England after the war, a Liverpool journalist professed disappointment in the appearance of the famous American general. He was small and not at all striking looking, said the Englishman. A Yankee who saw Beauregard on a train in New York and who was amazed to learn he was gazing on the hero of Manassas expressed a similar feeling in more pungent terms: "The little cuss looked worse whipped than a hen-pecked rooster." [2]

Almost until his death Beauregard was an alert and active individual and an important figure in the social life of his city. He was a member or a patron of the most exclusive clubs and organizations and played a prominent role in their social functions. When the Washington Artillery staged their dress ball in 1866, "the ball par excellence of the season," Beauregard headed the list of managers. He was a stockholder in the French Opera House and La Variété Association, a theatrical organization, and a frequent attendant at the programs of both.[3] On the sporting side, he was a member of the Louisiana Jockey Club and an enthusiastic follower of the races at the Fair Grounds track.[4]

[1] King, *Creole Families*, 459–60; letter by Jessica Hawthorne, in New Orleans *States*, April 1, 1888; New Orleans *Times-Democrat*, February 21, 1893.

[2] Liverpool *Daily Post*, quoted in New Orleans *Picayune*, June 19, 1866; New Orleans *Times*, September 7, 1867.

[3] New Orleans *Picayune*, April 10, 25, 1866, February 21, 1893.

[4] St. Louis *Republic*, February 3, 1889, clipping in Beauregard Papers (Louisiana State University); New Orleans *Picayune*, April 12, 1873.

319

He had a part too in the city's intellectual life. In 1869 he and other former Confederates in New Orleans organized the Southern Historical Society. After the society grew into a section-wide organization, its headquarters were removed to Richmond. For years Beauregard was a member of the executive committee and an enthusiastic delegate to its conventions.[5] He was also one of the founders of L'Athénée Louisianais, an organization devoted to cultivating the study of the French language. Beauregard served as president for eleven years. At its meetings, all conducted in French, the members read research papers, short stories, and poems which they had composed. Their tastes seem to have been fairly catholic. One session opened with a paper on the Hundred Years' War. Next followed a poem on literary comradeship. Two doctors then discussed a newspaper story in which a hen scared by a snake was supposed to have laid an egg with a snake embossed on the shell, and proved the hen could not have done it. Another doctor concluded the program by discussing suicide.[6]

One society Beauregard founded singlehanded to aid the family of a former comrade. In 1879 General Hood died, leaving several small children without means of support. Just before his death he had completed a manuscript on his war experiences which he had hoped to sell to a publisher. Touched by the plight of the young Hoods, Beauregard started subscription funds for their relief and induced a friend to adopt one child. Then he set out to get Hood's book published. He organized the Hood Memorial Association, which with the assistance of his lottery friends, published the memoirs. All the proceeds were turned over to a fund for the children.[7]

Not all of Beauregard's offices were in social or cultural organizations. In 1873 for a brief period he became president of the Louisiana Immigration and Homestead Company. This organization had as its purpose inducing white immigrants from Europe and the North to settle in Louisiana. At first the company hoped to buy land and sell it to the newcomers. Lacking the resources to do this, it converted

[5] Maury, *Recollections,* 251–52; printed circular of the Southern Historical Society (1869), in Beauregard Papers (Louisiana State University); New Orleans *Picayune,* August 7, 24, 1873.

[6] Henry Rightor (ed.), *Standard History of New Orleans, Louisiana* (Chicago, 1900), 628; New Orleans *Times-Democrat,* July 22, 1882.

[7] Beauregard to Early, September 4, 1879, in Early Papers; Hay, *Hood's Tennessee Campaign,* 215.

itself into a nonprofit society devoted to publishing pamphlets, circulars, and other materials depicting the advantages of the state. It hoped to secure funds for its work from planters and merchants. Not many contributions were received, and the company had to suspend operations. The reason for the lack of support was simple. Beauregard and his associates advocated that the large landowners break up their holdings and sell them in parcels to immigrants. The planters were not interested in a movement that threatened their estates.[8]

In 1879 Beauregard was appointed adjutant general of Louisiana. As the state's chief military officer he commanded the militia, the organization which after 1865 was called the National Guard. He held the post for nine years. He threw himself into his duties with his customary energy and enthusiasm, devoting particular attention to reorganizing the units in the country parishes. By all reports, he did a good job. On occasion, though, he could revert to the kind of thinking which had made him distrusted in the war. He concluded that the range and accuracy of the new firearms were making daytime fighting too dangerous. For future wars troops should be trained to fight at night. He proposed that the militia be supplied with uniforms with phosphorescent backs so that the men could be seen by their comrades in rear while remaining invisible in front![9]

After failing to win an elective office in his younger years, Beauregard was chosen for one in his old age. In 1888 he was elected Commissioner of Public Works—as the candidate of the Young Men's Democratic Association. Drainage and sanitation were two things he had been interested in all his mature life, and in this office he believed he could really make a contribution to the well-being of his town. He was to be bitterly disappointed.

Politically innocent as always, he thought the city fathers wanted him to clean up the filthy streets and gutters. Actually the public works department was viewed by the politicians as a patronage heaven, a place where the worst hacks could be given jobs. When Beauregard discharged some of the hacks and substituted men who

[8] *Address to the People in Behalf of the Louisiana Immigration and Homestead Company* (New Orleans, 1873), *passim.*, a pamphlet issued by the company. See also New Orleans *Picayune*, April 25, May 7, 9, 10, 11, 1873; New Orleans *Times*, August 16, November 2, December 20, 1873, January 20, 24, 1874.

[9] New Orleans *Democrat*, January 3, March 26, 1879; New Orleans *Times-Democrat*, March 23, 1884; New Orleans *Picayune*, February 21, 1893; New Orleans *States*, February 21, 1893.

knew their business, the council refused to confirm his appointments. He was told that if he employed some men suggested by the council members, some of his appointees would be approved. He resigned in disgust.[10]

When Beauregard returned from the war, he and his sons took rooms for a period in a dwelling at 279 Chartres Street. In 1868 he removed to 226 Royal Street; in later years he lived at residences on North Rampart, Chartres, St. Claude, Esplanade, Thalia, and St. Charles streets. In all he resided at ten different addresses between 1865-93. He purchased in 1889 a large house at 255 Esplanade Avenue. This was the house in which he died.[11]

Although Beauregard loved New Orleans, he could not stand the hot, humid Louisiana summers. Whenever he could, he spent a part or the whole of the warm season in a cooler climate. As he liked to say, he had to "unboil" himself. One of his favorite vacations spots was West Virginia and its famous springs. He delighted in taking the waters at White Sulphur Springs and Sweet Springs. At these resorts, much patronized by Southerners, he could loll the weeks away, talk about the war with old comrades, and utter gallantries to thrilled young ladies.[12]

Other places that drew him in the hot months were Asheville, North Carolina, the Maine coast, and northern Wisconsin.[13] In 1889 he went for the first time to Waukesha, Wisconsin, which liked to be called the Saratoga of the West. The guests at the resort, a few of whom were Louisianians, decided to tender a reception to the man who, in the words of a local reporter, was known as "the Sir Galahad of Southern Chivalry." At the meeting the spokesman for the group, a Northerner, welcomed Beauregard and said that twenty-five years

[10] New Orleans *Times-Democrat,* April 28, 29, May 1, 17, 1888; New Orleans *States,* April 28, 1888; New Orleans *Picayune,* April 29, May 8, 17, 1888, February 21, 1893.

[11] The information about Beauregard's addresses is drawn from New Orleans directories. He lived at two different places on St. Charles Avenue and at two on Chartres Street. The 279 Chartres house is the present 1113, and is the building now known as the Beauregard House. The residence at 255 Esplanade is now numbered 1631.

[12] Beauregard to Miles, July 26, 1869, July 8, 1874, in Miles Papers; New Orleans *Picayune,* August 22, 1873; Beauregard to Roman, April 12, 1887, in Roman Papers (Library of Congress).

[13] New Orleans *Republican,* August 7, 1873; New Orleans *Picayune,* August 17, 1873; Beauregard to Claiborne, July 23, 1878, in Claiborne Papers.

ago they did not feel very kindly toward him; but the past was dead and now they admired him. Modestly Beauregard replied that he had not expected to be so honored. "As to my past life," he said, "I have always endeavored to do my duty under all circumstances, from the time I entered West Point, a boy of seventeen, up to the present." This hardly conciliatory remark, which retracted nothing he had done, was greeted by loud applause. The North was becoming almost as proud of romantic Confederate heroes as the South.[14]

In addition to his trip to Europe for the Jackson Railroad, Beauregard made a purely social journey in 1888. In London he renewed old friendships, met new and important people, and was invited to the best clubs.[15] He was not too happy about his visit to France. The Empire was gone, and a new class of people was in power. In Paris he was invited to only one large social function, which he did not enjoy. He was the only man present not in evening dress. He had borrowed a frock coat for the occasion and a pair of English shoes weighing ten pounds each. He left France with sore feet and a conviction the Republic would not last.[16]

In his family circle Beauregard was a tender and loving patriarch. He was devoted to his children, and they to him. His first son, René, took a law degree after the war, and practiced in New Orleans and St. Bernard parish. He married Alice Cenas, of an old and numerous Creole family. To Beauregard's delight, René and Alice for long periods made their home with him. They had six children, five daughters and a son. The boy was named after Beauregard. Familiarly called "Guste," he was a great favorite with his grandfather.[17]

The second son, Henri, left New Orleans. He married Antoinette Harney of St. Louis and lived in that city for years. It would seem that while René prospered, Henri did not. Eventually, with financial aid from his father, he established a real estate business in San Diego, California. Beauregard was glad to hear that he seemed to be doing

---

14 New Orleans *States,* September 8, 1889.

15 J. A. Wardell to Beauregard, September 3, 1888, James Ferguson to Beauregard, September 4, 1888, Garnet Wolseley to Beauregard, September 5, 1888, Sir Henry Acland to Beauregard, October 5, 1888, in Beauregard Papers (Louisiana State University).

16 Beauregard to René Beauregard, September 19, 1888, *ibid.*

17 De Leon, *Belles, Beaux and Brains,* 297–98; New Orleans *Picayune,* December 15, 1910; Gustave Beauregard to Beauregard, October 15, 1888, in Beauregard Papers (Tulane University).

well. "So it seems that poor Henri is very happy which is a lot," he observed to Roman.[18]

The Beauregard and Cenas families were very close, and often they filled Beauregard's home to overflowing. But their favorite gathering place was "Buen Retiro," a country dwelling which René purchased. Situated about three miles below New Orleans, "Buen" was a lovely ante-bellum house hidden in a grove of live oaks, magnolias, and orange trees. Here the two families came to escape the city's heat and noise and to let the children play in the fields. In his later years Beauregard spent much of his time in the summers at "Buen." He liked to sit on the veranda and watch Guste run over the clover and under the great trees.[19]

Beauregard loved his sons and René's children, but for his daughter Laure he had a feeling close to worship. "Doucette" he called her, pronouncing the name like a caress. As a child and as a young lady she was his almost constant companion; no one who saw them together could doubt that she was the idol of his heart. All New Orleans was excited when she married Charles Larendon of Atlanta. Marriage did not separate her from her father, as Larendon accepted Beauregard's invitation to live with him.[20]

A daughter was born to the marriage, a beautiful child named Lilian. In the summer of 1884 Beauregard went to New York. Laure was expecting another baby and was apparently in fine health. A telegram was delivered to Beauregard informing him that she had given birth to a daughter and that all was well. Two days later another telegram came—Laure was desperately ill. He started for home immediately. As he walked up to his house, he saw crape on the door. She had died the day before his arrival. He entered the mortuary chamber to see her, as beautiful as ever and on her face what he thought was a smile of welcome for him.[21]

[18] René Beauregard to Beauregard, September 29, 1887, in Beauregard Papers (Louisiana State University); Beauregard to Roman, April 12, 1887, in Roman Papers (Library of Congress). The Henri Beauregards did not have children.
[19] William R. Spratling and Natalie Scott, *Old Plantation Houses in Louisiana* (New York, 1927), 159; Heloise Cenas to Gustave Beauregard, May 12, 1889, in Beauregard Papers (Louisiana State University); Beauregard to Laure Larendon, June 15, 1891, in Larendon Papers; Beauregard to Mrs. N. H. Beauregard, June 1, September 18, 1892, in Beauregard Papers (Missouri Historical Society).
[20] De Leon, *Belles, Beaux and Brains,* 298–300.
[21] Beauregard to Elizabeth W. Lay, July 19, 1884, in Clement C. Clay Papers (Duke University Library).

The terrible shock was almost too much for him to bear. Pouring out his grief to a friend, he wrote: "She was . . . a devoted daughter, wife, & mother! . . . She was indeed as perfect a human being as I have ever known." [22] For years after he remained in seclusion and was seldom seen in his accustomed social haunts.[23]

The second daughter was named Laure for her mother, and as he had the mother, Beauregard always addressed her as "Doucette." He was deeply devoted to both of the little girls. It became a familiar spectacle for people to see the old man and his granddaughters strolling on the streets. Lilian was a delicate and sensitive child. She never seemed to recover from the blow of her mother's death. She was always telling Beauregard that she wanted to go to her mother in Heaven and live among the the stars. When his face would sadden, she would add, "I'll come back again." [24]

The remains of Laure Larendon the first had been buried in a temporary resting place until Beauregard could have a granite tomb constructed in Metairie Cemetery. While the tomb was being erected, Lilian would coax him to take her every day to the pretty stone house in which her mother was going to live. On a March morning in 1887 the body of Mrs. Larendon was removed to the tomb. That same day Lilian died, and was buried beside her mother that evening. As the wind wailed through the flowers and rain fell on the coffin, Beauregard stood with his white head bowed in sorrow.[25]

After Lilian's death Beauregard concentrated much of his affection upon the second Laure. When she was in New Orleans, she lived at his house and was with him constantly. When he left town for any extended period, he corresponded with her frequently and carried with him pictures of her and Lilian—"so as to see you both all the time," he explained to her.[26]

Laure was not always in New Orleans. Sometimes her father took her with him to Atlanta or to other places where he thought he might settle. For some reason the Beauregards detested Charles

[22] *Ibid.*
[23] Beauregard to Roman, March 2, 1887, in Roman Papers (Library of Congress).
[24] Beauregard to V. P. Sisson, October 16, 1888, in Larendon Papers.
[25] Letter by Jessica Hawthorne, in New Orleans *States,* April 1, 1888.
[26] Beauregard to Laure Larendon, September 16, 1890, September 7, 1892, in Larendon Papers. This collection contains many letters from Beauregard to his granddaughter.

Larendon, probably because he moved around a great deal without working and was always asking Beauregard for money.[27] One of the Cenas women spoke of "poor little Doucette" being "sacrificed to her father's low minded ways of life. I rejoice now that poor little Lilian has been spared." [28] Once Larendon told Beauregard he was thinking of setting up a business on the Pacific coast and might be away for years. Beauregard advised him to go and predicted he would make a fortune. While Larendon was absent, Beauregard said he would take charge of Doucette. "Whenever you may wish to take Doucette with you can do so," he said to Larendon, "but I trust *not for good* as long as I am alive! I don't want to part with her, 'until death do us part.' " [29]

He seemed resigned to death. When they told him that his old enemy Ben Butler had died, he only said sadly, "Another of us has gone. Very soon there will not be many of us left." That very day he became ill with gastric cramps. He seemed to rally, and took the ladies of his family to a matinee of a play, "The Fair Rebel."

That night he took to his bed. For over a week he was seriously sick. Much of the time he was delirious, and his mind went back to the war. He would order René and Henri, who had rushed home from St. Louis, to mass the divisions—his old principle of concentration. "We will rout the enemy tomorrow," he would cry.

On Saturday, February 18, 1893, he seemed better, and dressed and came downstairs. The next day he complained of a feeling of oppression around his heart, and that night he did not sleep well. Still, he got up on Monday, the twentieth, and spent most of the day in the garden and on the balcony. He dined with the family and spoke cheerfully of his recovery. Before retiring that night, he wound his watch, saying that he was getting well enough to take his medicine unaided and wanted the watch so he could follow the doctor's orders. Henri and two nurses assisted him upstairs, and the son helped to undress him. Before Henri left, Beauregard said, "I will be well tomorrow if I sleep tonight." The nurses remained on duty in the

[27] Ruby M. Kennedy to Mrs. René Beauregard, February 1, 1893, in Beauregard Papers (Louisiana State University).

[28] Heloise Cenas to Mrs. René Beauregard, August 12, November 4, 1888, *ibid.*

[29] Beauregard to Charles Larendon, April 4, 1888, in Larendon Papers.

room. Shortly after ten they were startled to hear the death rattle in his throat. Before they could summon the family he was dead.[30]

Into the home on Esplanade Avenue the condolences and resolutions of respect poured in a flood. They came from Louisiana and from all over the South—from state and city officials, former comrades, the organizations of which he had been a member, chapters of the United Confederate veterans from Virginia to Texas.[31] Mayor John Fitzpatrick proclaimed a period of mourning until after the funeral and directed that all municipal buildings be closed. Governor Murphy F. Foster ordered the same arrangements at the capital in Baton Rouge. Both the governor and the mayor asked the family for permission to let the body lie in state at the City Hall, and consent was granted.[32]

On the afternoon of the twenty-second services were conducted in the home before the remains were taken to the hall. The only floral ornament in the room was a large palm leaf tied with a purple ribbon, Beauregard having requested that there be no flowers at his funeral. Father Joseph Subileau, an old friend, conducted the ceremony. In his sermon he said that Beauregard had possessed deep religious feelings, although he had not practiced his faith with the regularity which the priest would have desired.

Accompanied by an escort of National Guard units, the body, resting in a heavy casket finished in burl and ebony and adorned with silver handles, was conveyed to the council room at the City Hall. The walls of the dimly lit chamber were hung with black drapes and Confederate and United States flags. Three Confederate emblems, one of which belonged to the Washington Artillery, covered the casket. Flowers banked the bier, and in the coffin was a bunch of violets placed there by Doucette, who had picked them in Georgia. Above the catafalque stood the battle flag which Miss Hettie Cary

[30] New Orleans *Picayune*, February 21, 1893; New Orleans *Times-Democrat*, February 21, 1893; New Orleans *States*, February 21, 1893; New Orleans *Delta*, February 21, 1893; New Orleans *Sunday Figaro*, February 26, 1893. Several of these newspapers stated that on the Saturday before his death Beauregard attended a theatrical or operatic program. It would seem impossible that he did so. These accounts probably confused his activities on Saturday with those on the first day of his illness.

[31] Folders for February, 1893, in Beauregard Papers (Louisiana State University).

[32] New Orleans *Times-Democrat*, February 21, 1893; New Orleans *Picayune*, February 22, 1893.

had made for him from her own dress in 1861. All that night and throughout the next day, while an honor guard of Confederate veterans stood by, thousands of people passed through the room to gaze on the Creole hero.[33]

On the afternoon of the twenty-third the body was removed from the City Hall and taken for burial to the tomb of the Army of Tennessee in Metairie Cemetery. Under a cloudless sky, through streets packed with spectators, the funeral marchers moved to Canal and Claiborne streets, where a special train was to carry them to the cemetery. Two military bands led the procession. Behind them swung the Washington Artillery, National Guard units, the Louisiana Field Artillery, and veterans of the Army of Northern Virginia and of his old Army of Tennessee. Riding in a carriage was the chief mourner, Edmund Kirby Smith, now the only surviving full general of the Confederacy, who had come to New Orleans to attend a Confederate reunion. A month later he too would be dead. At the grave, priests chanted the requiem, three volleys were fired in a last salute, and taps were sounded. From above, the equestrian statue of Albert Sidney Johnston looked down on the scene.[34]

By the terms of Beauregard's will his property was to be divided equally among René, Henri, and little Laure. The sons were to administer Laure's share until she reached majority. To René and Henri he bequeathed his books and war relics; the items that they did not want were to be given to the Howard Memorial Library at Tulane University. Doucette was to receive his portraits of her grandmother and mother and Lilian, as well as the furniture in his bedroom. He left to Guste the gold watch he had always carried. Each grandchild and grandniece was to get $500 as a souvenir. A like sum was to go to a woman who had been a family servant for twenty-four years and to the Confederate Soldiers' Home in New Orleans.[35]

The lengthy inventory of his succession listed everything he owned. It was all there—his home and its belongings; his other property in Orleans Parish; land in Jefferson Parish; stocks in banks and corporations, some valuable, some worthless; stocks in opera and theater

---

[33] New Orleans *Picayune*, February 23, 1893; New Orleans *Times-Democrat*, February 23, 1893.

[34] New Orleans *Picayune*, February 24, 1893; New Orleans *States*, February 24, 1893; New Orleans *Times-Democrat*, February 24, 1893.

[35] New Orleans *Picayune*, March 1, 1893.

companies; property in other states; and promissory notes running into thousands of dollars. The first inventory of his estate placed a valuation of $86,439.46 on his Orleans property and $10,000 on the land in Jefferson. A second inventory, made a year later, reduced the Orleans total to $69,882.80 while retaining the $10,000 figure for Jefferson. Most of the decrease resulted from eliminating notes which the sons had given to their father and which were to form part of their inheritance. Neither analysis, however, appraised Beauregard's property out of the state. He owned a hotel in St. Louis, sections of lots in Chicago, and land and lots in California at Santa Barbara, San Diego, Los Angeles, and Corona Beach. By a most conservative estimate he was worth at least $150,000.[36] It seemed very wrong to some people. Confederate generals were not supposed to become that wealthy.

The enigma of his life was in that inventory. There in the painfully listed columns was the sword which the ladies of New Orleans had presented to him after he captured Fort Sumter, and the little red-topped artillery general's cap which he had worn at Manassas and when he rode before the ranks the night before Shiloh, and the battle flag made by Hettie Cary in the exultant days of 1861—the faded and pathetic relics of the Old South. There too, and more numerous and significant, were the stocks, the real estate, the promissory notes, the speculative investments—the glittering symbols of the New South. And so even to the last he was a paradox. Despite all that he seemed and all that he had fought for, he did not really look back to Contreras and the planting South and the mellow glories of the ancient regime, but forward to International House and the New Orleans industrial district and the bustling delta of tomorrow.

[36] Succession of Pierre Gustave Toutant Beauregard, No. 38,254, Civil District Court, Parish of Orleans, New Orleans. A photostatic record of this document was furnished me by Mr. Thomas S. Buckley, Clerk of the Civil District Court for the Parish of Orleans. For aid in analyzing the inventory, I am indebted to Mrs. George Herlitz of the Union Bond and Mortgage Company, Baton Rouge, Louisiana. Undoubtedly the real estate was appraised at a value lower than its actual worth; this procedure was customary in making an inventory. Estimating Beauregard's estate in terms of the dollar of the 1950's, it would seem that he was worth close to half a million dollars.

Critical Essay on Authorities

Manuscript Collections

No dearth of Beauregard manuscripts hindered the preparation of this biography. The general wrote voluminously, and most of his papers seem to have been preserved. In fact, I have sometimes been discouraged to have friends inform me, at exultant moments when I thought I had completed my research, that they knew of a new batch of letters that had turned up.

The largest and most valuable collection of Beauregard Papers is in the Division of Manuscripts, Library of Congress. Spanning his mature life, it includes fifty-one volumes and contains his letterbooks, which have copies of letters that otherwise would be unavailable. There are many Beauregard items in the National Archives in the Records of the Adjutant General's Office relating to West Point; in the Office of Chief of Engineer files; in the Adjutant General files, Letters Received; in the War Department Records, Letters Received; and in the War Department Collection of Confederate Records. The Archives records were of particular assistance in following Beauregard's military career before 1860. Another large collection is the Beauregard Papers in the Department of Archives, Louisiana State University; most of these papers relate to his career after the war.

There are smaller collections of Beauregard Papers at the following places: the Howard-Tilton Memorial Library, Tulane University; Duke University Library; Missouri Historical Society, St. Louis; Mirabeau B. Lamar Library, University of Texas; Confederate Collection, Emory University Library; Charleston Library Society, Charleston, South Carolina; Confederate Memorial Hall, New Orleans; the Cabildo, New Orleans; the North Carolina State Department of Archives and History, Raleigh; the Confederate Museum, Richmond; and the South Carolina Historical Society, Charleston.

Although not called the Beauregard Papers, a file of Beauregard letters is in the Yates Snowden Papers, South Caroliniana Library, University of South Carolina. Miss Laure Beauregard Larendon, of Atlanta, Georgia, granddaughter of the general, permitted me to examine her collection of family letters; later she presented some of them to Emory University and some to Louisiana State University. René Beauregard, older son of the general, wrote a manuscript account of his father and his family which he entitled "Magnolia." A typewritten copy of this document was given to me by Mr. Harnett Kane, New Orleans.

A substantial number of Beauregard letters are in each of the following collections: in the Southern Historical Collection, University of North Carolina Library, the Edward Porter Alexander Papers, the J. F. H. Claiborne Papers, the William Porcher Miles Papers, and the Marcus J. Wright Papers; at Duke University Library, the Rose O'Neal Greenhow Papers, the David B. Harris Papers, and the Alfred Roman Papers; at the Confederate Museum, Richmond, the Confederate Flag Correspondence; at Emory University Library, the Jefferson Davis Papers and the Gourdin-Young Papers; in the Division of Manuscripts, Library of Congress, the Jubal A. Early Papers, the Frankin Pierce Papers, and the Alfred Roman Papers; and at the Alderman Library, University of Virginia, the John Henshaw Papers.

The following collections contain one or a few Beauregard letters: in the Southern Historical Collection, University of North Carolina Library, the John F. Alexander Papers, the Mrs. S. Westray Battle Papers, the William Montgomery Gardner Papers, the Jeremy F. Gilmer Papers, the L. M. Hatch Papers, the Daniel Harvey Hill Papers, the Lafayette McLaws Papers, and the Williams-Chesnut-Manning Papers; at Duke University Library, the Clement C. Clay Papers, the Georgia Portfolio Papers, the Paul Hamilton Hayne Papers, the Charles C. Jones Papers, and the Francis W. Pickens Papers; at Emory University Library, the John H. Hewitt Papers, and the Alexander H. Stephens Papers; in the Department of Archives, Louisiana State University, the David F. Boyd Papers and the Charles Gayarré Papers; in the Division of Manuscripts, Library of Congress, the Andrew Johnson Papers; at the North Carolina State Department of Archives and History, Raleigh, the Robert F. Hoke Papers; at the Confederate Memorial Institute, Richmond, the Robert E. Lee Papers; and at the Florida Historical Society, St. Augustine, the John Milton Papers.

Important references to Beauregard and letters to him were located in these papers: at Duke University Library, the Braxton Bragg Papers, the Jefferson Davis Papers, the H. W. De Saussure and Wilmot Gibbs Papers, the Joseph E. Johnston Papers, and the Thomas Jordan Papers; in the Southern Historical Collection, University of North Carolina Library, the Peter W. Hairston Papers, the Edmund Kirby Smith Papers, the Pettigrew Family Papers, and the Polk-

Brown-Ewell Papers; at the Confederate Museum, Richmond, the C. McC. Reeve Papers; in the Department of Archives, Louisiana State University, the Ellis Family Papers and the Gras-Lauzin Family Papers; in the Division of Manuscripts, Library of Congress, the Robert E. Lee Papers, in the De Butts-Ely Collection; in the Confederate Memorial Institute, Richmond, the Robert E. Lee Papers; in the South Carolina Historical Society, Charleston, the Middleton Papers of the Cheves Collection; and at Howard-Tilton Memorial Library, Tulane University, the Mrs. Mason Barret Papers, which are really the papers of Albert Sidney Johnston and William Preston Johnston.

In the South Caroliniana Library, University of South Carolina, is an interesting manuscript by Thomas Smythe entitled "Memoranda of an interview with Gen. Beauregard in my own house on the evening of May 20th 1863." Mr. Vernon Munroe, New York City, gave me a typed copy of the journal of A. R. Chisolm, Beauregard's aide: "Journal of Events before and during the Bombardment of Fort Sumter—April 1861." The diary of Stephen R. Mallory, Secretary of the Navy, is in the Southern Historical Collection, University of North Carolina Library; its entries reflect the views of the Davis administration toward Beauregard.

Published Correspondence

Stan V. Henkels, auction commission merchant, published two valuable catalogs containing letters by Beauregard and letters to him. *The Beauregard Papers* ..., his Catalog 1148 (Philadelphia, 1915), Pt. I, contains documents of the war period. Most of the letters in his Catalog 1148, *The Beauregard Papers* ..., (Philadelphia, 1916), Pt. II, deal with the postwar years. A rich assortment of Confederate letters is in a volume prepared by the Historical Records Survey of the Works Progress Administration, *A Calendar of the Ryder Collection of Confederate Archives at Tufts College* (Boston, 1940).

There is much information about Beauregard, most of it hostile and inaccurate, in Dunbar Rowland (ed.), *Jefferson Davis, Constitutionalist, His Letters, Papers and Speeches*, 10 vols. (Jackson, Miss., 1923). Lee's relations with Beauregard can be followed in Douglas S. Freeman (ed.), *Lee's Dispatches, Unpublished Letters of General Robert E. Lee, C. S. A., to Jefferson Davis* ... (New York, 1915). Revealing glimpses of Beauregard at the beginning of the war are afforded in two collections of letters by Thomas R. R. Cobb: "Extracts from Letters to his Wife, February 3, 1861–December 10, 1862," in *Southern Historical Society Papers*, XXVIII (1900), 280–301; and "The Correspondence of Thomas Reade Rootes Cobb,

1860–1862," in *Publications of the Southern History Association*, XI (1907), 147–85, 233–60, 312–28. Significant references to Beauregard appear in Percy Gatling Hamlin (ed.), *The Making of a Soldier: Letters of General R. S. Ewell* (Richmond, 1935).

Diaries, Memoirs, Reminiscences, and Autobiographies

Most of the books written by Confederate leaders after the war contain material of varying importance about Beauregard. He is also mentioned frequently in the recollections of lower-echelon officers and enlisted men. Only those works which supplied much or valuable information are listed here.

Beauregard's own *A Commentary on the Campaign and Battle of Manassas . . .* (New York, 1891) gives his views of the first battle of the war; it also reprints an earlier pamphlet by him on the art of war. Two books by T. C. De Leon include many references to Beauregard: *Four Years in Rebel Capitals* (Mobile, 1892) ; and *Belles, Beaux and Brains of the Sixties* (New York, 1909). A revealing account by an officer who was very close to Beauregard is Johnson Hagood, *Memoirs of the War of Secession* (Columbia, S. C., 1910). Sensitive descriptions of Beauregard are found in Sir Arthur J. L. Fremantle, *Three Months in the Southern States, April–June, 1863* (New York, 1864) ; and William Howard Russell, *My Diary North and South* (Boston, 1863). Valuable for its summaries of Richmond gossip is J. B. Jones, *A Rebel War Clerk's Diary*, ed. by Howard Swiggett, 2 vols. (New York, 1935).

Other significant works are the following: E. P. Alexander, *Military Memoirs of a Confederate* (New York, 1907) ; Mary Boykin Chesnut, *A Diary from Dixie*, ed. by Ben Ames Williams (Boston, 1949) ; Mrs. Clement C. Clay, *A Belle of the Fifties* (New York, 1905) ; John Esten Cooke, *Wearing of the Gray . . .* (New York, 1867) ; Jefferson Davis, *Rise and Fall of the Confederate Government*, 2 vols. (New York, 1881) ; Quincy A. Gillmore, *Engineer and Artillery Operations against the Defenses of Charleston in 1863 . . .* (New York, 1865) ; Mrs. Rose Greenhow, *My Imprisonment and the First Year of Abolition Rule at Washington* (London, 1863) ; John B. Hood, *Advance and Retreat . . .* (New Orleans, 1880) ; Joseph E. Johnston, *Narrative of Military Operations . . .* (New York, 1874) ; James Longstreet, *From Manassas to Appomattox* (Philadelphia, 1896) ; Charles Marshall, *An Aide-de-Camp of Lee . . .*, ed. by Sir Frederick Maurice (Boston, 1927) ; Dabney H. Maury, *Recollections of a Virginian in the Mexican, Indian and Civil Wars,* (New York, 1894) ; William Miller Owen, *In Camp and Battle with the*

Washington Artillery of New Orleans (Boston, 1885); John H. Reagan, *Memoirs, with Special Reference to Secession and the Civil War* (New York, 1906); and Gustavus W. Smith, *Confederate War Papers* (New York, 1884).

The following accounts by soldiers provide interesting sidelights on Beauregard: [Napier Bartlett], *A Soldier's Story of the War* . . . (New Orleans, 1874); [F. G. De Fontaine], *Marginalia; or Gleanings from an Army Notebook* (Columbia, S. C., 1864); Thomas D. Duncan, *Recollections of Thomas D. Duncan* . . . (Nashville, 1922); and An English Combatant, *Battlefields of the South From Bull Run to Fredericksburg,* 2 vols. (London, 1863).

Biographies

Not all of the many biographies of Beauregard's contemporaries which I have read or consulted are cited in the footnotes. Only those that were most useful to my purposes are listed in this essay.

There have been two previous biographies of Beauregard: Alfred Roman, *Military Operations of General Beauregard,* 2 vols. (New York, 1884) and Hamilton Basso, *Beauregard, The Great Creole* (New York, 1933). Most of Roman's work was written by Beauregard; the characteristics of the biography I have described in Chapter Nineteen of this book. Basso's book is interesting and full of human interest, but it neglects or slights many important phases of Beauregard's career. An interesting contemporary sketch of Beauregard appeared in William Parker Snow, *Southern Generals* . . . (New York, 1866).

The three best biographies of Beauregard's great enemy are Hamilton J. Eckenrode, *Jefferson Davis, President of the South* (New York, 1923); Elizabeth Cutting, *Jefferson Davis, Political Soldier* (New York, 1930); and Robert McElroy, *Jefferson Davis, the Unreal and the Real,* 2 vols. (New York, 1937).

Douglas Southall Freeman has discussed Beauregard as a soldier in *R. E. Lee: A Biography,* 4 vols. (New York, 1934–35) and, more fully, in *Lee's Lieutenants: A Study in Command,* 3 vols. (New York, 1942–44). Dr. Freeman's descriptions of battles in which Beauregard participated are invaluable as background. His judgments on Beauregard are almost always hostile. With some of his opinions I agree; with others I differ.

Beauregard figures prominently if unfortunately in William Preston Johnston, *Life of Gen. Albert Sidney Johnston* . . . (New York, 1878). General Johnston's son was interested in proving that Beauregard's role in the Shiloh campaign was subordinate. Despite its violent bias, the book is valuable for its material on the war in the West. Significant information on Beauregard appears in Thomas Jordan and J. P. Pryor, *The Campaigns of Lieut.-General N. B. Forrest and of Forrest's Cavalry* (New Orleans, 1868) ; and William M. Polk, *Leonidas Polk, Bishop and General,* 2 vols. (New York, 1915).

Histories and Monographs

For Beauregard's Louisiana background I have found the following useful: Stanley C. Arthur and George C. H. de Kernion, *Old Families of Louisiana* (New Orleans, 1931) ; George W. Cable, *The Creoles of Louisiana* (New York, 1910) ; Hodding Carter, *Lower Mississippi* (New York, 1942) ; Henry E. Chambers, *A History of Louisiana,* 3 vols. (Chicago, 1925) ; Alcée Fortier, *A History of Louisiana,* 4 vols. (New York, 1903) ; Charles Gayarré, *History of Louisiana,* 4 vols. (New Orleans, 1903) ; Harnett T. Kane, *Deep Delta Country* (New York, 1944) ; John Smith Kendall, *History of New Orleans,* 3 vols. (Chicago, 1922) ; Grace King, *Creole Families of New Orleans* (New York, 1921) ; and Henry Rightor (ed.), *Standard History of New Orleans, Louisiana* (Chicago, 1900).

Background material for Beauregard's career at West Point was drawn from Edward C. Boynton, *Guide to West Point . . .* (New York, 1867) ; Edward C. Boynton, *History of West Point . . .* (New York, 1863) ; George W. Cullum, *Biographical Register of the Officers and Graduates of the U. S. Military Academy . . . ,* 2 vols. (New York, 1868) ; and Joseph P. Farley, *West Point in the Early Sixties* (Troy, N. Y., 1902).

Three works on the Mexican War that contain some references to Beauregard are Edward D. Mansfield, *The Mexican War* (New York, 1948) ; R. S. Ripley, *The War with Mexico,* 2 vols. (New York, 1849) ; and Justin H. Smith, *The War with Mexico,* 2 vols. (New York, 1919).

Of the myriad monographs on the Civil War, only those that deal specifically with Beauregard's campaigns can be cited here. Stanley F. Horn, *The Army of Tennessee* (Indianapolis, 1941), is excellent for the war in the West. Ellsworth Eliot, Jr., *West Point in the Confederacy* (New York, 1941), contains some Beauregard letters and other valuable information. All of Beauregard's battles are treated in the articles in Robert U. Johnson and Clarence C. Buel (eds.), *Battles and Leaders of the Civil War,* 4 vols. (New York, 1887). A similar compilation is *The Annals of the War Written by Leading Participants North and South* (Philadelphia, 1879) ; consisting of articles originally appearing in the Philadelphia *Weekly Times,* it contains an article by Beauregard, "Torpedo Service in Charleston Harbor." In the twelve volumes of gossip and trivia edited by Frank Moore, *The Rebellion Record* . . . (New York, 1864-68) there are many references to Beauregard.

Particular battles and operations are described in several good monographs: Samuel W. Crawford, *The Genesis of the Civil War: The Story of Sumter, 1860–1861* (New York, 1887) ; Thomas Robson Hay, *Hood's Tennessee Campaign* (New York, 1929) ; R. M. Johnston, *Bull Run: Its Strategy and Tactics* (Boston, 1913) ; John Johnson, *The Defence of Charleston Harbor* (Charleston, 1890); and Samuel Jones, *The Siege of Charleston* (New York, 1911).

For phases of Beauregard's postwar career, useful background material is in E. L. Corthell, *A History of the Jetties at the Mouth of the Mississippi River* (New York, 1880) ; Thomas D. Clark, *A Pioneer Southern Railroad From New Orleans to Cairo* (Chapel Hill, N. C., 1936) ; and John F. Stover, "The Development of Northern Financial Control over Southern Railroads, 1865–1900" (Ph. D. dissertation, University of Wisconsin, 1951).

Newspapers

Civil War newspapers rarely contain accurate or important information about generals or battles. But from their columns the researcher can learn how a particular general stood with the public and what his friends were doing to help him and his enemies to damage him. To secure such reactions concerning Beauregard, I have sampled files of the Charleston *Courier,* the Charleston *Mercury,* the Richmond *Dispatch,* the Richmond *Enquirer,* and the Richmond *Examiner.*

For the postwar activities of a general, newspapers are valuable sources of information. Indeed, it would be impossible to reconstruct the peacetime career of a man like Beauregard without a careful study of newspapers. Although I have not run completely the file of any one New Orleans paper from 1865–93, I have examined the files of several for many of the years in this period. The papers which I consulted are the New Orleans *Daily Crescent,* the New Orleans *Daily Democrat,* the New Orleans *Daily Picayune,* the New Orleans *Republican,* the New Orleans *States,* the New Orleans *Times,* and the New Orleans *Times-Democrat.*

Government and Official Documents

Material on Beauregard's career as a cadet at West Point is in Asbury Dickins and John W. Forney (eds.), *American State Papers,*

Military Affairs, V (Washington, 1860), VI (Washington, 1861), VII (Washington, 1861).

Many of his actions in the Mexican War can be traced in three publications of war reports: *Senate Executive Documents,* 30 Congress, 1 Session, Document No. 1, Document No. 65; *House Executive Documents,* 30 Congress, 2 Session, Document No. 1.

Important collections of Confederate documents, which also contain material on Beauregard, are James D. Richardson (ed.), *A Compilation of the Messages and Papers of the Confederacy . . . ,* 2 vols. (Nashville, 1905); *Journals of the Congress of the Confederate States of America, 1861–1865,* 7 vols. (Washington, 1904–1905). The greatest single source for the Civil War and for Beauregard's war career is, of course, *The War of the Rebellion: A Compilation of the Official Records of the Union and Confederate Armies,* 128 vols. (Washington, 1880-1901).

Articles and Periodicals

Beauregard's role in the municipal election of 1858 in New Orleans receives attention in John Smith Kendall, "The Municipal Elections of 1858," in *Louisiana Historical Quarterly,* V (1922), 357–76; and in James K. Greer, "Louisiana Politics, 1845–1861," *ibid.,* XIII (1930), 257–303.

As discussed in Chapter Nineteen of this book, all of Beauregard's articles on the Civil War except the one on Bull Run were written by Alfred Roman. These articles were later condensed or revised for publication in *Battles and Leaders.* In the following list the magazine citation of each article is given and the pages in *Battles and Leaders* in which the equivalent of the essay appears: "The First Battle of Bull Run," in the *Century Illustrated Monthly Magazine,* XIX (1884), 80–106 (*Battles and Leaders,* I, 196–227); "The Shiloh Campaign," in the *North American Review,* CXLII (1886), 1–24, 159–84 (*Battles and Leaders,* I, 569–93); "Defence of Charleston, South Carolina," *ibid.,* CXLII (1886), 419–36, 564–71, CXLIII (1886), 42–53 (*Battles and Leaders,* IV, 1–23); "Drewry's Bluff and Petersburg," *ibid.,* CXLIV (1887), 244–60 (*Battles and Leaders,* IV, 195–205); and "The Battle of Petersburg," *ibid.,* XLV (1887), 367–77, 506–15 (*Battles and Leaders,* IV, 540–44). Beauregard's article, "Torpedo Service in Charleston Harbor," in *Annals of the War,* 513–26, was apparently his own work.

Thomas Jordan, Beauregard's chief of staff, wrote an excellent account of his chief at Shiloh in his article, "Notes of a Confederate Staff-Officer at Shiloh," *Battles and Leaders,* I, 594–603. A vivid description of the Greensboro conference at which Johnston and

Beauregard advised Davis to surrender is in Stephen R. Mallory, "Last Days of the Confederate Government," in *McClure's Magazine*, XVI (1901), 239–48. Bits of information about Beauregard, many of them very important, are in *The Land We Love*, 6 vols. (Charlotte, N. C., 1866–69); and in *Southern Historical Society Papers*, 47 vols. (Richmond, 1876–1930).

A valuable account of the Louisiana Lottery is in Berthold C. Awes, "The History of the Louisiana State Lottery Company," in *Louisiana Historical Quarterly*, XXVII (1944), 2–156. The lottery is also treated in Clarence C. Buel, "The Degradation of a State," in the *Century Illustrated Monthly Magazine*, XLIII (1892), 618-32.

Index

Adams, Dan, 263-64
Aiken, William, 199
Ammonia Thermo-Specific Propelling Company, 287
Anderson, Robert, 8, 53, 54; and Fort Sumter, 54-58; surrenders Fort Sumter, 58-61
Appomattox River, 207, 220
Argentina, seeks Beauregard's services, 265-66
Atalaya, 20-21
Ayotla, 23
Aztec Club, 32

Barataria Bay, 9
Barnard, John G., 14, 30, 36-37, 44-45, 50
Battery Gregg, 187; evacuation of, 194
Battery Wagner, 187; Federal attacks on, in 1863, 188-89, 193-94; evacuation of, 194
Beauregard, Armand, brother of P. G. T. Beauregard, 198
Beauregard, Caroline Deslonde, second wife of P. G. T. Beauregard, 35-36; death of, 203-205
Beauregard, Henri, son of P. G. T. Beauregard, 10, 323-24, 326, 328
Beauregard, Jacques Toutant-, see Toutant-Beauregard, Jacques
Beauregard, Laure Villeré, daughter of P. G. T. Beauregard, 36; marriage of, to Charles Larendon, 324; death of, 324-25
Beauregard, Marie Laure Villeré, first wife of P. G. T. Beauregard, 10; death of, 35-36
Beauregard, P. G. T., summary of career of, 1-2; birth and early life

of, 3-5; education of, 5; goes to West Point, 5-8; esteems Napoleon, 5, 19, 39, 74-75, 93; accepts commission and first assignment, 8-9; at Fort Adams, Miss., 9; at Pensacola, 9; at Barataria Bay, 9; and mouths of Mississippi River, 9, 36-37, 288-89; first marriage of, 10; homes of, 10, 322; at Fort McHenry, 10-11; quarrels with J. C. Henshaw, 11-12; desires war with Mexico, 12-13; in Mexican War, 13-33; as engineer officer with Scott, 15; in siege of Vera Cruz, 15-19; irked at Scott, 19, 22, 33; at Cerro Gordo, 19-22; at Puebla, 23; scouts roads to Mexico City, 24-25; at the Pedregal, 25-27; scouts approaches to Mexico City, 27-28; at Piedad council, 28-30; at Chapultepec, 30; in capture of Mexico City, 31-32; in occupation of Mexico City, 32-33; assigned after Mexican War, 34-36; supports Franklin Pierce in elections of 1852, 38-39; and New Orleans customhouse, 39-41, 45; threatens to resign from army, 42-43; runs for mayor of New Orleans, 43-44; and superintendency of West Point, 44-46; resigns from army, 47; applies for service in Confederate army, 48; assigned to command at Charleston, 49-50; description of, 51-53; assumes command in Charleston, 53-56; demands surrender of Fort Sumter, 56-58; directs attack on Fort Sumter, 58-61; as first Confederate hero, 61-62; confers with Davis in Montgomery,